DATE DUE	
~~3/5/83~~	~~9/19/95~~

Looking Out/Looking In

Looking Out/Looking In

INTERPERSONAL COMMUNICATION Third Edition

RONALD B. ADLER
Santa Barbara City College

NEIL TOWNE
Grossmont College

Holt, Rinehart and Winston
New York   Chicago   San Francisco   Dallas
Montreal   Toronto   London   Sydney

To Janet Bollow,
our designer

Cover photograph: Stephen Hender

Library of Congress Cataloging in Publication Data

Adler, Ron, 1946–
  Looking out/looking in.

Bibliographies
  Includes index.
  1. Interpersonal communication.   I. Towne, Neil,
1928–   joint author.   II. Title. BF637.C45A34   1980
      158'.2   80-20801

ISBN 0-03-053836-X

Credits

ii, "Peanuts" cartoon by Charles Schulz. © 1970 United Feature Syndicate, Inc. viii, from *Will You Be My Friend* by James Kavanaugh. Copyright © 1971 by James Kavanaugh. Published by Nash Publishing Corporation, Los Angeles. vii–ix, Wayne Miller, Magnum. **Chapter 1:** x–1, Malcolm Perkins, Stock, Boston. 8, from p. 9 (under title "The Shields") in *Seven Arrows* by Hyemeyohsts Storm. Copyright © 1972 by Hyemeyohsts Storm. Reprinted by permission of Harper & Row, Publishers, Inc. 8, (top) Burk Uzzle, Magnum; (bottom) Robert Eckert, Ekm-Nepenthe. 12, Ellis Herwig, Stock, Boston. 13, "Dear Ann Landers" reprinted by permission of Ann Landers and Field Newspaper Syndicate. 14, "Human Eye" from *Sunflowers* by Ric Masten 1971, revised 1979, by permission of author, Sunflower Ink, Monterey, California. 14, Frank Siteman, Stock, Boston. 15, "Talk for Sale" Copyright 1973 by Newsweek, Inc. All rights reserved. Reprinted by permission. 16, © Lorraine Rorke, Icon. 17, "If You're Shy, Just Pay Lip Service." Reprinted by permission of the Associated Press. 18, Jill Freedman, Magnum. 19, "Reaching Out to the Inner Man." Reprinted by permission of the author and Suburban Features, Inc. 20, "1966 Graduates Rate Courses Most Useful." Reprinted by permission of United Press International. 27, MISS PEACH by Mell Lazarus. Courtesy of Mell Lazarus and Field Newspaper Syndicate. 33, Peress, Magnum. 39, Thelma Shumsky, Icon. 41, from *Group Processes: An Introduction to Group Dynamics* by Joseph Luft, by permission of Mayfield Publishing Company. Copyright © 1963, 1970 Joseph Luft. 43, MISS PEACH by Mell Lazarus. Courtesy of Mell Lazarus and Field Newspaper Syndicate. 44, from "Mending Wall" from *The Poetry of Robert Frost* edited by Edward Connery Lathem. Copyright 1930, 1939, © 1969 by Holt, Rinehart and Winston. Copyright © 1958 by Robert Frost. Copyright © 1967 by Lesley Frost Ballantine. Reprinted by permission of Holt, Rinehart and Winston, Publishers, and Jonathan Cape Ltd. 45, "Looking Out/Looking In" from *Stark Naked* by Ric Masten 1980, by permission of author, Sunflower Ink, Monterey, California. 45, Jack Prelutsky, Stock, Boston. **Chapter 2:** 50–51, © Erika Stone, Photo Researchers, Inc. 52, courtesy Datique, Inc., Pacifica, California. Reprinted with permission. 55, Cor-

nell Capa, Magnum. 56, Elliott Erwitt, Magnum. 57, from *Person to Person* by Barry Stevens. © 1967 Real People Press. Used by permission. 60, Constantine Manos, Magnum. 61, "Love and the Cabbie" by Art Buchwald. Reprinted by permission of the Los Angeles Times Syndicate. 62, SNUFFY SMITH cartoon by Fred Lasswell. Copyright © 1974 King Features. Used by permission. 64, "Peanuts" cartoon by Charles Schultz. © 1978 United Feature Syndicate, Inc. 65, cartoon by Chon Day. Used by permission of Chon Day. Copyright © by Saturday Review. 66, Patricia Hollander Gross, Stock, Boston. 67, "Cipher in the Snow" by Jean Mizer, from *Today's Education,* November 1964. Reprinted by permission of Jean Mizer Todhunter and *Today's Education.* 68, poem by Lenni Shender Goldstein. Used by permission of author. 72, Mark Chester. 73, "Hate Yourself? It May Not Be the Real You" by Ellen Goodman. Copyright 1977 The Boston Globe Newspaper Company. Reprinted by permission. 74, Broom-Hilda Cartoon by Russell Myers. © 1977 the Chicago Tribune–N.Y. News Syndicate. Reprinted by permission. 74, poetry by Leonard Nimoy. Reprinted by permission of International Creative Management. Copyright © Leonard Nimoy, 1978. 75, © 1980 Kent Reno, Jeroboam. 78, reprinted from Shyness: *What It Is and What To Do About It* by Philip G. Zimbardo, copyright © 1977, by permission of Addison-Wesley Publishing Co., Reading, Mass. 81, Bill Owens, Magnum. 83, Rick Smolan, Stock, Boston. 84, Burk Uzzle, Magnum. 86, from *The Velveteen Rabbit* by Margery Williams. Reprinted by courtesy of Doubleday & Co., and William Heinemann Ltd. Publishers (London). 86, from *Winnie-The-Pooh* by A. A. Milne, illustrated by Ernest H. Shepard. Copyright, 1926, by E. P. Dutton & Co.; renewal 1954, by A. A. Milne. Reprinted by permission of the publishers, E. P. Dutton and Curtis Brown Ltd. **Chapter 3:** 88–89, Gloria Carlson, 1980. 92, Norman Hurst, Stock, Boston. 96, permission of The Fine Arts Museums of San Francisco. 98, Susan Miller. 100, "i remember" from *Love View* by Bernard Gunther. Copyright © 1969 by Bernard Gunther. Reprinted by permission of Macmillan Publishing Co. and Bernard Gunther, c/o International Creative Management. 100, Rick Smolan, Stock, Boston. 102, David Wing 103, Robert Eckert,

Ekm-Nepenthe. 104, drawing from *Smile in a Mad Dog's i* by Richard Stine. Drawing by Richard Stine. Reprinted by permission of Carolyn Bean Publishing, Ltd. © 1974 Richard Stine. 105, "Ziggy" cartoon by Tom Wilson. Copyright © 1974, Universal Press Syndicate. Used by permission. 106, abridged from p. 127 in *Benchley Beside Himself* by Robert Benchley. Copyright © 1925 by Harper & Row, Publishers, Inc. Reprinted by permission of the publisher. 108, "Peanuts" cartoon by Charles Schultz. © 1963 United Feature Syndicate, Inc. 111, "Cathy" cartoon by Cathy Guisewite. Copyright © 1979, Universal Press Syndicate. All rights reserved. 117, Michael Hayman, Stock, Boston. 118, poem by Lenni Shender Goldstein. Used by permission of the author. 118, Dennis Stock, Magnum. **Chapter 4:** 122–123, Inge Morath, Magnum. 124, Leonard Freed, Magnum. 127, "Janus" by Charles Bragg. Reproduced by permission of Thought Factory. 129, Eugene Richards, Magnum. 130, "The Belfast Tiger" by Charles Bragg. Reproduced by permission of Thought Factory. 131, "Shooting an Elephant" from *Shooting an Elephant and Other Stories* by George Orwell, Copyright 1945, 1946, 1949, 1950 by Sonia Brownell Orwell. Reprinted by permission of Harcourt Brace Jovanovich, Inc., and by permission of Mrs. Sonia Brownell Orwell and Secker & Warburg. 135, poem by R. D. Lang, from *Knots* Copyright © 1970 Pantheon Books, a Division of Random House, Inc., New York, and Tavistock Publications Ltd. 135, Patricia Hollander Gross, Stock, Boston. 136, "Peanuts" cartoon by Charles Schulz. © 1964 United Feature Syndicate, Inc. 139, "I Am A Rock" by Paul Simon and Art Garfunkel. © 1965 Paul Simon. Used by permission. 141, Mark Chester. 142, © Alice Kandell, Rapho/ Photo Researchers, Inc. 143, Elliott Erwitt, Magnum. 144, Jules Feiffer cartoon. © 1967 Jules Feiffer. Used by permission. 145, From pp 79–80 in *An Empty Spoon* by Sunny Decker. Copyright © 1969 by Sunny Decker. By permission of Harper & Row, Publishers, Inc. 145, Eugene Richards, Magnum. 146, "What is This? Teacher said" from *Sunflowers* by Ric Masten 1971, revised 1979, by permission of author, Sunflower Ink, Monterey, California. 150, quotation by Hugh Prather from *Notes to Myself* by Hugh Prather. © 1970 Real People Press. 151,

The Gibb Categories from "Defensive Communication" by Jack R. Gibb from *Journal of Communication* Volume 11:3 (1961), pp. 141–148. Reprinted courtesy of *Journal of Communication* and the author. Cartoon by David Sipress. Reprinted by special permission of *Learning, The Magazine for Creative Teaching,* © 1979 by Education Today Company, Inc. 153, © Rose Skytta, Jeroboam. 156, Henri Cartier-Bresson, Magnum. 157, "Teens, Parents, and Conversation Gap" Reprinted by permission of United Press International. 160, Jeff Albertson, Stock, Boston. **Chapter 5:** 164–165, © Richard Bermack, Icon. 174–175, "Elephant" by Katsushika Hokusai from *The Hokusai Sketchbooks* by James A. Michner. Reproduced by permission of Charles E. Tuttle Co., Inc. 178, quotation to Estelle Ramsey from article that appeared in *Ms.* Magazine. Reprinted by permission of Estelle Ramsey. 180, cartoon by Jerry Marcus. © 1979. Reprinted by permission of *Redbook Magazine* and Jerry Marcus. 182, "Coming & Going" from *His & Hers* by Ric Masten, Copyright © 1978. Reprinted by permission of the author, Sunflower Ink, Monterey, California. 184, Charles Gatewood, Stock, Boston. 185, "Field Experiments: Preparation for the Changing Police Role" by Fred Ferguson. Reprinted by permission of the author. 186, "23 Judges Shaken by Night in Nevada Prison." Reprinted by permission of United Press International. 187, cartoon from *What's Funny About That?* compiled by the editors of *This Week* Magazine. Copyright © 1954 by E. P. Dutton and Co., Inc., and used with their permission. 188, Ian Berry, Magnum. 189, "Beware of a Crocodile Bag" by Peter Mayne from Punch November 2, 1960, pp. 638–39. © 1960 Punch (Rothco). 191, "Relativity" by artist M. C. Escher. Reproduced by permission of the Escher Foundation, Haaga Gemeentemuseum, The Hague. 192, Richard Kalvar, Magnum. 193, from *Black Like Me* by John Howard Griffin. Copyright © 1960, 1961 by John Howard Griffin. Reprinted by permission of Houghton Mifflin Company. 195, Rick Smolan, Stock, Boston. 199, quotation by Hugh Prather from *Notes to Myself* by Hugh Prather. © 1970 Real People Press. 200, Reni Burri, Magnum. 201, "Pillow Education in Rural Japan" from *Square Sun, Square Moon* by

(*Credits continue following index.*)

Preface

We once knew a college professor who talked about "my-mys." A my-my, he said, is a piece of information which may be quite interesting, but which doesn't change your life in any significant way. He called them my-mys because that's what you say when you hear them.

Although my-mys are often interesting, they aren't what *Looking Out/ Looking In* is all about. We won't judge this book as successful if, after finishing it, you know a great deal about how people in general communicate. For us—and we hope for you too—the real measure of success will come if you can use this book to improve *your own* communication and to help others do the same thing. Informative? Yes. Entertaining? Hopefully. But most important, change.

The reception which the first two editions of *Looking Out/Looking In* received tells us that we've done a decent job of reaching this goal. In this new edition we've tried to make the book even more useful. There is a new chapter on emotions, a vital topic in interpersonal communication. There are significant changes in the material on listening, language, and conflict resolution, as well as modifications in other areas.

Along with changes in the text, a greatly expanded instructor's manual accompanies this edition. Its most notable feature is a 153-page section of reproducible exercises that will help each student apply the principles introduced in *Looking Out/Looking In* to his or her own life. In addition, expanded quiz and test questions, suggestions on classroom activities, and syllabi should help make each instructor's class run more smoothly and efficiently.

As always, creating a book is a joint venture between the authors and many other people. We've been lucky to have top quality support and advice from many sources. Roth Wilkofsky and Kathleen Domenig were the ideal editors, making our job easier and our product better while also being good friends. The management in the college department at Holt, Rinehart and Winston gave us the freedom to develop a book which departed in many ways from more traditional ones. Pamela Forcey and Jeanette Ninas Johnson turned a potentially nerve-racking production schedule into a smooth, relatively painless effort—at least for us. And our designer, Janet Bollow, used her many talents to transform *Looking Out/Looking In* from a stack of dogeared manuscript pages into a visual delight.

We're also grateful to our reviewers for their suggestions about how to make the book meet student needs. Thanks to Stephen L. Coffman (Eastern Montana College, Billings), Dick Johnston (Diablo Valley College, Pleasant Hill, Calif.), Walter Kassoway (College of Marin, Kentfield, Calif.), Daniel O'Keefe (University of Illinois), Barbara Warnick (Tulane University), Phyllis Weinstein (Cuyauaga Community College, Cleveland), John Wiemann (University of California, Santa Barbara), Mary Wiemann (Santa Barbara City College), Larry Wise (Mt. Hood Community College, Gresham, Ore.), and Robert Wolterbeek (Contra Costa College, San Pablo, Calif.).

Ronald B. Adler
Neil Towne

What is the use of a book, thought Alice, without pictures or conversations?

Lewis Carroll
Alice's Adventures in Wonderland

v

Contents

Will You Be My Friend?

Will you be my friend?
There are so many reasons why you never should:
I'm sometimes sullen, often shy, acutely sensitive,
My fear erupts as anger, I find it hard to give,
I talk about myself when I'm afraid
And often spend a day without anything to say.
    But I will make you laugh
    And love you quite a bit
    And hold you when you're sad.
I cry a little almost every day
Because I'm more caring than the strangers ever know,
And if at times, I show my tender side
(The soft and warmer part I hide)
    I wonder,
    Will you be my friend?
A friend
    Who far beyond the feebleness of any vow or tie
    Will touch the secret place where I am really I,
    To know the pain of lips that plead and eyes that weep,
    Who will not run away when you find me in the street
    Alone and lying mangled by my quota of defeats
    But will stop and stay—to tell me of another day
    When I was beautiful.

Will you be my friend?
There are so many reasons why you never should:
Often I'm too serious, seldom predictably the same,
Sometimes cold and distant, probably I'll always change.
I bluster and brag, seek attention like a child,
I brood and pout, my anger can be wild,
    But I will make you laugh
    And love you quite a bit
    And be near when you're afraid.

I shake a little almost every day
Because I'm more frightened than the strangers ever know
And if at times I show my trembling side
(The anxious, fearful part I hide)
    I wonder,
    Will you be my friend?
A friend
    Who, when I fear your closeness, feels me push away
    And stubbornly will stay to share what's left on
        such a day,
    Who, when no one knows my name or calls me on
        the phone,
    When there's no concern for me—what I have
        or haven't done—
    And those I've helped and counted on have, oh so
        deftly, run,
    Who, when there's nothing left but me, stripped of
        charm and subtlety,
    Will nonetheless remain.

Will you be my friend?
    For no reason that I know
    Except I want you so.

James Kavanaugh

Chapter One

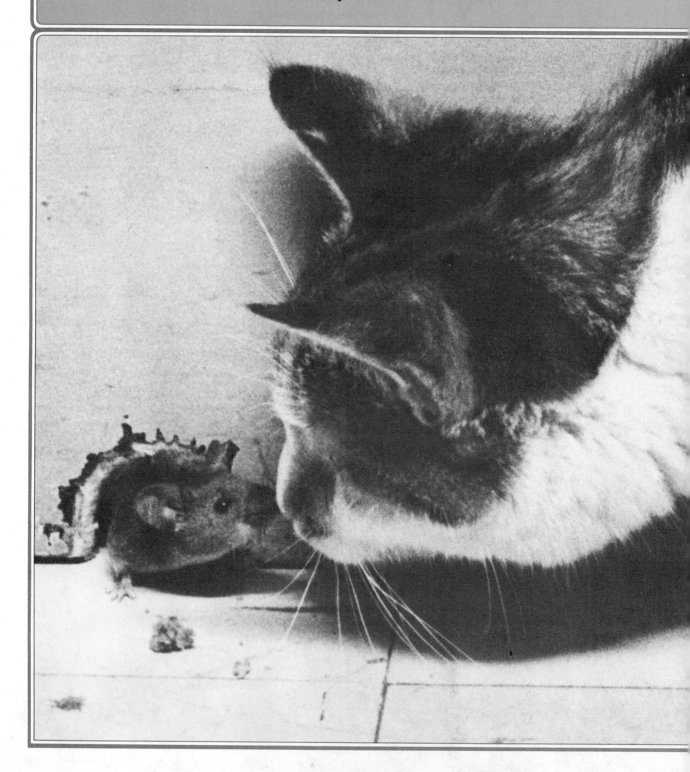

A First Look

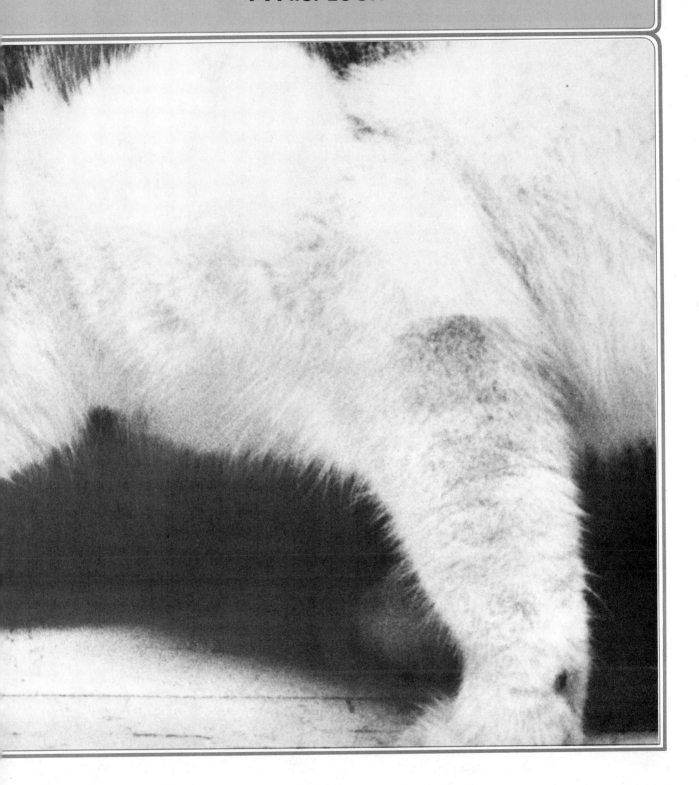

Right now I can only hypnotize you, persuade you, make you believe that I'm right. You don't know. I'm just preaching something. You wouldn't learn from my words. Learning is discovery. There is no other means of effective learning. You can tell the child a thousand times, "The stove is hot." It doesn't help. The child has to discover it for himself. And I hope I can assist you in learning, in discovering something about yourself.

Fritz Perls, Gestalt Therapy Verbatim

Introducing Ourselves

We want to begin by introducing ourselves. The word *we* you'll be reading throughout this book isn't just editorial: it refers to us, Ron Adler and Neil Towne. We live in Southern California, where we make our living teaching interpersonal communication at the college level. We like our work: it helps us grow, helps our students get along better, and is fun. In fact we often think that we get as many rewards from our students as they do from us. Although we do share many things in common, we want to tell you that there are differences, too.

As we write this Ron, the younger by fifteen years, lives near the ocean with his wife Sherri and two daughters, Robin and Rebecca, ages seven and four. Ron enjoys being a dad and husband most of the time, although he often longs for more quiet moments than he can find.

Ron likes trees, old houses, views, mail-order catalogs, and food, which he is able to enjoy without adding too many pounds. Daily jogging along the ocean and improving his skills at carpentry help him to relax and balance his life. In addition to coauthoring this book Ron has written two others by himself and has collaborated on a third. He enjoys having written books, but will admit that he has a hard time writing them. Ron always seems to be too busy but realizes that this is the life-style he's chosen for himself for the time being, and wouldn't choose to have it any other way. When all is said and done, Ron feels lucky to have a fine, caring family, his share of close friends, and work he enjoys.

Neil finds it difficult to believe that he has been teaching for more than twenty-two years, but that's apt to happen when you enjoy what you're doing. Neil has a love affair going with his family. Bobbi, his wife, is his number-one fan. Presently she manages the home front, is involved with foster parent education, and is completing a master's degree. Neil and Bobbi have six children, but since their ages range from thirteen to twenty-five, they'd probably dispute the use of the word "children."

Although only three of the offspring remain at home, life with the Townes is anything but dull. If it isn't soccer or baseball, it's applying for college scholarships or loans, taking guitar and drum lessons, worrying that someone isn't home yet, discussing report cards, spending a weekend at big brother's college, attending church and youth groups, working, skiing in Colorado, enduring a new diet, having friends stay overnight, finding a way to spend a year of college in Europe, talking, feeding friends, loving, dividing up the chores, quarreling, playing in the surf with boogie boards, studying, watching the sun come up from the jogging course, and leaving Dad alone to struggle with his book writing.

Both Neil and Bobbi are involved in designing and leading workshops and courses in marriage enrichment and couples' communication. With six young people trying to become independent, they constantly have the opportunity to work on interpersonal communication skills. Perhaps it's this ever-present opportunity at home and in the classroom that accounts for Neil's rapidly graying hair. On the other hand, it may be that he too often takes on more than he can comfortably handle. In any case the word *dull* has no place in this description.

Introducing This Book

We'll be sharing more about ourselves throughout the book. For now we hope this introduction has given you a brief idea about who we are. Our attempt to establish a personal style of writing is deliberate. We would like to think of our relationship with you as a conversation, a face-to-face meeting of real individuals, and not a treatise by faceless authors addressed to nameless students. We assume that you are in many ways like the people we get to know in our classes—so as you read on, realize that we are thinking of you.

Our goal in putting this book together was to provide a useful tool for helping you to improve your interpersonal communication skills. In other words our emphasis is practical rather than theoretical. Since this communication course may be the only one you ever take, we believe strongly that it needs to do more than "talk about" the subject: we hope it will actually help you find more satisfying ways to behave. If at the end of the course you have learned only to list the rules for good listening, identify defensive behaviors, or recite definitions of communication, we'll have failed to meet our goal. The kinds of results we are hoping for include relationships that run more smoothly, friendships that are becoming more meaningful, or a newfound ability to speak up when you want to.

Changes like these don't just happen magically. They come through new awareness, discovery, and learning on your part. To promote these goals we have filled *Looking Out/Looking In* with exercises and other activities, which you'll find printed in colored type. These activities fall into two categories. Some are designed to help you recognize more clearly your present styles of communicating, so that you can explore just how well they work for you. A second type of activity is aimed at showing you alternatives to those already existing styles. These are alternatives that research and experience suggest work well for most people, and we believe they will work for you if you are willing to learn them well.

You'll soon discover that there are many ways to communicate more effectively. While reading about them and carrying out the activities in the text should leave you feeling optimistic about improving your communication skill, we need to insert a note of caution at the beginning. Becoming a better communicator will require a good amount of time and effort on your part. Communication is a skill, and like other skills—playing a musical instrument or learning a sport, for example—it takes time to learn.

In the manual that accompanies their valuable book *Alive and Aware,* Sherod Miller, Elam Nunnally, and Daniel Wackman describe the steps necessary in learning any skill. The first stage is one of beginning awareness. This is the point at which you first learn that there is a new and better way of behaving. Reading this text should bring this sort of awareness to you.

The second stage is one of awkwardness. Just as you were clumsy when you first tried to ride a bicycle or drive a car, your initial attempts at communicating in new ways may also be awkward. This doesn't mean that there's anything wrong with the methods, but rather that you need more experience with them. After all, if it's reasonable to expect difficulty learning other skills, you ought to expect the same fumbling with the concepts in this book.

If you're willing to keep working at overcoming the awkwardness of your initial attempts, you will arrive at the third learning stage, which is one of skillfulness. At this point you'll be able to handle yourself well, although you will still need to think about what you're doing. In learning a new language, this is the time when you're able to speak grammatically and use the correct words, although you still need to think hard in order to express yourself well.

Finally, after a period of time in the skillful phase you'll find yourself at the final level, which is one of integration. This occurs when you're able to perform well without thinking about it. The behavior becomes automatic, a part of you. Integrated speakers of a foreign language can speak without translating mentally from their native tongue. Integrated cyclists ride skillfully and comfortably, almost as if the bike is an extension of their own body. And integrated communicators express themselves in skillful ways, not as an awkward act, but rather because that is who they have become.

It's important to keep these stages in mind as you try out the ideas in this book. Prepare yourself for the inevitable awkwardness, knowing that if you're willing to keep practicing the new skills, you will become more and more comfortable and successful with them. Realize that the effort is worth it, for once you have learned new methods of communicating, you'll be rewarded with far more satisfying relationships.

Becoming Acquainted with Your Group

Having introduced ourselves as authors and told you something about the book, it's time for you to meet the other people who make up your group. You'll soon find that they will be important to you.

Name Calling

1. Assemble your group, including instructor, so that everyone can see each other easily; a circle works well.

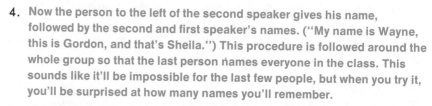

Gilly Caskey Lee
Hello Jay Mac Bobbi
Jane Eleanor Hello Ed
Jack Lois Neil Joe
Sherri Hello Jenny
Rich Sarah Karen Di
Hello Millie James
Don John Rebecca Hello Candy Al Wayne Frank Giles Ole Hello
Jeannie Sheila Robin Dave Mark Hello Wanda Gordon Audrey
Sean Gene Hello Joan Linda Dani Janet Patty Etta Steven
Hello Emmett Rabbit
Bill Greg Mimi Bob
Luke Hello Laura
Roth Matthew Lee
Marc Shayne Hello
Chevvie Vala Reda

MY
NAME
IS
ZEKE

2. The first person (ask for a volunteer) begins by giving his or her* name to the whole group, speaking loudly enough to be heard clearly by everyone. ("My name is Sheila.") The instructor may want to repeat what he's heard to check whether the speaker has been heard correctly. If you're not sure of a name, ask to have it repeated.

3. The group member seated on the first speaker's left will then give his own name followed by the first speaker's. ("My name is Gordon, and this is Sheila.")

4. Now the person to the left of the second speaker gives his name, followed by the second and first speaker's names. ("My name is Wayne, this is Gordon, and that's Sheila.") This procedure is followed around the whole group so that the last person names everyone in the class. This sounds like it'll be impossible for the last few people, but when you try it, you'll be surprised at how many names you'll remember.

5. Things to watch for:
   a. If you forget a name, don't worry: that person will help you after you've had a little time to think.
   b. If you don't catch the speaker's name, ask to have it repeated.
   c. You may want the person who begins the activity to end it also. After that, anyone who wants to should try to "name 'em all."
   d. Above all, keep the atmosphere informal. As you know, personal comments and humor have a way of lessening pressure.

Now that you have started to become acquainted with the others in your class, let's look at some of the benefits of working in such a group. First, the sharing of thoughts and experiences that you'll find here can show you that you're not the only person who wants to communicate better. It's probable that many of the people you encounter every day are trying to appear more confident and skillful than they feel. They most likely put on this show of "having it all together" in the belief that others will like them better if they appear nearly perfect. If you're fooled by such acts, you probably think that you are the only one who sometimes finds it difficult to express yourself comfortably and well. In reality this most certainly isn't true, and in this group you'll find that most members share the same goals as you and have the same difficulty reaching them. This isn't because the people here are less well adjusted than those you'll find elsewhere, but simply because there will be more honesty here.

A second advantage of belonging to your group is the amount you will be

---

* It's difficult to find a way of handling pronouns that doesn't discriminate against one sex or the other. For the rest of the book we'll shift back and forth between *he* and *she* as a way of both preventing bias and maintaining word economy. (See Chapter 8 for more thoughts on sexism in language.)

able to learn from other members. Many will have found ways of overcoming difficulties you now have, and hearing their experiences can often give you new ideas about how to handle issues in your life. Some members might also serve as especially good models of desirable ways of communicating, so that you can learn a great deal simply by watching the way they behave.

A third benefit of exploring interpersonal communication in a group will become clear when you begin practicing the new skills presented throughout this book. Then you'll see that your classroom can become a kind of safe laboratory in which to try out new ways of behaving. This advantage of working with others is valuable because it helps you avoid the risk and anxiety that would come if you had to try out these new styles in the "outside world," where people might not look at your first and possibly fumbling attempts with much understanding. Since most of the techniques that follow will be new to the group, you'll all be able to try out new behaviors, make mistakes, and adapt accordingly with members of the group who understand what's going on.

To continue the process of getting to know one another, here's an exercise that will add some new information to go with the names you've already learned.

Introductions

1. Form dyads (groups of twos). If possible, pair up with someone you've *not* known previously. The instructor or facilitator should use himself to even out the dyads if necessary. In any event, someone should introduce the instructor.

2. Each member of a dyad will interview the other. Try to allow about twenty minutes for this.
   a. You should find *three* unique things to tell the group about the person you're introducing. These may be actions, characteristics, or experiences that set your partner apart from other people. (For example, the fact that he graduated from Lincoln High School probably isn't so important as the fact that he's thinking about getting married, quitting school, or planning an interesting career.) Remember that most people feel uncomfortable talking about themselves, so you'll have to probe to get those *unique* aspects from your partner.
   b. Use the *name* of the person you're introducing instead of the pronoun *he* or *she.* This will help everyone learn names.

3. After you've interviewed each other, get the group back together and proceed around the room introducing your partners until everyone has been introduced.

4. Unpacking: Discussing the Activity.
   a. This experience was different from the usual way you get to know someone. What parts of it did you like? Were there parts that you didn't like? Why?
   b. Now that you know more about each other, have your feelings changed about any of the individuals? How? Have your feelings changed in regard to the group? How?

THE SHIELDS

Among the People, every person possessed a Shield of one kind or another. One of the most important things to understand about these Shields is that they were never intended to give physical protection in battle. They were not made to turn away arrows or bullets, or for people to hide behind. Usually they were much too thin and fragile for this. Sometimes they were made from the tough hides of bears or buffalo bulls, but more often they were covered only with the soft skins of deer, antelope, coyote, otter, weasel, or even mice. They were then hung with eagle plumes, cedar pouches, tassels of animal fur, and many other things. They were also painted with various symbolic figures.

In the case of the Personal Shields, all of these different things represented the individual

Medicines and Clan Signs of the men who carried them. These Signs told who the man was, what he sought to be, and what his loves, fears and dreams were. Almost everything about him was written there, reflected in the Mirror of his Shield. . . .

These Shields were carried by the men among the People in order that anyone they met might know them. Even when they rested in their lodges, their Shields were always kept outside where all could see them. They might be hung up by the lodge door, or up by the smoke hole, or on a tripod near the lodge, according to each person's own Medicine Way. But they were always kept outside, where the People might see and learn from them.

Hyemeyohsts Storm, *Seven Arrows*

Why We Communicate

Sometimes we are only vaguely aware of those things that are the closest to us. Just as we usually take the air around us for granted because it's always there and not visible, we often ignore the process by which we express ourselves and understand others. But just as the atmosphere can slowly become polluted without our noticing it and thus affect our physical health, the manner in which we communicate can break down and in so doing lead to many problems. In the next few pages we want to show you the critical role communication plays in meeting everyday needs, and then point out how some present styles of relating to each other fail to satisfy many of those needs.

Anthropologists tell us that language developed to meet the needs of early man in his struggle to survive in a hostile environment. Robert Ardrey in his book *The Social Contract* suggests that it was the ability to communicate that made it possible for our distant ancestors to hunt and kill for food, to protect themselves against larger and stronger animals, and to organize their efforts in a manner that made civilization possible. If you think about it for a moment, it becomes apparent that none of these accomplishments would have occurred without the ability to work and plan together, which in turn depends on the ability to communicate.

Today as much as in the past our ability to survive and prosper depends on the same ability. The success of our family, social, and commercial relationships hinges on effective communication. Psychologist Abraham Maslow in his book *Motivation and Personality* identifies five basic types of human needs that each of us must satisfy if we are to live a safe and satisfying life in today's world.

Physical Needs We must have sufficient air, water, food, and rest in order to live. As a species, we must reproduce in order to survive. Unless these basic physical needs are met, we have no future to be concerned with.

Safety Needs Moving up Maslow's needs ladder, the next necessity is safety. Once we know we won't starve or suffocate, we have to look for ways to protect ourselves from less immediate threats. Shelter and clothing become concerns, and we do whatever is necessary to prevent harm from other sources that threaten our well-being. At various times in human history these have included dangerous animals, threatening people, and diseases.

How do we satisfy these needs in our lives? For the most part it means getting and holding a job that earns us the money to put food on the table, clothes on our backs, and a roof over our heads. In order to accomplish this we *must* communicate—we have no other choice. Even if you were to spend the rest of your life on public welfare, you'd have to convince the eligibility worker of your need.

Social Needs Maslow believed that once we've satisfied our first two levels of needs, we turn to our social needs. Included at this need level is our desire to belong, to be accepted, to be loved and appreciated, and to have friends. Most of us become lonely when we don't have other humans to interact with. Therefore, when we have time and energy that is not required for satisfying our physiological and safety needs, we tend to seek companionship.

Psychologist William Schutz identifies three interpersonal needs that we must satisfy at this social need level. He says that we want to be included in what other people do and to include them in our activities (inclusion); we desire to exercise some control over others (control); and we need to have others care about us, and we also need to care about them (affection). Like Maslow, Schutz argues that our needs to achieve inclusion, control, and affection aren't just desirable, they are essential. If we are unable to interact with others, we become lonely, isolated, and sometimes disturbed. We might add emphasis to this by taking some liberty with the lyrics of a recently popular song: "People who need people" aren't the luckiest people in the world, they're the *only* people in the world, since building relationships with people is one of our basic human needs.

Self-esteem Needs   As you'll read in Chapter 2, defining and confirming our personal identity provides the foundation for much of our behavior. Maslow recognized this behavior as the need to promote our self-esteem. This need explains why we need to keep proving to ourselves that we are o.k. We want to believe that what we do is satisfactory and valuable. You can identify with how important it is for us to have evidence that we're succeeding at school, in our jobs, or in our special relationships.

Self-actualization Needs   At the top of Maslow's ladder of human needs we find the drive to develop our potential to its maximum, to become everything we are capable of becoming. We might add here that this need is open-ended because no matter how much we accomplish there is still the urge to go on— to reach for the stars. This need to be self-actualized explains why people who seem to "have it made" will risk their security and sometimes even their lives by changing careers in mid-life, attempting to earn a new academic degree at age 65, crossing the ocean in a small boat, or climbing a dangerous mountain. If you ask why, you may receive an answer like "I haven't done that before, it was there," or "It's something I've always wanted to do." We suspect that it was partly this drive that prodded us to write this book. We're both successful in our teaching and could have settled for that, but somehow we felt challenged—we had to find out "if we had it in us" to be successful textbook authors, too.

The order in which these needs are listed is important, for Maslow suggests that we must satisfy the basic ones before moving on to higher categories. For example, a person who is suffocating must find air to breathe before worrying about freezing, and someone who is threatened by a physical attack will seek safety before worrying about being lonesome.

A Day in the Life

From our standpoint it is significant that each of these levels of needs depends on effective communication for its satisfaction. Physiological survival, safety, social contact, self-esteem and self-actualization all require the ability to express yourself and understand others. To see how true this is, take a look at some of the activities that might occur in an ordinary day.

Social need *6:15 a.m.* Your clock radio comes on playing a song which reminds you of a special friend you haven't seen in some time. You make a mental note to phone this person and make plans to get together.

Physiological and safety needs *7:00 a.m.* You are somewhat rushed this morning and ask to have a sandwich made for your lunch. You grab your heavy coat but can't find your gloves. It's cold out so you inquire as to their whereabouts. After a moment of discussion, others at home help you recall where you left the gloves.

Social need *7:30 a.m.* You're on your way to the college. You stop and pick up your friends. The conversation centers on an exam you will all be taking, and how you are all dreading the ordeal. You make plans to get together for some studying. You feel better now for knowing that you'll be prepared for the test and that you're not facing the experience alone. Misery loves company!

Social and self-esteem needs *8:00 a.m.* You're in class and smile at the interesting, attractive person across the room. The smile is returned, and you drift off into a pleasant daydream. . . . You're not paying attention to the lecture and suddenly realize that the instructor has asked you a question. When you don't know how to respond, the instructor makes a sarcastic remark about students who don't pay attention. Your face suddenly feels hot. You wish you could find the words to apologize to the professor and at the same time request that if he has any complaints about your behavior he share them in a less humiliating way.

Safety need *12:00 noon* You stop by the auto repair shop to see about an ominous sound coming from one of your car's wheels. Of course, when the service manager goes out for a test drive the noise isn't there. You do your best to describe the problem, stating that it's important you have the problem taken care of before you wind up in an accident. After much discussion the manager begins to decipher the problem and makes an appointment to fix it the next day.

Physiological, safety, and self-esteem needs *2:00 p.m.* Now you're at work. Today is the day you are going to talk to your boss about a raise. You're convinced that your work has improved enough so that your services are worth more to the company. Finally you get up enough nerve to actually make your request. After considering your reasoning, your boss agrees with you and announces that the raise will be more than you had hoped for. Elated, you phone home to share the good news, receiving congratulations from your family.

Social and self-actualization needs *8:00 p.m.* During your guitar lesson the teacher praises you for catching on so rapidly. While this pleases you, you believe you could still do a better job, and ask for more help in mastering a new technique.

As you read this account and think about your own daily activities you can see that you are continually communicating. Whether asking for food, smiling at another person, listening to instructions, or requesting help, you're constantly sending and receiving messages in order to satisfy your various needs. How successfully are you communicating to meet your needs?

This model of human motivations isn't a totally accurate representation of how people operate. The distinction between one category of needs and another is sometimes blurred, and we frequently strive to satisfy several needs simultaneously. However, Maslow states that the bulk of our energy is directed at satisfying different needs at different times.

The Need for Better Communication

The human needs we've just discussed are obviously important. If we were able to satisfy these needs on our own, there would be no reason for us to write this book, for you to be reading it, or for much of the misery that exists in people's lives. The truth is, however, that few of us communicate well enough to completely satisfy our physiological, social and ego needs; and many fall so short of these goals that they lead troubled lives. In the next few pages we'll look at some of the evidence found in contemporary society to support this conclusion. We'll investigate the connections between good interpersonal communication and life and health, better relationships, and self-understanding.

Life and Health It is obvious that failure to satisfy our physiological needs is fatal. It would be an overstatement to say that there are many cases where people communicate so poorly that they starve, suffocate, or meet some similar fate, but consider the other types of needs we've discussed. What happens if we don't satisfy our desire for inclusion, control, or affection? Do we die? You're probably thinking, ''Of course not,'' but, in fact, there does seem to be a connection between social interaction and physical health—and even longevity. In a nine-year study of 7,000 subjects Lisa Berkman, an epidemiologist working for the California Department of Health, found that people with few or no strong social relationships died at a rate from two to four and one-half times greater than more socially oriented people. The context in which social interaction occurred did not seem to matter: some of the longer-lived subjects gained satisfaction for their social needs from marriages, others had friendships, and still others were members of some organization. But people with no such affiliations apparently failed to have a life-sustaining need met.

Suicide figures are also indicative of people's inability to meet interpersonal needs. In the United States in 1975 there were 12.6 deaths by suicide for every 100,000 population. A decade before there were 11.6 suicides per 100,000. The increase amounts to a significant increase of 8 percent in only ten years. Although making the connection of a person's death by suicide and that person's failure to meet the need for social interaction isn't as clearcut as death from failing to meet a physiological need (i.e., no food to eat), it seems reasonable to assume that some relationship exists.

Perhaps more immediate to many college students is the depressing fact that there has been a 90 percent increase in suicides among young people between the ages of fifteen and twenty-one in the last decade. Suicide ranks second only to automobile accidents as a cause of death for this age group.

And this probably isn't the whole picture: the number of suicides disguised as auto accidents, poisonings, and so on can never be known. Moreover, sociologists working in this area estimate that seven to eight times the number who succeed in committing suicide attempt it. This means that about 175,000 to 200,000 individuals each year in this country make the choice to give up the struggle to live a satisfying life. The evidence of suicide notes, relatives, and experts in this area points to loneliness, alienation, and unhappy relationships as the chief causes for this desperate decision. How many of these suicides could have been prevented had the victims had the communication skills necessary to establish meaningful interpersonal relationships?

Of course, not everyone who has trouble communicating interpersonally dies prematurely. But unless something happens to help these people relate better, their lives are likely to be troubled. Looking at the figures on mental illness we discover that one in ten of all Americans is considered maladjusted or mentally ill. New laws make it mandatory for teachers and health personnel to report all cases of suspected child abuse to the authorities. A look at any

put me in your human eye
come taste
the bitter tears
that i cry
touch me
with your human hand
hear me with your ear
but notice me
damn you
notice me
i'm here.

Ric Masten

Talk for Sale

Even talk isn't cheap any more. In the San Francisco suburb of Kensington, talk is going for $8 an hour in a sadly modern kind of coffeehouse called "Conversation." The café offers a troupe of twenty "conversationalists" for hire at $5 for the first 30 minutes and $3 for each additional half hour, along with fourteen soundproofed booths to chat in. The owners, Dick Braunlich and his wife, Chris, opened Conversation last month. They insist that they are not dispensing therapy, but simply providing the customer with "a nice person to talk to." Says Chris Braunlich: "Most of our patrons want to discuss their philosophy of life. They don't need a psychiatrist."

Indeed, even the hint of therapy is discouraged. When more than 100 applications for the conversationalist job came in, those who stressed guidance and counseling—even those with degrees in psychology—were turned down. "We hired those we felt were good, warm people," says Dick Braunlich. Engel Devendorf, 57, one of the café's more popular professional talkers, recalls a blond divorcée who, stricken with terminal loneliness, wandered in after dropping her children off at a movie matinee. "She was new to California and didn't know anyone here," he says. "She didn't stop talking from the moment she came in." There are many other places—such as churches—where lonely people can find companionship. But, as Chris Braunlich points out, "people think if you're not paying, you're not getting anything."

Newsweek Magazine

authorities. A look at any medical text concerned with these problems makes it clear that child abusers are motivated in great part by unsatisfying relationships in which little effective communication has occurred. It's additionally sad that many people who experience such difficulties suffer greatly from guilt and remorse but are either afraid or don't know how to ask for help.

Better Relationships   "What's this to do with me?" you may be asking. "I'm alive, and neither suicidal nor mentally ill. Why should I worry about communicating?" We can answer these questions by suggesting that while your life might not be terrible, it's probably not as good as it could be. One reason why you may be less than totally satisfied is that your important relationships are sometimes unrewarding. And one of the main sources of relationship problems is the difficulty many have in communicating.

Family relationships certainly suffer when members cannot communicate effectively. Professionals who counsel troubled families consistently state that one of the most common problems they hear from their clients is "we can't communicate with each other." Sometimes this inability to communicate successfully is symptomatic of other problems; but in many cases families who learn some of the skills described in this book find that problems that formerly seemed unsolvable can be dealt with.

While family relationships may be of major importance to parents, to teenagers the associations with peers become primary. Teenagers need to break away from the family (usually to reestablish emotional ties later), while parents often want to hang onto their children. As this struggle develops, family unity is shaken—typical patterns of interaction are disrupted, and the stability that was most likely one of the prime benefits of family life is shattered. During this stressful period the friction between family members grows, often becoming intolerable.

Tosh and I were walking back down the trail, our run completed, when we encountered a young woman walking up the road. Tosh automatically sprinted toward her, wagging his tail. Sensing that his advance might frighten her, I called, "Don't worry, he's friendly." She regarded him for a moment, then dropped her eyes to the ground and walked past him. As she approached, I started to say something but thought better of it. There was no face to address. The nearer she got, the more bowed her head became. The best gesture seemed to be to make eye contact and offer a silent, perfunctory nod. We were now only a few feet apart; still all I could see was the top of her head. I waited for her to lift her head, ready to meet her eyes. Nothing. We were almost opposite one another. If there was to be any mutual recognition, it would have to happen now. It didn't. Though there couldn't have been more than two feet between us, we passed each other without a word or a glance.

Her behavior perplexed me. It wasn't that I felt snubbed. It just seemed perverse for two persons to meet on a narrow, isolated road and not acknowledge one another. She had seemed almost to cower, as if intimidated by my presence. Perhaps she had reason to fear or hate men. Still, it might have been an extreme case of self-consciousness or depression. The possible explanations were endless. But none satisfied me, then or now.

Mace Perona

Although learning to communicate effectively certainly won't make these generational differences evaporate, it can help family members cope with them in a way that doesn't threaten their relationships with each other. If families had communication skills such as those that this book describes and that you'll be working to improve, their ability to share and adapt to each others' needs could provide a basis for dealing positively with these turbulent and stressful periods.

Married couples often have as much trouble communicating with each other as with their children. In 1975 there were 2.1 million marriages and a million divorces officially recorded. That works out to about one marriage dissolved for every two started. Just ten years earlier, in 1965, there was one divorce for every four marriages. In California in 1975 there were 130,000 divorces and 160,000 marriages. In part these figures stem from the fact that more people are willing to abandon an unsuccessful relationship rather than continue the charade of an unhappy marriage. But it is also fair to say that many couples end their marriages reluctantly, having been unable to overcome the difficulties that came between them. If some of these partners could learn better communication skills, then perhaps their chances for success in future relationships—both within and outside of marriage—will increase.

REACHING OUT TO THE INNER MAN

Two dozen men of all ages sat or sprawled on the carpet in a rough circle. Joe wasn't sure he liked this setup. He hadn't got down on the floor in years. Serious men sat in chairs around a table, they looked each other in the eye, and they got something done. Didn't they?

These men were talking to each other, but they didn't seem to have an objective. They were telling each other how they were feeling—good and bad. Joe didn't see the point of it. He felt slightly embarrased and thought of an old joke: What's the definition of a bore? It's when you ask somebody "How are you?" . . . and he tells you.

It was Sunday night, and Joe mentally began to sort through the TV schedule. If he left now, maybe . . . But a man was saying. "I'm lonely—that's it, pure and simple. I talk to people all week. I talk up a storm, but it's like I'm walking around encased in a giant ice cube. I can never get close."

Astonishing. Joe had never heard another man admit he was lonely.

Depressed over lost job Someone else was speaking. He was depressed because he'd lost his job. Aha, Joe thought, this is a collection of losers. They come here to cry on each other's shoulders.

But then, moving around the circle, three men in a row had good feelings to report: A son had finally been accepted in the college he desperately wanted; a man who had just celebrated an anniversary was thinking out loud about all the reasons his relationship with his wife continued to be so satisfying; and the next man was gleefully reporting how he'd just found the perfect new job after a two-year search.

He had some words of comfort for the man who'd just lost his, and they agreed to get together later to talk about resumes.

Joe began to relax a little. There was something easy in the air—nobody trying to look good or protect his rear.

It didn't seem to matter that every man had something different on his mind. The group was there to share tangibly the burden of an unhappy man, and it was equally ready to enhance and make real the joy another might feel.

A sense of sharing Joe began to think back to other male groupings. The basketball team of long ago? The bowling league, the poker gang? Of course he'd felt a sense of sharing, but always in a competitive framework. Camaraderie? Yes, but how often did it lead to truly serious talk? You can't tell another man—even your best friend—what you're afraid of.

And yet that's exactly what this group was doing. Here he was a stranger, and they were telling him all their secrets. A young man was saying, "I didn't really want to have sex with her, but I pushed it like crazy—I was a madman. Then when she finally give in, I couldn't make it. Why can't I get it through my head that I'm looking for somebody to love?"

Another man began to talk about a divorce action he was going through and suddenly Joe, without thinking about it, was giving him reassurance from his own experience. He stopped in midsentence, recognizing the emotion in his voice. This was something he hadn't sorted out himself. It's risky for a man to admit that he feels so emotionally torn up that he can't even perform his job very well.

Dimly he realized that another man was talking about the pain of ending a 10-year relationship. A mental alarm bell went off in Joe. This man was telling about a homosexual breakup! Joe had never heard a gay man talk about his personal life.

Fear, curiosity, hostility He studied other faces in the circle. Was this a discovery for them too? Had they known about this alien sitting here among them? How many other gay men were in the circle? Fear, curiosity, hostility flitted through his head, and yet the group remained as open and receptive as before.

Joe forced himself to listen, and it came to him finally: The pain, the sense of loss this man was describing was exactly the same as his own. The stereotype was broken. He felt himself reaching out, expressing his support to a troubled fellow man, a brother.

As he drove home that night, Joe tried to assess the meaning of this "men's liberation" experience. He felt good, warmed, and he thought he might try it again. But what had this group actually accomplished? He couldn't pin it down.

All he knew was that for the first time in his life he had heard adult men talk with absolute candor about their innermost feelings; and the ice cube that shielded him had melted a little.

Jim Sanderson, *Los Angeles Times*

Outside of the family, communication difficulties keep many people from having the number and quality of friendships they desire. In a survey of students at Pennsylvania State University Gerald Phillips and Nancy Metzger explored the relationship between communication and friendship. The responses of their subjects indicated a strong need for better communication skills. A majority of the people Phillips and Metzger questioned reported that their friendships needed improving. Of these, many expressed frustration over their efforts to explain their behavior to others, while another group had trouble explaining to others how they wanted them to behave. The three main sources of pain in friendships were all communication-related: failure of friends to live up to promises, betrayal of confidences, and the friends' use of confessed weaknesses to intimidate the subjects.

The October, 1979, issue of *Psychology Today* reports an extensive survey on friendship in America. When asked what friends do together, those answering the survey wrote more often than anything else that they "had an intimate talk." It would seem, then, that the very basis of friendship stems from the interpersonal communication that such relationships provide.

1966 Graduates Rate Courses Most Useful

BETHLEHEM, PA. (UPI)—According to a study released by the college Placement Council in cooperation with the National Institute of Education, more than 4,100 college graduates who completed their degrees in 1966 ... cited communication, administration, interpersonal relations, and mathematical ability as desirable skills. "The implication is that persons with competencies in these areas are better prepared for whatever career they choose," the council said. . .

San Diego Union

> *People don't get along because they fear each other.*
> *People fear each other because they don't know each other.*
> *They don't know each other because they have not properly*
> *communicated with each other.*
>
> Martin Luther King, Jr.

Perhaps one of our students described the benefits of effective interpersonal communication best:

> I am also blessed with more than my share of good relationships. Relationships do not seem to be easy for people to build. I seem to be good at it, and I am deeply grateful for that. After all, it doesn't matter if I am no good at mechanics, for I can always find someone to fix my car. I could never hire someone to build and maintain my relationships. A car is something I could live without, if it came to that. But where would I be without the important people in my life?

Self-understanding   So far we've seen the importance of communication in building and maintaining relationships between couples, parents and children, and friends. In addition to these areas, there is one final reason for learning to communicate more skillfully. By relating clearly with others we can understand ourselves better.

Communication can lead to better self-understanding in two ways. First, by becoming open to the way others view us, we can learn more about ourselves. As you'll read in Chapter 2, the reflected appraisals of others serve as a kind of mirror in which we view ourselves. The more we open ourselves up to such appraisals, the better idea we'll have of how we appear.

We also learn about ourselves by speaking. Virtually all people have had the experience of understanding their own position better after they have explained it to another person. The value of talking about one's ideas is true of almost any subject, from the process for factoring a quadratic equation to whether to stay in school to why you are or aren't in love. Probably the most dramatic validation of self-expression as a road to understanding is evidenced by the handsome living that many psychotherapists earn primarily by allowing their clients to talk themselves into better mental health. Of course, it would be an oversimplification to suggest that the only skill a therapist must possess is to keep quiet and let the patient rattle on, but few therapists would dispute the value of a supportive, empathetic listener.

The Process of Communication

So far we've been talking about communication as if the actions described by this word were perfectly clear. We've found, however, that most people aren't aware of all that goes on whenever two people share ideas. Before going further we want to show you exactly what does happen when one person expresses a thought or feeling to another. By doing so we can introduce you to a common working vocabulary that will be useful as you read on, at the same time previewing some of the activities we'll cover in later chapters.

Since we need to begin somewhere, let's start with you wanting to express an idea. If you think about it for a moment, you'll realize that most ideas you have don't come to you already put into words. Rather, they're more like mental images, often consisting of unverbalized feelings (anger, excitement, etc.), intentions (wants, desires, needs), or even mental pictures (such as how you want a job to look when it is finished). We can represent your mental image like this.

Since people aren't mind readers, you have to translate this mental image into symbols (usually words) that others can understand. No doubt you can recall times when you actually shuffled through a mental list of words to pick exactly the right ones to explain an idea. This process, called *encoding,* goes on every time we speak. Chapter 8 will deal in some detail with the problems and skills of being an effective encoder.

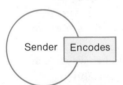

Once you've encoded an idea, the next step is to send it. We call this step the *message* phase of our model. You have a number of ways by which you can send a message. For instance, you might consider expressing yourself in a letter or over the telephone. In this sense writing and speaking words are two of the *channels* through which we send our messages. In addition to these channels we transfer our thoughts and feelings by touch, posture, gestures, distance, clothing, and many other ways as described in Chapter 7. The important thing to realize now is that there are a number of such channels.

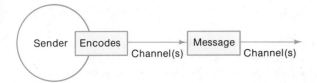

When your message reaches another person, much the same process we described earlier occurs in reverse. The receiver must make some sense out of the symbols you've sent by *decoding* them back into feelings, intentions, or thoughts that mean something to him.

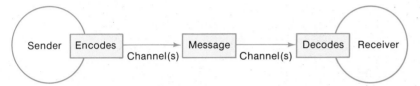

Ideally, at this point the mental images of the sender and receiver ought to match. If this happens, we can say that an act of successful communication has occurred. However, as you know from your own experience, things often go wrong somewhere between sender and receiver. For instance:

your constructive suggestion is taken as criticism

your carefully phrased question is misunderstood

your friendly joke is taken as an insult

your hinted request is missed entirely

And so it often goes. Why do such misunderstandings occur? To answer this question we need to add more detail to our model.

First, it's important to recognize that communication always takes place in an environment. By this term we don't mean simply a physical location, but also the personal history that each person brings to a conversation. The problem here is that each of us has a different environment because of our differing backgrounds. While we certainly have some things in common, we also see each situation in a unique way. For instance, consider how two individuals' environments would differ if

A was well rested and *B* was exhausted

A was rich and *B* was poor

A was rushed and *B* had nowhere special to go

A had lived a long, eventful life and *B* was young and inexperienced

A was passionately concerned with the subject and *B* was indifferent to it

Obviously this list could go on and on. Because the problem of differing environments is so critical to effective communication, Chapter 5 is devoted to showing you the many different ways people can perceive a single event. Even now, though, you can see from just these few items that the world is a different place for sender and receiver. We can represent this idea on our model in this manner.

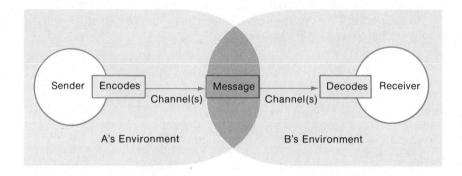

Notice that we've overlapped the environments of *A* and *B*. This overlapping represents those things that our communicators have in common. This is an important point because it is through the knowledge that we share that we are able to communicate. For example, you are able at least partially to understand the messages we are writing on these pages because we share the same language, however imprecise it often may be.

Different environments aren't the only cause of ineffective communication. Communicologists use the term *noise* to label other forces that interfere with the process, and point out that it can occur in every stage.

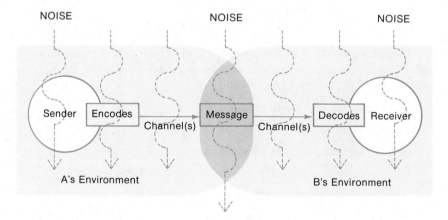

There are three types of noise that can block communication. The first, external noise, includes those obvious things that make it difficult to hear, as well as many other kinds of distractions. For instance, too much cigarette smoke in a crowded room might make it hard for you to pay attention to another person, and sitting in the rear of an auditorium might make a speaker's remarks unclear. External noise can disrupt communication almost anywhere in our model—in the sender, channel, message, or receiver.

The second type of noise is physiological. A hearing disorder is probably the most obvious type of physiological barrier, although many more exist. Consider, for instance, the difficulty you experience as a listener when you are suffering from a cold or are very tired. In the same way you might speak less when you have a sore throat or a headache.

Psychological noise refers to forces within the sender or receiver that make these people less able to express or understand the message clearly. For instance, an outdoorsman might exaggerate the size and number of fish caught in order to convince himself and others of his talents. In the same way, a student might become so upset upon learning that she failed a test that she would be unable (perhaps unwilling is a better word) to clearly understand where she went wrong. Psychological noise is so important a problem in communication that we have devoted Chapter 4 to investigating its most common form, defensiveness.

So far we've only talked about one-way communication, consisting of a single sender and receiver who never switch roles. There certainly are situations in which this is an accurate picture of what goes on. Television, radio, and newspapers represent one-way communication, as do some unfortunate families where parents expect to do all the talking while their kids are placed in the position of being merely listeners.

At this point you can probably recognize that there are also cases where communication must be *two-way,* with each participant both sending and receiving. Two-way communication is appropriate and important in many situations, not only because it gives us a chance to share our ideas with others, but also because it helps us check and verify our understanding of the messages others have sent. This use of two-way communication for verification is termed *feedback.* To see its role in effective communication, consider the following brief conversations.

Anne   So I'll be by to pick you up as soon as I get off work.

Becca   Good! I'll be in front about six.

Anne   Better make it closer to six-thirty. I've got to stop by the market on my way home.

Charlie   What are you looking at me like that for? I said I was sorry, didn't I?

Dave   Hold it a second! I accepted your apology. What's the problem?

Charlie   Well, it seemed to me that you gave me one of your dirty looks.

Dave   What dirty looks?

Charlie   Well, a lot of the time you kind of smile and shake your head at the same time. It looks to me like you're disagreeing with whatever I've said.

You can see from these examples that if Becca and Charlie had simply accepted their decoding of the sender's message without checking back, a misunderstanding would have occurred. For this reason it's important to realize that being an effective receiver demands that you often use active feedback, and not just passively assume that you understand the sender. We'll cover this essential set of skills in Chapter 6.

So far we've talked about sending and receiving as if a communicator played only one of these roles at a time. In fact, it's more accurate to say that most of the time we are sending and receiving messages simultaneously. Consider, for instance, what happens when you are debating a political issue with a friend. You begin by expressing your ideas, but while your friend is listening (receiving), he begins to shake his head in what you interpret as disagreement. This feedback is a message in itself, which might cause you to modify your remarks. This brief incident should show you that much of the time each of us is involved in transactions where we are both senders and receivers. Thus, we can say that communication is an ongoing process, rather than a linear activity in which one person talks, gestures, or writes while the other passively absorbs the message.

Keeping these facts in mind, we now have a detailed model of the communication process.

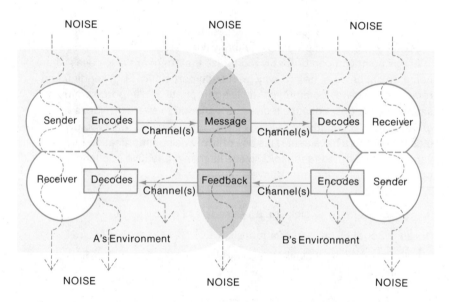

As we said earlier, this picture is probably more complicated than the definition you might have once given. But now you can probably see that every step is important and can't be omitted. Given this model, perhaps you can better understand why effective communication is often so difficult, and why spending some time learning the skills that make it possible can be worth your while.

Make Your Own Model

Check your understanding of the communication model by applying it to your own life.

1. In a group of three, share two important messages you intend to express within the next week.

2. For each message, describe
   a. The idea you want to send and the various ways you could encode it.
   b. Channels by which you could send it.
   c. Problems your receiver might have in decoding it.
   d. Possible differences between your environment and that of the receiver, and how those differences might make it difficult to understand your full message.
   e. Likely sources of external, physical and psychological noise that might make it difficult for you to phrase your message clearly or for your receiver to understand it.
   f. Ways you can make sure your receiver uses feedback to verify an accurate understanding of the message.

Elements of a Clear Message

After studying the previous model, you should see that effective communication requires you to express completely and accurately what's happening for you in such a way that the other person receives exactly the message you intended to send.

   If you think about it for a moment, you'll recognize that our definition implies that as a sender you must *know* what's happening for you. After all, it's difficult to clearly express an idea that you're not aware of having.

Surprisingly, failure to meet this simple requirement of knowing what you want to say is the cause of many communication problems. To put it another way, many communicators aren't aware of some important things about themselves that they must share if others are to fully understand their messages.

In the following pages we will describe several elements of a message that sometimes go ignored, and thus unsent. As we do so, you'll probably see that you often fail to recognize one or more of these elements in yourself, and thus make it hard for others to understand your message.

Sensing   Sensing provides the raw material upon which you react. Sense data includes the things you see, hear, touch, smell, and feel with your skin. For instance, a camera records visual sense data and an audio tape recorder picks up and stores sounds.

For our purpose the important thing to recognize about sense data is that it is *objective.* A record of pure sensory information would simply describe an event without interpreting it.

Two examples of purely sensory records of events might look like this:

Example 1
One week ago John promised me that he would ask my permission before smoking in the same room with me. Just a moment ago he lit up a cigarette without asking for my o.k.

Example 2
When I walked into the room, there were about fifteen people there. They were gathered into several groups, all of which were involved in some sort of conversation. As I approached one group the speaker smiled briefly at me and then went on talking. The other members all looked at me and said hello, moved aside, creating space for me to join their circle, and then returned their gaze to the speaker.

Note that in both cases the description records only data that is available through the senses. The observer has not attached any meaning to the behaviors so far. This is the essense of sensing.

Interpreting   Interpretation is the process of attaching meaning to sense data. The important thing to realize about interpretations is that they are *subjective.* That is, there is more than one interpretation that we can attach to any set of sense data. For example, look at these two different interpretations of each descriptin above:

Example 1
Interpretation A: "John must have forgotten about our agreement that he wouldn't smoke without asking me first. I'm sure he's too considerate to go back on his word on something he knows I feel strongly about."

Interpretation B: "John is a rude inconsiderate person. After promising not to smoke around me without asking, he's just deliberately done so. This shows that he only cares about himself. In fact, I bet he's deliberately doing this to drive me crazy!"

Example 2
Interpretation A: "I can tell that the people in this group are glad to see me, for they all took a moment out of what was obviously an interesting story to say hello. Naturally they want to hear the speaker through to the end before talking about anything else, so I'll stick around and see what the topic is so I can talk about it when he's finished."

Interpretation B: "The people in the group must think I'm a jerk for butting into their conversation when they already had something going. Oh, they were polite enough to smile at me, but it's obvious that they don't have any interest in an outsider nosing into their private conversation. I'm getting out of here!"

It's clear from these examples that interpretations clearly are made on more than simple sense data. They also grow out of the following:

Our past experience   "John has always (never) kept his promises in the past." or "A friend once told me to mind my own business (feel welcome) when I joined what turned out to be a private conversation."

Our assumptions   "An unkept promise is a sign of uncaring (forgetfulness)." or "At parties people don't (do) expect to discuss private subjects.

Our expectations   "John probably wants (doesn't want) to fight." or "I think these guests will (won't) like me."

Our knowledge   "Long-time, habitual cigarette smokers often aren't even aware of lighting up." or "Social psychologists have observed that, as a rule, if members of a group acknowledge a new person by smiling and moving aside to make room, they are willing to have that person join the group."

Our current mood   "I feel good about John and about life in general," or "I've been feeling insecure lately, and so I imagine that the guests won't like me."

Once you become aware of the difference between sense data and interpretation, some of the reasons for communication breakdowns become clear. Many problems occur when a sender fails to share the sense data upon which an interpretation is based. For instance, imagine the difference between hearing a friend say

"You are a tightwad!" (No sense data)

. . . and explaining

"When you never offer to pay me back for the coffee and snacks I often buy you, I think you're a tightwad." (Sense data plus interpretation)

The first speaker's failure to specify sense data would probably confuse the receiver, who has no way of knowing what prompted the sender's remarks. This failure to describe sense data also reduces any chance that the receiver will change the offensive behavior, which, after all, is unknown to her.

Just as important as specifying sense data is the need to label an interpretation as such, instead of presenting it as a matter of fact. Consider the difference between saying

"It's obvious that if you cared for me you'd write more often." (Interpretation presented as fact)

. . . and

"When you didn't write, I thought that you didn't care for me." (Interpretation made clear)

As you'll learn in Chapter 3, your comments a e much less likely to arouse defensiveness in others when you present them in a tentative, provisional manner.

A third important rule is to avoid making statements that appear to report sense data but are in fact interpretations. For instance, don't mistake these kinds of statements as objective descriptions:

"I see you're tired." (*Tired* is an interpretation. Your sense data might have been "I see your eyes closing and your head nodding.")

"I see you're in a hurry." (*Hurry* is an interpretation. The sense data could have been, "I see you gathering up your books and looking at the clock.")

"I hear that you're hungry." (*Hungry* is an interpretation. The sense data you heard was the sound of your friend's stomach growling.)

"You look eager to get started." *Eager* is an interpretation. What could the sense data be in this case? The short time it took her to answer the doorbell? The outside clothing in which she was already dressed?)

There's nothing wrong with making these interpretations. In fact, this is a necessary step because only by interpreting sense data do you arrive at a meaning. However, we often make inaccurate interpretations, and when we don't separate sense data from our interpretations we fool ourselves into believing that our interpretations are reality—that is, what we *think* is what exists.

Sense Statements

Form a circle with a few other group members. Each person in turn should take one minute to report the sense data he is receiving *as it occurs*. Don't worry about your perceptions being in any logical order—simply describe them as they come to you. Try to be aware of all your senses: seeing, hearing, touching, feeling, and tasting.

A sample report might begin "Now I'm aware of all of you looking at me . . . now I'm aware of a dry taste in my mouth . . . this chair feels uncomfortable . . . and I'm seeing a smile on Kathy's face . . . I feel warm . . . now I'm aware of the hum of the air conditioner. . . ."

Notice how difficult it may be simply to describe what you perceive without attaching interpretations. Does this same problem occur in your everyday life?

Sensing and Interpreting

1. Share with two other group members several interpretations you have recently made about other people in your life. For each interpretation, describe the sense data upon which you based your remarks.

2. With your partners' help, consider some alternate interpretations of your sense data that might be as plausible as your original one.

3. After considering the alternate interpretations, decide
   a. Which one was most reasonable
   b. How you might share that interpretation (along with the sense data) with the other person involved in a tentative, nondogmatic way.

Feelings   What emotions can you identify? Without looking at the list on page 96, try to jot down all the feelings you can think of. Go ahead and make your list now, before going on. Many of our readers who try this activity have a hard time coming up with more than a few vague emotions, such as "good" or "bad," "terrible" or "great." Now take a moment and compare your list with the one on page 96 and see if you've been able to recall all the emotions there.

Feelings add an extremely important dimension to a message. For example, consider the difference between saying

"When you kiss me and nibble on my ear while we're watching television (sense data), I think you probably want to make love (interpretation), *and I feel excited.*"

"When you kiss me and nibble on my ear while we're watching television, I think you probably want to make love, and *I feel disgusted.*"

There's quite a difference between these two statements, isn't there? Notice how the expression of different feelings can change the meaning of another message.

"When you laugh at me (sense data), I think you find my comments foolish (interpretation), and *I feel embarrassed.*"

"When you laugh at me, I think you find my comments foolish, and *I feel angry.*"

No doubt you can supply other examples in which different feelings can radically affect a speaker's meaning. Recognizing this, it seems logical to say that we should identify the feelings we're experiencing in our conversations with others. Yet, if you pay attention to the everyday acts of communication you observe, you'll see that no such sharing goes on.

It's important to recognize that some statements *seem* as if they're expressing feelings but are really interpretations or statements of intention. For instance, it's incorrect to say "I feel like leaving" (really an intention) or "I feel like you're wrong" (an interpretation). Statements like these obscure the true expression of feelings and should be avoided.

What prevents people from sharing their feelings? Certainly one cause is that making such statements can bring on a great deal of anxiety. It's often frightening to come right out and say "I'm angry," "I feel embarrassed," or "I love you," and often we aren't willing to take the risks that come with such clear-cut assertions. We'll have more to say about the issue of taking risks in a few pages.

A second reason why people don't express their feelings is simply because they don't recognize them as they occur. If this seems strange to you, take another look at the list of emotions you just recorded. Most likely you'll find that it was much less comprehensive than even the incomplete one we've included in this book. If this was so, you'll begin to see that most of our emotional vocabularies are limited.

Why is it that people sometimes have such trouble recognizing how they feel? This doesn't seem to be a problem we're born with. If you've spent any time with babies or young children, you know that for them there's no gap between feeling and acting. When a one-year-old is happy, she laughs, not just with her face but with her whole body. When she feels pain, she cries; when she's angry, you know it right away. Children this age don't follow the feel-think-act pattern that's so common with grownups; instead it seems that they just *are*.

What happens to get in the way of this easy expression of feelings? Part of the gap between thinking and feeling almost certainly comes from the lessons we learn while growing up. Usually without being aware of it, and almost inevitably, adults send message after message telling a child which emotions are acceptable and which aren't. In a house where angry words are taboo, the child gets the idea that anger is a "not o.k." thing. If sex is never discussed except with great discomfort, then the child will learn to stop talking about—and even stop consciously feeling—emotions that center around the body. If the parents only talk about trivial subjects and never share their deeper feelings, the child's conversation and thinking will tend to follow the same path.

Kids don't stop getting angry, having sexual thoughts, or intense feelings; emotions can't be turned off or on at will like water from a faucet. But because we're taught that certain feelings aren't o.k., we learn to push them out of our consciousness so that pretty soon they become hard to recognize.

As we said earlier, this lack of spontaneity in expressing feelings can become a real problem as we grow up. But what can you do if you want to get

to not
be aware
is no aware

Bernard Gunther

more closely in touch with your emotions? When you're not sure how you feel, one thing you can do is analyze yourself. Are you really happy in your job, or should you look for a new one? You can list all the reasons for each decision. Do you really love him or her? (It's possible to think this one to death.) Sometimes, after analyzing yourself this way, it's likely that you wind up even more confused than when you began. You start trying to figure out all the ways you *could* be feeling or you ask yourself how you *should* feel, but you never really come up with a satisfying answer.

Fortunately there's another, often better, way to get in touch with those unclear emotions. Unlike the approaches we've been used to, this one relies very little on your intellect. Instead of thinking about how you are, all you need to do with this technique is to listen, to pay attention to your own body. By becoming aware of the messages it sends, you can often find out more clearly what's really going on between you and other people. Try this experience and see what you can learn from your own body.

Identifying Feelings

1. Divide your group into triads.
2. In turn each person should share with the other two members of the triad a feeling she has experienced in the last few days.
3. Share also the inner and outer physical signs that accompanied the feeling.
4. Explain what you did with the feeling. Did you ignore it, deny it, let it tell you what it could, or deal with it? What happened? Were you satisfied with the outcome?
5. Share feelings for three rounds, trying to introduce as large a variety of feelings as you can.
6. When you have finished sharing a minimum of three feelings each, move into the large group and report the different feelings that were identified in your group. Have someone in the group record all the different feelings mentioned, and post the list so that everyone can see it.

Once you're aware of your feelings, the question becomes whether or not to share them with the other people involved. While we're convinced that most of us don't express our emotions often enough, we don't want to suggest that you should always share your feelings as soon as they come up. For instance, while you might become angry upon being stopped for speeding by a police officer or after being unfairly criticized by an employer, you might be better off to keep quiet in these situations.

In deciding when to share your emotions, it's a good idea to consider the realistic consequences that would come from speaking out.

1. Ask yourself what might result if you remained quiet. Will your silence encourage the continuation of an unpleasant situation or the end of a satisfying one?

2. Consider the probable result that would occur if you *did* speak out. Would such an action stop the unpleasant behavior or make it worse? Would it help to maintain a pleasant situation or stop it?

3. Whether or not your assertiveness would influence the other person's behavior, decide what impact this sharing would have on yourself. Sometimes the costs of keeping quiet are high enough in terms of psychological wear and tear that simply getting an emotion off your chest is reason enough to speak out.

We will have a great deal more to say about emotions in Chapter 3.

Consequences A consequence statement explains what happens as a result of the sense data you've described. There are three types of consequences:

1. What happens to you, the speaker
   —When you forgot to give me the phone message yesterday (sense data), *I didn't know that my doctor's appointment was delayed and I wound up sitting in the office for an hour when I could have been studying or working* (consequences). It seems to me that you don't care enough about how busy I am to even write a simple note (interpretation), and that really makes me mad (feeling).
   —I appreciate (feeling) the help you've given me on my term paper (sense data). It tells me you think I'm on the right track (interpretation), and *this gives me a boost to keep working on the idea* (consequences).

2. What happens to the person you're addressing
   —When you have four or five drinks at a party after I've warned you to slow down (sense data), *you start to act strange: you make crude jokes which offend everybody, and on the way home you drive poorly* (consequences). *For instance, last night you almost hit a phone pole* while you were backing out of the driveway (more sense data). I don't think you realize how differently you act (interpretation), and I'm worried (feeling) about what will happen if you don't drink less.

3. What happens to *others*
   —You probably don't know because you couldn't hear her cry (interpretation), but when you play your stereo that loudly (sense data), *the baby can't sleep* (consequence). I'm especially concerned (feeling) about her because she's had a cold lately.
   —I thought you'd want to know (interpretation) that when you kid Bob about his accent (sense data), he gets embarrassed (feeling) and *usually quiets down or leaves* (consequences).

Consequence statements are valuable for two reasons. First, they help you understand more clearly why you are bothered or pleased by another's behavior. Just as importantly, telling others about the consequences of their actions can clarify for them the results of their behavior. As with interpretations, we often think others *should* be aware of consequences without being told; but the fact is that they often aren't. By explicitly stating consequences, you can be sure that you or your message leaves nothing to the listener's imagination.

When stating consequences, it's important simply to describe what happens without moralizing. For instance, it's one thing to say "When you didn't call to say you'd be late, I stayed up worrying," and another to rant on "How can I ever trust you? You're going to drive me crazy!" Remember, it's perfectly legitimate to express your thoughts and feelings, but it's important to label them as such. And when you want to request change from someone, you can use intention statements, which we'll now describe.

Intentions   We can best identify intentions as statements about where you stand on an issue, what you want, or how you plan to act in the future.

Sometimes your intentions involve *making requests of others*.

"When you didn't call last night (sense data) I thought you were mad at me (interpretation). I've been thinking about it ever since (consequence), and I'm still worried (feeling). I'd like to know whether you are angry (intention)."

"I really enjoyed (feeling/consequence) your visit (sense data), and I'm glad you had a good time too (interpretation). I hope you'll come again (intention)."

In other cases intention statements can describe *how you plan to act* in the future.

"I've asked you to repay the $25 I loaned you three times now (sense data). I'm getting the idea that you've been avoiding me (interpretation), and I'm pretty angry about it (feeling). I want you to know that unless we clear this up now, you shouldn't expect me ever to loan you anything again (intention)."

"I'm glad (feeling) you liked (interpretation) the paper I wrote. I'm thinking about taking your advanced writing class next term (intention)."

Why is it so important to make your intentions clear? Because failing to do so often makes it hard for others to know what you want from them or how to plan to act. Consider how confusing the following statements are because they lack a clear statement of intention.

"Wow! A frozen Snickers. I haven't had one of those in years." (Does the speaker want a bite or is she just making an innocent remark?)

"Thanks for the invitation, but I really should study Saturday night." (Does the speaker want to be asked out again, or is he indirectly suggesting that he doesn't ever want to go out with you?)

"To tell you the truth, I was asleep when you came by, but I should have been up anyway." (Is the speaker saying that it's o.k. to come by in the future, or is she hinting that she doesn't appreciate unannounced visitors?)

You can see from these examples that it's often hard to make a clear interpretation of another person's ideas without a direct statement of intention. Notice how much more direct each of the above statements would be if each speaker had made his or her position clear.

"Wow! A frozen Snickers. I haven't had one of those in years. If I hadn't already eaten, I'd sure ask for a bite."

"Thanks for the invitation, but I really should study Saturday night. I hope you'll ask me again soon."

"To tell you the truth, I was asleep when you came by, but I should have been up anyway. Maybe the next time you should phone before dropping in so I'll be sure to be awake."

As in the above cases we are often motivated by one single intention. Sometimes, however, we act from a combination of intentions, which may even be in conflict with each other. When this happens, your conflicting wants often make it difficult for you to reach decisions.

"I want to be truthful with you, but I don't want you to know where I was last weekend."

"I want to continue to enjoy your friendship and company, but I don't want to get too attached right now."

"I want to have time to study and get good grades, but I also want to have a job with some money coming in too."

While sharing your conflicting intentions isn't a guaranteed way to clear up confusion, there are times when an outright statement such as the ones above can help you come to a decision. Even when you remain mixed up, expressing your contrary wants has the benefit of letting others know where you stand.

Of course, you can't expect others always to make their intentions clear to you, so you'll often have to ask them questions such as "What do you want?" or "What do you intend to do about that?" As long as you ask such questions in a sincere spirit and not in an accusing tone, you'll find that both you and the sender will have a better idea of what's going on between you.

Once you start making your intentions clear and seeking the same clarity from others, you'll be surprised at how much more direct your communication becomes.

Before you try to deliver messages using the sense-interpret-feel-consequences-intention format, there are a few points you should remember. First, it isn't necessary or even wise always to put the elements in the order described here. As you can see from reviewing the examples on the preceding pages, it's sometimes best to begin by stating your feelings, intentions, interpretations, or the consequences.

You also ought to word your message in a way that suits your style of speaking. Instead of saying "interpret your behavior to mean," you might choose to say "I think . . . ," "it seems to me . . . ," or perhaps "I get the idea . . .". In the same way you can express your intentions by saying "I hope you'll understand (or do) . . . ." or perhaps "I wish you would . . .". It's important that you get your message across, but you should do it in a way that sounds and feels genuine to you.

Realize that there are some cases in which you can combine two elements in a single phrase. For instance, the statement ". . . and ever since then I've been wanting to talk to you'' expresses both a consequence and an intention. In the same way saying ''. . . and after you said that I felt confused'' expresses a consequence and a feeling. Whether you combine elements or state them separately, the important point is to be sure that every one is present in your statement.

Finally, you need to realize that it isn't always possible to deliver messages such as the ones here all at one time, wrapped up in neat paragraphs. It will often be necessary to repeat or restate one part many times before your receiver truly understands what you're saying. As you've already read in this chapter, there are all sorts of psychological and physical noise that make it difficult for us to understand each other. Just remember: You haven't communicated successfully until the receiver of your message understands everything you've said. In communication, as in many other activities, patience and persistence are essential.

Now try your hand at combining all these elements in this exercise:

Putting Your Message Together

1. Join with two other class members. Each person in turn should share a message they might want to send to another person, being sure to include sensing, interpreting, feeling, consequence and intention statements in the remarks.

2. The others in the group should help the speaker by offering feedback about how the remarks could be made more clear if there is any question about the meaning.

3. Once the speaker has composed a satisfactory message, she should practice actually delivering it by having another group member play the role of the intended receiver. Continue this practice until the speaker is confident that she can deliver the message effectively.

4. Repeat this process until each group member has had a chance to practice delivering a message.

Self-Disclosure and Risk in Communication

You can probably see that the kind of communication that results when you express your sense data, interpretations, feelings, and intentions is much more direct and revealing than the messages people typically send and receive. There is certainly risk in sharing yourself so completely; so now we need to talk about the costs and benefits of self-disclosure. How much should you say, and how much should you keep to yourself? When is it appropriate to share your thoughts, feelings, and intentions? What do you stand to gain from being a more open and direct communicator?

Before answering these questions we need to define our terms. Self-disclosure refers to the process of deliberately revealing information about ourselves that is significant and that would not normally be known by others. Let's take a closer look at some parts of this definition. Self-disclosure must be *deliberate*. If you accidentally mentioned to a friend that you were thinking

about quitting a job or proposing marriage, that information would not fit into the category we are examining here. On the other hand, if you intentionally shared information that wasn't *significant*—the fact that you like fudge, for example—it's obvious that no important disclosure occurred. Our third requirement is that the information being disclosed would *not be known by others.* There's nothing noteworthy about telling others that you are depressed or elated if they already know how you're feeling.

One way to look at the important part self-disclosure plays in interpersonal communication is by means of a device called the Johari Window.* Imagine a frame inside which is everything there is to know about you: your likes and dislikes, your goals, your secrets, your needs—everything.

* The Johari Window was originated by Joseph Luft and Harry Ingham during a summer laboratory in group development at UCLA in 1955. The model takes its name from the first names of the two men, Joe and Harry.

Figure 1-1

Of course, you aren't aware of everything about yourself. Like most people you're probably discovering new things about yourself all the time. To represent this we can divide the frame containing everything about you into two parts: the part you know about and the part you're not aware of, as in Figure 1-2.

Figure 1-2

We can also divide this frame containing everything about you in another way. In this division one part represents the things about you that others know, and the second part contains the things about you that you keep to yourself. Figure 1-3 represents this view.

Figure 1-3

When we impose these two divided frames one atop the other, we have a Johari Window. By looking at Figure 1–4 you can see that the Johari divides everything about you into four parts.

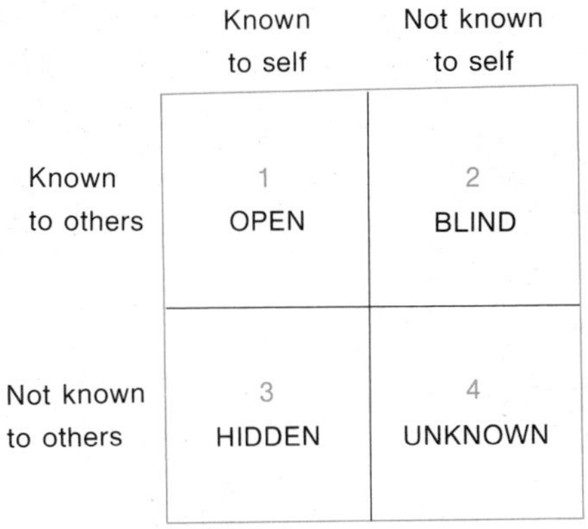

	Known to self	Not known to self
Known to others	1 OPEN	2 BLIND
Not known to others	3 HIDDEN	4 UNKNOWN

Figure 1–4

Part 1 represents the part of you that both you and others are aware of. This area is labeled your *open* area. Part 2 represents the part of you that you're not aware of but others are. This is called your *blind* area. Part 3 represents your *hidden* area; you're aware of this part of yourself, but you don't allow others to know it. Part 4 represents the part of you that is known neither to you nor to others and is therefore referred to as the *unknown* area.

You can construct a model of your own Johari Window: Draw a square, then locate your boundaries in the positions you think would best fit you. For example, if you think you're an open person, then obviously Part 1 of your window would be larger than the other areas. Such a window would look like the one in Figure 1–5.

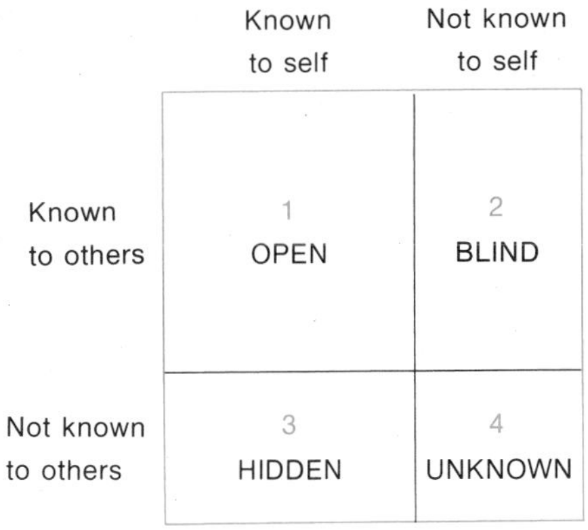

	Known to self	Not known to self
Known to others	1 OPEN	2 BLIND
Not known to others	3 HIDDEN	4 UNKNOWN

Figure 1–5

So far we've been looking at the disclosing behavior of a single communicator. We can use the same principle to show the relationship between two people by juxtaposing two Johari windows, as in Figure 1–6. Note that we've set up A's window in reverse so that the open areas of A's and of B's Joharis appear next to each other.

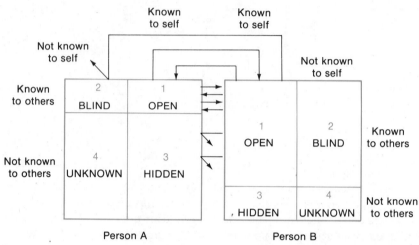

Figure 1–6

Characteristics of Self-disclosure   The Johari Window suggests several characteristics of self-disclosure.*

1. Self-disclosure usually occurs in dyads   While it is possible for people to disclose a great deal about themselves in groups, such communication usually occurs in one-to-one settings. Since revealing significant information about one's self involves a certain amount of risk, limiting the disclosure to one person at a time minimizes the chance that your revelations will lead to unhappy consequences.

2. Self-disclosure is usually symmetrical   Note in Figure 6 that the amount of successful, two-way communication (represented by the arrows connecting the two open areas) is dictated by the size of the smaller open area of A. The arrows that are originating from B's open area and being turned aside by A's hidden and blind areas represent unsuccessful attempts to communicate. In situations such as this it's easy to imagine how B would soon limit the amount of disclosure to match that of A. On the other hand, if A

* Taken from Charles M. Rossiter and Barnett Pearce *Communicating Personally.* (Indianapolis: Bobbs-Merrill, 1975), pp. 214–218.

was willing to match the degree of disclosure given by B, the relationship would move to a new level of intimacy. In either case we can expect that most often the degree of sharing between partners will soon stabilize at a symmetrical level.

3. *Self-disclosure occurs incrementally* While occasions do occur in which partners start their relationship by telling everything about themselves to each other, such instances are rare. In most cases the amount of sharing increases over time. We begin relationships by revealing relatively little about ourselves, then, if our first bits of self-disclosure are well received and bring on similar responses from the other person, we're willing to reveal more. This principle is important to remember. It would usually be a mistake to assume that the way to build a strong relationship would be to reveal the most private details about yourself when first making contact with another person. Unless the circumstances are unique, such baring of your soul would be likely to scare potential partners away rather than bring them closer.

4. *Relatively few transactions involve high levels of self-disclosure* Just as it's unwise to seek great self-disclosure too soon, it's also unproductive to reveal yourself too much. Except for unique settings—such as in therapy—there's usually no need to disclose frequently or steadily.

5. *Self-disclosure usually occurs in the context of positive relationships* This principle makes sense. We're generally more willing to reveal information about ourselves when we feel accepted by the other person. This doesn't mean that you should avoid making disclosing statements that contain negative messages (e.g., "I feel uncomfortable about what happened last night."). Such explanations are likely to be successful if they're designed to be constructive, to help your relationship grow. On the other hand, disclosure that has the effect of attacking the other person ("You

take a chance
on getting slapped
you might
get kissed

Bernard Gunther

MISS PEACH

By Mell Lazarus

> *Before I built a wall I'd ask to know*
> *What I was walling in or walling out.*
> *And to whom I was like to give offense.*
> *Something there is that doesn't love a wall,*
> *That wants it down.*
>
> Robert Frost

sure aren't very bright'') are almost guaranteed to be destructive. For this reason, it's especially important to phrase negative messages in the sense-think-feel-consequence-want format described earlier in this chapter.

When to Disclose?   The case for appropriate self-disclosure seems overwhelming. Why then do we have a problem doing it? Sidney M. Jourard in his book *The Transparent Self* wrote:

> . . . When you permit yourself to be known, you expose yourself not only to a lover's balm, but also to a hater's bombs. When he knows you, he knows just where to plant them for maximum effect.

Jourard's message is clear. There is *risk* involved in self-disclosure: the risk of facing disapproval, being criticized, laughed at, and rejected. Although the thought of these possible consequences often makes self-disclosure pretty frightening, failure to do so is also undesirable. If you don't share yourself with others, you stand little chance of establishing meaningful relationships with others—without sharing yourself, it's difficult for others to help meet your basic social needs of belonging, being accepted, and being loved. Once you understand the connection between sharing knowledge of self and meaningful interpersonal relationships, it becomes apparent that you must take the risk that comes with self-disclosure. The question then becomes, when to open up and when to remain quiet.

One way of deciding when and what to disclose is to consider the risks and benefits involved. The first step here is to ask yourself what you stand to gain by disclosing yourself. Is the other person someone whose friendship, approval, or help is important to you? It might not be wise to share personal information with someone to whom you didn't feel especially close to in the first place. Such openness would be much more worthwhile if the potential for a new and important relationship existed.

he stripped
the dark circle
of mystery off
revealed his eyes
and thus
he waited
exposed

and I
did sing the song
around
until I found
the chorus
that speaks
of windows

looking out
means looking in
my friend
and I'm all right
now
I'm fine
I have seen
the beauty
that is mine

you can
watch the sky
for signals
but look
to the eyes
for signs

Ric Masten

You also should take a realistic look at the potential risks of self-disclosure. Even if the probable benefits are great, opening yourself up to almost certain rejection is simply asking for trouble. For instance, it might be foolhardy to share your important feelings with someone you know is likely to betray your confidences or ridicule them. On the other hand, knowing that your partner is trustworthy and supportive makes the prospect of speaking out more reasonable. In anticipating risks, be sure that you are realistic. It's sometimes easy to indulge in catastrophic expectations, in which you begin to imagine all sorts of disastrous consequences of your opening up, when in fact such horrors are very unlikely to occur.

A third point to realize is that there are *degrees* of self-disclosure, so that telling others about yourself isn't an all-or-nothing decision you must make. It's possible to share some facts, opinions, or feelings with one person while reserving riskier ones for others. In the same vein, before sharing very important information with someone who does matter to you, you might consider testing their reactions by disclosing less personal data.

In any case it's important to realize that any information you disclose about yourself should be relevant to your relationship with the person at hand. Self-disclosure isn't a long confession about your past life or current thoughts that is unrelated to the now. On the contrary, it ought to be directly pertinent to your present conversation. It's ludicrous to picture the self-disclosing person as someone who blurts out intimate details of every past experience. Instead, our model is someone who, when the time is appropriate, trusts us enough to share the hidden parts of himself that affect our relationship.

By this time we hope that you know your classmates pretty well. We hope that the activities you've tried have helped build a comfortable atmosphere for the weeks ahead. In this chapter we've tried to introduce topics and methods you can expect to see throughout the course. Unless we're mistaken, the subjects you'll be exploring in the following chapters will hold considerable interest for you. Each will concern a specific area of interpersonal communication; both the problems that may exist and suggestions for coping with them are presented. If you're willing to apply the ideas you find here to your own life, there's a good chance that this can be a very useful experience for you, not only now but in the years to come.

I should not talk so much about myself if there were anybody else whom I knew as well.

Henry David Thoreau

Roads Not Taken

At the end of each chapter in this book you'll find a list of topics for further investigation. Any book has a limit on how much can be included, and this one is no exception. Therefore, many aspects of human communication are only mentioned here. Our hope is that this list may encourage you to pursue some area that interests you.

1. Explore the history of human communication. When did it begin? Has the human ability to communicate successfully changed from the time of early man to today?

2. How does human communication differ from that of animals?

3. What evidence can you gather that demonstrates the contemporary need for better interpersonal communication?

4. What are the various models of human communication that communicologists have developed?

5. What research exists on risk and trust in interpersonal relationships?

6. Keep a journal that records the degree to which you engage in self-disclosure. Report your opportunities for sharing important information about yourself, the risks and benefits involved, the amount of disclosing you do, and your level of satisfaction.

7. To what degree do people you observe identify and report sense data, make interpretations, experience and share feelings, describe consequences, and state intentions?

8. What are the similarities and differences between interpersonal, group, public, and mass communication?

9. Begin a Significant Learning Journal.'' During the term of this course you will be asked to keep a journal in which you record your "significant learnings." We have borrowed this term from Carl Rogers, who defines it in his book, *On Becoming a Person:*

> By significant learning I mean learning which is more than an accumulation of facts. It is learning which makes a difference—in the individual's behavior, in the course of action he chooses in the future, in his attitudes and in his personality. It is a pervasive learning which is not just an accretion of knowledge, but which interpenetrates with every portion of his existence.

We want this to be a practical course and we believe this journal can help you focus on what, if anything, you are studying in the classroom that you can apply to the real world.

Your entries should consist of whatever you have learned that has made a difference or will make a difference in the way you relate or communicate with others. *Caution:* Don't pass judgment on what you write in your journal. Even thinking "That's silly" or "Everybody else probably knows that already" will tend to start you censoring those things that you think you want to include. Try to include anything and everything that you consider significant.

Nothing you write will be made available to anyone other than your instructor. The mechanics of how you will handle making entries, how often, and where the journals will be kept should be worked out within your group. It sometimes helps if the journals are kept together and a regular time is allotted each week for writing in them.

More Readings

Bensman, Joseph, and Robert Lilienfeld. "Friendship and Alienation." *Psychology Today,* 13:4 (October 1979) 4.
Two sociologists look at friendship at various stages in life. They confirm everyone's need for intimacy and suggest that an erosion of family, community, and traditional institutions contributes to our drift toward alienation.

Buscaglia, Leo F. *Love.* Thorofare, NJ: Charles B. Slack, Inc., 1972.
The author speaks with warmth, sincerity, and enthusiasm on the importance of love and intimacy. He understands people's confusions and depressions and believes that communicated love is the creative force for change.

Harris, Thomas A. *I'm O.K., You're O.K.* New York: Harper & Row, 1967.
The most understandable introduction to transactional analysis we've found. This book may give you another model for looking at the process of interpersonal communication.

Holtzman, Paul D., and Donald Ecroyd. *Communication Concepts and Models.* Skokie, IL: National Textbook Co., 1976.
This programmed text gives a thorough treatment of communication models in understandable terms.

Jourard, Sidney M. *The Transparent Self.* New York: Van Nostrand Reinhold, 1971.
This is probably the best-known treatment of self-disclosure in print. Jourard writes well about its role in the helping relationship, particularly the nursing profession.

Kavanaugh, James. *Will You Be My Friend?* Los Angeles: Nash Publishing, 1971.
Kavanaugh's poems speak to many of the rewards and problems contained in this book.

Keyes, Ralph. *We, The Lonely People: Searching For Community.* New York: Harper & Row, 1973.
Keyes makes a strong case for the necessity of community, and describes its absence in contemporary society.

Lazarus, Arnold, and Allen Fay. *I Can If I Want To.* New York: Morrow, 1975.
Lazarus and Fay give a detailed list of the many faulty inerpretations people often place on their own behavior and that of others, as well as providing more sensible ways of thinking. We recommend this book highly.

Luft, Joseph. *Of Human Interaction.* Palo Alto, CA: National Press Books, 1969.
A clear, detailed introduction to the Johari Window, with an analysis of how various degrees of openness influence communication.

Maslow, Abraham H. *Toward a Psychology of Being.* New York: Van Nostrand Reinhold, 1968.
This is a collection of lectures Maslow has given to explain his humanistic psychology. He carefully works out his hierarchy of basic human needs.

Miller, Sherod, Elam Nunnally, and Daniel B. Wackman. *Alive and Aware.*
Minneapolis: Interpersonal Communication Programs, Inc., 1975.
This book gives a detailed description of the sensing-interpreting-feeling-intending messages discussed in Chapter 1.

Parlee, Mary Brown, and Editors of *Psychology Today.* "The Friendship
Bond." *Psychology Today,* 13:4 (October 1979).
A report on the survey conducted by P.T. on what people look for in close friendships; 40,000 readers responded.

Rubin, Zick. "Seeking a Cure for Loneliness." *Psychology Today,* 13:4
(October 1979).
This article concerns latest research on loneliness as reported at the first national research conference on loneliness.

Chapter Two

The Self-Concept: Key to Communication

1. Name _____ First _____ Last _____ City _____

2. Address _____ Apt. No. _____ Occupation _____

3. Height _____ Weight _____ Hair Color _____ Eye Color _____

4. Appearance
I am considered:
- ☐ Very good looking
- ☐ Above average
- ☐ Average

5. Astrological Sign
Circle if known:
Aquarius Aries Cancer
Capricorn Gemini Leo
Libra Pisces Sagittarius
Scorpio Taurus Virgo

6. Racial Origin
- ☐ Caucasian (white)
- ☐ Black
- ☐ Oriental
- ☐ Other_____

7. Ethnic Background
Check one or more:
- ☐ U.S. / Canadian
- ☐ European
- ☐ Latin
- ☐ Asian
- ☐ Middle Eastern
- ☐ African
- ☐ Other_____

8. Religion
- ☐ None
- ☐ Protestant
- ☐ Catholic
- ☐ Jewish
- ☐ Buddhist
- ☐ Hindu
- ☐ Other_____

9. Religious Beliefs
- ☐ None at all
- ☐ Medium
- ☐ Strong

10. Education
Circle last year completed:
- ☐ High School 1 2 3 4
- ☐ College 1 2 3 4 5+
- ☐ Other_____

11. Marital Status

12. Dependent Children
- ☐ None
- ☐ Yes, living with me
- ☐ Yes, living elsewhere

13. Tobacco Use
- ☐ Never
- ☐ Light
- ☐ Moderate
- ☐ Heavy

14. Liquor Use
- ☐ Not at all
- ☐ On occasion
- ☐ Socially
- ☐ Regularly

15. Miscellaneous Qualities
Circle the words or phrases that best describe you:
Outgoing, quiet, punctual, sensitive, flexible, aware, politically liberal, politically moderate, politically conservative, adventurous, affectionate, considerate, open minded, imaginative, independent, sense of humor, self confident, sexy, relaxed, trusting, changeable, serious, athletic, friendly, loyal, optimistic, loving, neat, sincere, clean, good dresser, creative, talkative, understanding, tolerant.

16. Musical Preference
Check favorites:
- ☐ Classical
- ☐ Opera
- ☐ Easy listening
- ☐ Folk
- ☐ Popular
- ☐ Rock
- ☐ Jazz
- ☐ Country

17. Social Activity
Enjoy going out:
- ☐ 2 or more times a week
- ☐ Once a week
- ☐ Rarely

18. Leisure Time Interests
Circle appropriate ones:
Theater, dining out, concerts, movies, dancing, parties, travel, museums, art, lectures, politics, tennis, golf, bowling, swimming, boating, skiing, skindiving, horseback riding, archery, volleyball, ping pong, billiards, spectator sports, hunting, camping, hiking, exploring, fishing, motorcycling, auto racing, flying, bicycling, trips, picnics, beach, physical fitness, yoga, awareness & self-improvement group, meditation, astrology, photograph, chess, interior decorating, electro, arts and crafts, CB radio, garde, working around home, cars, relaxing at home, entertaining, poetry, reading, TV, writing, collecting, painting, cookin, sewing, musical instruments, cards, volunteer work.

If you wish, give more additional interests, li looking for in the opr

_____

_____

_____

W ho are you? Take a moment now to answer this question.

How did you define yourself? As a student? A man or woman? By your age? Your religion? Your occupation? Of course there are many ways of identifying yourself.

Take a few more moments and list as many ways as you can to identify who you are. You'll need this list later on in this chapter, so be sure to complete it now. Try to include all the characteristics that describe you:

> **your moods or feelings**
>
> **your appearance and physical condition**
>
> **your social traits**
>
> **talents you possess or lack**
>
> **your intellectual capacity**
>
> **your strong beliefs**
>
> **your social roles**

Now take a look at what you've written. You'll probably see that the words you've chosen represent a profile of what you now view as your most important characteristics. In other words, if you were required to describe the "real you," this list ought to be a pretty accurate summary.

What you've done in developing this list is to give a partial description of your *self-concept*. There are many different ways of defining this term, but probably the clearest way to think of your self-concept is as the image you hold of yourself. If you could imagine a special mirror that not only reflected physical features, but also allowed you to view other aspects of yourself— emotional states, talents, likes, dislikes, values, roles, and so on—then the reflection you'd see looking back at you in that mirror would be your self-concept.

You probably recognize that the self-concept list you recorded above is only a partial one. To make the description of your self complete you'd have to keep adding items until your list ran into hundreds of words.

Take a moment now to demonstrate the many parts of your self-concept by simply responding to the question "Who am I?" over and over again. Add these responses to the list you started above.

Of course, not every item on your self-concept list is equally important. For example, the most significant part of one person's self-concept might consist of social roles, while for another it might be physical appearance, health, friendships, accomplishments, or skills.

You can discover how much you value each part of your self-concept by rank-ordering the items on the list you've compiled. Try it now: Place number 1 next to the most fundamental thing about you, number 2 next to the second most important term, and continue on in this manner until you've completed your list.

This self-concept you've just described is extremely important. To see just how fundamental it is, try the following exercise.

Take Away

1. Look over the list of words you've just made describing yourself. If you haven't already done so, pick the ten items that describe the most fundamental aspects of who you are. Be sure you've organized these items so that the most fundamental one is in first place and the one that is least central to your identity is number ten, arranging the words or phrases in between in their proper order.

2. Now find a comfortable spot where you can think without being interrupted. You can complete this exercise in a group with the leader giving instructions or you can do it alone by reading the directions yourself when necessary.

3. Close your eyes and get a mental picture of yourself. Besides visualizing your apearance, your image should also include your less observable features: your disposition, your hopes, your concerns . . . of course including all the items you described in step 1.

4. Keep this picture in mind, but now imagine what would happen if the tenth item on your list disappeared from your makeup. How would you be different? Does the idea of giving up that item leave you feeling better or worse? How hard was it to let go of that item?

5. Now, without taking back the item you just abandoned, go on to give up the ninth item on your list, and see what difference this makes to you. After pausing to experience your thoughts and feelings, go on and give up each succeeding item on your list one by one.

6. After you've abandoned the number-one feature of who you are, take a few minutes to regather the parts of yourself that you abandoned, and then read on.

For most people this exercise dramatically illustrates just how fundamental the concept of self is. Even when the item being abandoned is an unpleasant one, it's often hard to give it up. And when they are asked to let go of their most central feelings or thoughts, most people balk. ''I wouldn't be *me* without that,'' they insist. Of course, this proves our point: The concept of self is perhaps our most fundamental possession. Knowing who we are is essential, for without a self-concept it would be impossible to relate to the world.

To be nobody—but—yourself in a world which is doing its best, night and day, to make you everybody—else means to fight the hardest battle which any human being can fight, and never stop fighting.

E. E. Cummings

Will the Real Me Please Stand Up?

In the beginning, I was one person, knowing nothing but my own experience.

Then I was told things, and I became two people: the little girl who said how terrible it was that the boys had a fire going in the lot next door where they were roasting apples (which was what the woman said)—and the little girl who, when the boys were called by their mothers to go to the store, ran out and tended the fire and the apples because she loved doing it.

So then there were two of I. One I always doing something that the other I disapproved of. Or other I said what I disapproved of. All this argument in me so much.

In the beginning was I, and I was good.

Then came in other I. Outside authority. This was confusing. And then other I became very confused because there were so many different outside authorities.

Sit nicely. Leave the room to blow your nose. Don't do that, that's silly. Why, the poor child doesn't even know how to pick a bone! Flush the toilet at night because if you don't it makes it harder to clean. DON'T FLUSH THE TOILET AT NIGHT—you wake people up! Always be nice to people. Even if you don't like them, you mustn't hurt their feelings. Be frank and honest. If

you don't tell people what you think of them, that's cowardly. Butter knives. It is important to use butter knives. Butter knives? What foolishness! Speak nicely. Sissy! Kipling is wonderful! Ugh! Kipling (turning away).

The most important thing is to have a career. The most important thing is to get married. The hell with everyone. Be nice to everyone. The most important thing is sex. The most important thing is to have everyone like you. The most important thing is to be sophisticated and say what you don't mean and don't let anyone know what you feel. The most important thing is a black seal coat and china and silver. The most important thing is to be clean. The most important thing is to always pay your debts. The most important thing is not to be taken in by anyone else. The most important thing is to love your parents. The most important thing is to work. The most important thing is to be independent. The most important thing is to speak correct English. The most important thing is to go to the right plays and read the right books. The most important thing is to do what others say. And others say all these things.

All the time, I is saying, live with life. That is what is important.

But when I lives with life, other I says no, that's bad. All the different other I's say this. It's dangerous. It isn't practical. You'll come to a bad end. Of course . . .

everyone felt that way once, the way you do, but *you'll learn*.

Out of all the other I's some are chosen as a pattern that is me. But there are all the other possibilities of patterns within what all the others say which come into me and become other I which is not myself, and sometimes these take over. Then who am I?

I does not bother about who am I. I is, and is happy being. But when I is happy being, other I says get to work, do something worthwhile! I is happy doing dishes. "You're weird!" I is happy being with people saying nothing. Other I says talk. Talk, talk, talk. I gets lost.

I know that things are to be played with, not possessed. I likes putting things together, lightly. Taking things apart, lightly. "You'll never have anything!" Making things of things in a way that the things themselves take part in, putting themselves together with surprise and delight to I. "There's no money in that!"

I is human. If someone needs, I gives. "You can't do that! You'll never have anything for yourself! We'll have to support you!"

I loves. I loves in a way that other I does not know. I loves. "That's too warm for friends!" "That's too cool for lovers!" "Don't feel so bad, he's just a friend. It's not as though you loved him." "How can you let him go? I thought you loved him?" So cool the warm for friends and hot up the love for lovers, and I gets lost.

So both I's have a house and a husband and children and all that, but both I's are confused because other I says, "You see? You're lucky," while I goes on crying. "What are you crying about? Why are you so ungrateful?" I doesn't know gratitude or ingratitude, and cannot argue. I goes on crying. Other I pushes it out, says "I am happy! I am very lucky to have such a fine family and a nice house and good neighbors and lots of friends who want me to do this, do that." I is not reason-able either. I goes on crying.

Other I gets tired, and goes on smiling, because that is the thing to do. Smile, and you will be rewarded. Like the seal who gets tossed a piece of fish. Be nice to everyone and you will be rewarded. People will be nice to you, and you can be happy with that. You know they like you. Like a dog who gets patted on the head for good behavior. Tell funny stories. Be gay. Smile, smile, smile. . . . I is crying. . . . "Don't be sorry for yourself! Go out and do things for people!" "Go out and be with people!" I is still crying, but now, that is not heard and felt so much.

Suddenly: "What am I doing?" "Am I to go through life playing the clown?" "What am I doing, going to parties that I do not enjoy?" "What am I doing, being with people who bore me?" "Why am I so hollow and the hollowness filled with emptiness?" A shell. How has this shell grown around me? Why am I proud of my children and unhappy about their lives which are not good enough? Why am I disappointed? Why do I feel so much waste?

I comes through, a little. In moments. And gets pushed back by other I.

I refuses to play the clown any more. Which I is that? "She used to be fun, but now she thinks too much about herself." I lets friends drop away. Which I is that? "She's being too much by herself. That's bad. She's losing her mind." Which mind?

Barry Stevens, *Person to Person*

How the Self-Concept Develops

"All right," you say, "now I know pretty clearly what my self-concept is, but what does this have to do with the way I communicate?" We can begin to answer this question by looking at how you came to possess your present self-concept.

You can begin to understand how your self-concept came to be by trying the accompanying exercise.

Uppers and Downers

1. Either by yourself or aloud with a partner, recall someone you know or once knew who was an "upper"—who helped enhance your self-concept by acting in a way that made you feel accepted, worthwhile, important, appreciated, or loved. Your upper needn't have played a crucial role in your life, as long as the role was positive. Often one's self-concept is shaped by many tiny nudges as well as a few giant events.

Some uppers we have known are
a. Sam, who when Ron was six or seven years old treated him to "special days"—a morning spent together exploring the treasures in Sam's jewelry store, followed by a lunch in a restaurant.

b. Marge, a student who recently approached us after completing our class to report her success at a new job and to insist that it wouldn't have been possible without our help.

c. Miss Gardner, Neil's high school history teacher, who invited him to join her in entering a **Contemporary History Contest**, and repeatedly told him that she was confident he would do an excellent job.

2. After thinking about your upper, take time to recall a "downer" from your life—some person who acted in either a big or small way to diminish your self-esteem.

At this time we can recall downers such as

a. Students who yawn in the middle of our classes. (They may be tired, but it's difficult to avoid the thought that we're not teaching as effectively as we might be.)

b. Ken, a junior high school classmate of Ron's who seemed to enjoy making Ron look bad by challenging him to fight, elbowing him in the ribs constantly in basketball games, and trying to steal away girlfriends, among other things.

c. Joyce, a former girlfriend of Neil's, who shrugged off his romantic overtures by refusing to take them seriously.

3. Now that you've thought about people who were uppers to you, recall the last time you were an upper to someone else. What ways have you acted that helped build others' self-esteem?

Don't merely settle for a recent instance in which you were *nice:* Look for a time when your actions had the effect of letting another know that he was valued, loved, needed, and so on.

For instance, we can recall recently being uppers by

a. Spending time with our children. Taking the time to listen with full attention to their account of a day's events or play a game with them.

b. Buying gifts for our wives for no special occasion.

c. Saying "thanks" to students who have offered valuable comments in class.

4. Finally, recall a recent instance in which you were a downer for someone else. What did you do to diminish another's self-concept?

Some of our recent downers are

a. Yesterday Ron was caught sneaking a look at the clock by a friend who was describing in great detail her recent vacation.

b. Being involved in writing this book, we failed to return the call of a colleague who wanted to talk with us.

c. When Neil questioned his son Steve's explanation, he was asked, "How come you can't ever believe me, Dad?"

Love and the Cabbie

I was in New York the other day and rode with a friend in a taxi. When we got out my friend said to the driver. "Thank you for the ride. You did a superb job of driving."

The taxi driver was stunned for a second. Then he said:

"Are you a wise guy or something?"

"No, my dear man, and I'm not putting you on. I admire the way you keep cool in heavy traffic."

"Yeh," the driver said and drove off.

"What was that all about?" I asked.

"I am trying to bring love back to New York," he said. "I believe it's the only thing that can save the city."

"How can one man save New York?"

"It's not one man. I believe I have made the taxi driver's day. Suppose he has twenty fares. He's going to be nice to those twenty fares because someone was nice to him. Those fares in turn will be kinder to their employees or shop-keepers or waiters or even their own families. Eventually the goodwill could spread to at least 1,000 people. Now that isn't bad, is it?"

"But you're depending on that taxi driver to pass your goodwill to others."

"I'm not depending on it," my friend said. "Im aware that the system isn't foolproof so I might deal with 10 different people today. If, out of 10, I can make three happy, then eventually I can indirectly influence the attitudes of 3,000 more."

"It sounds good on paper," I admitted, "but I'm not sure it works in practice."

"Nothing is lost if it doesn't. I didn't take any of my time to tell that man he was doing a good job. He neither received a larger tip nor a smaller tip. If it fell on deaf ears, so what? Tomorrow there will be another taxi driver whom I can try to make happy."

"You're some kind of a nut," I said.

"That shows you how cynical you have become. I have made a study of this. The thing that seems to be lacking, besides money of course, for our postal employees, is that no one tells people who work for the post office what a good job they're doing."

"But they're not doing a good job."

"They're not doing a good job because they feel no one cares if they do or not. Why shouldn't someone say a kind word to them?"

We were walking past a structure in the process of being built and passed five workmen eating their lunch. My friend stopped. "That's a magnificent job you men have done. It must be difficult and dangerous work."

The five men eyed my friend suspiciously.

"When will it be finished?"

"June," a man grunted.

"Ah. That really is impressive. You must all be very proud."

We walked away. I said to him, "I haven't seen anyone like you since 'The Man from La Mancha.' "

"When those men digest my words, they will feel better for it. Somehow the city will benefit from their happiness."

"But you can't do this all alone!" I protested. "You're just one man."

"The most important thing is not to get discouraged. Making people in the city become kind again is not an easy job, but if I can enlist other people in my campaign. . ."

"You just winked at a very plain looking woman," I said.

"Yes, I know," he replied. "And if she's a schoolteacher, her class will be in for a fantastic day."

Art Buchwald

After completing the "upper and downer" exercise (you *did* complete it, didn't you?) you should begin to see that your self-concept is shaped by those around you. To the extent that you have received upper messages, you have learned to appreciate and value yourself. To the degree that others have communicated downer signals, you are likely to feel less valuable, lovable, and capable. In this sense it's possible to see that the self-concept you partially described in your list on page 53 is a product of the upper and downer messages you've received throughout your life.

To further illustrate this point, let's start at the beginning of life. A newborn child isn't born with any sense of identity: She only learns to judge herself through the way others treat her.

At first the evaluations aren't linguistic. Nonetheless, even the earliest days of life are full of messages that constitute the first uppers and/or downers that start to shape her self-concept. The amount of time parents allow their child to cry before attending to her needs nonverbally communicates over a period of time how important she is to them. Their method of handling her

also speaks volumes: Do they affectionately toy with her, joggling her gently and holding her close, or do they treat her like so much baggage, changing diapers, feeding and bathing her in a brusque, businesslike manner? Does the tone of voice with which they speak to her express love and enjoyment or disappointment and irritation?

Of course, most of these messages are not intentional ones. It is rare when a parent will deliberately try to tell a child she's not lovable; but whether they're intentional or not doesn't matter—nonverbal statements play a big role in shaping a youngster's feelings of being "o.k." or "not o.k."

As the child learns to speak and understand language, verbal messages also contribute to her developing self-concept. Every day a child is bombarded with scores of messages about herself. Some of these are uppers . . .

"You're so cute!"

"I love you."

"What a big girl!"

"It's fun to play with you."

. . . while other messages are downers.

"Can't you do anything right?"

"What's the matter with you?"

"You're a bad girl!"

"Leave me alone. You're driving me crazy!"

As we've said, the evaluations others make of us are the mirrors by which we know ourselves; and since children are trusting souls who have no other way of viewing themselves, they accept at face value both the positive and negative evaluations of the apparently all-knowing and all-powerful adults around them.

These same principles of self-concept formation continue in later life, especially when messages come from what sociologists term "significant others"—those people whose opinions we especially value. A look at the uppers and downers you described in the previous exercise (as well as others you can remember) will show that the evaluations of a few especially important people can have long-range effects. A teacher from long ago, a special friend or relative, or perhaps a barely known acquaintance whom you respected can all leave an imprint on how you view yourself. To see the importance of significant others, ask yourself how you arrived at your opinion of yourself as a student . . . as a person attractive to the opposite sex . . . as a competent worker . . . and you'll see that these self-evaluations were probably influenced by the way others regarded you.

In additon to specific influential individuals, each of us also formulates a self-concept based on the influence of various reference groups to which we are exposed. A youngster who is interested in ballet and who lives in a setting

Children Learn What They Live

If a child lives with criticism
he learns to condemn.
If a child lives with hostility
he learns to fight.
If a child lives with ridicule
he learns to be shy.
If a child lives with shame
he learns to feel guilty.
If a child lives with tolerance
he learns to be patient.
If a child lives with encouragement
he learns confidence.
If a child lives with praise
he learns to appreciate.
If a child lives with fairness
he learns justice.
If a child lives with security
he learns to have faith.
If a child lives with approval
he learns to like himself.
If a child lives with acceptance
and friendship
he learns to find love
in the world.

Dorothy Law Nolte

We are not only our brother's keeper; in countless large and small ways, we are our brother's maker.

Bonaro Overstreet

where such preferences are regarded as weird will start to accept this label if there is no support from significant others. Adults who want to share their feelings but find themselves in a society that discourages such sharing might after a while think of themselves as oddballs, unless they get some reassurance that such a desire is normal. Again, the idea of knowing ourselves through the mirrors of others stands out. To a great degree we judge ourselves by the way others see us.

You might argue that not every part of one's self-concept is shaped by others, insisting there are certain objective facts that are recognizable by self-observation. After all, nobody needs to tell a person that she is taller than others, speaks with an accent, has acne, and so on. These facts are obvious.

While it's true that some features of the self are immediately apparent, the *significance* we attach to them—the rank we assign them in the hierarchy of our list and the interpretation we give them—depends greatly on the opinions of others. After all, there are many of your features that are readily observable, yet you don't find them important at all because nobody has regarded them as significant.

Recently we heard a woman in her eighties describing her youth. ''When I was a girl,'' she declared, ''we didn't worry about weight. Some poeple were skinny and others were plump, and we pretty much accepted the bodies God gave us.'' In those days its unlikely that weight would have found its way onto the self-concept list you constructed, since it wasn't considered significant. Compare this attitude with what you find today: It's seldom that you pick up a popular magazine or visit a bookstore without reading about the latest diet fads, and television ads are filled with scenes of slender, happy people. As a result you'll rarely find a person (especially female) who doesn't complain about the need to ''lose a few pounds.'' Obviously the reason for such concern has more to do with the attention paid to slimness these days than with any increase in the number of people in the population who are overweight. Furthermore, the interpretation of characteristics such as weight depends on the way people important to us regard them. We generally see fat as undesirable because others tell us it is. In a society where obesity is the ideal (and there are such societies) a person who regards herself as extremely heavy would be a beauty. In the same way, the fact that one is single or married, solitary or sociable, aggressive or passive takes on meaning depending on the interpretation society attaches to those traits. Thus, the importance of a given characteristic in your self-concept has as much to do with the significance you and others attach to it as with the existence of the characteristic.

By now you might be thinking, ''Adler and Towne are telling me it's not my fault that I've always been shy or unconfident. Since I developed a picture of myself as a result of the way others have treated me, I can't help being what I am.'' While it's true that to a great extent you are a product of your environment, to accept yourself as being forever doomed to possess a poor self-concept would be a big mistake. Having held a poor self-image in the past is no reason for continuing to do so in the future. You *can* change your attitudes and behaviors, as you'll shortly read. So don't despair, and most of all don't use the fact that others have shaped your self-concept as an excuse for self-pity or acting helpless. Now that you know the effect that overly negative evaluations have had on you in the past, you'll be in a better position to revise your perception of yourself more favorably in the future.

''Guess who Miss Price picked to play poison ivy in the class play.''

CIPHER IN THE SNOW

It started with tragedy on a biting cold February morning. I was driving behind the Milford Corners bus as I did most snowy mornings on may way to school. It veered and stopped short at the hotel, which it had no business doing, and I was annoyed as I had to come to an unexpected stop. A boy lurched out of the bus, reeled, stumbled, and collapsed on the snowbank at the curb. The bus driver and I reached him at the same moment. His thin, hollow face was white even against the snow.

"He's dead," the driver whispered.

It didn't register for a minute. I glanced quickly at the scared young faces staring down at us from the school bus. "A doctor! Quick! I'll phone from the hotel. . . ."

"No use, I tell you he's dead." The driver looked down at the boy's still form. "He never even said he felt bad," he muttered. "Just tapped me on the shoulder and said, real quiet, 'I'm sorry. I have to get off at the hotel.' That's all. Polite and apologizing like."

At school, the giggling, shuffling morning noise quieted as the news went down the halls. I passed a huddle of girls. "Who was it? Who dropped dead on the way to school?" I heard one of them half-whisper.

"Don't know his name; some kid from Milford Corners" was the reply.

It was like that in the faculty room and the principal's office. "I'd appreciate your going out to tell the parents," the principal told me. "They haven't a phone and, anyway, somebody from school should go there in person. I'll cover your classes."

"Why me?" I asked. "Wouldn't it be better if you did it?"

"I didn't know the boy," the principal admitted levelly. "And, in last year's sophomore personalities column I note that you were listed as his favorite teacher."

I drove through the snow and cold down the bad canyon road to the Evans place and thought about the boy, Cliff Evans. His favorite teacher! I thought. He hasn't spoken two words to me in two years! I could see him in my mind's eye all right, sitting back there in the last seat in my afternoon literature class. He came in the room by himelf and left by himself. "Cliff Evans," I muttered to myself, "a boy who never talked." I thought a minute. "A boy who never smiled. I never saw him smile once."

The big ranch kitchen was clean and warm. I blurted out my news somehow. Mrs. Evans reached blindly toward a chair. "He never said anything about bein' ailing.

His stepfather snorted. "He ain't said nothin' about anything since I moved in here."

Mrs. Evans pushed a pan to the back of the stove and began to untie her apron. "Now hold on," her husband snapped. "I got to have breakfast before I go to town. Nothin' we can do now anyway. If Cliff hadn't been so dumb, he'd have told us he didn't feel good."

After school I sat in the office and stared blankly at the records spread out before me. I was to close the file and write the obituary for the school paper. The almost bare sheets mocked the effort. Cliff Evans, white, never legally adopted by stepfather, five young half-brothers and sisters. These meager strands of information and the list of D grades were all the records had to offer.

Cliff Evans had silently come in the school door in the mornings and gone out the school door in the evenings, and that was all. He had never belonged to a club. He had never played on a team. He had never held an office. As far as I could tell he had never done one happy, noisy kid thing. He had never been anybody at all.

A true story. "Cipher in the Snow" by Jean Mizer from *Today's Education*, November, 1964.   Reprinted by permission of the author and publisher.

How do you go about making a boy into a zero? The grade-school records showed me. The first and second grade teachers' annotatons read "sweet, shy child," "timid but eager." Then the third grade note had opened the attack. Some teacher had written in a good, firm hand, "Cliff won't talk. Uncooperative. Slow learner." The other academic sheep had followed with "dull"; "slow-witted"; "low I.Q." They became correct. The boy's I.Q. score in the ninth grade was listed as 83. But his I.Q. in the third grade had been 106. The score didn't go under 100 until the seventh grade. Even shy, timid, sweet children have resilience. It takes time to break them.

I stomped to the typewriter and wrote a savage report pointing out what education had done to Cliff Evans. I slapped a copy on the principal's desk and another in the sad, dog-eared file. I banged the typewriter and slammed the file and crashed the door shut, but I didn't feel much better. A little boy kept walking after me, a little boy with a peaked, pale face; a skinny body in faded jeans; and big eyes that had looked and searched for a long time and then had become veiled.

I could guess how many times he's been chosen last to play sides in a game, how many whispered child conversations had excluded him, how many times he hadn't been asked. I could see and hear the faces and voices that said over and over, "You're a nothing, Cliff Evans."

A child is a believing creature. Cliff undoubtedly believed them. Suddenly it seemed clear to me: When finally there was nothing left at all for Cliff Evans, he collapsed on a snowbank and went away. The doctor might list "heart failure" as the cause of death, but that wouldn't change my mind.

We couldn't find ten students in the school who had known Cliff well enough to attend the funeral as his friends. So the student body officers and a committee from the junior class went as a group to the church, being politely sad. I attended the services with them, and sat through it with a lump of cold lead in my chest and a big resolve growing through me.

I've never forgotten Cliff Evans nor that resolve. He has been my challenge year after year, class after class. I look for veiled eyes or bodies scrouged into a seat in an alien world. "Look, kids," I say silently, "I may not do anything else for you this year, but not one of you is going to come out of here a nobody. I'll work or fight to the bitter end doing battle with society and the school board, but I won't have one of you coming out of here thinking himself a zero."

Most of the time—not always, but most of the time—I've succeeded.

Jean Mizer

PREMIER ARTISTE

Watch me perform!
I walk a tightrope of unique design.
I teeter, falter, recover
  And bow.
    You applaud.

I run forward, backward, hesitate
  And bow.
    You applaud.
If you don't applaud
  I'll Fall.
Cheer me! Hurray me!
Or you push me
Down.

Lenni Shender Goldstein

Characteristics of the Self-Concept

Now that you have a better idea of how your self-concept has developed, we can take a closer look at some of its characteristics.

The Self-Concept Is Not Objective   The way you see yourself isn't always the same as the way others view you. Sometimes the image you hold of yourself might be more favorable than the way others regard you. You might, for instance, see yourself as a witty joketeller when others can barely tolerate your attempts at humor. You might view yourself as highly intelligent while one or more instructors would see your scholarship as substandard. Perhaps you consider yourself an excellent worker, in contrast to the employer who wants to fire you.

There are several reasons why some people have a self-concept that others would regard as being unrealistically favorable. First, a self-estimation might be based on obsolete information. Perhaps your jokes used to be well received, or your grades were high, or your work was superior, and now the facts have changed. As you'll soon read, people are reluctant to give up a familiar self-image; this principle makes especially good sense when it's possible to avoid the unpleasant truth of the present by staying in the more desirable past.

A self-concept might also be excessively favorable due to distorted feedback from others. A boss may think of himself as an excellent manager because his assistants lave him with false praise in order to keep their jobs. A child's inflated ego may be based on the praise of doting parents.

A third reason for holding what appears to be an unrealistically high self-concept has to do with the expectations of a society that demands too much of its members. Much of the conditioning we receive in our early years implies that anything less than perfection is unsatisfactory, so that admitting one's mistakes is often seen as a sign of weakness. Instructors who fail to admit they don't know everything about a subject are afraid they will lose face with their colleagues and students. Couples whose relationships are beset by occasional problems don't want to admit that they have failed to achieve the "ideal" relationship they've seen portrayed in fiction. Parents who don't want to say, "I'm sorry, I made a mistake," to their children are afraid they'll lose the youngsters' respect. Once you accept such an irrational idea—that to be less than perfect is a character defect—admitting your frailties becomes difficult. Such a confession equates with admitting one is a failure—and failure is not an element of most peoples' self-concept. Rather than label themselves failures, many people engage in self-deception, insisting to themselves and to others that their behavior is more admirable than the circumstances indicate. We'll have more to say about the reasons behind such behavior and its consequences in Chapter 4, when we discuss defense mechanisms.

In contrast to the cases we've just described are times when we view ourselves *more* harshly than the objective facts suggest. You may have known people, for instance, who insist that they are unattractive or incompetent in spite of your honest insistence to the contrary. In fact, you

. . . for the love of one's neighbor is not possible without the love of ones-self.

Herman Hesse

have probably experienced feelings of excessively negative self-evaluation yourself. Recall a time when you woke up with a case of the "uglies," convinced that you looked terrible. Remember how on such days you were unwilling to accept even the most sincere compliments from others, having already decided how wretched you were. While many of us only fall into the trap of being overly critical occasionally, others constantly have an unrealistically low self-concept.

What are the reasons for such excessively negative self-evaluations? As with an unrealistically high self-esteem, one source for an overabundance of self-putdowns is obsolete information. A string of past failures in school or social relations can linger to haunt a communicator long after they have occurred, even though such events don't predict failure in the future. Similarly, we've known slender students who still think of themselves as fat and clear-complexioned people who still behave as if they were acne-ridden.

Distorted feedback can also create a self-image that is worse than a more objective observer would see. Having grown up around overly critical parents is one of the most common causes of a negative self-image. In other cases the remarks of cruel friends, uncaring teachers, excessively demanding employers, or even memorable strangers can have a lasting effect. As you read earlier, the impact of significant others and reference groups in forming a self-concept can be great.

A third cause for a very negative self-concept is again the myth of perfection, which is common in our society. From the time most of us learn to understand language we are exposed to models who appear to be perfect at whatever they do. This myth is most clear when we examine the most common stories children are told. In them the hero is wise, brave, talented, and victorious, while the villain is totally evil and doomed to failure. This kind of model is easy for a child to understand, but it hardly paints a realistic picture of the world, in which whatever heroes are identifiable are definitely not faultless. Unfortunately, many parents perpetuate the myth of perfection by refusing to admit that they are ever mistaken or unfair. Kids, of course, accept this perfectionist facade for a long time, not being in any position to dispute the wisdom of such powerful beings. And from the behavior of the adults around them comes the clear message: "A well-adjusted, successful person has no faults." Thus children learn that in order to gain acceptance, it's necessary to pretend to "have it all together," even though they know this isn't the case. Given this naive belief that everyone else is perfect and the knowledge that you aren't it's easy to see how one's self-concept would suffer.

Don't get the mistaken impression that we're suggesting it's wrong to aim at perfection as an *ideal.* We're only suggesting that achieving this state is usually not possible, and to expect that you should do so is a sure ticket to an inaccurate and unnecessarily low self-concept.

A final reason people often sell themselves short is also connected to social expectations. Curiously, the perfectionistic society to which we belong rewards those people who downplay the strengths we demand they possess (or pretend to possess). We term these people "modest" and find their behavior agreeable. On the other hand, we consider those who honestly appreciate their strengths to be "braggarts" or "egotists," confusing them with the people who boast about accomplishments they do not possess. This convention leads most of us to talk freely about our shortcomings while downplaying our accomplishments. It's all right to proclaim that you're miserable if you have failed to do well on a project, while it's considered boastful to express your pride at a job well done. It's fine to remark that you feel unattractive, but egocentric to say that you think you look good.

After a while we begin to believe the types of statements we repeatedly make. The self-putdowns are viewed as modesty and become part of our self-concept, while the strengths and accomplishments go unmentioned and are thus forgotten. And in the end we see ourselves as much worse than we are.

To contrast this kind of distortion, try the following exercise. It will give you a chance to suspend the rules we've just discussed by letting you appreciate yourself publicly for a change.

Group Bragging

1. Everyone should be seated so they can see each other.

2. Starting at one point of the circle, proceed to your right. In turn, each person should give three brags about herself. These brags needn't be about areas where you are an expert, and they don't have to be concerned with momentous feats. On the contrary, it's perfectly acceptable to brag about some part of yourself or thing you've done about which you're pleased or proud. For instance, you might share the fact that for once you completed a school assignment before the last minute, that you made the final payment on your car, that you bake a fantastic chocolate fudge cake, that you're proud to express your religious faith, or that you frequently drive hitchhikers to their destinations although it's out of your way.

3. If you're at a loss for brags, ask yourself
   a. What are some ways in which you've grown in the past year? How are you wiser, more skillful, or a better person than you previously were?
   b. Why do certain friends or family members care about you? What features do you possess that makes that person appreciate you?

4. If you're at a loss to think of brags, there's a penalty. You must sit and listen without protesting while other group members give you compliments. What a terrible fate!

5. After everyone has finished bragging, discuss the experience. How did you feel as you shared parts of yourself that you feel good about? Was this difficult? Did you have a hard time thinking of things to say? Consider whether you would have found it easier to think of a list of the things that are *wrong* with you. If this would have been less difficult, ask yourself whether this is because you truly are a wretched person or rather because you are in the habit of stressing your defects and ignoring your strengths. Consider the impact of such a habit on your self-concept, and ask yourself whether it wouldn't be wiser to place your self-appreciations and self-putdowns into more balance.

Hate Yourself? It May Not Be the Real You

Call it gossip, call it character analysis, call it what you will, the demand for private information about public people is running full throttle. We want to know who they *really* are. We want to know what they're *really* like.

We want the warts, and nothing but the warts.

We have come to associate character revelations with Digging Up the Dirt, and we are currently convinced that only the dirt is real. In short, we think the worst of ourselves. We think the worst *is* ourself.

This rampant pessimism comes up in all kinds of little ways. It came up one night when I visited a friend in a state of terminal grubbiness—matched only by the condition of her apartment. She put one hand on her hair rollers, pointed to the laundry with the other hand and grimaced, "Well, now you've seen the Real Me." This woman, who relines her kitchen drawers twice a year, was sure that she had revealed the secret inner soul of a slob.

But why is it that we are all so sure the *real me* is the one with the dirty hair, the one in dire need of a tube of Clearasil, the one screaming at the children, the one harboring thoughts of dismembering the driver behind us?

Why isn't the *real me* the one who remembers birthdays, keeps the scale within the limits of self-hate and plays "Go Fish" with the kids? Doesn't that count? Why are we so convinced that anything good about us is a civilized shell hiding the *real me*?

The *real me* problem is horribly destructive. If one assumes that the truth about ourselves is too bad to be false, then of course we have to hide it from others. They in turn can't truly love us because they don't know the real us. The unlovable real us.

Our belief in the bad comes from religion on the right and Freud on the left—original sin and original id. Between psychology and theology we've had a double-whammy that's convinced us that way down deep there in the old subconsicious or whatever, we are a mass of grasping, greedy, destructive, angry and rather appalling characteristics.

Abraham Maslow, who was one of the few psychologists to try and help us out of this pessimistic view, once observed that not only do we associate our nature with animal nature, but with the worst of the animals.

"Western civilization has generally believed that the animal in us was a bad animal, and that our most primitive impulses are evil, greedy, selfish and hostile," he said, adding that we have chosen to identify with "wolves, tigers, pigs, vultures or snakes, rather than with at least milder animals like the elephants or chimpanzees."

Maslow was one of those who tried to convince us that the *real me* is no more angry than loving, selfish than generous. He also tried to show us that people are motivated not just by neurotic needs, impulses and fears, but also out of a positive desire to grow, and out of a sense of fun and pleasure.

But we are not yet convinced. The common street-wisdom of the day is that the most successful of us are "compensating" for some lack, and that the happiest-seeming of us are really "repressing" some unhappiness.

Now, I hate to sound like Little Mary Sunshine, and I am not advocating that we accept everyone at face value. We've been plagued by masked men. But maybe we can get off the hook by letting others off it. The things we hate about ourselves, from the roll around the stomach to the bad temper, aren't more real than the things we like about ourselves. The good isn't a fake. Even if we have to dig for it.

Ellen Goodman

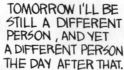

A Healthy Self-Concept Is Flexible   People change. From moment to moment we aren't the same. We wake up in the morning in a jovial mood and turn grumpy before lunch. We find ourselves fascinated in a conversational topic one moment, then suddenly lose interest. One moment's anger often gives way to forgiveness the next. Health turns to illness and back to health. Alertness becomes fatigue, hunger becomes satiation, and confusion becomes clarity.

We also change from situation to situation. You might be a relaxed conversationalist with people you know but at a loss for words with strangers. You might be patient when explaining things on the job and have no tolerance for such things at home. You might be a wizard at solving mathematical problems but have a terribly difficult time putting your thoughts into words.

Over longer stretches of time we also change. We grow older, learn new facts, adopt new attitudes and philosophies, set and reach new goals, and find that others change their way of thinking and acting toward us.

Since we change in these and many other ways, to keep a realistic picture of ourselves our self-concept must also change. Thus an accurate self-portrait of the type described on page 53 would probably not be the same as it would have been a year or a few months ago or even the way it would have been yesterday. This doesn't mean that you will change radically from day to day. There are certainly fundamental characteristics of your personality that will stay the same for years, perhaps for a lifetime. It is likely, however, that in other important ways you are changing—physically, intellectually, emotionally, and spiritually.

Like a snapshot
  You develop
Unlike a snapshot . . .
  You never stop

Leonard Nimoy

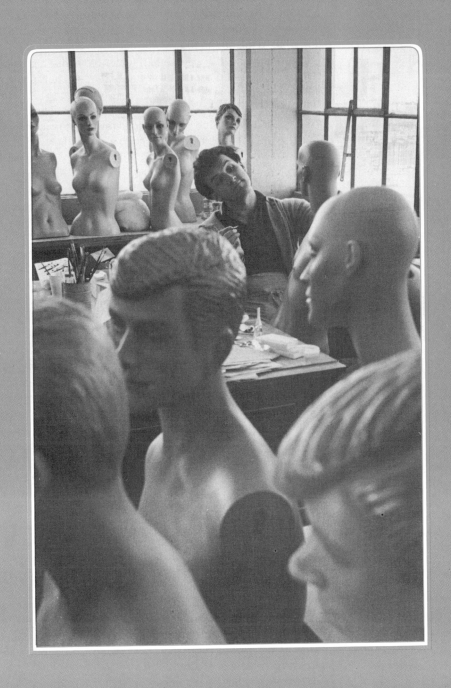

The Self-Concept Resists Change   In spite of the facts that we change and that a realistic self-concept should reflect this, the tendency to resist revision of our self-perception is strong. When confronted with facts that contradict the mental picture we hold of ourselves, the tendency is to dispute the facts and cling to the outmoded self-perception.

It's understandable why we're reluctant to revise a previously favorable self-concept. As we write these words, we recall how some professional athletes doggedly insist that they can be of value to the team when they are clearly past their prime. It must be tremendously difficult to give up the life of excitement, recognition, and financial rewards that comes with such a talent. Faced with such a tremendous loss, it's easy to see why the athlete would try to play one more season, insisting that the old skills are still there. In the same way a student who did well in earlier years but now has failed to study might be unwilling to admit that the label "good scholar" no longer applies, and a previously industrious worker, pointing to past commendations in a personnel file and insisting that she is a top-notch employee might resent a supervisor's mentioning increased absences and low productivity. (Remember that the people in these and other examples aren't *lying* when they insist that they're doing well in spite of the facts to the contrary; they honestly believe that the old truths still hold precisely because their self-concepts have been so resistant to change.)

Curiously, the tendency to cling to an outmoded self-perception also holds when the new image would be more favorable than the old one. We recall a former student who almost anyone would have regarded as being beautiful, with physical features attractive enough to appear in any glamour magazine. In spite of her appearance, in a class exercise this woman characterized herself as "ordinary" and "unattractive." When questioned by her classmates, she described how as a child her teeth were extremely crooked, and how she had worn braces for several years in her teens to correct this problem. During this time she was often kidded by her friends, who never let her forget her "metal mouth," as she put it. Even though the braces had been off for two years, our student reported that she still saw herself as ugly, and brushed aside our compliments by insisting that we were just saying these things to be nice—she knew how she *really* looked.

Examples like this show one problem that occurs when we resist changing an inaccurate self-concept. Our student denied herself a much happier life by clinging to an obsolete picture of herself. In the same way some communicators insist that they are less talented or worthy of friendship than others would suggest, thus creating their own miserable world when it needn't exist. These unfortunate souls probably resist changing because they aren't willing to go through the disorientation that comes from redefining themselves, correctly anticipating that it *is* an effort to think of one's self in a new way. Whatever their reasons, it's sad to see people in such an unnecessary state of affairs.

A second problem that comes from trying to perpetrate an inaccurate self-concept is self-delusion and lack of growth. If you hold an unrealistically favorable picture of yourself, you won't see the real need for change that may exist. Instead of learning new talents, working to change a relationship, or

"Who are you?" said the caterpillar. This was not an encouraging opening for a conversation. Alice replied rather shyly, "I hardly know, sir, just at present—at least I knew who I was when I got up this morning, but I think I must have changed several times since then."

Lewis Carroll, *Alice's Adventures in Wonderland*

improving your physical condition, you'll stay with the familiar and comfortable delusion that everything is all right. As time goes by this delusion becomes more and more difficult to maintain, leading to a third type of problem.

To understand this problem you need to remember that communicators who are presented with information that contradicts their self-perception have two choices: They can either accept the new data and change their perception accordingly, or they can keep their original viewpoint and in some way refute the new information. Since most communicators are reluctant to downgrade a favorable image of themselves, their tendency is to opt for refutation, either by discounting the information and rationalizing it away or by counterattacking the person who shared it. While Chapter 4 will go into details of such defensive communication, it's enough to say now that these sorts of responses are usually quite destructive, and most often lead to increased hard feelings and weakened relationships.

The Self-Fulfilling Prophecy and Communication

The self-concept is such a powerful force on the personality that it not only determines how you see yourself in the present, but can actually influence your future behavior and that of others. Such occurrences come about through a phenomenon called the self-fulfilling prophecy.

A self-fulfilling prophecy occurs when a person's expectation of an event makes the outcome more likely to occur than would otherwise have been true. Self-fulfilling prophecies occur all the time, although you might never have given them that label. For example, think of some instances you may have known.

You expected to become nervous and botch a job interview and later did so.

You anticipated having a good (or terrible) time at a social affair and found your expectations being met.

A teacher or boss explained a new task to you, saying that you probably wouldn't do well at first. You did not do well.

A friend described someone you were about to meet, saying that you wouldn't like the person. The prediction turned out to be correct—you didn't like the new acquaintance.

In each of these cases there is a good chance that the event happened because it was predicted to occur. You needn't have botched the interview, the party might have been boring only because you helped make it so, you might have done better on the job if your boss hadn't spoken up, and you might have liked the new acquaintance if your friend hadn't given you preconceptions. In other words, what helped make each event occur was the expectation that it would happen.

Friday in Mrs. Gainey's sixth-grade class at P.S. 25 in New York City was the weekly day of reckoning for us. The mornings were spent taking tests which she graded during lunch period (who ate?). When we reassembled after recess, all thirty of us cleared out our belongings from the "old" desks and stood at attention around the perimeter of the classroom. We waited to discover for whom the bells would toll and for whom the chimes would ring out. On the basis of a combined average of the test scores, each child was ranked from one to thirty and seated accordingly. The best and the brightest would be placed up front from left to right in the first row closest to the teacher's desk. There would always be a lot of tension between these ambitious little hotshots to determine if they would keep their exalted places or move even further toward Row 1 Seat 1. There was also the sex thing: would a boy beat our Joanie this week or would the girls continue their stranglehold on the top spot?

After the first ten names were sung out by the teacher and the pupils took their seats, the tension eased somewhat as the insignificant middle-level kids were put into their places. As Mrs. Gainey got down to the final ten kids already standing nervously at the back of the room, all forty eyes were riveted on them. Accompanying each name called was the math grade, spelling grade, history grade, and science grade. Smiles broke into snickers as these grades got lower and lower. Sometimes you'd have to bite the inside of your mouth not to laugh out loud as these unfortunates squirmed in agony. It didn't help to have the teacher remind us not to laugh at them because one day we might be in the same boat and then we'd be sorry. Unimaginable! As usual, "Baby" Gonzales brought up the rear. I was sure he did so on purpose as a status thing to hear the teacher say, "And last again this week, Mr. Gonzales." No one laughed or looked his way; "Baby" was the biggest kid in the class and did not "work and play well with others."

Philip Zimbardo, Shyness

© 1977 by Addison-Wesley

There are two types of self-fulfilling prophecies. The first occurs when your own expectations influence your behavior. Like the job interview and the party described above, there are many times when an event that needn't have occurred does happen because you expect it to. In sports you've probably psyched yourself into playing either better or worse than usual, so that the only explanation for your unusual performance was your attitude that you'd behave differently. Similarly, you've probably faced an audience at one time or another with a fearful attitude and forgotten your remarks, not because you were unprepared, but because you said to yourself, "I know I'll blow it."

Certainly you've had the experience of waking up in a cross mood and saying to yourself, "This will be a 'bad day'." Once you made such a decision, you may have acted in ways that made it come true. If you approached a class expecting to be bored, you most probably did lose interest, due partly to a lack of attention on your part. If you avoided the company of others because you expected that they had nothing to offer, your suspicions would have been confirmed—nothing exciting or new did happen to you. On the other hand, if you approached the same day with the idea that it had the potential to be a good one, this expectation probably would also have been met. Smile at people, and they'll probably smile back. Enter a class determined to learn something, and you probably will—even if it's how not to instruct students! Approach many people with the idea that some of them will be good to know, and you'll most likely make some new friends. In these cases and ones like them your attitude has a great deal to do with how you see yourself and how others will see you.

A second type of self-fulfilling prophecy occurs when the expectations of one person govern another's actions. The classic example was demonstrated by Robert Rosenthal and Lenore Jacobson in a study they described in their book, *Pygmalion in the Classroom:*

> 20 percent of the children in a certain elementary school were reported to their teachers as showing unusual potential for intellectual growth. The names of these 20 percent were drawn by means of a table of random numbers, which is to say that the names were drawn out of a hat. Eight months later these unusual or "magic" children showed significantly greater gains in IQ than did the remaining children who had not been singled out for the teachers' attention. The change in the teachers' expectations regarding the intellectual performance of these allegedly "special" children had led to an actual change in the intellectual performance of these randomly selected children.

In other words, some children may do better in school, not because they are any more intelligent than their classmates, but because they learn that their teacher, a significant other, believes they can achieve.

To put this phenomenon in context with the self-concept, we can say that when a teacher communicates to a child the message, "I think you're bright," the child accepts that evaluation and changes her self-concept to include that evaluation. Unfortunately, we can assume that the same principle holds for students whose teachers send the message, "I think you're stupid."

This type of self-fulfilling prophecy has been shown to be a powerful force for shaping the self-concept and thus the behavior of people in a wide range of settings outside the schools. In medicine patients who unknowingly use

. . . the difference between a lady and a flower girl is not how she behaves, but how she's treated. I shall always be a flower girl to Professor Higgins, because he always treats me as a flower girl, and always will; but I know I can be a lady to you, because you always treat me as a lady, and always will.

G. B. Shaw, *Pygmalion*

placebos—substances such as injections of sterile water or doses of sugar pills that have no curative value—often respond just as favorably to treatment as people who actually received a drug. The patients believe they have taken a substance that will help them feel better, and this belief actually brings about a "cure." In psychotherapy Rosenthal and Jacobson describe several studies which suggest that patients who believe that they will benefit from treatment do so, regardless of the type of treatment they receive. In the same vein, when a doctor believes a patient will improve, the patient may do so precisely because of this expectation, while another person for whom the physician has little hope often fails to recover. Apparently the patient's self-concept as sick or well—as shaped by the doctor—plays an important role in determining the actual state of health.

In business the power of the self-fulfilling prophecy was proved as early as 1890. A new tabulating machine had just been installed at the U.S. Census Bureau in Washington, D.C. In order to use the machine the bureau's staff had to learn a new set of skills that the machine's inventor believed to be quite difficult. He told the clerks that after some practice they could expect to punch about 550 cards per day; to process any more would jeopardize their psychological well-being. Sure enough, after two weeks the clerks were processing the anticipated number of cards, and reported feelings of stress if they attempted to move any faster.

Some time later an additional group of clerks was hired to operate the same machines. These workers knew nothing of the devices, and no one had told them about the upper limit of production. After only three days the new employees were each punching over 2,000 cards per day with no ill effects. Again, the self-fulfilling prophecy seemed to be in operation. The original workers believed themselves capable of punching only 550 cards and so behaved accordingly, while the new clerks had no limiting expectations as part of their self-concepts and so behaved more productively.

The self-fulfilling prophecy operates in families as well. If parents tell a child long enough that she can't do anything right, her self-concept will soon incorporate this idea, and she will fail at many or most of the tasks she attempts. On the other hand, if a child is told she is a capable or lovable or kind person, there is a much greater chance of her behaving accordingly.

The self-fulfilling prophecy is an important force in interpersonal communication, but we don't want to suggest that it explains all behavior. There are certainly times when the expectation of an event's outcome won't bring about that occurrence. Your hope of drawing an ace in a card game won't in any way affect the chance of that card turning up in an already shuffled deck, and your belief that good weather is coming won't stop the rain from falling. In the same way, believing you'll do well in a job interview when you're clearly not qualified for the position is unrealistic. Similarly, there will probably be people you don't like and occasions you won't enjoy, no matter what your attitude. To connect the self-fulfilling prophecy with the "power of positive thinking" is an oversimplification.

In other cases your expectations will be borne out because you're a good predictor, and not because of the self-fulfilling prophecy. For example, children are not equally well equipped to do well in school, and in such cases

it would be wrong to say that the child's performance was shaped by a parent or teacher, even though the behavior did match that which was expected. In the same way, some workers excel and others fail, some patients recover and others don't, all according to our predictions but not because of them.

Keeping these qualifications in mind, it's important to recognize the tremendous influence that self-fulfilling prophecies play in our lives. To a great extent we are what we believe we are. In this sense we and those around us constantly create our self-concepts and thus ourselves.

Changing Your Self-Concept

After reading this far you know more clearly just what the self-concept is, how it is formed, and how it affects communication. But we still haven't focused directly on perhaps the most important question of all: How can you change the parts of your self-concept with which you aren't happy? There's certainly no quick method for becoming the person you'd like to be: Personal growth and self-improvement is a lifetime process. But we can offer several suggestions which will help you move closer to your goals.

Have Realistic Expectations   It's extremely important to realize that some of your dissatisfaction might come from expecting too much of yourself. If you demand that you handle every act of communication perfectly, you're bound to be disappointed. Nobody is able to handle every conflict productively, to be totally relaxed and skillful in conversations, to always ask perceptive questions, or to be 100 percent helpful when others have problems. Expecting yourself to reach such unrealistic goals is to doom yourself to unhappiness at the start.

Sometimes it's easy to be hard on yourself because everyone around you seems to be handling themselves so much better than you. It's important to realize that much of what seems like confidence and skill in others is a front to hide uncertainty. They may be suffering from the same self-imposed demands of perfection that you place on yourself.

Even in cases where others definitely seem more competent than you, it's important to judge yourself in terms of your own growth, and not against the behavior of others. Rather than feeling miserable because you're not as talented as an expert, realize that you probably are a better, wiser, or more skillful person than you used to be and that this is a legitimate source of satisfaction. Perfection is fine as an ideal, but you're being unfair to yourself if you expect actually to reach that state.

Self-Appreciation Exercise

As a means of demonstrating the self-appreciation that can come from recognizing that you're growing, do the following:

1. Form a circle in your group. Your group size may be the group as a whole or several small groups.

2. Each group member in turn should complete the following statement:
   "Im a long way from being perfect at _____,
   but I'm slowly getting better by _____."

   Here are some examples:
   "I'm a long way from being perfect at *my job,* but I'm slowly getting better by *taking on just one task at a time and persisting until I finish.*"

   "I'm a long way from being perfect at *approaching strangers,* but I'm slowly getting better by *going to more parties and once in a while actually starting to talk to people I don't know.*"

Have a Realistic Perception of Yourself One source of a poor self-concept is an inaccurate self-perception. As you've already read, such unrealistic pictures sometimes come from being overly harsh on yourself, believing that you're worse than the facts indicate. By sharing the self-concept list you recorded on page 53 with others who know you, it will be possible to see whether you have been selling yourself short. Of course, it would be foolish to deny that you could be a better person than you are, but it's also important to recognize your strengths. A periodic session of bragging such as you tried earlier in this chapter is often a good way to put your strengths and shortcomings into perspective.

An unrealistically poor self-concept can also come from the inaccurate feedback of others. Perhaps you are in an environment where you receive an excessive number of "downer" messages, many of which are undeserved, and a minimum of upper messages. We've known many housewives, for example, who have returned to college after many years spent in homemaking where they received virtually no recognition for their intellectual strengths. It's amazing that these women have the courage to come to college at all, so low are their self-concepts; but come they do, and most are thrilled to find that they are much brighter and more competent intellectually than they suspected. In the same way, workers with overly critical supervisors, children with cruel "friends," and students with unsupportive teachers all are prone to suffering from low self-concepts due to excessively negative feedback.

If you fall into this category, it's important to put the unrealistic evaluations you receive into perspective and then to seek out more supportive people who will acknowledge your assets as well as point out your shortcomings. Doing so is often a quick and sure boost to the self-concept.

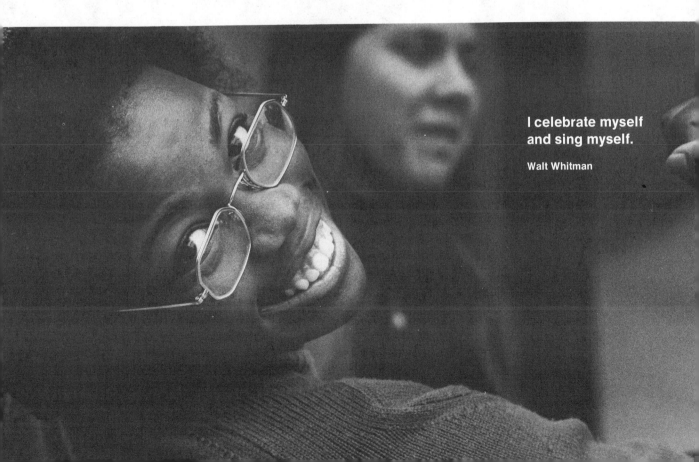

I celebrate myself
and sing myself.

Walt Whitman

Probably a crab would be filled
with a sense of personal outrage
if it could hear us class it without
ado or apology as a crustacean,
and thus dispose of it. "I am no
such thing," it would say; "I am
myself, myself alone."

William James

Have the Will To Change   Often we say we want to change but we aren't willing to do the necessary work. You might, for instance, decide that you'd like to become a better conversationalist. Taking the advice offered in the next section of this book, you ask your instructor or some other communication adviser how to reach this goal. You receive two pieces of advice. First, you're instructed to spend the next three weeks observing people who handle themselves well in conversations and to record exactly what they do that makes them so skillful. Second, your adviser suggests that you read several books on the subject of conversational skills. You begin these tasks with the best intentions, but after a few days the task of recording conversations becomes a burden—it would be so much easier just to listen to others talk. And your diligent reading program becomes bogged down as the press of other work fills up your time. In other words, you find you just "can't" fit the self-improvement plan into your busy schedule.

Let's be realistic. Becoming a better communicator is probably one of many goals in your life. It's possible that you'll find other needs are more pressing, which is completely reasonable. However, you should realize that changing your self-concept often requires a good deal of effort, and without that effort your good intentions alone probably won't get you much closer to this goal. In communication, as in most other aspects of life, "there's no such thing as a free lunch."

Have The Skill Needed To Change   Often trying isn't enough. There are some cases where you would change if you knew of a way to do so. To see if this is the case for you, go back to your list of "can'ts" and "won'ts" and see if any items there are more appropriately "don't know how." If so, then the way to change is to learn how. You can do so in two ways.

First, you can seek advice—from books such as this one, the references listed at the end of each chapter, and other printed sources. You can also get advice from instructors, counselors and other experts, as well as friends. Of course, not all the advice you receive will be useful, but if you read widely and talk to enough people, you have a good chance of learning the things you want to know.

A second method of learning how to change is to observe models—people who handle themselves in the ways you would like to master. It's often been said that people learn more from models than in any other way, and by taking advantage of this principle you will find that the world is full of teachers who can show you how to communicate more successfully. Become a careful observer. Watch what people you admire do and say, not so that you can copy them, but so that you can adapt their behavior to fit your own personal style.

At this point you might be overwhelmed at the difficulty of changing the way you think about yourself and the way you act. Remember, we never said that this process would be an easy one (although it sometimes is). But even when change is difficult, you know that it's possible if you are serious. You don't need to be perfect, but you can improve your self-concept if you choose to.

WHAT IS REAL?

The Skin Horse had lived longer in the nursery than any of the others. He was so old that his brown coat was bald in patches and showed the seams underneath, and most of the hairs in his tail had been pulled out to string bead necklaces. He was wise, for he had seen a long succession of mechanical toys arrive to boast and swagger, and by-and-by break their mainsprings and pass away, and he knew that they were only toys, and would never turn into anything else. For nursery magic is very strange and wonderful, and only those playthings that are old and wise and experienced like the Skin Horse understand all about it.

"What is REAL?" asked the Rabbit one day, when they were lying side by side near the nursery fender, before Nana came to tidy the room. "Does it mean having things that buzz inside you and a stick-out handle?"

"Real isn't how you are made," said the Skin Horse, "it's a thing that happens to you. When a child loves you for a long, long time, not just to play with, but REALLY loves you, then you become Real."

"Does it hurt?" asked the Rabbit.

"Sometimes," said the Skin Horse, for he was always truthful. "When you are Real you don't mind being hurt."

"Does it happen all at once, like being wound up," he asked. "or bit by bit?"

"It doesn't happen all at once," said the Skin Horse. "You become. It takes a long time. That's why it doesn't often happen to people who break easily, or have sharp edges, or who have to be carefully kept. Generally, by the time you are Real, most of your hair has been loved off, and your eyes drop out and you get loose in the joints and very shabby. But these things don't matter at all, because once you are real you can't be ugly, except to people who don't understand."

"I suppose *you* are Real?" said the Rabbit. And then he wished he had not said it, for he thought the Skin Horse might be sensitive. But the Skin Horse only smiled.

"The Boy's Uncle made me Real," he said. "That was a great many years ago; but once you are Real you can't become unreal again. It lasts for always."

Margery Williams, *The Velveteen Rabbit*

Roads Not Taken

1. What implications do recent self-concept studies have for teachers and educators? parents? supervisors?

2. What is the relationship between self-esteem and the process of self-disclosure and feedback?

3. What is meant by the statement that role definition is usually the product of the value system of a society, a group, or an individual?

4. Where does self-concept fit into the explanation of the fact that girls outperform boys in mathematics up to about twelve years of age, after which boys show superior abilities?

5. Can you trace the development of your self-concept, naming persons, places, incidents, and dates?

More Readings on the Self-Concept

Briggs, Dorothy C. *Your Child's Self-Esteem.* Garden City, NY: Doubleday, 1975.
This is a down-to-earth guide for parents and other adults who work with children. It reminds us of the critical role we play in shaping the self-concept of youngsters.

Campbell, Colin. "Our Many Versions of the Self: An Interview With M. Brewster Smith." *Psychology Today,* 9 (February, 1976), 74–79.
Psychologist Smith discusses the many ways to view the self, and the consequences of each.

Gergen, Kenneth J. "The Healthy, Happy Human Being Wears Many Masks." *Psychology Today,* 5 (May, 1972), 31–35, 64–66.
This article makes it clear that the idea of a single "self" may be overly simplistic; perhaps we are different people in different contexts. This article makes a good companion to Campbell's interview with M. Brewster Smith, cited above.

Hayakawa, S. I. *Symbol, Status and Personality.* New York: Harcourt, Brace Jovanovich, 1953.
Hayakawa's description of the self-concept in Chapter 4 may have been written over twenty-five years ago, but it is still one of the clearest and most interesting ones around.

Insel, Paul M., and Lenore Jacobson. *What Do You Expect? An Inquiry into Self-Fulfilling Prophecies.* Menlo Park, CA: Cummings Publishing Co., 1975.
This collection of essays and research articles describes some of the many ways the self-fulfilling prophecy operates. Especially valuable for educators.

Rosenthal, Robert, and Lenore Jacobson. *Pygmalion in the Classroom.* New York: Holt, Rinehart and Winston, 1968.
This book contains a fascinating description of how self-fulfilling prophecies operate in education, social science research, medicine, and everyday life.

Chapter Three

Emotions: Thinking and Feeling

I t's hard to talk about communication without realizing the importance of emotions. Think about it for yourself: Feeling confident can make the difference between success and failure in everything from giving a speech to asking for a date, while insecurity can ruin your chances. Being angry or defensive can spoil your time with others, while feeling and acting calm will help prevent or solve problems. The way you share or withhold your feelings of liking or affection can affect the future of your relationships. On and on the list of feelings goes: appreciation, loneliness, joy, insecurity, curiosity, irritation . . . the point is clear: Communication shapes our feelings, and feelings influence our communication.

Because this subject of emotions is so important, we'll spend this chapter taking a closer look. Just what are feelings, and how can we recognize them? How are feelings caused, and how can we control them, increasing the positive ones and decreasing the negatives? When and how can you best share your feelings with others? Read on and see.

What Are Emotions?

Suppose that a visitor from the planet Vulcan or Ork asked you to explain emotions. How would you answer? You might start by saying that emotions are things that we feel. But this doesn't say much, since in turn you would probably describe feelings as synonymous with emotions. Social scientists who have studied the role of affect generally agree that there are four components to the phenomena we label as feelings.

Physiological Changes   When a person experiences strong emotions, many bodily changes occur. For example, the physical components of fear include an increased heartbeat, a rise in blood pressure, an increase in adrenaline secretions, an elevated blood sugar level, a slowing of digestion, and a dilation of pupils in the eyes. Some of these changes are recognizable to the person experiencing them. These sensations are termed *proprioceptive stimuli*, meaning that they are activated by movement of internal tissues. Proprioceptive messages can offer a significant clue to your emotions once you become aware of them. For instance, we know a woman who began focusing on her internal messages and learned that every time she returned to the city from a vacation she felt an empty feeling in the pit of her stomach. From what she'd already learned about herself, she knew that this sensation always accompanied things she dreaded; and once aware of this knowledge, she realized she was much happier in the country. Now she is trying to find a way to make the move she knows is right for her.

Another friend of ours had always appeared easygoing and agreeable in even the most frustrating circumstances. But after focusing on internal messages, he discovered his mild behavior contrasted strongly with the tense

. . . Every thought, gesture, muscle tension, feeling, stomach gurgle, nose scratch, fart, hummed tune, slip of the tongue, illness—everything is significant and meaningful and related to the now. It is possible to know and understand oneself on all these levels, and the more one knows the more he is free to determine his own life.

If I know what my body tells me, I know my deepest feelings and I can choose what to do. . . . Given a complete knowledge of myself, I can determine my life; lacking that mastery, I am controlled in ways that are often undesirable, unproductive, worrisome, and confusing.

William Schutz, Here Comes Everybody

muscles and headaches that he got during trying times. This new awareness led him to realize that he did indeed experience frustration and anger—and that he somehow needed to deal with these feelings if he was going to feel truly comfortable.

How Does It Feel?

Here's a way to learn more about yourself from your body. You can do this exercise with a group or individually outside the classroom. If you do it alone, read all the steps ahead of time so that you can work through the whole experience without interrupting yourself. However, the exercise will have more impact if you do it for the first time in a group because in this way your facilitator can read the instructions for you. Also, in a group your feelings can be shared and compared.

The ellipses (. . .) in the instructions indicate points where you should pause for a moment and examine what you're experiencing.

1. Wherever you are, find yourself a comfortable position, either lying or sitting. You'll need to find a quiet place with no distractions. You'll find the exercise works better if you dim the lights.

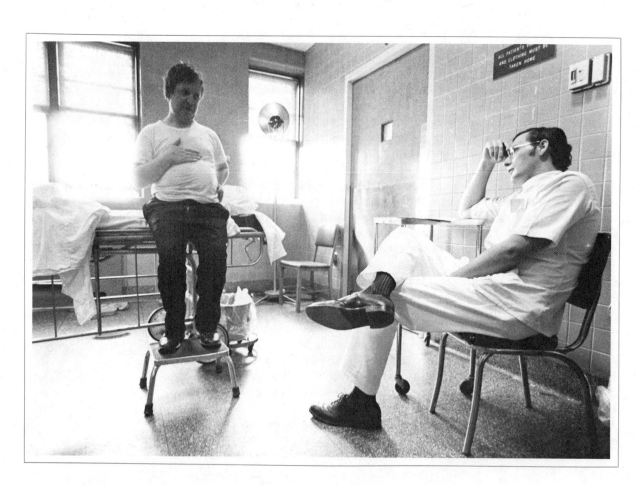

2. Close your eyes. The visual sense is so dominant that it's easy to neglect your other senses.

3. Now that your eyes are closed and you're comfortable, take a trip through your body and see how the various parts of it are. As you focus on each part, don't try to change what you find . . . just notice how you are, how you feel.

4. Now let's begin. Start with your feet. How do they feel? Are they comfortable, or do they hurt? Are your toes cold? Do your shoes fit well, or are they too tight?

   Now move your attention to your legs . . . . Is there any tension in them, or are they relaxed? . . . Can you feel each muscle and see how it is? . . . Are your legs crossed? Is there pressure where one presses against the other? . . . Are they comfortable?

   Now pay attention to your hips and pelvis . . . the area where your legs and backbone join. Do you feel comfortable here or are you not as relaxed as you'd like to be? If you're seated, direct your attention to your buttocks. . . . Can you feel your body's weight pressing against the surface you're sitting on?

   Now move on to the trunk of your body. How does your abdomen feel? . . . What are the sensations you can detect there? . . . Is anything moving? . . . Focus on your breathing. . . . Do you breathe off the top of your lungs, or are you taking deep, relaxed breaths? . . . Does the air move in and out through your nose or your mouth? Is your chest tight, or is it comfortable?

   Checking out your breathing has probably led you to your throat and neck. Is your throat comfortable, or do you feel a lump there you need to keep swallowing? . . . How about your neck? . . . Can you feel it holding your head in its present position? . . . Perhaps moving your head slowly from side to side will help you feel these muscles doing their work. . . . Is there tension in your neck or shoulders?

   Now let's move to your face. . . . What expression are you wearing? . . . Are the muscles of your face tense or relaxed? Which ones? Your mouth . . . brow . . . jaw . . . temples? Take a few moments and see. . . .

   Finally, go inside your head and see what's happening there. . . Is it quiet and dark, or are things happening there? . . . What are they? Does it feel good inside your head, or is there some pressure or aching? . . .

   You've made a trip from bottom to top. Try feeling your whole body now. . . . See what new awareness of it you've gained. . . . Are there any special parts of your body that attract your attention now? . . . What are they telling you?

   Now there's another very important part of your body to focus on. It's the part of you where you *feel* when you're happy or sad or afraid. Take a moment and find that spot. . . See how you are now in there. . . . See what happens when you ask yourself "How am I now? How do I feel?" . . . See what happens in that place when you think of a personal problem that's been bothering you lately. . . . Be sure it's something that's important to your life now. . . . Now see if you can get the feel of this problem there in the place where you feel things. . . . Let yourself feel all of it. . . . If the feeling changes as you focus on it, that's o.k. Just stay with the feeling wherever it goes and see how it is. . . . If what you feel now makes a difference to you, see what that difference is. . . . Now, take a few minutes to use in whatever way you like, and then slowly open your eyes.

5. Now think about the following questions. If you're with your group, you may want to discuss them there.
   a. Did you find out things about your body that you hadn't noticed before? Did you discover some tensions that you'd been carrying around? How long do you think you've been this way? Did recognizing them make any difference to you?
   b. Could you find the part of yourself where you usually feel things? Where was it? Or are there different spots for different feelings? Did focusing on your problem make some kind of difference to you?

Nonverbal Manifestations   A quick comparison between the emotionless Mr. Spock of *Star Trek* and full-blooded humans tells us that feelings show up in many nonverbal behaviors. Postures, gestures, facial expressions, body positioning and distance all provide clues that suggest our emotional state. We'll have a great deal to say about the value of observing nonverbal messages as clues to emotion—both yours and others'—in Chapter 7.

Cognitive Interpretations   A moment ago you read that some physiological components of fear are a racing heart, perspiration, tense muscles, and a boost in blood pressure. Interestingly enough, the symptoms are similar to the physical changes that accompany excitement, joy, and other emotions. In other words, if we were to measure the physical condition of someone experiencing a strong emotion, we would have a hard time knowing whether she was trembling with fear or quivering with excitement. The recognition that the bodily components of most emotions are similar led Norman Schachter and some other psychologists to conclude that the experience of fright, joy, or anger comes primarily from the *label* we give to the same physical symptoms at a given time. This cognitive explanation of emotion has been labeled *attribution theory.* Psychologist Philip Zimbardo offers a good example of attribution in action.

> I notice I'm perspiring while lecturing. From that I infer I am feeling nervous. If it occurs often, I might even label myself a "nervous person." Once I have the label, the next question I must answer is "Why am I nervous?" Then I start to search for an appropriate explanation. I might notice some students leaving the room, or being inattentive. I am nervous because I'm not giving a good lecture. That makes me nervous. How do I know it's not good? Because I'm boring my audience. I am nervous because I am a boring lecturer and I want to be a good lecturer. I feel inadequate. Maybe I should open a delicatessen instead. Just then a student says, "It's hot in here, I'm perspiring and it makes it tough to concentrate on your lecture." Instantly, I'm no longer "nervous" or "boring."

In his book *Shyness* Zimbardo discusses the consequences of making inaccurate or exaggerated attributions. In a survey of more than 5,000 subjects, over 80 percent described themselves as having been shy at some time in their lives, while more than 40 percent considered themselves presently shy. Most significantly, these "not shy" people behaved in virtually the *same way* as their shy counterparts. They would blush, perspire, and feel their hearts pounding in certain social situations. The biggest difference between the two groups seemed to be the label with which they describe themselves. This is a significant difference. Someone who notices the symptoms we've described and thinks, "I'm such a shy person!" will most likely feel more uncomfortable and communicate less effectively than another person with the same symptoms who thinks, "Well, I'm a bit shaky here, but that's to be expected."

We'll take a closer look at ways of reducing unpleasant emotions through cognitive processes a bit later in this chapter.

Verbal Expression   A fourth component of emotions involves verbal expression. There are several ways to express a feeling verbally. The first is through single words: "I'm angry (excited, depressed, curious, and so on)." While this point seems obvious, many people suffer from impoverished emotional vocabularies. They have a hard time describing more than a few basic feelings, such as "good" or "bad," "terrible" or "great." Take a moment now and see how many feelings you can write down. After you've done this, look at the list on page 96 and see which ones you've missed.

Another way of expressing feelings verbally is by using descriptive phrases: "I feel all jumbled up," "I'm on top of the world," and so on. As long as such phrases aren't too obscure, e.g., "I feel somnolent," they can be an effective way of describing your emotional state.

It's also possible to express emotions by describing what you'd like to do: "I feel like singing," "I'd like to cry," "I feel like running away," and so on. Often expressions like these capture the emotion clearly, but in other cases they can be confusing. For instance, if somebody told you, "Every time I see you I want to laugh," you might have a hard time knowing whether you were an object of enjoyment or ridicule.

As you read in Chapter 1, the ability to express emotions verbally is a critical element in effective communication. To recall why, notice the difference between the following statements:

"Ever since we had our fight, I've been avoiding you."

and

"Ever since our fight, I've been avoiding you *because I've been so embarrassed* (*or so angry*)."

Many communicators think they're expressing their feelings when in fact their statements are emotionally counterfeit. For example, it sounds emotionally revealing to say "I feel like going to a show" or "I feel we've been seeing too much of each other." But in fact neither of these statements has any emotional content. In the first sentence the word *feel* really stands for an intention: "I *want* to go to a show." In the second sentence the "feeling" is really a *thought:* "I *think* we've been seeing too much of each other." You can recognize the absence of emotion in each case by adding a genuine feeling word to them. For instance, "I'm *bored* and I want to go to a show," or "I think we've been seeing too much of each other and I feel *confined.*"

accepted	edgy	intense	restless
afraid	elated	intimidated	sad
annoyed	embarrassed	irritable	sensual
anxious	enthusiastic	jazzed	sentimental
angry	envious	jealous	sexy
ashamed	estatic	joyful	shaky
bashful	excited	lonely	shy
bewildered	fearful	loving	silly
bitter	foolish	mean	strong
bored	free	miserable	subdued
brave	frustrated	needed	tender
calm	furious	neglected	tense
confident	glum	nervous	terrified
confused	good	passionate	tight
concerned	guilty	peaceful	tired
defeated	happy	pessimistic	trapped
DEFENSIVE	helpless	playful	ugly
depressed	high	pleased	uneasy
detached	hopeful	pressured	uptight
disappointed	hostile	protective	VULNERABLE
disgusted	humiliated	puzzled	warm
disturbed	hurt	rejected	weak
eager	inadequate	relieved	wonderful
	inhibited	resentful	worried

Most people would be able to express their emotions (and intentions) more clearly if they were able to describe them to themselves first. How many times have you stopped what you were going to say because you couldn't "find the words"? Identifying your feeling for yourself can help you communicate with others.

Recognizing Your Emotions

Keep a three-day record of your feelings. You can do this by spending a few minutes each evening recalling what emotions you felt during the day, what other people were involved, and the circumstances in which the emotion occurred.

At the end of the three-day period you can understand the role emotions play in your communication by answering the following questions:

1. **How did you recognize the emotions you experienced: Through proprioceptive stimuli, nonverbal behaviors, cognitive processes, and/or verbal expression?**

2. **Did you have any difficulty deciding which emotion you were feeling?**

3. **What emotions do you experience most often? Are there any emotions that you didn't experience as much as you would have expected?**

4. **In what circumstances do/don't you express the feelings you experience? What factors influence your decision to share or not share your feelings? The type of emotion? The person(s) involved? The situation (time, place)? The subject that the emotion involves (money, sex, etc.)?**

5. **What are the consequences of the type of communicating you just described in step 4? Are you satisfied with these consequences? If not, what can you do to become more satisfied?**

Benefits of Expressing Emotions

Now that you better understand just what emotions are, the next step is to see why expressing them is a good idea. There are several benefits of effectively communicating feelings.

You Learn More About Others   Feelings, like other kinds of behavior, are shared on a reciprocal basis. In other words, you're likely to get what you give. This principle of reciprocity has important implications for your relationships. If you'd like to know how others are feeling about you, your best chance of learning will come from sharing your own feelings. It's sad to think about how many times two people have failed to grow closer because each one was waiting for the other to make the first move. Of course, the principle of reciprocity doesn't guarantee you'll like what you hear in return for sharing your feelings. You might find out that others have some negative

feelings about you. But even a genuinely negative reaction is often better than living with another person's stiff, uncomfortable silence while you wonder what he or she might be thinking about you.

Others Understand You Better   It's frustrating to be ignored or misunderstood, and yet you may be creating these sad circumstances yourself by not sharing your feelings. When you let others know how you feel, you have a far better chance of being understood. We often think that people *should* know that we care for them or that we are upset by something they've done, but the fact is that humans aren't mind readers, and that even the best of us can be downright insensitive at times. Thus, if you want others to be aware of what you're feeling, you'll probably have to tell them.

Your Relationships Will Grow Stronger   One characteristic that distinguishes deep relationships from superficial ones is the amount of genuine feelings that the partners express. The benefits of sharing generally go beyond simply understanding each other better, for sharing usually leads to stronger bonds between people. To recognize the truth of this statement, think about the relationships you have that consist of basically superficial, emotion-free conversations. At best, such relationships can be exchanges of factual information—useful but impersonal. In other cases they are to communication what junk food is to nutrition—an imitation of the real thing. On the other hand, when emotions begin to be shared, a relationship begins to deepen. This is obviously true when the feelings are positive, but even negative emotions can deepen a relationship when they're shared.

This principle doesn't mean that every sentence you speak needs to be loaded with feelings, or that the feelings you do express all have to involve your partner. Even emotional expressions that involve other people or subjects can improve the depth and quality of a relationship. Whatever the subject, the important point to remember is that relationships grow stronger when nourished with feelings.

Physical Health Benefits   Sharing emotions is healthy. Or to put it differently, keeping your feelings pent up can lead to psychosomatic illness. To see how this happens, remember the bodily changes that accompany strong emotions: digestion slows, heartbeat increases, adrenaline is secreted, and respiration grows quicker. Whereas these conditions are short-lived for people who can express their feelings, the failure to act on these impulses can lead to a constant state of physiological tension that damages the digestive tract, lungs, circulatory system, muscles, joints, and the body's ability to resist infections. One example of how the stress that accompanies the poor communication of emotions can damage health involves hypertension, or high blood pressure. Over a five-year period Flanders Dunbar studied a random sample of 1,600 cardiovascular patients at Columbia Presbyterian Medical Center in New York City. She found that four out of five patients shared common emotional characteristics, many of which are representative of either nonassertive or aggressive communicators. For instance, most of her patients were argumentative, had trouble expressing their feelings, and kept people at a distance. Difficulty in expressing feelings crops up in other characteristics of cardiovascular sufferers—easily upset but unable to handle upsetting situations, anxious to please but longing to rebel, alternately passive and irritable.

Besides suffering from these conditions in disproportionate numbers, there is evidence that nonasserters sometimes face another physical problem. The immunological system, which protects the body against infection, seems to function less effectively when a person is under stress. Sometimes the body doesn't respond quickly enough to infection; at other times it responds incorrectly, as in the case of allergic reactions. Stress has even been diagnosed as one cause of the common cold. It is important to realize that stress or anxiety alone are not sufficient to cause these disorders; there must

". . . My head is stuffed with straw, you know, and that is why I am going to Oz to ask him for some brains."

"Have you any?" inquired the Scarecrow.

"No, my head is quite empty," answered the Woodman; "but once I had brains, and a heart also; so, having tried them both, I should much rather have a heart."

L. Frank Baum, *The Wizard of Oz*

I remember
when my body knew
when it was time
to cry
and it was all
right then

to explode
the world
and melt
everything
warm

and start new
washed clean

Bernard Gunther

also be a source of infection present. But as research by Swiss physiologist Hans Selye suggests, persons subjected to stress have an increased chance of contracting infectious disease. As Selye states, ''If a microbe is in or around us all the time and yet causes no disease until we are exposed to stress, what is the cause of our illness, the microbe or the stress?''

All this talk about psychosomatic illness is not to suggest that a life of nonassertion automatically leads to ulcers, heart trouble, and cancer. Obviously, many unexpressive people never suffer from such ailments, and many assertive people do. And just as clearly there are many other sources of stress in our society besides emotional unexpressiveness. Nonetheless, an increasing amount of evidence suggests that the person who is unwilling or unable to be fully expressive stands a greater risk of developing physical disabilities. Just as nonsmokers are less likely to contract lung cancer than their pack-a-day counterparts, skillful communicators would seem to have a better chance of living a healthy life.

You Feel Relieved and More Authentic   There are many times when unexpressed feelings become a heavy load to carry around. Whether the emotions are loving, fearful, or angry, there's a great feeling of relief when you finally deliver your message. Of course, there are cases where the relief doesn't justify speaking out, but most of the time sharing emotions can do no harm to others and much good for you.

In addition to relieving some emotional pressure, sharing your feelings also often gives a boost to your self-esteem. There are many times when it's easy to feel critical of yourself for not speaking out—to a boss, instructor, friend, or stranger—and when you do finally express yourself, you experience a rush of self-pride. It's a good feeling to face another person and know that you've represented yourself completely and honestly.

Reasons for Emotional Sterility

In spite of all these advantages, most people do very little sharing of their feelings. You can verify this by counting the number of genuine emotional expressions you hear over a two- or three-day period. You'll probably discover that these sorts of expressions are extremely rare. People are generally comfortable making statements of fact and often delight in expressing their opinion, but they rarely disclose how they feel.

Why is it that people fail to express their feelings? Let's take a look at several reasons.

Modeling and Instructions   Our society discourages the expression of most feelings. From the time children are old enough to understand language, they learn that the range of acceptable emotions is limited. Do these sound familiar to you?

''Don't get angry.''

''There's nothing to worry about.''

"That isn't funny."

"There's no reason to feel bad."

"Control yourself—don't get excited."

"For God's sake, don't cry!"

Notice how each of these messages denies the right to experience a certain feeling. Anger isn't legitimate, and neither is fear. There's something wrong with finding certain situations humorous. Feeling bad is silly. Excitement isn't desirable, so keep your emotions under control. And finally, don't make a scene by crying.

Often such parental admonitions are nothing more than a coded request for some peace and quiet. But when repeated often enough, the underlying instruction comes through loud and clear—only a narrow range of emotions is acceptable to share or experience.

In addition, the actions of most adults create a model suggesting that grownups shouldn't express too many feelings. Expressions of affection are fine within limits: A hug and kiss for mother is all right, though a young man should instead shake hands with Dad. Affection toward friends becomes less and less frequent as we grow older, so that even a simple statement such as "I like you" is seldom heard between adults.

Social Roles   Expressing of emotions is also limited by the requirements of many social roles. Salespeople are taught to always smile at customers, no matter how obnoxious. Teachers are portrayed as paragons of rationality, supposedly representing their field of expertise and instructing their students with total impartiality. Students are rewarded for asking "acceptable" questions and otherwise being submissive creatures.

Furthermore, stereotyped sexual roles discourage people from freely expressing certain emotions. Men don't cry and are rational creatures. They must be strong, emotionally and physically. Aggressiveness is a virtue ("the Marine Corps builds men"). Women, on the other hand, are supposedly flighty, prone to tears and other emotional outbursts. They are often irrational and intuitive. A certain amount of female determination and assertiveness is appealing, but when faced with a man's resistance they ought to defer, lest they be accused of being a "bitch," or worse.

Inability to Recognize Emotions   The result of all these restrictions is that many of us lose the ability to feel deeply. Just as a muscle withers way when it is unused, our capacity to recognize and act on certain emotions decreases without practice. It's hard to cry after spending most of one's life fulfilling the role society expects of a man, even when the tears are inside. After years of denying your anger, the ability to recognize that feeling takes real effort. For someone who has never acknowledged love for one's friends, accepting that emotion can be difficult indeed.

Fear of Self-Disclosure   In a society that discourages the expressions of feelings, emotional self-disclosure can be risky. For a parent, boss, or teacher whose life has been built on the image of confidence and certainty, it may be frightening to say, "I'm sorry, I was wrong." A person who has made a life's work out of not relying on others has a hard time saying, "I'm lonesome. I want your friendship."

Moreover, someone who musters up the courage to share feelings such as these still risks suffering unpleasant consequences. Others might misunderstand: An expression of affection might be construed as a romantic come-on, and a confession of uncertainty might appear to be a sign of weakness. Another risk is that emotional honesty might make others feel uncomfortable. Finally, there's always a chance that emotional honesty could be used against you, either out of cruelty or thoughtlessness.

Thinking and Feeling

By now you might think that it's always beneficial to experience and express emotions. Actually this position is too extreme: There are some feelings that do little good for anyone. For instance, depression, rage, terror, and jealousy do little to help you feel better or to improve your relationships. We need to make a distinction, then, between *facilitative* emotions, which contribute to effective functioning, and *debilitative* ones, which keep us from feeling and relating effectively.

One big difference between facilitative and debilitative emotions is their *intensity.* For instance, a certain amount of anger or irritation can be constructive, since it often provides the stimulus that leads you to improve the unsatisfying conditions. Rage, on the other hand, will usually make matters worse. The same holds true for fear. A little bit of nervousness before an important athletic contest or job interview might give you the boost that will improve your performance. (After all, mellow athletes or employees usually don't do well.) But total terror is something else.

A second characteristic that distinguishes debilitative feelings from facilitative ones is their extended *duration.* Feeling depressed for a while after the breakup of a relationship or the loss of a job is natural. But spending the rest of your life grieving over your loss would accomplish nothing. In the same way, staying angry at someone for a wrong inflicted long ago can be just as

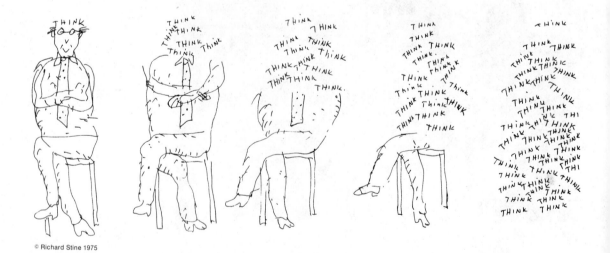

© Richard Stine 1975

punishing to you as to the wrongdoer. Our goal, then, is to find a method for getting rid of debilitative feelings while remaining sensitive to your more facilitative emotions, which can improve your relationships. Fortunately, there is such a method. Developed by cognitive psychologists such as Aaron Beck and Albert Ellis, it is based on the idea that the key to changing feelings is to change unproductive thinking. Let's see how it works.

For most people, emotions seem to have a life of their own. You wish you could feel calm when approaching strangers, yet your voice quivers. You try to appear confident when asking for a raise, yet your eye twitches nervously.

At times like these it's common to say that strangers or your boss *make* you feel nervous, just as you would say that a bee sting causes you to feel pain. The apparent similarities between physical and emotional discomfort become clear if you look at them in the following way:

Activating event	Causes	Consequences
bee sting	causes	physical pain
meeting strangers	causes	nervous feelings

When looking at your emotions in this way, it seems as if you have little control over how you feel. However, this apparent similarity between physical pain and emotional discomfort (or pleasure) isn't as great as it seems to be. Cognitive psychologists and therapists argue that it is not *events* such as meeting strangers or being jilted by a lover that cause people to feel bad, but rather the *beliefs they hold* about these events.

Albert Ellis, who developed the cognitive approach called Rational-Emotive Therapy, tells a story that makes this point clear. Imagine yourself walking by a friend's house and seeing your friend stick his head out of a window and call you a string of vile names. (You supply the friend and the names.) Under these circumstances it's likely that you would feel hurt and upset. Now imagine that instead of walking by the house you were passing a mental institution when the same friend, who was obviously a patient there, shouted the same offensive names at you. In this case, your feelings would probably be quite different; most likely, sadness and pity. You can see that in this story the activating event of being called names was the same in both cases, yet the emotional consequences were very different. The reason for the different feelings you experience has to do with your thinking in each case. In the first instance you would most likely think that your friend was very angry with you; further, you might imagine that you must have done something terrible to deserve such a response. In the second case you would probably assume that your friend had experienced some psychological difficulty, and most likely you would feel sympathetic.

From this example you can start to see that it's the *interpretations* people make of an event that determine their feelings. Thus, the model for emotions looks like this:

Activating event	Interpretation, thought or belief	Consequences
being called names	"I've done something wrong"	hurt, upset
being called names	"My friend must be sick"	concern, sympathy

Talking to Yourself

You can become better at understanding how your thoughts shape your feelings by completing the following steps.

1. Take a few minutes to listen to the silent voice you use when thinking. Close your eyes now and listen to it. . . . Did you hear the voice? Perhaps it was saying, "What voice? I don't have any voice . . ." Try again, and pay attention to what the voice is saying.

2. Now think about the following situations and imagine how you would react in each. How would you interpret them with your little voice? What feelings would follow from each interpretation?
   a. While sitting on a bus, in class, or on the street, you notice an attractive person sneaking glances at you.
   b. During a lecture your professor asks the class, "What do you think about this?" and looks toward you.
   c. You are telling friends about your vacation and one yawns.
   d. You run into a friend on the street and ask how things are going. Fine," he replies and rushes off.

3. Now recall three recent times when you experienced a strong emotion. For each one, recall the activating event and then the interpretation that led to your emotional reaction.

This process of self-talk is the key to understanding debilitative feelings. Albert Ellis suggests that many debilitative feelings come from accepting a number of irrational beliefs—we'll call them fallacies here—which lead to illogical conclusions and in turn to debilitating feelings.

The fallacy of perfection   People who accept this myth believe that a worthwile communicator should be able to handle any situation with complete confidence and skill.

Once you accept the belief that it's desirable and possible to be a perfect communicator, the next step is to assume that people won't appreciate you if you are imperfect. Admitting your mistakes, saying "I don't know" or sharing feelings of uncertainty, seem like social defects when viewed in this manner.

> *I never was what you would call a fancy skater—and while I seldom actually fell, it might have been more impressive if I had. A good resounding fall is no disgrace. It is the fantastic writhing to avoid a fall which destroys any illusion of being a gentleman. How like life that is, after all!*
>
> Robert Benchley from *Benchley Beside Himself*, Harper & Row

Given the desire to be valued and appreciated, it's tempting to try to *appear* perfect, but the costs of such deception are high. If others ever find you out, they'll see you as a phony. Even when your act isn't uncovered, such a performance uses up a great deal of psychological energy and thus makes the rewards of approval less enjoyable.

Subscribing to the myth of perfection not only can keep others from liking you, it can also act as a force to diminish your own self-esteem. How can you like yourself when you don't measure up to the way you ought to be? How liberated you become when you can comfortably accept the idea that you are not perfect, that:

like everyone else, you sometimes have a hard time expressing yourself;

like everyone else, you make mistakes from time to time, and there is no reason to hide this;

you are honestly doing the best you can to realize your potential, to become the best person you can be.

The fallacy of approval　This mistaken belief is based on the idea that it is not just desirable, but *vital* to get the approval of virtually every person. People who accept this belief go to incredible lengths to seek acceptance from others, even when they have to sacrifice their own principles and happiness to do so. Accepting this irrational myth can lead to some ludicrous situations:

feeling nervous because people you really don't like seem to disapprove of you;

feeling apologetic when others are at fault;

feeling embarrassed after behaving unnaturally to gain another's approval.

In addition to the obvious discomfort that comes from denying your own principles and needs, the myth of acceptance is irrational because it implies that others will respect and like you more if you go out of your way to please them. Often this simply isn't true. How is it possible to respect people who have compromised important values just to gain acceptance? How is it possible to think highly of people who repeatedly deny their own needs as a means of buying approval? While others may find it tempting to use these individuals to suit their ends or amusing to be around them, genuine affection and respect are hardly due such characters.

In addition, striving for universal acceptance is irrational because it's simply not possible. Sooner or later a conflict of expectations is bound to occur; one person will approve if you behave only in a certain way, while another will only accept the opposite course of action. What are you to do then?

Don't misunderstand: abandoning the fallacy of approval doesn't mean living a life of selfishness. It's still important to consider the needs of others and to meet them whenever possible. It's also pleasant—we might even say necessary—to strive for the respect of those people you value. The point here is that when you must abandon your own needs and principles in order to seek these goals, the price is too high.

I believe that courage is all too often mistakenly seen as the absence of fear. If you descend by rope from a cliff and are not fearful to some degree, you are either crazy or unaware. Courage is seeing your fear in a realistic perspective, defining it, considering the alternatives and choosing to function in spite of risk.

Leonard Zunin, *Contact: The First Four Minutes*

The fallacy of shoulds   One huge source of unhappiness is an inability to distinguish between what *is* and what *should be*. You can see the difference by imagining a person who is full of complaints about the world:

> there should be no rain on weekends
>
> people ought to live forever
>
> money should grow on trees
>
> we should all be able to fly

Beliefs like these are obviously foolish. However pleasant wishing may be, insisting that the unchangeable should be changed won't affect reality one bit. And yet many people torture themselves by engaging in this sort of irrational thinking when they confuse ''is'' with ''ought.'' They say and think things like

> that guy should drive better
>
> she shouldn't be so inconsiderate
>
> they ought to be more friendly
>
> you should work harder

The message in each of these cases is that you would *prefer* people to behave differently. Wishing that things were better is perfectly legitimate, and trying to change them is, of course, a good idea; but it's unreasonable to *insist* that the world operate just as you want it to or to feel cheated when things aren't ideal.

Becoming obsessed with shoulds has three bad consequences. First, it leads to unnecessary unhappiness, for people who are constantly dreaming about the ideal are seldom satisfied with what they have. A second drawback is that merely complaining without acting can keep you from doing anything to change unsatisfying conditions. A third problem with shoulds is that this sort of complaining can build a defensive climate in others, who will resent being carped at. It's much more effective to tell people about what you'd like than to preach: say "I wish you'd be more punctual" instead of "You should be on time." We'll discuss ways of avoiding defensive climates in Chapter 4.

The fallacy of overgeneralization   There are two types of overgeneralization. The first occurs when we base a belief on a *limited amount of evidence.* For instance, how many times have you found yourself saying something like

"I'm so stupid! I can't even understand how to do my income tax."

"Some friend I am! I forgot my best friend's birthday."

In cases like these we focus on a limited type of shortcoming as if it represented everything about us. We forget that along with our difficulties we also have solved tough problems, and that while we're sometimes forgetful, at other times we're caring and thoughtful.

A second related category of overgeneralization occurs when we *exaggerate shortcomings:*

"You *never* listen to me."

"You're *always* late."

"I can't think of *anything.*"

Upon closer examination, absolute statements like these are almost always false and usually lead to discouragement or anger. You'll feel far better when you replace overgeneralizations with more accurate messages to yourself and others:

"You often don't listen to me."

"You've been late three times this week."

"I haven't had any ideas I like today."

As you'll read in Chapter 8, many overgeneralizations are based on abuse of the verb "to be." For example, unqualified thoughts such as "He *is* an idiot [all the time?]" and "I *am* a failure [in everything?]" will lead you to see yourself and others in an unrealistically negative way, thus contributing to debilitative feelings.

The fallacy of causation   People who live their lives in accordance with this myth believe that it is their duty to do nothing that might possibly hurt or in

A man said to the universe:
"Sir, I exist!"
"However," replied the universe,
"The fact has not created in me
A sense of obligation."

Stephen Crane

any way inconvenience others. This attitude leads to guilty and resentful feelings in cases such as:

visiting friends or family out of a sense of obligation rather than a genuine desire to see them

keeping quiet when another person's behavior is bothering you

pretending to be attentive to a speaker when you are already late for another engagement or are feeling ill

praising and reassuring others who ask for your opinion, even when your honest response is a negative one.

A reluctance to speak out in situations like these is often based on the assumption that you are the cause of others' feelings: that you hurt, confuse, or anger them. Actually, such a position isn't correct. You don't *cause* feelings in others; rather, they *respond* to your behavior with feelings of their own. For example, consider how strange it sounds to suggest that you make others fall in love with you. Such a statement simply doesn't make sense. It would be closer to the truth to say that you act in one way or another, and some people might fall in love with you as a result of these actions, while others wouldn't. In the same way it's incorrect to say that you *make* others angry, upset—or happy, for that matter. It's better to say that others' responses are as much or more a function of their own psychological makeup as they are determined by our own behavior.

Restricting your communication because of the fallacy of causation can result in three types of damaging consequences. First, as a result of your caution you often will fail to have your own needs met. After all, there's little likelihood that others will change their behavior unless they know that it's affecting you in a negative way.

A second consequence is that you're likely to begin resenting the person whose behavior you find bothersome. Obviously this reaction is illogical, since you never have made your feelings known, but logic doesn't change the fact that keeping your problem buried usually leads to a buildup of hostility.

Even when your withholding of feelings is based on the best of intentions, it often damages relationships in a third way; for once others find out about your deceptive nature, they will find it difficult ever to know when you really are upset with them. Even your most fervent assurances that everything is fine sound suspicious, since there's always the chance that you may be covering up for resentments you're unwilling to express. Thus, in many respects taking responsibility for others' feelings is not only irrational, it's also counterproductive.

The fallacy of helplessness   This irrational idea suggests that satisfaction in life is determined by forces beyond your control. People who continuously see themselves as victims make unhappiness-producing statements such as:

''There's no way a woman can get ahead in this society. It's a man's world, and the best thing I can do is to accept it.''

''I was born with a shy personality. I'd like to be more outgoing, but there's nothing I can do about that.''

"I can't tell my boss that she is putting too many demands on me. If I did, I might lose my job."

The mistake in statements like these becomes apparent once you realize that there are many things you can do if you really want to. As you read in Chapter 2, most "can't" statements can be more correctly rephrased either as *"won't"* ("I can't tell him what I think" becomes "I won't be honest with him.") or as *"don't know how"* ("I can't carry on an interesting conversation" becomes "I don't know what to say") Once you've rephrased these inaccurate "can'ts," it becomes clear that they're either a matter of choice or an area that calls for your action—both quite different from saying that you're helpless.

When viewed in this light, it's apparent that many "can'ts" are really rationalizations to justify not wanting to change. Once you've persuaded yourself that there's no hope for you, it's easy to give up trying. On the other hand, acknowledging that there is a way to change—even though it may be difficult—puts the responsibility for your predicament on your shoulders. You *can* become a better communicator—this book is one step in your movement toward that goal. Don't give up or sell yourself short!

The fallacy of catastrophic failure   Fearful communicators who subscribe to this irrational belief operate on the assumption that if something bad can possibly happen, it will. Typical catastrophic fantasies include:

"If I invite them to the party, they probably won't want to come."

"If I speak up in order to try and resolve a conflict, things will probably get worse."

"If I apply for the job I want, I probably won't be hired."

"If I tell them how I really feel, they'll probably laugh at me."

While it's naive to think that all of your interactions with others will meet with success, it's just as damaging to assume that you'll fail. One way to

CATHY   **by Cathy Guisewite**

escape from the fallacy of catastrophic failure is to think about the consequences that would follow even if you don't communicate successfully. Keeping in mind the folly of trying to be perfect and of living only for the approval of others, realize that failing in a given instance usually isn't as bad as it might seem. What if people do laugh at you? Suppose you don't get the job? What if others do get angry at your remarks? Are these matters really *that* serious?

How Irrational Are You?

1. Return to the situations described in the exercise *Talking to Yourself* on page 106. Examine each one to see whether your self-talk contains any irrational thoughts.

2. Keep a two- or three-day record of the debilitative feelings you experience. Are any of them based on irrational thinking? Examine your conclusions and see if you repeatedly use any of the fallacies described in the preceding section.

3. Take a class poll to see which irrational fallacies are most "popular." Also, discuss what subjects seem to stimulate most of this irrational thinking (e.g., schoolwork, dating, jobs, family, etc.).

Feeling Better

How can you overcome such irrational thinking? Albert Ellis and his associates have developed a simple yet effective approach. When practiced conscientiously, it can help you cut down on the self-defeating thinking that leads to many debilitative emotions.

Monitor Your Emotional Reactions   The first step is to recognize when you're experiencing debilitative emotions. (Of course it's also nice to be aware of pleasant feelings when they occur!) As we suggested earlier, one way to notice feelings is through proprioceptive stimuli: butterflies in the stomach, racing heart, hot flashes, and so on. While such reactions might be symptoms of food poisoning, more often they reflect a strong emotion. You can also recognize certain ways of behaving that suggest your feelings: stomping instead of walking normally, being unusually quiet, or speaking in a sarcastic tone of voice are some examples.

It may seem strange to suggest that it's necessary to look for emotions—they ought to be immediately apparent. The fact is however, that we often suffer from debilitating feelings for some time without noticing them. For example, at the end of a trying day you've probably caught yourself frowning and realized that you've been wearing that mask for some time without realizing it.

Note the Activating Event Once you're aware of how you're feeling, the next step is to figure out what activating event triggered your response. Sometimes this activating event is obvious. For instance, a common source of anger is being accused unfairly (or fairly) of foolish behavior; being rejected by somebody important to you is clearly a source of hurt, too. In other cases, however, the activating event isn't so apparent. A friend of ours recently reported feeling much more irritable than usual, though he couldn't figure out what led to these emotions. After some analysis he realized that his grumpiness increased shortly after his roommate began carrying on with a new woman. Their infatuation left him feeling like an intruder in his own apartment when he walked in to find the two lovers expressing their feelings in various ways.

Sometimes there isn't a single activating event, but rather a series of small incidents that finally build toward a critical mass and trigger a debilitative feeling. This sort of thing happens when you're trying to work or sleep and are continually interrupted by a string of interruptions, or when you suffer a string of small disappointments.

The best way to begin tracking down activating events is to notice the circumstances in which you experience debilitative feelings. Perhaps they occur when you're around *specific people.* In other cases you might be bothered by certain *types of individuals* due to their age, role, background, or some other factor. Or perhaps certain *settings* stimulate unpleasant emotions: parties, work, school. Sometimes the *topic* of conversation is the factor that sets you off, whether it be politics, religion, sex, or some other subject.

"There is nothing good or bad but thinking makes it so."

Shakespeare, *Hamlet*

Record Your Self-Talk This is the point at which you analyze the thoughts that are the link between the activating event and your feeling. If you're serious about getting rid of debilitative emotions, it's important actually to write down your self-talk when first learning to use this method. Putting your thoughts on paper will help you see whether or not they actually make any sense.

Monitoring your self-talk might be difficult at first. This is a new skill, and any new activity seems awkward. If you persevere, however, you'll find you will be able to identify the thoughts that lead to your debilitative feelings. Once you get in the habit of recognizing this internal monolog, you'll be able to identify your thoughts quickly and easily.

Dispute Your Irrational Beliefs This step is the key to success in the rational-emotive approach. Use the list of irrational fallacies on pages 106–111 to discover which of your internal statements are based on mistaken thinking.

You can do this most effectively by following three steps. First, decide whether each belief you've recorded is rational or irrational. Next, explain why the belief does or doesn't make sense. Finally, if the belief is irrational, you should write down an alternative way of thinking that is more sensible and that can leave you feeling better when faced with the same activating event in the future.

Activating Event

I was at my boyfriend Mike's house the other night when he received a phone call from his ex-wife (they've been separated about a year). After some superficial conversation she asked him if he was happy. His response was, "Yes, I'm happy for now". (emphasis mine). Toward the end of the conversation she asked him to tell her that he loved her. His response was, "I'd rather not. I don't want to talk now. I'll talk to you tomorrow when you call about shipping the furniture."

Beliefs and Self-Talk

1. *I wish she wouldn't call him! Why can't she leave him alone?*
2. *I wish she didn't exist!*
3. *What does he mean, "I'm happy for now?" Does he have doubts about us?*
4. *Why can't he tell her firmly that it's over between them? And why does he want to talk to her tomorrow about it? Maybe he has something to say that he wants to keep from me.*
5. *If he went back to her I would die.*

Consequences

I felt angry toward Mike's wife and toward Mike. I felt hurt and jealous. I was also very fearful about losing Mike.

Disputing Irrational Beliefs

1. *My question, "Why can't she leave him alone?" is really another way of saying I wish she would quit phoning. This is a rational thing for me to want.*
2. *It's irrational to wish that she didn't exist. She does exist, and I can't change that. I have to learn to deal with it and quit trying to wish her away.*
3. *I'm not sure whether this is rational or not. Maybe Mike's "for now" meant nothing. On the other hand, that did seem like an odd thing to say. The only way I can find out whether he has doubts about our future is to ask him. It's stupid for me to worry before I see whether there's any reason for doing it.*
4. *What I'm really saying here is that he should tell her that it's over. While I wish he'd do that, there's no reason why he should. He'll handle this the way he thinks is best. He doesn't want to hurt her, and he's trying to let her off lightly. He sees her in a different light than I do, of course, and so he'll speak to her in a different way. My fear that Mike is keeping things from me is irrational catastrophizing. Why do I always—oops! often—assume the worst?*
5. *I would definitely be hurt and sad if he went back to her, but I wouldn't die. I sure do get dramatic at times!*

Activating Event

My friend Betsy dropped by last night when I was studying for an important exam. This is typical of her: she seems to be phoning or coming over to my place constantly, and usually at times when I'm busy or have other guests.

Beliefs and Self-Talk

1. After all the hints I've dropped she should get the idea and leave me alone.
2. She's driving me crazy.
3. I'm a coward for not speaking up and telling her to quit bothering me.
4. If I do tell her, she'll be crushed.
5. There's no solution to this mess. I'm damned if I tell her to leave me alone and damned if I don't.

Feelings

I felt mad at Betsy and myself. I also felt cruel and heartless for wanting to turn away such a lonely person. I was frustrated at not being able to study.

Disputing Irrational Beliefs

1. This is irrational. If Betsy was perfect she would be more sensitive and get my hints. But she's an insensitive person, and she's behaving just like I'd expect her to do. I'd like her to be more considerate, though. That's rational!
2. This is a bit melodramatic. I definitely don't like her interruptions, but there's a big difference between being irritated and going crazy. Besides, even if I was losing my mind, it wouldn't be accurate to say that she was driving me crazy, but rather that I'm letting her get to me. (It's fun to feel sorry for myself sometimes, though.)
3. This is an exaggeration. I am afraid to tell her, but that doesn't make me a coward. It makes me a less than totally self-assured person. This confirms my suspicion that I'm not perfect.
4. There's a chance that she'll be disappointed if she knows that I've found her irritating. But I have to be careful not to catastrophize here. She would probably survive my comments and even appreciate my honesty, once she gets over the shock. Besides, I'm not sure that I want to take the responsibility of keeping her happy if it leaves me feeling irritated. She's a big girl, and if she has a problem, she can learn to deal with it.
5. I'm playing helpless here. There must be a way I can tell her honestly while still being supportive.

After reading about this method for dealing with unpleasant emotions, some readers have objections.

"This rational-emotive approach sounds like nothing more than trying to talk yourself out of feeling bad." This accusation is totally correct. After all, since we talk ourselves *into* feeling bad, what's wrong with talking ourselves *out* of them, especially when the bad feelings are based on irrational thoughts? Rationalizing may be a cop-out and a self-deception, but there's nothing wrong with being rational.

"The kind of disputing we just read sounds phony and unnatural. I don't talk to myself in sentences and paragraphs." There's no need to dispute your irrational beliefs in any special literary style. You can be just as colloquial as you want. The important thing is to get a clear understanding of what thoughts led you into your debilitative feeling so you can clearly dispute them. When the technique is new for you, it's a good idea to write or talk out your thoughts in order to make them clear. After you've had some practice, you'll be able to do these steps in a quicker, less formal way.

"This approach is too cold and impersonal. It seems to aim at turning people into cold-blooded, calculating, emotionless machines." This is simply not true. There's nothing wrong with having facilitative emotions: they're the stuff that makes life worth living. The goal of the rational-emotive approach is to get rid of the debilitative, harmful emotions that keep us from functioning well. Just as you remove the weeds in your garden in order to let your vegetables and flowers reach their maximum potential, you can use rational thinking to get rid of your unproductive, harmful feelings and leave room for the productive, positive ones that help you grow and enjoy life.

"This technique promises too much. There's no chance I could rid myself of all unpleasant feelings, however nice that might be." We can answer this by assuring you that rational-emotive thinking probably won't totally solve emotional problems. What it can do is to reduce the amount, intensity, and duration of your debilitative feelings. This method is not the answer to all your problems, but it can make a significant difference—not a bad accomplishment.

Rational Thinking

1. Return to the diary of irrational thoughts you recorded on page 112. Dispute the self-talk in each case, and write a more rational, accurate interpretation of the event.

2. Now try out your ability to think rationally on the spot. You can do this by acting out the scenes listed below. You'll need three players for each one: a subject, the subject's "little voice"—his or her thoughts—and a second party.

3. Play out each scene by having the subject and second party interact, while the "little voice" stands just behind the subject and speaks the thoughts that the subject is probably having. For example, in a scene where the subject is asking an instructor to reconsider a low grade, the voice might say, "I hope I haven't made things worse by bringing this up.

Maybe he'll lower the grade after rereading the test. I'm such an idiot! Why didn't I keep quiet?"

4. Whenever the voice expresses an irrational thought, the observers who are watching the skit should call out "foul." At this point the action should stop while the group discusses the irrational thought and suggests a more rational line of self-talk. The players should then replay the scene with the voice speaking in a more rational way.

Here are some scenes. Of course, you can invent others as well.
a. A couple is just beginning their first date.
b. A potential employee has just begun a job interview.
c. A teacher or boss is criticizing the subject for showing up late.
d. A student and instructor run across each other in the market.

Sharing Feelings: When and How?

So far we've talked about how to deal with debilitative feelings. But what about facilitative ones: how do you go about sharing them in the best way? It's obvious that sharing every feeling of boredom, fear, affection, and so on could often get you into trouble. On the other hand, you can almost certainly do a better job of sharing how you feel. Here are some guidelines you can use to decide when and how to express your emotions in ways that will give you the best chances for improving your relationships.

Recognize Your Feelings   You can best share your feelings when you're aware of what they are. As we've already said, there are a number of ways in which feelings become recognizable. Physiological changes can be a clear sign of your emotional state. Monitoring nonverbal behaviors is another excellent way to keep in touch with your feelings. We'll have a great deal to say about this in Chapter 7. You can also recognize your feelings by monitoring your self-talk as well as the verbal messages you send to others. It's not far from the verbal statement "I hate this!" to the realization that you're angry (or bored, nervous, or embarrassed).

Distinguish Between Primary and Secondary Feelings   Many times the feeling you express isn't the only one you're experiencing. For example, you might often express your anger but overlook the confusion, disappointment, frustration, sadness, or embarrassment that preceded it.

Recognize the Difference Between Feeling and Acting   Just because you feel a certain way doesn't mean you must always act it out. This distinction is important, for it can liberate you from the fear that acknowledging and sharing a feeling will commit you to some disastrous course of action. If, for instance, you say to a friend, "I feel so angry that I could punch you in the nose," it becomes possible to explore exactly why you feel so furious and then to resolve the problem that led to your anger. Pretending that nothing is the matter, on the other hand, will do nothing to diminish your resentful feelings, which can then go on to contaminate the relationship.

There are, I know, cats that purr loudly.
    Mine can be heard only when your cheek
    rests against the soft fur on her back
    —so afraid is she to share her pleasure
    with you.

The tree I fed, nurtured, watered so faithfully
    that it grew taller than the house, never
    bowed in the breeze to me as I passed under
    it—only sprinkled pale yellow flowers in
    my hair that later greeted me when I glanced
    in a mirror.

People, too, keep within them their purrs, their
    faintly scented flowers, not returning a
    sign that your stroking of their egos has
    been noted and appreciated—and a little
    bit more to the left, please.

Lenni Shender Goldstein

Accept Responsibility for Your Feelings   It's important to make sure that your language reflects the fact that you're responsible for your feelings. Instead of "You're making me angry," say "I'm getting angry." Instead of "You hurt my feelings," say "I feel hurt when you do that." People don't make us like or dislike them, and pretending that they do denies the responsibility each of us has for our own emotions.

Choose the Best Time and Place to Express Your Feelings   Often the first flush of a strong feeling is not the best time to speak out. If you're awakened by the racket caused by a noisy neighbor, storming over to complain might result in your saying things you'll regret later. In such a case it's probably wiser to wait until you have thought out carefully how you might express your feelings in a way that would be most likely to be heard.

Even after you've waited for the first flush of feeling to subside, it's still important to choose the time that's best suited to the message. Being rushed, or tired, or disturbed by some other matter are probably all good reasons for postponing the sharing of your feeling. Often dealing with your emotions can take a great amount of time and effort, and fatigue or distraction will make it difficult to devote your energy to follow through on the matter you've started. In the same manner you ought to be sure that the recipient of your message is ready to hear you out before you begin your sharing.

Share Your Feelings Clearly and Unambiguously   Either out of confusion or discomfort we sometimes express our emotions in an unclear way. One key to making your emotions clear is to realize that you most often can summarize a feeling in a single word—hurt, glad, confused, excited, resentful, and so on. In the same way, with a little thought you can probably describe any reasons you have for feeling a certain way very briefly.

In addition to excessive length, a second way in which you can confuse the expression of a feeling is to discount or qualify it—"I'm a *little* unhappy," or "I'm *pretty* excited," or "I'm *sort* of confused." Of course, not all emotions are strong ones. We do experience degrees of sadness and joy, for example, but some communicators have a tendency to discount almost every feeling. Do you?

A third way to confuse the expression of an emotion is to send it in a coded manner. This most often happens when the sender is uncomfortable about sharing the feeling in question. Some codes are verbal ones, as when the sender hints more or less subtly at the message. For example, an indirect way to say "I'm lonesome" might be "I guess there isn't much happening this weekend, so if you're not busy, why don't you drop by?" Such a message is so indirect that the chances of your real feeling being recognized are slim. For this reason people who send coded messages stand less of a chance of having their emotions understood and their needs met.

Finally, you can express yourself clearly by making sure that both you and your partner understand that your feeling is centered on a specific set of circumstances, rather than being indicative of the whole relationship. Instead of saying, "I resent you," say, "I resent you when you don't keep your promises.'' Rather than, "I'm bored with you," say, "I'm bored when you talk about your money.''

After thinking about these guidelines, you can probably agree that expressing feelings isn't as natural or as simple as most people think—that communicating emotions effectively is a skill. We hope you recognize the importance of expressing feelings clearly, both because of the benefits that can come from doing so and the dangers that come from failing to do so. With some practice the information in this chapter should both help you to experience more facilitative feelings and fewer debilitating ones to share your important feelings when the time is right. Is this material useful? Yes. Will you use it? It's up to you.

Roads Not Taken

1. Explore the degree to which emotions are expressed in this society by observing the number of genuine feeling statements made in the following situations:
   a. Social interaction between strangers or acquaintances during conversations (e.g., at parties, on dates)
   b. job-related communication (boss-subordinate, among coworkers, and worker to public)
   c. between parents and children (of various ages)
   d. between partners of a couple (when enjoying each other's company, during conflicts, and while carrying on ordinary business)
   e. among children at play

2. Increase the number of feeling statements you express, either to a specific person or in a certain type of situation. What effect does this change have on your relationships? Do you feel any differently after the change?

3. Interview several people to determine which irrational fallacies seem to be most commonly used. Develop a theory about the ways in which these fallacies are learned.

More Readings on Emotions

Beck, Aaron T. *Cognitive Therapy and the Emotional Disorders.* New York: International Universities Press, 1976.
Beck is one of the leading figures in the exploration of how thinking shapes emotions. While this book is written for professionals, it gives a clear picture of one way to handle debilitative feelings.

Ellis, Albert. *A New Guide to Rational Living.* North Hollywood, CA: Wilshire Books, 1977.
Ellis is probably the best known advocate of changing feelings by thinking rationally, and this is his most widely read book.

Harris, Lance, and Chris Meriam. *Feeling Good About Feelings.* Palo Alto, CA: Bull Publishing Co., 1979.

This readable, useful workbook is divided into three parts. The first explains the nature and sources of feelings as well as arguing that it is acceptable to feel. The second part describes methods of expressing and responding to feelings. The third section provides a step-by-step method for dealing with personal emotions in a constructive way.

Izard, Carroll E. *Human Emotions.* New York: Plenum Press, 1977.

While Izard spends a major part of the book defending his own theories about emotions, there is also a good explanation of the subject for interested readers.

Kranzler, Gerald. *You Can Change How You Feel.* Eugene, OR: RETC Press, 1974.

Many readers find the tone of this book somewhat irritating, but it does provide a brief and clear summary of the information in this chapter.

Jakubowski, Patricia, and Arthur Lange. *The Assertive Option.* Champaign, IL: Research Press, 1978.

Jakubowski and Lange offer both a good review of the principles in this chapter and some specific suggestions on how to express feelings assertively.

Plutchik, Robert. ''A Language for the Emotions.'' *Psychology Today,* 13 (February, 1980), 68–78.

Plutchik offers a series of classifications for describing and understanding human emotions. Based on his research, he identifies eight primary emotions, which he suggests occur in varying combinations and intensities.

Chapter Four

W e all know what it's like to be defensive.

After teaching courses in interpersonal communication to thousands of students, we've yet to find a single person who hasn't experienced this feeling. When asked to report the sensations and actions that come with such an attitude, practically everyone describes similar experiences—tense muscles, upset stomach, high-pitched and argumentative tone of voice, a rush of adrenaline, and a temptation either to rush away from the situation at hand or to stay and fight. And just as most people report the same symptoms for defensiveness, they also describe similar consequences—hurt feelings, damaged relationships, personal frustration, and lack of satisfying resolution to the conflicts that brought on the defensiveness in the first place. In fact, defensiveness is such a problem that our students invariably list reducing its occurrence in their lives as one of the major goals of our courses.

What exactly is defensiveness? When and why does it occur? What are you defending? How can you learn to respond less defensively? What can you do to arouse less defensiveness in others? These are the questions we'll try to answer in Chapter 4.

What Is Defensiveness?

The very word defensiveness suggests protecting one's self from attack, but what kind of attack? Surely, few of the times when you become defensive involve a threat to your physical safety; so if you're not threatened by that sort of injury, what can it be that you *are* guarding against? To answer this question we need to talk more about the notion of the self-concept, which we introduced in Chapter 2.

You'll recall that the self-concept consists of your perceptions of yourself, including physical characteristics, personality traits, strengths and weaknesses, as well as a large number of other characteristics and beliefs you see yourself as possessing.

Right now turn to the list you compiled for the exercise in Chapter 2 on page 53. Review the list of terms you used to describe your self-concept.

As you read in Chapter 2, this self-concept is nothing less than the sum of your personal identity, and as such it is extremely important. Consider, for example, the value you attach to the following parts of your self-concept:

Social roles

Intelligence

Ethical standards

Physical appearance

Job-oriented abilities

Of course, not all parts of your self-concept are equally important to you. For example, the fact that you see yourself as a resident of a particular state or having been born in a certain month is probably less important than your identity as a female or male or the kind of friend you are.

Imagine what might happen if someone attacked a part of your self-concept that was particularly important to you. Suppose, for instance, that

An instructor labeled you as an idiot when you regard yourself as reasonably bright.

A friend accused you of being snobbish when you believe you are a friendly person.

An employer called you lazy, when you see yourself as a hard worker.

What are your choices in such situations? One alternative would be to accept the new information and change your self-concept accordingly, relabeling yourself as stupid, snobbish, or lazy. On the other hand, given the human tendency to perpetuate an existing self-concept, a more likely choice is in some way to discount the critical information in order to maintain your old picture of yourself. You might do so by ignoring this dissonant information (pretending you didn't hear it, forgetting it, avoiding the critic, and so on), or by disputing it (offering evidence to the contrary or counterattacking the critic). In any case, it's important to see that we often act to protect a self-concept that has been threatened.

Public and Private Selves   So far, then, we've said that people become defensive when they perceive others attacking their self-concept. While this statement explains much defensive behavior, it doesn't account for every case. Often there are times when others offer an evaluation that coincides with your self-concept, and yet you *still* become defensive. For example, consider the many times when you have failed to meet your obligations before the last moment, so that you've had to rush in order to get the job done. Certainly if you are like most people you would probably admit to including the word *procrastinator* in your self-concept. When confronted with this failure to meet deadlines, however, you might not willingly admit your habit of stalling, instead making all sorts of excuses to justify your tardiness. In the same way there are probably other parts of your self-concept that you might not readily own up to when others point them out—perhaps the tendency to tell an occasional lie, a periodic streak of unreasonableness, or tendencies toward selfishness.

To understand what's going on here you need to recognize the existence of two selves, one public and the other private. Your public self is the face you show to the world, while your private self is the person you see in moments of self-honesty. These two selves are similar in many ways. For instance, you might see yourself as a perfectionist or a person who dislikes opera and be perfectly willing to publicly express these attitudes. On the other hand, there are some cases in which the face you show to the world is quite different from the one you see when you stare at yourself in the mirror. Perhaps you sometimes feel insecure but try to act in a confident manner. Maybe you find yourself feeling angry when you want to appear calm and happy. Or perhaps you sometimes feel stupid but try to look bright to others. Take a few minutes now to explore your public and private selves by completing the following exercise.

Please Hear What I'm Not Saying

Don't be fooled by me.
Don't be fooled by the face I wear
For I wear a mask. I wear a
    thousand masks,
    masks that I'm afraid to take off
    and none of them are me.

Pretending is an art that's second
    nature with me
But don't be fooled, for God's
    sake don't be fooled.
I give you the impression that I'm
    secure
That all is sunny and unruffled
    with me
    within as well as without,
    that confidence is my name
    and coolness my game.
    that the water's calm
    and I'm in command,
    and that I need no one.
But don't believe me. Please!

My surface may be smooth but my
    surface is my mask,
My ever-varying and ever-
    concealing mask.
Beneath lies no smugness, no
    complacence.
Beneath dwells the real me in
    confusion, in fear, in
    aloneness.
    But I hide this.
    I don't want anybody to know it.
    I panic at the thought of my
    weaknesses
    and fear exposing them.
That's why I frantically create my
    masks to hide behind.
They're nonchalant, sophisticated
    facades to help me pretend,
To shield me from the glance that
    knows.
But such a glance is precisely my
    salvation,

my only salvation,
    and I know it.
That is, if it's followed by
    acceptance, if it's followed by
    love.
It's the only thing that can liberate
    me from myself
    from my own self-built prison
    walls
    from the barriers that I so
    painstakingly erect.
That glance is the only thing that
    assures me
    of what I can't assure myself,
    that I'm really worth something.
But I don't tell you this.
    I don't dare.
    I'm afraid to.

I'm afraid you'll think less of me,
    that you'll laugh
    and your laugh would kill me.
I'm afraid that deep-down I'm
    nothing, that I'm just no good
    and you will see this
    and reject me.
So I play my game, my desperate,
    pretending game
With a facade of assurance
    without
And a trembling child within,
So begins the parade of masks
The glittering but empty parade of
    masks,

And my life becomes a front.
I idly chatter to you in suave tones
    of surface talk.
I tell you everything that's nothing
And nothing of what's everything,
    of what's crying within me.
So when I'm going through my
    routine
Do not be fooled by what I'm
    saying.
Please listen carefully and try to
    hear
    what I'm *not* saying.
Hear what I'd like to say
    but what I can not say.

I dislike hiding.
    Honestly.
I dislike the superficial game I'm
    playing
    the superficial phony game.
I'd really like to be genuine
    and spontaneous
    and me.
But I need your help, your hand to
    hold
Even though my masks would tell
    you otherwise.
It will not be easy for you.
Long felt inadequacies make my
    defenses strong.
The nearer you approach me
The blinder I may strike back.
Despite what books say of men, I
    am irrational;
I fight against the very thing that I
    cry out for.

You wonder who I am?
You shouldn't
    For I am everyman
    And everywoman
    Who wears a mask.
Don't be fooled by me.
At least not by the face I wear.

Defining My Two Selves

1. Divide a sheet of paper into two halves, top and bottom.

2. On the top half write the ten words that best describe your private self—the person you know yourself to be, although you might or might not share this self with others.

3. Now make some kind of drawing that represents the essential nature of your private self. Don't worry about being an artist: The idea is to put something on paper that captures the feeling of the private you. We've had students draw trees, automobiles, stick people, or even abstract designs. There's no "wrong" way to do this, so use your imagination.

4. Now repeat the process on the bottom half of the paper. This time select ten words and draw something to represent your public self—the person you want others to see. If you find you want to use some of the same terms you used above the line, that's fine.

5. After you have finished, take a moment to notice the relationship between the two halves of your paper. What similarities are there? What differences? In what ways do you act to reflect the public image you've drawn here? How satisfied are you with the selves you've represented? What might you do to change them?

My Two Selves in 3D

1. Another way to illustrate your two selves is by constructing a self-portrait in three dimensions. Perhaps the simplest method is to use a cardboard box, carton, or even a paper bag. The idea is that you've both an outside and an inside to represent the public and private self.

2. Decorate your container in any way you see fit to describe your selves. Clipping pictures or words from magazines and newspapers or attaching or including articles that are meaningful are two possibilities.

3. The style you choose to represent yourself will probably make a statement about you. There's no correct way—any way you choose will be acceptable. You're limited only by your imagination.

4. Before you begin work, decide with your instructor what you'll be doing with your portraits: Should they be kept private, should the owner show his to the group, or should they be collected anonymously with attempts at guessing the artist's identity?

Be sure you've completed one of these exercises before reading on. What did you discover about your two selves? Were they mostly similar? In what ways did they differ? Most people find that the face they present to the public is more favorable than their private one. Was this true for you? If so, the reason is probably a social one. From the time most of us are quite young we're taught that certain kinds of behavior are the only way to gain acceptance. In such environments perfection is the model: One should

always act in a pleasant manner, be reasonable, selfless, and kind. This stress on perfection is carried on in most forms of entertainment, where the models are characters who are always self-assured, knowledgeable, and socially talented. The message here is that the kind of person who gains the approval of others is *perfect.* Of course, privately each of us knows that we're not perfect, so we are faced with the choices of sharing our private self and risking rejection or putting on a public mask and gaining what we think will be social rewards.

John Powell speaks to the problem of fear and defensiveness with a question that also serves as the title to his book *Why Am I Afraid to Tell You Who I Am?* One of the answers he recorded from an actual conversation says ". . . if I tell you who I am, you may not like who I am, and it is all that I have." So one reason we wear masks is to show the world an acceptable public or "ideal" self, trying to be the kind of person others think we should be instead of the person we truly are.

With this explanation it becomes easy to see why we get defensive at times when a critic makes an evaluation that does match our private image: for the concept that we most strongly defend is our public one. Thus, we can finally say that *defensiveness is the attempt to protect a public image that we perceive is being attacked.*

The extremes we'll go to for the sake of making a "good" appearance are illustrated well in the following account by George Orwell.

They defend their errors as if they were defending their inheritance.

Edmund Burke

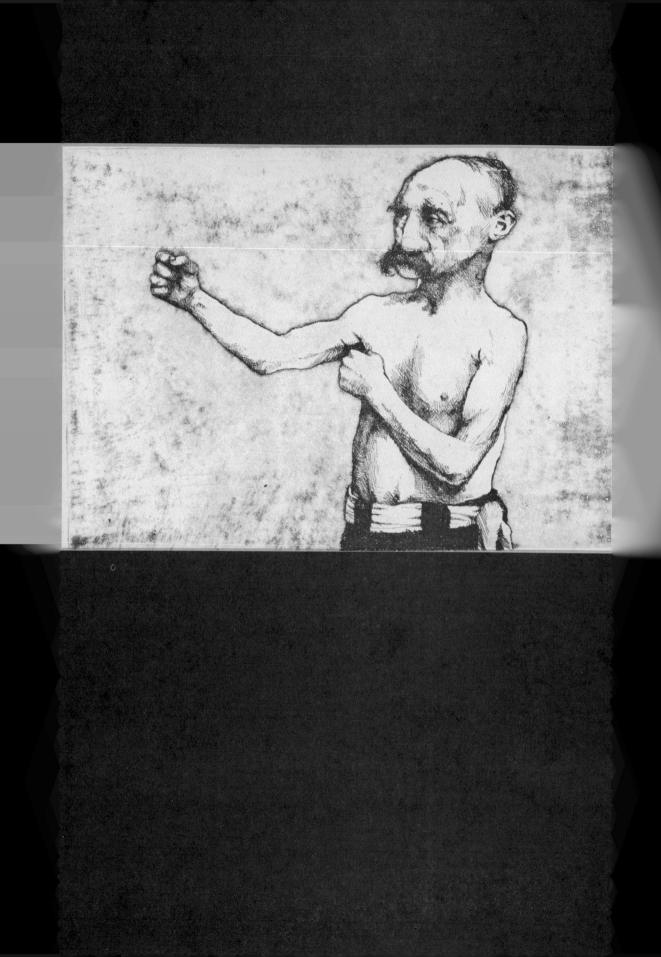

SHOOTING AN ELEPHANT

In Moulmein, in Lower Burma, I was hated by large numbers of people—the only time in my life that I have been important enough for this to happen to me. I was sub-divisional police officer of the town, and in an aimless, petty kind of way anti-European feeling was very bitter. No one had the guts to raise a riot, but if a European woman went through the bazaars alone somebody would probably spit betel juice over her dress. As a police officer I was an obvious target and was baited whenever it seemed safe to do so. When a nimble Burman tripped me up on the football field and the referee (another Burman) looked the other way, the crowd yelled with hideous laughter. This happened more than once. In the end the sneering yellow faces of young men that met me everywhere, the insults hooted after me when I was at a safe distance, got badly on my nerves. The young Buddhist priests were the worst of all. There were several thousands of them in the town and none of them seemed to have anything to do except stand on street corners and jeer at Europeans.

All this was perplexing and upsetting. For at that time I had already made up my mind that imperialism was an evil thing and the sooner I chucked up my job and got out of it the better. Theoretically—and secretly, of course—I was all for the Burmese and all against their oppressors, the British. As for the job I was doing, I hated it more bitterly than I can perhaps make clear. In a job like that you see the dirty work of Empire at close quarters. The wretched prisoners huddling in the stinking cages of the lock-ups, the grey, cowed faces of the long-term convicts, the scarred buttocks of the men who had been flogged with bamboos—all these oppressed me with an intolerable sense of guilt. But I could get nothing into perspective. I was young and ill-educated and I had to think out my problems in the utter silence that is imposed on every Englishman in the East. I did not even know that the British Empire is dying, still less did I know that it is a great deal better than the younger empires that are going to supplant it. All I knew was that I was stuck between my hatred of the empire I served and my rage against the evil-spirited little beasts who tried to make my job impossible. With one part of my mind I thought of the British Raj as an unbreakable tyranny, as something clamped down, in *saecula saeculorum,* upon the will of prostrate peoples; with another part I thought that the greatest joy in the world would be to drive a bayonet into a Buddhist priest's guts. Feelings like these are the normal by-products of imperialism; ask any Anglo-Indian official, if you can catch him off duty.

One day something happened which in a round-about way was enlightening. It was a tiny incident in itself, but it gave me a better glimpse than I had had before of the real nature of imperialism—the real motives for which despotic governments act. Early one morning the sub-inspector at a police station the other end of the town rang me up on the phone and said that an elephant was ravaging the bazaar. Would I please come and do something about it? I did not know what I could do, but I wanted to see what was happening and I got on to a pony and started out. I took my rifle, an old .44 Winchester and much too small to kill an elephant, but I thought the noise might be useful *in terrorem.* Various Burmans stopped me on the way and told me about the elephant's doings. It was not, of course, a wild elephant, but a tame one which had gone "must." It had been chained up, as tame elephants always are when their attack of "must" is due, but on the previous night it had broken its chain and escaped. Its mahout, the only person who could manage it when it was in that state, had set out in pursuit, but had taken the wrong direction and was now twelve hours' journey away, and in the morning the elephant had suddenly reappeared in the town. The Burmese population had no weapons and were quite helpless against it. It had already destroyed somebody's bamboo hut, killed a cow and raided some fruit-stalls and devoured the stock; also it had met the municipal rubbish van and, when the driver jumped out and took to his heels, had turned the van over and inflicted violences upon it.

The Burmese sub-inspector and some Indian constables were waiting for me in the quarter where the elephant had been seen. It was a very poor quarter, a labyrinth of squalid bamboo huts, thatched with palm-leaf, winding all over a steep hillside. I remember that it was a cloudy, stuffy morning at the beginning of the rains. We began questioning the people as to where the elephant had gone and, as usual, failed to get any definite information. That is invariably the case in the East; a story always sounds clear enough at a distance, but the nearer you get to the scene of events the vaguer it becomes. Some of the people said that the elephant had gone in one direction, some said that he had gone in another, some professed not even to have heard of any elephant. I had almost made up my mind that the whole story was a pack of lies, when we heard yells a little distance away. There was a loud, scandalized cry of ''Go away, child! Go away, child! Go away this instant!'' and an old woman with a switch in her hand came round the corner of a hut, violently shooing away a crowd of naked children. Some more women followed, clicking their tongues and exclaiming; evidently there was something that the children ought not to have seen. I rounded the hut and saw a man's dead body sprawling in the mud. He was an Indian, a black Dravidian coolie, almost naked, and he could not have been dead many minutes. The people said that the elephant had come suddenly upon him round the corner of the hut, caught him with its trunk, put its foot on his back and ground him into the earth. This was the rainy season and the ground was soft, and his face had scored a trench a foot deep and a couple of yards long. He was laying on his belly with arms crucified and head sharply twisted to one side. His face was coated with mud, the eyes wide open, the teeth bared and grinning with an expression of unendurable agony. (Never tell me, by the way, that the dead look peaceful. Most of the corpses I have seen looked devilish.) The friction of the great beast's foot had stripped the skin from his back as neatly as one skins a rabbit. As soon as I saw the dead man I sent an orderly to a friend's house nearby to borrow an elephant rifle. I had already sent back the pony, not wanting it to go mad with fright and throw me if it smelt the elephant.

The orderly came back in a few minutes with a rifle and five cartridges, and meanwhile some Burmans had arrived and told us that the elephant was in the paddy fields below, only a few hundred yards away. As I started forward practically the whole population of the quarter flocked out of the houses and followed me. They had seen the rifle and were all shouting excitedly that I was going to shoot the elephant. They had not shown much interest in the elephant when he was merely ravaging their homes, but it was different now that he was going to be shot. It was a bit of fun to them, as it would be to an English crowd; besides they wanted the meat. It made me vaguely uneasy. I had no intention of shooting the elephant—I had merely sent for the rifle to defend myself if necessary—and it is always unnerving to have a crowd following you. I marched down the hill, looking and feeling a fool, with the rifle over my shoulder and an ever-growing army of people jostling at my heels. At the bottom, when you got away from the huts, there was a metalled road and beyond that a miry waste of paddy fields a thousand yards across, not yet ploughed but soggy from the first rains and dotted with coarse grass. The elephant was standing eight yards from the road, his left side towards us. He took not the slightest notice of the crowd's approach. He was tearing up bunches of grass, beating them against his knees to clean them and stuffing them into his mouth.

I had halted on the road. As soon as I saw the elephant I knew with perfect certainty that I ought not to shoot him. It is a serious matter to shoot a working elephant—it is comparable to destroying a huge and costly piece of machinery—and obviously one ought not to do it if it can possibly be avoided. And at that distance, peacefully eating, the elephant looked no more dangerous than a cow. I thought then and I think now that his attack of "must" was already passing off; in which case he would merely wander harmlessly about until the mahout came back and caught him. Moreover, I did not in the least want to shoot him. I decided that I would watch him for a little while to make sure that he did not turn savage again, and then go home.

But at that moment I glanced round at the crowd that had followed me. It was an immense crowd, two thousand at the least and growing every minute. It blocked the road for a long distance on either side. I looked at the sea of yellow faces above the garish clothes—faces all happy and excited over this bit of fun, all certain that the elephant was going to be shot. They were watching me as they would watch a conjurer about to perform a trick. They did not like me, but with the magical rifle in my hands I was momentarily worth watching. And suddenly I realized that I should have to shoot the elephant after all. The people expected it of me and I had got to do it; I could feel their two thousand wills pressing me forward, irresistibly. And it was at this moment, as I stood there with the rifle in my hands, that I first grasped the hollowness, the futility of the white man's dominion in the East. Here was I, the white man with his gun, standing in front of the unarmed native crowd—seemingly the leading actor of the piece; but in reality I was only an absurd puppet pushed to and fro by the will of those yellow faces behind. I perceived in this moment that when the white man turns tyrant it is his own freedom that he destroys. He becomes a sort of hollow, posing dummy, the conventionalized figure of a sahib. For it is the condition of his rule that he shall spend his life in trying to impress the "natives," and so in every crisis he has got to do what the "natives" expect of him. He wears a mask, and his face grows to fit it. I had got to shoot the elephant. I had committed myself to doing it when I sent for the rifle. A sahib has got to act like a sahib; he has got to appear resolute, to know his own mind and do definite things. To come all that way, rifle in hand, with two thousand people marching at my heels, and then to trail feebly away, having done nothing—no, that was impossible. The crowd would laugh at me. And my whole life, every white man's life in the East, was one long struggle not to be laughed at.

But I did not want to shoot the elephant. I watched him beating his bunch of grass against his knees, with that preoccupied grandmotherly air that elephants have. It seemed to me that it would be murder to shoot him. At that age I was not squeamish about killing animals, but I had never shot an elephant and never wanted to. (Somehow it always seems worse to kill a *large* animal.) Besides, there was the beast's owner to be considered. Alive, the elephant was worth at least a hundred pounds; dead, he would only be worth the value of his tusks, five pounds, possibly. But I had got to act quickly. I turned to some experienced-looking Burmans who had been there when we arrived, and asked them how the elephant had been behaving. They all said the same thing: he took no notice of you if you left him alone, but he might charge if you went too close to him.

It was perfectly clear to me what I ought to do. I ought to walk up to within, say, twenty-five yards of the elephant and test his behavior. If he charged, I could shoot; if he took no notice of me, it would be safe to leave him until the mahout came back. But also I knew that I was going to do no such thing. I was a poor shot with a rifle and the ground was soft mud into which one would sink at every step. If the elephant charged and I missed him, I should have about as much chance as a toad under a steam-roller. But even then I was not thinking particularly of my own skin, only of the watchful yellow faces behind. For at that moment, with the crowd watching me, I was not afraid in the ordinary sense, as I would have been if I had been alone. A white man mustn't be frightened in front of "natives"; and so, in general, he isn't frightened. The sole thought in my mind was that if anything went wrong those two thousand Burmans would see me pursued, caught, trampled on and reduced to a grinning corpse like that Indian up the hill. And if that happened it was quite probable that some of them would laugh. That would never do. There was only one alternative. I shoved the cartridges into the magazine and lay down on the road to get a better aim.

The crowd grew very still, and a deep, low, happy sigh, as of people who see the theatre curtain go up at last, breathed from innumerable throats. They were going to have their bit of fun after all. The rifle was a beautiful German thing with cross-hair sights. I did not then know that in shooting an elephant one would shoot to cut an imaginary bar running from ear-hole to ear-hole. I ought, therefore, as the elephant was sideways on, to have aimed straight at his ear-hole; actually I aimed several inches in front of this, thinking the brain would be further forward.

When I pulled the trigger I did not hear the bang or feel the kick—one never does when a shot goes home—but I heard the devilish roar of glee that went up from the crowd. In that instant, in too short a time, one would have thought, even for the bullet to get there, a mysterious, terrible change had come over the elephant. He neither stirred nor fell, but every line of his body had altered. He looked suddenly stricken, shrunken, immensely old, as though the frightful impact of the bullet had paralyzed him without knocking him down. At last, after what seemed a long time—it might have been five seconds, I dare say—he sagged flabbily to his knees. His mouth slobbered. An enormous senility seemed to have settled upon him.

One could have imagined him thousands of years old. I fired again into the same spot. At the second shot he did not collapse but climbed with desperate slowness to his feet and stood weakly upright, with legs sagging and head dropping. I fired a third time. That was the shot that did for him. You could see the agony of it jolt his whole body and knock the last remnant of strength from his legs. But in falling he seemed for a moment to rise, for as his hind legs collapsed beneath him he seemed to tower upward like a huge rock toppling, his trunk reaching skywards like a tree. He trumpeted, for the first and only time. And then down he came, his belly towards me, with a crash that seemed to shake the ground even where I lay.

I got up. The Burmans were already racing past me across the mud. It was obvious that the elephant would never rise again, but he was not dead. He was breathing very rhythmically with long rattling gasps, his great mound of a side painfully rising and falling. His mouth was wide open—I could see far down into caverns of pale pink throat. I waited a long time for him to die, but his breathing did not weaken. Finally I fired my two remaining shots into the spot where I thought his heart must be. The thick blood welled out of him like red velvet, but still he did not die. His body did not even jerk when the shots hit him, the tortured breathing continued without a pause. He was dying, very slowly and in great agony, but in some world remote from me where not even a bullet could damage him further. I felt that I had got to put an end to that dreadful noise. It seemed dreadful to see the great beast lying there, powerless to move and yet powerless to die, and not even to be able to finish him. I sent back for my small rifle and poured shot after shot into his heart and down his throat. They seemed to make no impression. The tortured gasps continued as steadily as the ticking of a clock.

In the end I could not stand it any longer and went away. I heard later that it took him half an hour to die. Burmans were bringing dahs and baskets even before I left, and I was told they had stripped his body almost to the bones by the afternoon.

Afterwards, of course, there were endless discussions about the shooting of the elephant. The owner was furious, but he was only an Indian and could do nothing. Besides, legally I had done the right thing, for a mad elephant has to be killed, like a mad dog, if its owner fails to control it. Among the Europeans opinion was divided. The older men said I was right, the younger men said it was a damn shame to shoot an elephant for killing a coolie, because an elephant was worth more than any damn Coringhee coolie. And afterwards I was very glad that the coolie had been killed; it put me legally in the right and it gave me a sufficient pretext for shooting the elephant. I often wondered whether any of the others grasped that I had done it solely to avoid looking a fool.

George Orwell

There is something I don't know
    that I am supposed to know.
I don't know what it is I don't know,
    and yet am supposed to know,
and I feel I look stupid
    if I seem both not to know it
    and not know what it is I don't know.

Therefore I pretend I know it.
    This is nerve-wracking
    since I don't know what I must pretend to know
Therefore I pretend to know everything!

R. D. Laing, *Knots*

Defense Mechanisms

You now recognize that defensiveness is likely to occur whenever it appears that another person's view of us doesn't match the image we want to present. In these cases it's as if the other person has peeked behind our mask and seen who we really are. Before going any further, it's important to point out that there's usually an element of self-deception in such mask wearing. Much of the time that we're defending ourselves to others, we also want desperately to believe the act we're putting on. It's unpleasant and anxiety-producing to admit that we're not the person we'd like to be (even if our ideal image is totally unrealistic), and faced with a situation where the truth might hurt, it's tempting to convince ourselves that we do fit this superhuman picture we've constructed for others.

How do we manage this self-deception? In the following pages you'll read about some of the methods we use. They are generally referred to as defense mechanisms. Just as the two methods of protecting yourself from physical attack are to flee or to fight, the mechanisms for psychological defense involve either avoidance or counterattack. The fact that these defense mechanisms operate unconsciously and have as their goal the avoidance of, or escape from, threat and anxiety makes them difficult to recognize in ourselves. And when we fail to realize that we're distorting the reality that makes up our lives, communication with others suffers.

Defense mechanisms are not always undesirable. There are times when protecting a private self is desirable, particularly when such disclosure would be treated cruelly by others. Also, confronting too many unpleasant truths or perceptions of one's self too quickly can be unmanageable, and thus these mechanisms serve as protective gear for handling the process of self-discovery at a safe rate. However, your own experience will show that, most often, acting in the following defensive ways can damage your relationships with others. We therefore believe that acquainting you with some of the most common defense mechanisms—with the hope of reducing them in your life—is a valuable step in helping you become a better communicator.

Rationalization   One of the most common ways of avoiding a threat to our self-concept is to *rationalize,* that is, to think up a logical but untrue explanation that protects the unrealistic picture we hold of ourselves.

Have you ever justified cheating in school by saying the information you were tested on wasn't important anyway or that everybody cheats a little?

© 1964 United Feature Syndicate, Inc.

Rationalization Reader for Students

Situation	What to say
When the course is the lecture type:	We never get a chance to say anything.
When the course is the discussion type:	The professor just sits there. We don't know how to teach the course.
When all aspects of the course are covered in class:	All he does is follow the text.
When you're responsible for covering part of the course outside class:	He never covers half the things we're tested on.
When you're given objective tests:	They don't allow for any individuality for us.
When you're given essay tests:	They're too vague. We never know what's expected.
When the instructor gives no tests:	It isn't fair! He can't tell how much we really know.
When you have a lot of quizzes instead of a midterm and final:	We need major exams. Quizzes don't cover enough to really tell anything.
When you have only two exams for the whole course:	Too much rides on each one. You can just have a bad day.

Were those your real reasons, or just excuses? Have you ever shrugged off hurting someone's feelings by saying she'll soon forget what you've done? In cases like these it's often tempting to explain behavior you feel guilty about by justifying it in terms that fit your self-concept.

It is in the ability to deceive oneself that the greatest talent is shown.

Anatole France

Compensation   This is another technique people use for avoiding what they think is a personal shortcoming. Rather than face a problem head on, compensators stress a strength in some other area of their personality, hoping that it will camouflage what they feel is their fault.

A good example of compensation is the man whose home life is unhappy but refuses to do anything about it; instead, he puts all his energy into becoming successful in his business. Another example, is the girl who can't make friends with other women and compensates by attracting as many boyfriends as she can, rather than working on the real problem.

There are many instances when people try to compensate for the lack of good interpersonal relationships with material things. Parents in broken families may attempt to replace their missing relationships with their children by loading them up with toys, sporting equipment, clothes, and so on. This solution is hardly helpful to either the child or parent. Perhaps even more tragic is today's drug scene. Many individuals attempt to compensate for voids in their lives with alcohol and narcotics. In these cases, compensation keeps the problem covered so that it is never brought into the open, and consequently there is no possibility for a solution.

Reaction Formation   People who use reaction formation avoid facing an unpleasant truth by acting exactly opposite from the way they truly feel. The common expression that describes this behavior is "whistling in the dark."

For example, you may have known somebody who acts like the life of the party, always laughing and making jokes, but who you suspect is trying to fool everybody—including himself—into missing the fact that he is sad and lonely. Another example of reaction formation involves the person who goes overboard to be openminded, insisting, "I'm not prejudiced! Why, some of my best friends are ———!" It's easy to suspect that someone who makes such a fuss about being tolerant may be unwilling to admit that just the opposite is true.

At first, reaction formation might seem identical to compensation, but there is a difference. In compensation a communicator makes up for a perceived weakness by excelling in an entirely different area, whereas reaction formation involves behaving in an opposite manner about the bothersome subject. For instance, someone feeling bad about being shy around strangers could compensate for this problem by being especially attentive to close friends; whereas a reaction formation response to the same shyness would involve acting in an extroverted way toward new people. (Of course, there's nothing wrong with being outgoing if it leads to a genuine relationship. The problem with reaction formation is that the seemingly acceptable behavior is really an unnatural, uncomfortable act.)

Projection   In projection you avoid an unpleasant part of yourself by disowning that part and attributing it to others. For instance, on the days when as instructors we aren't as prepared for class as we might be, it's tempting to claim that the hour hasn't gone well because the students didn't do *their* homework. Similarly, you may have found yourself accusing others of being dishonest, lazy, or inconsiderate when in fact such descriptions fit your behavior quite well. In all of these cases we project an unpleasant trait of our own onto another, and in so doing we avoid facing it in ourselves. It doesn't matter whether the accusation you make about others is true or not: In projection the important point is that you are escaping from having to face the truth about yourself.

The mechanism of projection explains the common experience of taking an instant dislike to someone you've just met and realizing later that the traits you found so distasteful in that person are precisely those you dislike in yourself. By criticizing the new acquaintance you can put the undesirable characteristic "out there," and not have to admit it belongs to you.

A surefire test to determine whether you are using projection to fool yourself is to take every attack you make on others and substitute "I" for the words you use to identify the other person. For example, "She talks too much" Becomes "I talk too much," or "They're being unfair" is instead "I'm being unfair." When you try this simple experiment and your accusation of another seems to be true of you, you are projecting.

I AM A ROCK

A winter's day
In a deep and dark December
I am alone
Gazing from my window
To the streets below
On a freshly fallen silent shroud of snow
I am a rock
I am an island.

I built walls
A fortress deep and mighty
That none may penetrate
I have no need of friendship
Friendship causes pain
Its laughter and its loving I disdain
I am a rock
I am an island.

Don't talk of love
Well, I've heard the word before
It's sleeping in my memory
I won't disturb the slumber
Of feelings that have died
If I'd never loved I never would have cried
I am a rock
I am an island.

I have my books
And my poetry to protect me.
I am shielded in armor
Hiding in my room
Safe within my womb
I touch no one and no one touches me
I am a rock
I am an island

And a rock feels no pain
And an island never cries.

Paul Simon and Art Garfunkel

Identification   Sometimes when we're unsure or don't like ourselves, we hide our feelings by imitating someone we admire. The problem with identification of this sort is that it's artificial. We get so involved in "being like" another person that we can't respond to a situation genuinely; instead, we react as we think our "hero" would, often denying our own feelings in the process. Thus, when we use the mechanism of identification, our life becomes an act.

Many families only relate to each other in artificial ways. Without being conscious of it they pick up a mental picture of the "ideal, troublefree family" from television shows and other clichés. Then when real problems occur—as they're bound to do—nobody is willing to admit it for fear that something is wrong with them. Instead, everyone goes on acting a role, while the problem usually grows because of neglect.

Fantasy   When a person's desires or ambitions are frustrated, he often resorts to a fantasy world to satisfy them. We often daydream ourselves out of our "real" world into one that is more satisfying. A good example of this is the young career woman who finds herself bored with her dull life as a typist. To insulate herself from this unbearable existence she escapes into the excitement of her own fantasies. She becomes the leading lady in the romance magazine stories, the television dramas, and the movies she frequents. No matter how exciting and glamorous these fantasies are, they're not connected to the problem of her reality and therefore can't help her make changes to improve her life.

There is much to be said for the short daydream that lifts the boredom of an unpleasant task, or the fantasies that can be creative tools to help us think up new solutions to problems. But as with all defense mechanisms, the danger of fantasizing is that it keeps us from dealing squarely with what's bothering us by providing a temporary escape which doesn't really solve the problem.

Repression   Sometimes rather than facing up to an unpleasant situation and trying to deal with it, we protect ourselves by denying its existence. Quite simply, we "forget" what would otherwise be painful. Take a couple, for example, who can't seem to agree about how to handle their finances. One partner thinks that money is meant to be spent, while the other believes that it's important to save for the future. Rather than working to solve this important problem, the husband and wife pretend nothing is wrong. This charade may work for a while, but as time goes by each partner will probably begin to feel more and more uncomfortable and will likely begin to build up resentments about the way the other one uses their common money. Eventually these resentments are almost sure to leak into other areas of the marriage.

In the same way, we've seen families with serious problems—an alcoholic parent, a teenager into drugs, a conflict between members—try to pretend that everything is perfectly all right, as if acting that way will make it so. Of course, it's unlikely that they'll solve these problems without admitting that they exist.

Dependency or Regression   Sometimes rather than admit we *don't want* to do something, we convince ourselves that we *can't* do it. We resort to behavior that is more characteristic of an earlier age, an age when we were more helpless. This behavior is known as *regression* or *dependency*.

The person who says, "Gee, I'd really like to have a relationship with you, but I'm not ready" might really be hiding the truth: that she simply doesn't care enough about the relationship to make it grow. The pitiful soul who says "I'd really like to improve my life, but I can't" could be hiding from the fact that he isn't willing to put in the work necessary to change his present situation.

Emotional Insulation and Apathy   Often, rather than face an unpleasant situation, people will avoid hurt by not getting involved or pretending they don't care. Probably the most common example of *emotional insulation* is the person who develops a strong attachment to someone only to have the relationship break up. The pain is so great that the sufferer refuses to become involved like this again. At other times people who are hurt in this way defend their feeling of self-worth by becoming *apathetic*, by saying they don't care about whoever hurt them.

The sad thing about emotional insulation and apathy is that they prevent the person who uses them from doing anything about dealing with the cause of the defensiveness. As long as I say I don't care about dating when I really do, I can't go out with anyone because this would be inconsistent with my artificial self-concept. As long as I don't admit that I care about you, our relationship has little chance of growing.

Displacement   This occurs when we vent aggressive or hostile feelings against people or objects that are seen as less dangerous than the person or persons who caused the feelings originally. The child who is reminded that she has to clean up her room before she can play may get rid of some of her hostility by slamming the door to her bedroom or beating up a younger brother or sister. She knows it might cause her more pain if she expressed this hostility against her parents. In the same way, displacement occurs when, for example, a workman gets angry at the boss but doesn't want to risk getting fired and so takes out his frustration by yelling at his family.

What part of the self-concept do we defend when using displacement? Almost always the image we're trying to maintain is one of powerfulness or potency: "I'm not a pushover," we insist, and prove it by using force on people who don't threaten us. While in fact such acts don't change the fact that we have been pushed around by others, we conveniently ignore the truth.

Undoing   In undoing we make up for an act that doesn't fit with our ideal self-concept by offering a symbolic token of apology, usually to the person we've hurt. For example, the boy who is constantly late picking up his date may bring her gifts to show that he's not so bad after all. A parent who punishes his child and then feels guilty may be "extra" nice to the child for a while to raise his own self-esteem.

We should point out that symbolic gestures that really *do* signal a change in behavior aren't undoing. But these gestures become defense mechanisms when we use them to fool ourselves into thinking we've turned over a new leaf when we really haven't.

Verbal Aggression Sometimes, when we can get away with it, the easiest way to avoid facing criticism is to drown it out. Verbal aggression illustrates the old saying "The best defense is a good offense." Counterattacking somebody who threatens our self-concept tends to relieve tension and helps the defensive person feel better because his fireworks probably cover up whatever it was in the original remark that threatened him.

A good example of verbal aggression is the "so are you" defensive maneuver. When a person says something we feel is too critical, we counterattack by telling her all her faults. Our remarks may be true, but they don't answer her criticism and only wind up making her more defensive.

Temper tantrums, hitting below the belt, and bringing up past grievances are some other types of verbal aggression. (For more on these "crazymakers," see Chapter 9.)

Now that you've had a look at several ways people defend an unrealistic self-concept, we hope you'll be able to detect the role defense mechanisms play in your life. We want to repeat that these mechanisms aren't usually destructive unless they're practiced to the point where an individual's view of

reality becomes distorted. We also hope that you don't instantly become a self-appointed psychiatrist, analyzing the defense mechanisms in others. Rarely will you find an individual's behavior so transparent and uncomplicated that it can be diagnosed from casual observation. What appears on the surface as a defense mechanism in operation may be authentic, honest behavior. Our hope is that you can look at *yourself* with a little more knowledge of how you operate when you detect a threat to your self-concept.

Finally, you'll find defensive mechanisms don't usually appear as simple, clear-cut behaviors. We usually use them in combination because it's only natural to protect one's self in as many ways as possible.

Defense Mechanism Inventory

List the three defense mechanisms you use most often and describe three recent examples of each. You can arrive at your list both by thinking about your own behavior and by asking others to share their impressions of your behavior. As in the previous journal, conclude your inventory by describing the people with whom you become defensive most often, the parts of your public image that you frequently defend, the usual consequences of using defense mechanisms, and any more satisfying behavior you could promote in the future.

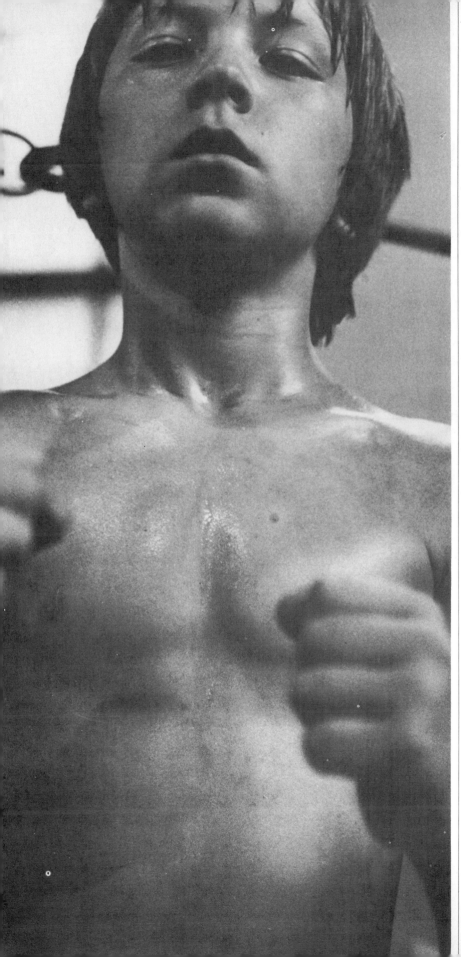

It's not all that hard to do the right thing. But it takes so much effort to think of the kid first, especially when you really need to explode. Arthur Wesson sat in my class for a month and never opened his mouth.

One day when I was feeling ugly, I asked him a question about the book we were reading. He didn't say a word. I thought of all the things I should have done, but no—I had to get belligerent. I asked the question again. Then I waited for an interminable length of time. Nothing.

"If you can't answer when you're spoken to, you can leave."

I hated the way I sounded. But I was too wrapped up in my own frustration to cope with anything Arthur might feel. He left. And I had to find out from a far more patient teacher than I that there wasn't anything personal in the kid's apathy. He couldn't read. His mother was insane, and there was no place to send her. The two babies at home hadn't eaten in a couple of days. I was just a very small ugliness in Arthur Wesson's ugly world. At least he'd found someone in school he could cry to. Except for selfishness, it might have been me. Everytime I saw him, I hated myself all over again. I was too ashamed to look him in the eye.

Sunny Decker, *An Empty Spoon*

145

years ago it was there
your beauty
on something as simple
as a square of paper
remember kindergarten
and the yellow spot
the sun
the splash of blue
the sky
the curving
dripping green line
of the hills
and the perfect
red stripe
i remember
how you looked
at your work
and saw
that it was good

what is this
teacher said
questioning the red

why
it's a fire engine
and then you looked
at your work
again
and then you
hurled your brush
into the corner
of the room
and stomped off
defeated

later
out on the playground
you hit barbara jenkins
in the head
with a kickball
and now
you sit
in the barber chair
running figures
through your mind
hating yourself
and the sight of my hair
waiting
for some kind
of good fairy
to come down
and save your ass

but i remember
i wish you did

Ric Masten

A Child's Garden of Defense Mechanisms

Dependency-regression

"Childlike behavior" is what I call avoiding a situation by pretending I'm not mature enough to handle it, or that I don't understand it. When there's a homework assignment I'm not particularly thrilled over, I try to convince myself that I'm not smart enough to handle it, thus excusing myself from any guilt feelings over the skipped assignment.

Verbal aggression

I was with my boyfriend a few months ago when this man ran a red light and smashed into the side of our van. It was definitely his fault—there were cars stopped in the lane next to him.

Even though this guy must have known he was guilty he jumped out of his car and began yelling at us. He called us "dirty hippies" and "bums."

He let out all that verbal aggression just to cover up the truth—that he was wrong.

Repression

Repression is my "favorite" way of facing up to myself and blocking my communication. I'm especially good at repressing my feelings about my parents. It's not that we hate each other or anything—I really dig them and they like me. But there are some problems that keep coming up. The big one is that they want me to go out with girls who are the same religion as we are. I don't think it matters what religion my dates are—I'm not ready to get married or anything.

Anyhow, the problem is that instead of talking the whole thing over, we all try to pretend that there's no problem when there really is. We wind up being so damn polite to each other that it drives us crazy.

Projection

I found out I do a lot of projecting. The most classical one I've done was Friday night at my boyfriend's house. His mom fixed tacos (lots of them), the company was good, the beer was plentiful. I had told myself earlier that week that I was going to start cutting down on my food intake for fear of gaining unwanted pounds. I told Joe about it so he was quite aware of it. But that night somehow I couldn't hold to my decision! Beer and tacos taste so-o-oo good together, that somehow it took four and a half to finish off my beer with!! (I was going to have one). So automatically after Joe commented on the number, I said "Well, you should have told me I couldn't have any more, but you didn't say anything, you just let me go right on eating!!" He seems to always be the one I project upon.

Rationalization

A guy I know broke up with his girlfriend not too long ago, and the way he handled the thing really shows how rationalization can hurt communication. The reason he gave her for splitting was that he'd be going away to Europe soon and he didn't want to break off suddenly when he left. But the truth was that he was just tired of her. She knew this, and I think his rationalization hurt her way more than if he'd been honest.

And I know he was only fooling himself because he wants to think he's a great guy who is thinking only of her welfare!

Reaction formation

It's really too bad, but I've never gotten along with my husband's mom. Ever since Jim and I met she's acted like I'm not good enough for him. I've always said that I didn't care what she thought about me but the other day I found out that I was kidding myself.

The way I found out was through a reaction formation. You see, neither Jim or I care that much about cooking. We're happy enough eating hamburgers or frozen dinners, but I just realized that everytime Bea (that's his Mom's name) comes over I break my back to fix a fancy dinner. It's almost like I was trying to show her (and myself) that I do take good care of Jim.

Displacement

Yesterday at work I used the defense mechanism of displacement. My supervisor had given me a bunch of static about a problem that was really his fault. He's an unrealistic old S.O.B. to begin with, and there's no use arguing with him. So I guess because I was so mad, when one of the guys on my crew asked me if he could take off a little early that afternoon I chewed him out for being a lazy so-and-so. But all it was was my anger at the boss being displaced.

I was really sorry and apologized later, but it'll take a few days for the guy to let the chip melt off his shoulder.

Identification

When I was in high school there was always a "popular" group of girls that I wanted to get into but they never seemed to notice me or like me very much, even though I tried to act just the way they did. I always bought the same kinds of clothes and I tried to make the same kinds of jokes that they did. I guess I thought if I could act like them they'd accept me. Now that I'm in college I realize how unhappy I was then and how foolish they seemed, but then I would have given anything to be one of them.

Emotional insulation

I think of all the defense mechanisms I can relate to, emotional insulation is the main one.

One example of emotional insulation in all its glory is concerning a friend that was very close but now even though we live in the same house, very little communication goes on between us. Sometimes when I let my pride down, I really feel the full impact of hurt on my part and wonder if she even cares. I've asked myself many times why I can't discuss it with her. And the deep-down reason is because I'm afraid that she won't respond and that would hurt me even worse than it does now; so I've chosen to ignore the situation which has worked only to the degree of convincing myself not to talk it out but so far it hasn't convinced me not to feel.

Undoing

I'm terrible about doing chores around the house. My wife has to bug me for weeks before I even change a lightbulb. We were talking about defense mechanisms last night and she suddenly exclaimed "Gordon, every time you don't do a job we end up going out to dinner!"

I always thought I was just being a nice guy by taking us out, but now I see that I've been buying my way back into my wife's good grace!

Compensation

The other night I was at a party when the subject turned to politics. I'm really turned off by that whole thing, even though I know it's important to know what's going on in Washington, etc. So when somebody brought up the election I tried to change the subject to motorcycles, which I know a lot about.

I do this a lot. When there's something I don't understand or don't like, I try to change the conversation over to an area where I'm an authority.

Fantasy

I've been having troubles at work lately with my boss. I know he thinks I dress too casually, but since no customers ever come into our office I don't see what difference it makes as long as I'm clean. There's been a lot of friction between us because of this dress thing, and it's gotten to the point where I sit at my desk and fantasize having the whole thing out with him. Sometimes I quit, sometimes we become friends—but all this is in my mind, since we never have it out. It's a real bummer.

Defensiveness Ruins Communication

If you've read carefully this far and tried to understand the role defense mechanisms play in your life, you've certainly seen how defensiveness can damage communication. If we're lucky, the damage we create in this way is short-lived and heals with time; but in some cases a single defensive outburst can destroy an entire relationship.

What Makes Us Defensive? The Gibb Categories

Many people think they are acting the way they feel when they tell someone off. Someone is critical of me and I answer by calling him an S.O.B. My feeling is not that he is an S.O.B.; my feeling is that he has hurt me: "You have hurt my feelings and now I want to hurt yours." Launching a verbal attack covers up my feeling of being hurt with an appearance of strength. I get angry when I think someone has hurt me in a way I am helpless to do anything about.

Hugh Prather

We've been talking about the defense mechanisms we use to protect our idealized self-concept and the more consciously applied masks we wear to gain acceptance. But what makes us defensive in the first place?

We've already said that the cause of defensiveness is threat to our self-concept; but thanks to the research of Dr. Jack Gibb we can be more specific. After observing groups for eight years, Gibb was able to isolate six defense-causing types of behavior. His work suggests that when another sees us as acting in one or more of these six ways, the threat to our self-concept is increased to a degree that defensiveness is likely to result.

But Gibb's work didn't stop here. He identified six contrasting behaviors that seemed to reduce the level of threat and defensiveness in communication. He termed these ways of responding as supportive behaviors.

In his research Gibb also found that defensiveness is *reciprocal.* That is, when Person *A* in a relationship becomes threatened and begins to use defense mechanisms and masks to protect herself, much of the time her behavior will begin to cause Person *B* to begin putting up his defenses. This in turn threatens Person *A* even more, and so a spiraling defensive cycle is started, making communication more and more difficult.

Fortunately, just the opposite is also true. When Person *A* behaves in a supportive way, *B* has less cause to feel threatened and so usually lowers his defenses; in turn this openness encourages *A* to become even more supportive. In other words, both defensive behaviors and supportive behaviors are cyclical: You get back what you give in a relationship.

In the next few pages we've listed the six pairs of contrasting behaviors that Gibb developed. Each set contains a description of the way people act that's likely to cause defensiveness, and the behavior that tends to reduce it. As you read about these behaviors, keep two things in mind: First, none of the following behaviors will bring on defensive reactions unless the receiver perceives them as threatening. Insecure receivers may be threatened by almost anything that's said to them, while on the other hand the more secure people are much less easily threatened.

The second thing to keep in mind is that even though we're talking about these behaviors as if they were distinct from one another, in actuality you may run into them in various combinations. The six-part division is made for clarity, but don't be misled by it.

The Gibb Categories of Defensive and Supportive Behaviors

Defensive behaviors	Supportive behaviors
1. Evaluation	1. Description
2. Control	2. Problem orientation
3. Strategy	3. Spontaneity
4. Neutrality	4. Empathy
5. Superiority	5. Equality
6. Certainty	6. Provisionalism

Evaluation vs. Description   A message that's received as evaluative or judgmental increases defensiveness in the receiver and is likely to make him behave in a way that will protect his self-concept. Most of us dislike any situation where we will be evaluated—even positively—because there's always the chance that the outcome will be unfavorable. How do you react when you learn that you'll be evaluated . . . in one of your college courses . . . for a driver's license . . . a job promotion? If you've competed in sports, for a scholarship, or for a job, you've probably felt the pressure evaluation by others can place on you. It seems we must be on guard whenever we suspect we're being rated or judged.

It is well, when one is judging a friend, to remember that he is judging you with the same godlike and superior impartiality

Arnold Bennett

"Just pretend we're not here, Ms. Robinson . . ."

Larry has just accidentally upset a glass of milk all over the dinner table. He was reaching for his salad.

Mother   Larry, how old are you anyway? When are you going to be able to go through a meal without spilling your milk?

Father   He can't help it, it looks like he was born clumsy.

Larry   _____

You can certainly fill in an appropriate response for Larry. And in thinking what Larry would say, you've identified with the defensiveness that he felt after his parents' negative evaluations of him as a person.

Sarah has been bothered lately by the pressure of school work and problems with her boyfriend.

Mother   (crossly) You haven't been fit to live with lately. You've been so thoughtless and moody. You'll just have to stop running around with that crowd of friends and get busy on your schoolwork.

Now even if Sarah had been thinking exactly the same things, how do you think she would have responded to these comments? She probably would have acted by arguing and protecting herself because evaluative language is almost certain to whip up hostility between people. This is the problem with all the defense-arousing behaviors we'll discuss here: Even if the sender's ideas are good ones, the way they're phrased blocks communication.

Psychologist Thomas Gordon has a good way of recognizing evaluative speech. He calls it "you" language because most of it's prefaced by that word, usually spoken in an accusing tone of voice: "You're wrong," "You're sloppy," "You're stupid," "You're being obnoxious," et cetera. And if you listen to your conversations for a day or so, you'll probably be surprised to find how many of your statements that contain "you are" carry evaluative messages that usually cause defensiveness.

In contrast to evaluative "you" language is what Gibb calls descriptive communication. Gordon labels this style of speaking as "I" language. Instead of putting the emphasis on judging another's behavior, the descriptive speaker simply explains how the other's action affects him. Referring back to our example of Sarah and her mother, imagine how much easier it would have been for Sarah to respond if her mother had said something like

I don't know what's happening between us lately, but I've been deeply hurt by some things you've said and done. . . .

and then continued to describe what actions of Sarah's she was thinking of and how they made her feel. This kind of approach doesn't put a lot of pressure on Sarah to change; it simply lets her know how her mother feels and allows her to go from there.

Take a minute to imagine yourself sending "I" and "you" messages to people in your life, and see what difference the two styles of communication would probably make.

Control vs. Problem Orientation   Communication that we sense is aimed at controlling our thoughts or behavior produces defensiveness. We're motivated to react defensively because the speaker seems to be saying that he knows what's best for us.

When was the last time you felt you were being controlled? How do you feel about TV commercials and aggressive salesmen? What about public employees who treat you as if you were some kind of moron? Or how do you react to teachers or parents who lead you into "discussions" when they have the "right" answer all along? All these are examples of controlling behavior in which the sender acts as if his mind is already made up about a course of action before talking takes place.

Needless to say, people who act in controlling ways create a defensive climate. Nobody likes to feel their ideas aren't worth anything and that nothing they say will change the other's determination to have his way—yet this is precisely the attitude a controller communicates. Whether he does it with his words, gestures, tone of voice, or some other channel; whether he controls through his status, insistence on obscure or irrelevent rules, or physical power, the controller generates hostility wherever he goes. The unspoken message his behavior communicates is "I know what's best for you, and if you do as I say we'll get along."

Unlike control, the supportive behavior of problem orientation projects to the listener a willingness to share in the solution of a problem rather than forcing a preconceived idea upon him. The problem-oriented person acts with the attitude "Let's find a solution that works for both of us." As you'll see in Chapter 9, when we talk about the no-lose approach to problem solving, it's often easier than you might think to solve difficulties by finding an answer

that's acceptable to everyone. In the end, even if you can't find the perfect solution, the mere fact that you're willing to try can create a far better climate than can the hostility that comes from two people trying to control each other.

If you're in an environment where control is often used (and who isn't!), don't be too surprised if your first attempts at problem orientation meet with some doubt from others. They may suspect that your willingness to look for a mutually satisfactory solution is some kind of trick, just another way to control them. Remember that defensiveness is reciprocal, and keeping your good humor can prevent the start of an ugly upward spiral of mistrust and hostility.

Strategy vs. Spontaneity   One of the surest ways to make people defensive is to get caught trying to manipulate them into doing something for you. The fact that you tried to trick them instead of just asking for what you wanted is enough to build mistrust. Nobody likes to be a guinea pig or a sucker, and even well-meant manipulation can cause bad feelings.

A teenager reported that his dad was tricky. It seems that whenever the father wanted to criticize the boy he'd always say something nice first, and then somewhere along the way let the axe fall. This stratagem has been referred to as the "psychological sandwich," two pieces of praise with criticism between.

It didn't take too many repeats of this strategy before the son cringed every time he heard praise from his dad because he learned it was only given to soften criticism. Probably it would have been better for the relationship if the son received honest praise or honest criicism rather than a strategy that seemed a dishonest mixture of both.

Have you ever wanted to go somewhere and not had a way of getting there? Have you ever tried to manipulate a friend, who had transportation, into wanting to go too? Think back to the different relationships you've had. Have any of them ended because you felt you were being used? Do you suppose anyone has stopped his association with you for the same reason?

> *I seem to get the most defensive when I think something I have done is "bad." The judgment as to what is bad is a judgment of mine as well as others around me. It cuts the most when someone else's judgment of me agrees with my own bad impression of myself. I seem very susceptible to a "bady boy" thing. I can get pouty and withdraw just like a bad boy would. When I get that way or get an impression of someone reacting to me in that way, I quickly blame them for being judgmental and not understanding me. I begin to feel misunderstood, unloved, unknown, and alone.*
>
> John T. Wood

Spontaneity is the behavior that contrasts with strategy. Spontaneity simply means being honest, reporting that which you're feeling right now rather than planning your words to get the best response. Often the spontaneous response won't get what you want, but in the long run it's usually better to be candid and yourself and perhaps miss out on some small goal than to say all the right things and become a fraud. More than once we've heard people say "I didn't like what he said, but at least I know he was being honest."

Although it sounds paradoxical at first, spontaneity can be a strategy too. Sometimes you'll see people using honesty in a calculating way, being just frank enough to win someone's trust or sympathy. This kind of "leveling" is probably the most defense-arousing strategy of all because once we've learned someone is using frankness as a manipulation there's almost no chance we'll ever trust him again.

While reading this chapter you might get the idea that using supportive behaviors described here is a great way to manipulate others. Before going any further we want to say loudly and clearly that if you ever act supportively without being sincere in what you're saying, you've misunderstood the idea behind this chapter, and you're running a risk of causing even more defensiveness than before. None of the ideas we present in this book can go into a "bag of tricks" that can be used to control others: If you ever find yourself using them this way, beware!

Neutrality vs. Empathy   Probably a better word to describe Gibb's idea of the defense-arousing behavior he calls neutrality is *indifference*. Acting with a neutral attitude communicates a lack of concern for the welfare of another and implies that he isn't very important to you. This perceived indifference is likely to promote defensiveness because no one likes to think of himself as worthless, and he'll protect a self-concept that pictures him as worthwhile.

The small child who has urgent things to tell a parent but is met with an indifferent response may be expected to become upset. The physician who seems clinical and detached to his patients may wonder why they find another doctor.

Gibb has found that empathy helps rid communication of the indifferent quality. When someone shows that he cares for the feelings of another there's little chance that a self-concept will be threatened. Empathy means accepting another's feelings, putting yourself in his place. This doesn't mean you need to agree with him; by simply letting someone know you care and respect him, you'll be acting in a supportive way.

In his research Gibb observed the importance of nonverbal messages in communicating empathy. Facial and bodily expressions of concern often are more important to the receiver than the words used.

The worst sin towards our fellow creatures is not to hate them, but to be indifferent to them; that's the essence of inhumanity

George Bernard Shaw

Superiority vs. Equality   How many interpersonal relationships have you dropped because you couldn't stand the superiority that the other person projected? Like the other behaviors we've talked about, an individual who communicates superiority arouses feelings of inadequacy in the recipients.

We're not particular as to the type of superiority presented to us; we just become defensive. Money, power, intellectual ability, physical appearance, and athletic prowess are areas in which we learn it's important to excel in our culture. Consequently we often feel a need to express our superiority along these lines.

The individual who acts superior communicates that he doesn't want to relate on equal terms with the other(s) in the relationship. Furthermore, he seems to imply that he doesn't want feedback nor will he need help because the help would be coming from someone inferior to him. This message of superiority alerts the listener to be on guard because the sender is likely to attempt to reduce the receiver's worth, power, or status to maintain or advance his own superiority.

An example you may have come across is the classmate who questions other members of the class to find out their grades. He's delighted each time he discovers another classmate who has received a grade lower than his. His degree of superiority is closely related to the number of fellow students who received marks lower than his. Have you ever been made defensive by this type of person?

Perhaps you've had a professor who continually reminded his students of his superior intellectual ability and position. Remember how delighted you were when you or a classmate caught him making a mistake? Why do you suppose it was so satisfying to let him know of his error? Some might argue that this is a good strategy to keep students awake, but in reality much of the student's effort is directed to defending his own worth rather than pursuing the objectives of the course.

Whenever we detect someone communicating superiority to us we react. We "turn her off," justify ourselves, or argue with her in our minds. Sometimes we choose to verbally change the subject or physically walk away, and of course there is always the counterattack, which includes an attempt to belittle the sender of the superiority message. We'll go to great lengths "to cut her down to size." All these defensive reactions to projected superiority are destructive to an interpersonal relationship.

There are many situations in our lives when we're in relationship with individuals who possess talents greater than ours. But is it necessary for these persons to project superiority? Your own experiences will tell you that it isn't. Gibb has found ample evidence that many people who possess superior skills and talents are capable of projecting feelings of *equality* rather than superiority. Such people communicate that although they may have greater talent in certain areas, they see others as having just as much worth as human beings.

Certainty vs. Provisionalism   Have you run into the person who is certain she's right, certain hers is the only or proper way of doing something, or certain that she has all the facts and needs no additional information? If you

Teens, Parents and Conversation Gap

NEW YORK (UPI)—Expect the communications gap between parent and teen-ager to worsen when you have a confidential talk with son or daughter—then blab contents of same.

The same will happen if every conversation takes on the tone of a courtroom interrogation.

Many of the teen-agers who stand charged with being sparse in the word department on the homefront really long for conversation with parents.

A report in the Christian Herald makes that point, adding that the youngsters keep the exchanges of words on a superficial level for many reasons.

In "How to Talk to a Teen-ager—Maybe," youngsters gave the following reasons for avoiding conversations in depth with adults:

—The youngsters have learned their confidences are not respected. Their parents tell each other, or other relatives, what has been revealed in private, or make jokes, or discuss their opinions with outside friends. Child reacts by clamming up.

—Parents do not accept their children's feelings as real, but attempt to change their moods without sitting down and trying to find out exactly what bothers them.

—Parents substitute advice and orders for real conversation dodging the issue when it comes to telling their children what they really think about such subjects as petting, cheating on examinations, politics or religion.

—Parents talk pompously, or too knowingly, stressing only what they think without listening to the youngster's ideas. Youngsters find such talks boring.

—Parents pretend to be authorities on subjects about which they really are ignorant. They make fools of themselves especially when parading their ignorance in front of child's friends.

—In the middle of a discussion, parents lose patience yelling at child—"You'd better do what I say" or "I know best." That puts the clamps on the child's tongue, cutting off communication.

Parents who have not lost the word battle with their teen-agers, meanwhile, have certain things in common.

They are patient while trying to catch a teenager's attention. They win their interest before attempting to start a conversation.

One way to bridge the gap, according to the report in the Christian Herald,—arrange for youngsters to help with household chores which give opportunity for normal conversation.

Los Angeles Times

have, you've met an individual who projects the defense-arousing behavior Gibb calls *certainty*.

How do you react when you're the target of such certainty? Do you suddenly find your energy directed to proving the dogmatic individual wrong? If you do, you're reacting normally, if not very constructively.

George Smith, a machine operator, was called into his supervisor's office after his third assistant in three weeks had asked for a transfer. When asked by his boss what was happening, George told him that the young guys he was getting couldn't be told anything. Actually all three assistants had given the same reason for having to "get away" from George. George "knew it all," and he was certain his was the only way any job could be done. He'd get mad if they didn't do exactly as he showed them even when they found a method as good or better than his. George made them feel like idiots. The supervisor was successful in getting George to replace his certainty with some provisionalism, and at last report George's latest assistant has been with him more than a year.

What is this provisionalism the supervisor so strongly suggested George practice? George's boss told him he'd have to do something about his attitude that his was the only way a job could be done. He explained that it was possible his assistant could see another method of doing a piece of work, and he should be willing to listen and perhaps even try it out. He needed to

stop trying so hard to teach and to treat his assistant as a coworker, not as someone inferior to himself.

Have you noticed that the person who projects certainty is usually more interested in winning an argument than solving a problem? Gibb points out that the individual who works hard at demonstrating his certainty usually communicates inward feelings of inferiority, a reaction formation that we mentioned earlier in the chapter.

When we exhibit provisionalism instead of certainty we communicate an openness to receiving new information and ideas. And this behavior seldom results in making a person defensive. We're not suggesting that you shouldn't express an opinion or take a position on an issue. We're suggesting, however, that when you practice provisionalism you're interested in that which is new or not yet known to you. The provisional attitude encourages participation and communication, whereas certainty discourages them.

Defensiveness, the Great Barrier

It's our belief that defensiveness is the greatest single barrier to effective interpersonal communication. The sooner you become aware of your part in producing defensiveness or reacting defensively, the sooner you'll find your interpersonal relationships more satisfying. Making another person defensive interferes with interpersonal communication. It may only make communication more difficult, or on the other hand it may make it impossible!

Defensiveness Feedback

1. Approach an important person in your life and request some help in learning more about yourself. Inform the other person that your discussion will probably take at least an hour, and make sure both of you are prepared to invest this amount of time.

2. Begin by explaining all twelve of the Gibb behaviors to your partner. Be sure to give enough examples so that each category is clearly understood.

3. When your explanation is complete and you've answered all your partner's questions, ask her to tell you which of the Gibb categories *you use with her.* Seek specific examples so that you are certain to understand the feedback fully. (Since you are requesting an evaluation, be prepared for a little defensiveness on your own part at this point.) Inform your partner that you are interested in discovering both the defense-arousing and the supportive behaviors you use, and that you are sincerely interested in receiving a candid answer. (Note: If you don't want to hear the truth from your partner, don't try this exercise.)

4. As your partner speaks, record the categories she lists in sufficient detail for both of you to be sure that you have understood her comments.

5. When you have finished your list, show it to your partner. Listen to her reactions and make any corrections that are necessary to reflect an accurate understanding of her comments. When your list is accurate, have your partner sign it to indicate that you have understood her clearly.

6. In a concluding statement note
   a. how you felt as your partner was describing you
   b. whether you agree with the evaluation
   c. what effect your use of the various Gibbs categories has on your relationship with your partner

Defensiveness Groups

1. Divide the class into six small groups, keeping the numbers as even as possible.

2. Each group selects one pair of the Gibb defensive and supportive behaviors.

3. Each group should study the explanation of categories given in the text and then compile a list of examples from the members' own experiences. Each group member should share at least one personal experience that illustrates the behavior being studied.

4. The instructor will act as a resource person, answering any questions the groups may have.

5. When each group has understood their particular defensive and supportive behaviors and armed themselves with good, fresh examples,

form new groups with six members. This time each group is to contain a member from each of the different behavior groups. You'll probably not be fortunate enough to have this work out evenly, but each of the new groups should have at least one person representing each of the six Gibb categories.

6. Each member of the new group is to acquaint the others in his group with the defensive and supportive behaviors he has studied. They should use the best examples they heard to illustrate them.

7. As the group proceeds they may have questions. Again, the instructor should be considered as a resource member of each group.

8. You may find that you're hearing examples that could fit into other categories. Don't let this bother you. Remember that we prefaced the materials on defensiveness by saying that Gibb's behaviors were categorized for convenience of investigation. An individual may experience these behaviors in many combinations. The important thing is to become aware of defensive behavior as it occurs in our daily communication, not to memorize the textbook terminology.

9. When each group has finished there should be a chance for anyone who has questions to throw them out to the group as a whole for possible answers.

By now we hope you've a clearer idea of the role defensiveness plays in your life. We've tried to help you become aware of the times you consciously wear masks to protect the self you fear others won't accept. We've pointed out some of the defense mechanisms you probably use unconsciously to protect an unrealistic self-concept from attack; and finally, we've shown how defensiveness is caused by certain kinds of behaviors and reduced by others.

Even if you've tried long and hard, you've almost certainly found that it isn't easy to strip away defenses. On the other hand, the people who make the greatest strides in improving their communication are those who will accept the risk involved in discarding their defenses. We feel strongly that this willingness is the key to more satisfying communication. We hope you can begin to look at your own defensiveness and start the process of opening yourself to those with whom you communicate.

"This all sounds fine" you say, "but let the other guy drop his defenses first!" This attitude would probably please an instructor teaching classes in a war college, but it's hardly growth promoting in the area of interpersonal communication. We've already written about the self-fulfilling prophecy in connection with our self-concept; now we can apply the same principle to dropping our defenses. If you're open and supportive in your behavior toward others, they'll tend to respond in a like manner. If you decide to wait for your partner to lower his defenses first, you can expect that again he'll respond in the same fashion; the defensive behavior spiral is set in motion.

Behold the turtle who makes progress only when he sticks his neck out.

Cecil Parker

Roads Not Taken

1. Make a study of the level of defensive communication in a particular part of your life—on the job, at school, at home, and so on. In your observations note

   a. which attacking and supporting categories as described by Gibb each person uses

   b. the response that each person gives in response to the behaviors described in step a above

   c. the consequences that come from the behaviors you have described in steps a and b.

2. Based on your knowledge gained in this chapter, describe in specific terms the ways you must act to arouse less defensiveness in others and to be less defensive yourself. Keep a record of your successes in using these behaviors and note the benefits of your doing so.

3. Observe models in your life who are rarely defensive and observe how they behave when attacked by others. How might you learn from their actions?

4. Comment on which of the mistaken ideas described in Chapter 4 you have been living by, noting the defensive consequences that can come from accepting such ideas.

5. Expand your knowledge of defense mechanisms by doing a thorough investigation of the subject in your library.

More Readings on Defensiveness

Adler, Ronald B. *Confidence in Communication: A Guide to Assertive and Social Skills.* New York: Holt, Rinehart and Winston, 1977.
Chapter 7 deals extensively with nondefensive ways of coping with criticism. In it you'll find detailed, step-by-step instructions for including these skills in your everyday life. Students often find that once they've learned these coping skills, they welcome and enjoy criticism, even when it's totally unfair and mistaken!

Gergen, Kenneth J. "Multiple Identity: The Healthy, Happy Human Being Wears Many Masks." *Psychology Today* (May 1972).
This article suggests that we wear a series of masks; instead of a single identity there are a whole series of "you's" which emerge in various situations. Although the ideas suggested in this article don't totally agree with the ones presented in this book, we recommend you consider them.

Gibb, Jack R. "Defensive Communication." *The Journal of Communication* 11:3 (September 1961).
This is the original article in which the six categories of defensive and supportive behaviors discussed in this book appeared.

Lazarus, Arnold, and Allen Fay. *I Can If I Want To.* New York: Morrow, 1975.
This brief, extremely readable book lists many mistaken ideas by which people try to run their lives and in so doing create tremendous potential for becoming defensive. We're positive that recognizing these mistaken ideas and eliminating them from your public image can lead to a great decrease in your own defensive behavior.

Powell, John. *Why Am I Afraid To Tell You Who I Am?* Chicago: Argus Communications, 1969.
Powell's brief, attractive book attempts to answer the question its title proposes. This is a simple but effective introduction to many issues discussed in this book, including defensiveness.

Shostrom, Everett L. *Man, the Manipulator.* New York: Bantam Books, 1968.
A description of the whys and hows of many masks people wear as well as an argument about the reasons for dropping them.

Wells, Theodora. *Keeping Your Cool Under Fire: Communicating Non-Defensively.* New York: McGraw-Hill, 1980.
This is a lengthy but readable treatment of defensiveness. In addition to amplifying the material in this chapter, Wells discusses defensiveness in organizations and relates the subject to some of the principles of emotions you read about in Chapter 3 of this book.

Chapter Five

Perception: What You See Is What You Get

Study the drawing on the opposite page. What does it look like to you? Do you see a half view of an old woman with a big nose? Or do you see a young woman looking away from you to the left? If you can't see them both, let us help you. The long vertical line that makes up the old lady's nose is the cheek and jaw of the girl; the old woman's mouth is the girl's neckband, and her left eye is the girl's ear. Can you see them both now?

Suppose you saw only one picture at first, the way most people do. What would you have thought about someone who saw the other one? If you weren't familiar with this type of experiment, if you didn't particularly like the person, or if you happened to be feeling impatient that day, you might be tempted to call anyone who disagreed with you wrong, or even crazy. It's possible that you could end up in a nasty argument over who was right, with each of you pushing your own view, never recognizing or admitting that both interpretations are correct.

A lot of communication problems follow this pattern: we tend to ignore the fact that all of us are different and that these differences equip us to view the world from our very own vantage points. Usually we spend more energy defending our own position than understanding another's.

In this chapter we want to help you deal with these problems by giving you some practice in seeing the world through other people's eyes as well as your own. We'll take a look at some of the reasons things appear different to each of us. In our survey we'll explore several areas: How our psychological makeup, personal needs, interests, and biases shape our perceptions; the physiological factors that influence our view of the world; the social roles that affect our image of events, and finally the role culture plays in creating our ideas of what behavior is proper. In doing so we'll cover many of the types of physiological and psychological noise that were described in the communication model you studied in Chapter 1.

The Perception Process

We need to begin our discussion of perception by talking about the gap between ''what is'' and what we know. At one time or another you've probably seen photos of sights not visible to the unaided eye: perhaps an infrared photo of a familiar area or the vastly enlarged image of a minute object taken by an electronic microscope. You've also noticed how certain animals are able to hear sounds and smell odors that are not apparent to humans. Experiences like these remind us that there is much more going on in the world than we are able to experience with our limited senses; that our idea of reality is in fact only a partial one.

Even within the realm of our senses we're only aware of a small part of what is going on around us. For instance, most people who live in large cities find that the noises of traffic, people, and construction soon fade out of awareness. Others can take a walk through the forest without distinguishing one bird's call from another or noticing the differences between various types of vegetation. On a personal level, we've all had the experience of failing to notice something unusual about a friend—perhaps a new hair style or a sad expression—until it's called to our attention.

Sometimes our failure to recognize some events while noticing others comes from not paying attention to important information. But in other cases it simply isn't possible to be aware of everything, no matter how attentive we might be: there is just too much going on for us to attend to everything.

William James said that "to the infant the world is just a big blooming, buzzing confusion." One reason for this is the fact that infants are not yet able to sort out the myriad impressions with which we're all bombarded. As we grow we learn to manage all this data, and as we do so, we begin to make sense out of the world.

Since this ability to organize our perceptions in a useful way is such a critical factor in our ability to function, we need to begin our study of perception by taking a closer look at this process. We can do so by examining the three steps by which we attach meaning to our experiences.

Selection   Since we're exposed to more input than we can possibly manage, the first step in perceiving is to select what data we will attend to. There are several factors that cause us to notice some messages and ignore others.

Stimuli that are *intense* often attract our attention. Something that is louder, larger, or brighter stands out. This explains why—other things being equal—we're more likely to remember extremely tall or short people, and why someone who laughs or talks loudly at a party attracts more attention (not always favorable) than do more quiet guests.

Repetitious stimuli, repetitious stimuli, repetitious stimuli, repetitious stimuli, repetitious stimuli, repetitious stimuli also attract attention.* Just as a quiet but steadily dripping faucet can come to dominate our awareness, people to whom we're frequently exposed become noticeable.

ATTENTION IS ALSO FREQUENTLY RELATED TO contrast OR change IN STIMULATION. Put differently, unchanging people or things become less noticeable. This principle gives an explanation (excuse?) for why we come to take wonderful people for granted when we interact with them frequently. It's only when they stop being so wonderful or go away that we appreciate them.

Motives also determine what information we select from our environment. If you're anxious about being late for a date, you'll notice whatever clocks may be around you, and if you're hungry, you'll become aware of any restaurants, markets, and billboards advertising food in your path. Motives also determine how we perceive people. For example, someone on the lookout for a romantic adventure will be especially aware of attractive potential partners, whereas the same person at a different time might be oblivious to anyone but police or medical personnel in an emergency.

*We borrowed the graphic demonstrations in this and the following paragraph from Dennis Coon's *Introduction to Philosophy* (St. Paul, MN; West Publishing Co., 1977).

Organization   Along with selecting information from the environment, we must arrange that data in some meaningful way. You can see how the principle of organization works by looking at Figure 5–1. A little examination shows that you can either view the picture as one of a vase or two twins, depending on whether you focus on the white or the black areas. In instances such as this we make sense of stimuli by noticing some data that stands out as a ''figure'' against a less striking ''ground.'' The ''vase-face'' drawing is interesting because it allows us to choose between two sets of figure-ground relationships.

This principle of figure-ground organization operates in nonvisual ways, too. Recall, for instance, how certain speech can suddenly stand out from a babble of voices. Sometimes the words are noticeable because they include your name, while at other times they might be spoken by a familiar voice.

In examples like the ones we just mentioned the process of organization is relatively simple. But there are other cases in which messages are ambiguous, having more than one possible way of being organized. You can see a visual example of such an ambiguous stimulus in Figure 5–2. How many ways can you view the boxes? One? Two? Three? Keep looking!

We can see the principle of alternative organizing patterns in human interaction. At ages six and three Ron's children don't yet classify people according to their skin color. They are just as likely to identify a black person, for example, as being tall, wearing glasses, or being a certain age. As they become more socialized, they'll doubtless learn that one common organizing principle used in today's society is race, and when they do, their perceptions of others will change. In the same way it's possible to classify people or behaviors according to many schemes, each of which will result in different

Figure 5–1

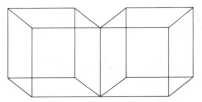

Figure 5–2

consequences. Do you organize according to age, education, occupation, physical attractiveness, astrological sign, or some other scheme? Imagine how different your relationships would be if you didn't use the organizing methods that you just identified.

Interpretation   We've already talked about interpretations in Chapter 1. We stated that there are many ways to interpret a single event. Is the person who smiles at you across a crowded room interested in romance or simply being polite? Is a friend's kidding a sign of affection or an indication of irritation? Should you take an invitation to "Drop by any time" literally or not?

You'll recall that there are several factors that cause us to interpret an event in one way or another:

—*past experience* What meaning have similar events held? If, for example, you've been gouged by landlords in the past, you might be skeptical about an apartment manager's assurances that careful housekeeping will assure the refund of your cleaning deposit.

—*assumptions about human behavior* "People generally do as little work as possible to get by." "In spite of their mistakes, people are doing the best they can." Beliefs like these will shape the way we interpret another's actions.

—*expectations* Anticipation shapes interpretations. If you imagine that your boss is unhappy with your work, you'll probably feel threatened by a request to "see me in my office first thing Monday morning." On the other hand, if you imagine that your work will be rewarded, your weekend will probably be a pleasant one as you anticipate a reward from the boss.

> *I've always admired those reporters who can descend on an area, talk to key people, ask key questions, take samplings of opinions, and then set down an orderly report very much like a road map. I envy this technique and at the same time do not trust it as a mirror of reality. I feel that there are too many realities. What I set down here is true until someone else passes that way and rearranges the world in his own style. In literary criticism the critic has no choice but to make over the victim of his attention into something the size and shape of himself. . . .*
>
> *So much there is to see, but our morning eyes describe a different world than do our afternoon eyes, and surely our wearied evening eyes can only report a weary evening world.*
>
> John Steinbeck, *Travels with Charley*

—*knowledge* If you know that a friend has just been jilted by a lover or been fired from a job, you'll interpret her aloof behavior differently than if you were unaware of what had happened. If you know that an instructor speaks sarcastically to all students, then you won't be as likely to take his remarks personally.

—*personal moods* When you're feeling insecure, the world is a very different place than when you're confident. The same goes for happiness and sadness or any other opposing emotions. The way we feel determines how we interpret events.

Of course, interpretations aren't always accurate; but whether they're correct or not, they shape our thoughts and behavior.

Physiological Influences on Perception

Now that we've explored the psychological process by which we perceive, it's time to look at some of the influences that cause us to select, organize, and interpret information. The first set of influences we need to examine involves our physical makeup. Within the wide range of human similarities, each of us perceives the world in a unique way due to physiological factors. In other words, although the same world exists "out there," each of us receives a different image of it because of our perceptual hardware.

Taste   The sense of taste depends upon a chemical reaction for its information. Taste receptors (*buds*) located in pores in the mouth respond to food that enters each pore by sending a message to the brain. Although we may *think* there are an infinite variety of tastes (recall the last good meal you had), there are only four: sweet, sour, salty, and bitter. Each part of the tongue is sensitive to only one taste.

The degree to which each of us possesses the four different types of taste buds determines how things taste. Not everyone tastes the same things the same way. Older people, for example, taste a wide variety of things as predominantly bitter. This is because the taste buds for sweet, salty, and sour die off and are not as readily replaced, leaving the taste buds for bitter as the primary sources of information.

Differences are not merely a function of age; heredity also plays a role. You can test this by trying the following experiment. From your biology department or a chemical supply house obtain strips of litmus paper treated with the chemical phenyl-thio-carbamide (PTC). (They're very inexpensive.) Give one strip to each member of your group, and have everyone taste their paper at the same time. Now immediately conduct a survey: how many people found the paper salty? How many found it sweet? How many found it bitter? How many found no taste at all? Did anyone find a different taste?

Chances are that to some people the paper tasted bitter, while to others it was sweet, sour, or salty. Somewhat less than half your group probably didn't taste anything at all. If you've inherited a dominant "taster" gene from someone in your family, you'll get one taste or another. Otherwise, the treated paper won't seem any different from the untreated type.

The fact that the paper has different tastes for different people is interesting in itself, but it also has important implications for communication. You can imagine that something similar is true for our taste in foods. Do you remember having a conversation that went something like this:

"Eat your liver, dear, it tastes so good."

"But Ma! I hate liver! It tastes horrible!"

"Don't be foolish, dear. I spent a lot of time in the kitchen fixing it. It's delicious."

"But every time I eat it, it makes me choke! I don't want any."

"You listen to me. This is the best liver money can buy. Now be quiet and eat your dinner. All this 'not liking it' is just in your mind."

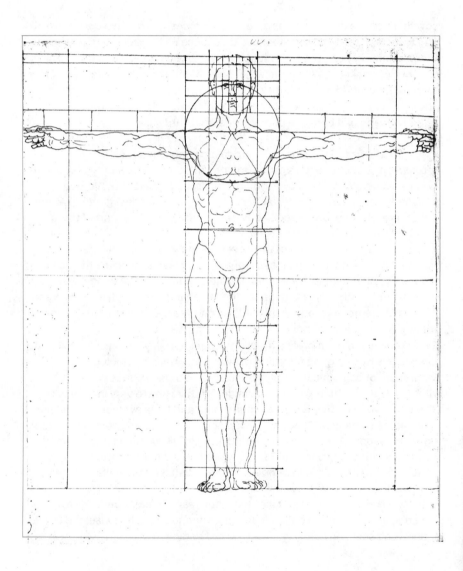

This kind of dialog probably sounds familiar to you. In view of the PTC experiment, you can see its flaw: both mother and child are arguing as if liver tastes the same to everyone. Either the food tastes good or it doesn't—so somebody's wrong. But when you think about the experiment, you begin to get the idea that maybe it just tastes *different.*

What's your favorite food? When was the last time you told someone he was crazy because he didn't like it? How did your remarks affect your communication?

Odor   What's true for taste is also true for your sense of smell. Most people can easily agree about what odors they like the least (burnt rubber or vomit, for example), and to a lesser degree the ones they especially like (fresh strawberries, honeysuckle), but there's no real consistency about whether most smells are good or bad. For example, in one study people ranked their preferences among 132 different odors. Bay leaf (a spice commonly used in cooking) ranged from 9th to 98th; peppermint from 1st to 76th; and raw onion from 5th to 110th. Age and sex seem to play some part in people's odor preferences. Children and men generally like sweeter fruit odors, while women prefer them less sweet; men ranked musky-smelling perfumes higher than women did; and children tolerate odors such as those from feces more than adults do.

Differences like these demonstrate that smells or tastes pleasing to one person can be repulsive to somebody else. So whether it's your perfume, ladies, or your aftershave lotion, men, that provokes the comment "What stinks?" don't be upset—the other person may only be perceiving the odor differently than you do.

Temperature   Like the other senses, sensitivity to temperature varies from person to person; forgetting this can block communication. For example, think of the times you've called someone "chicken" who thought the water was too cold for swimming or gotten angry at someone for turning the heat up or down when you were comfortable.

Again, the root of the problem may be biological. People's sensitivity to temperature varies greatly. Thus, if you're less sensitive to cold, it might be that sixty-five degrees to you feels like fifty-five to somebody else. If people could keep this in mind, they'd have less reason to disagree over who's right about the temperature. Rather than fighting, they could figure out alternative behaviors that would suit everyone involved. (That's why electric blankets with dual controls are so popular.)

It was six men of Indostan
 To learning much inclined,
Who went to see the elephant
 Though all of them were blind
That each by observation
 Might satisfy his mind.

The first approached the elephant
 And, happening to fall
Against the broad and sturdy side,
 At once began to bawl:
"Why, bless me! But the elephant
 Is very much like a wall!"

The second, feeling of the tusk,
 Cried: "Ho! What have we here
So very round and smooth and sharp?
 To me, 'tis very clear,
This wonder of an elephant
 Is very like a spear!"

The third approached the animal,
 And, happening to take
The squirming trunk within his hands
 Thus boldly up he spake:
"I see," quoth he, "the elephant
 Is very like a snake!"

The fourth reached out his eager hand
    And felt about the knee:
"What most this wondrous beast is like
    Is very plain," quoth he:
'Tis clear enough the elephant
    Is very like a tree!"

The fifth who chanced to touch the ear
    Said: "E'en the blindest man
Can tell what this resembles most —
    Deny the fact who can:
This marvel of an elephant
    Is very like a fan!"

The sixth no sooner had begun
    About the beast to grope
Than, seizing on the swinging tail
    That fell within his scope,
"I see," quoth he, "the elephant
    Is very like a rope!"

And so these men of Indostan
    Disputed loud and long,
Each in his own opinion
    Exceeding stiff and strong;
Though each was partly in the right,
    And all were in the wrong.

John G. Saxe

Hearing   Let's continue our study of the senses by examining hearing. We'll try to give you some feeling for how the world sounds to people who hear differently than you do, and then we'll examine the implications this has for communication.

Suppose you have normal hearing. You can represent this visually by holding your book at arm's length and reading what's written below:

LOUDNESS

You should have no trouble reading this comfortably, just as the person with normal hearing has no difficulty understanding others in a conversation. However, it's possible to have a hearing loss without ever knowing it; in fact, it's likely that you know someone who does. To these people the same sounds you hear so easily would be difficult to understand. You can represent how a person with the most common type of loss might hear a word by again holding your book at arm's length and reading this word:

LOU NESS

You probably had to magnify these letters or move closer and also mentally fill in the blanks to understand the word. Likewise, hard-of-hearing people try to understand sounds by magnifying the volume (often with a hearing aid) or by getting closer to the source; they utilize clues in the situation and context to "fill in" sounds they can't hear or are unable to read on a speaker's lips.

The increased noise of our civilization has caused permanent damage to the ears of many people, especially those who spend much of their time in noisy environments—factories, war zones, rock bands, and so on. These people with hearing losses are usually the ones who may have to turn up the television or radio at a level that's uncomfortable for the rest of us.

Forgetting the difference between people's sensitivity to sound can lead to sad consequences. Audiologists and physicians report many cases of children being held back in school for being "slow learners" and punished at home for "not paying attention" when the real problem was that they simply couldn't hear what was going on.

Spend a day experiencing a hearing loss. Put a wad of cotton in each ear (don't push it in too deeply), and notice the difference this makes to your communication. Do you find your mind wandering when you can't follow a conversation clearly? Do you develop the annoying habit of needing to have everything repeated? Do you turn up the radio and TV to a "normal" level and blast others out of the room?

Have you ever wondered how many people you know may have some degree of hearing loss?

Vision   It's obvious that people with uncorrected visual problems see differently than the rest of us. Let Sherri, Ron's wife, tell you how poor vision can affect communication.

I started wearing glasses when I was eight years old, and my eyesight continued to deteriorate until I was about seventeen. So practically all my life I've had to account for communication difficulties because of my very poor vision. (In my last eye test I couldn't even read the big "E" at the top of the chart without my contact lenses!)

When I was young I went through the embarrassment of having "four eyes" and would only put my glasses on to sneak a look at the blackboard. Asking the teacher if I could sit closer to the front would have solved part of the problem, but also would have singled me out again as a glasses-wearer. I stayed quiet, and my grades declined.

I used to love swimming, having grown up with a swimming pool and then living near the ocean. As my vision became worse I swam less and less, though my friends and family would spend whole summers on the beach. I just recently discovered that by wearing a face mask and my contact lenses I could swim again! Those weird, dark things floating in the water really are seaweed! No more explanations to people who just couldn't understand that it's scary to swim when you can hardly see!

Since I've known Ron we've had some experiences that have caused communication problems because of our differences in vision: He has perfect eyesight, and even when I'm wearing contacts he can see better than I.

A few summers ago we drove to Colorado. I would get angry (and frightened) when he continuously passed cars on narrow two-lane roads, and he would get mad at me for following slow-moving cars for thirty minutes without passing. When I explained that I just couldn't see as far up the road as he could, we realized that we didn't see things the same way and that our safety would be threatened if I was to drive the way he wanted me to.

This same problem occurs with freeway and street signs. I can't plan ahead when to turn because I can't see the signs until I'm practically on top of them! Because of this I'm a rather poor navigator, and Ron and I have to be careful to avoid fights when driving together.

I have to sit in the front half of a movie theater to be able to see well. Ron has adjusted to this, but he says he always sat in the back before he met me.

On a camping trip, lying in sleeping bags outdoors:
Ron: "Aren't the stars fantastic?"
Me: "What stars?"

We were camping in Mexico, and Ron had constructed a makeshift shelter with a tarp to cover our sleeping bags in case of bad weather. In the middle of the night it started to pour, and our shelter soon had a puddle of water overflowing onto us. Ron told me to get out, keep dry, get our clothes so they wouldn't get wet, put something on so I wouldn't get wet, help with the tarp, find the flashlight . . . While he was wet and angry at me for being so slow, I was practically in tears trying to explain I couldn't move that fast because I couldn't see!

Sex So far we've taken a look at how your five senses can make the world seem a different place to you and to other people. Now let's talk about another physiological factor that causes us to perceive things differently and show you how it can affect communication.

For some women, the menstrual cycle plays an important role in shaping feelings, and thus affects communication. But women aren't the only ones whose communication is affected by periodic changes in mood. Men, too, go through recognizable mood cycles, even though they aren't marked by obvious physical changes. Although they may not be aware of it, many men seem to go through biologically regulated periods of good spirits followed by equally predictable times of depression. The average length of this cycle is about five weeks, although in some cases it's as short as sixteen days or as

More than 40 years ago, the late Dr. Rex Hersey believed that male factory workers were incorrectly thought to be stable and unchanging in their daily capabilities. For a year, he observed both management and workers, concentrating on a group of men who seemed particularly well-adjusted and at ease in their jobs. Through a combination of four-times-a-day interviews with the workers, regular physical examinations, and a supplementary set of interviews with their families, he arrived at charts for each individual, showing that emotions varied predictably within the rhythm of 24 hours, and within the larger rhythm of a near-monthly cycle of four to six weeks. Low periods were character-ized by apathy, indifference, or a tendency to magnify minor problems out of all proportion. High periods were often marked by a feeling of well-being energy, a lower body weight, and a decreased need for sleep.

Each man tended to deny that he was more or less irritable, more or less amiable, at different points in his cycle, but standardized psychological tests established clearly that he responded very differently to the same life stresses at different times of his cycle. This denial by men of a cyclicity traditionally accepted by women may be an important factor: a two-edged sword for both men and women.

Estelle Ramey, Ph.D., Ms. Magazine

long as two months. However long it may be, this cycle of ups and downs is quite regular.

If you were to ask most men why they were feeling so bad during the low part of their mood cycle, you'd get plenty of reasons: troubles with the family, troubles at work, the state of the economy, the "cussedness" of politicians, or a million other explanations. However reasonable these woes may sound, they're often not the real cause of the problem. Although extremely good or bad events can alter our feelings, more often they're governed by the internal clock each of us carries around.

Although neither men nor women can change these emotional cycles, simply learning to expect them can be a big help in improving communication. When you understand that the cause of a bad mood is predictable and caused by physiological causes, you can plan for it. You'll know that every few weeks your patience will be shorter, and you'll be less likely to blame your bad moods on innocent bystanders. The people around you can also learn to expect your periodic lows. If they can attribute them to biology, maybe they won't get angry at you.

Other Physiological Factors   So far we've only looked at the most obvious physical differences that influence our perception. Even a casual second look shows that there are many other ways in which the state of our bodies determine how we perceive the world and thus shape the way we communicate.

Health   Recall the last time you came down with a cold, flu, or some other ailment. Do you remember how different you felt? You probably had much less energy. It's likely that you felt less sociable, and your thinking was probably a bit slower than usual. It's easy to see that these kinds of changes have a strong impact on how you relate to others. Obvious as this seems, it's easy to forget that someone else may be behaving differently due to illness. In the same way, it's important to let others know when you don't feel well so they can give you the understanding you need.

Fatigue   Just as being ill can affect your relationships, so too can being overly tired. Again we don't want to belabor an obvious point, but it's important to recognize the fact that you or someone else may behave differently when fatigued. Trying to deal with important issues at such a time can get you into trouble.

Age   One reason older people view the world differently than younger ones is because of their generally greater scope and number of experiences. But there are also age-related physical differences that shape perceptions. Although neither Ron nor Neil is exactly an old geezer, each of us has had his share of troubles with his kids due to age. If you've been around children, you know that their energy level is quite high, to put it mildly. To us it often seems as if our children are superactive—"little maniacs," we've sometimes called them. To the children, of course, adults must often seem like old bores. What's wrong with someone who doesn't want to wrestle or play hide and seek five hours a day?

Height To see the role height plays in perception, imagine two people attending a parade: one is six feet three inches tall, the other five feet two. Clearly what could be an enjoyable time for the first person would probably be a frustrating experience for the shorter companion. Countless other activities are affected by height, such as dancing, attending the theatre, and participation in many sports. What does all this have to do with interpersonal communication? It's easy to see how failing to recognize the different worlds in which shorter and taller people live can lead to unnecessary frustration. Think, for instance, of the troubles children encounter in a world designed for people twice their size. Drinking from a fountain, climbing into a chair, or even going to the bathroom can be chores. Parents would be wise to remember these difficulties before blaming kids for not being quick or tidy.

Hunger This factor is an obvious one, at least once you consider it. People often get grumpy when they haven't eaten and sleepy after stuffing themselves. Yet how often do we forget these simple facts and try to conduct important business at times when our stomachs are running our lives?

Daily cycles Are you a "morning person" or a "night person"? Most of us can answer this question pretty easily, and there's a good physiological reason for doing so. Each of us is in a daily cycle in which all sorts of changes constantly occur: body temperature, sexual drive, alertness, tolerance to stress, and mood. Most of these changes are due to hormonal cycles. For

"This is nothing. When I was your age, the snow was so deep it came up to my chin!"

instance, adrenal hormones, which affect feelings of stress, are secreted at higher rates during some hours. In the same manner the male and female sex hormones enter our systems at variable rates. We often aren't conscious of these changes, but they surely govern the way we relate toward each other. Once we're aware that our own cycles and those of others govern our feelings and behavior, it becomes possible to run our lives so that we deal with important issues at the most effective times.

Social Roles

So far you've seen how everyone's physiological makeup varies and how these variations can block communication if we're not careful. But besides our physical makeup there's another set of perceptual factors that can lead to communication breakdowns. From almost the time we're born, each of us is indirectly taught a whole set of roles that we'll be expected to play. In one sense this collection of prescribed parts is necessary because it enables a society to function smoothly and provides the security that comes from knowing what's expected of you. But in another way having roles defined in advance can lead to wide gaps in understanding. When roles become unquestioned and rigid, people tend to see the world from their own viewpoint, having no experiences that show them how other people view it. Naturally, in such a situation communication suffers.

Sex Roles   In every society one of the most important factors in determining roles is sex. How should a woman act? What kinds of behavior go with being a man? Until recently most of us never questioned the answers our society gave to these questions. Boys are made of "snips and snails and puppy-dog tails" and grow up to be the breadwinners of families; little girls are "sugar and spice and everything nice," and their mothers are irrational, intuitive, and temperamental. Not everyone fits into these patterns, but in the past the patterns became well established and were mainly unquestioned by most people.

But in recent years many men and women have found that following these roles caused them to live in different worlds that only partially meet, and they've found this kind of life unsatisfying. People are more and more willing to see themselves and others as *androgynous*—possessing a mixture of traits that have previously been considered exclusively masculine and feminine. Thus, it is becoming more common and acceptable for women to behave assertively, pursue careers, and choose not to take primary responsibility for raising children, while many men are beginning to feel comfortable expressing their emotions, becoming deeply involved in child care, and so on.

Occupational Roles   The kind of work we do often governs our view of the world. Imagine five people taking a walk through the park. One, a botanist, is fascinated by the variety of trees and plants. The zoologist is on the lookout for interesting animals. The third, a meteorologist, keeps an eye on the sky, noticing changes in the weather. The fourth companion, a psychologist, is

I have noticed
that men
somewhere around forty
tend to come in from the field
with a sigh
and removing their coat in the hall
call into the kitchen

> you were right
> grace
> it ain't out there
> just like you've always said

and she
with the children gone at last
breathless
puts her hat on her head

> the hell it ain't

coming and going
they pass
in the doorway

Ric Masten

totally unaware of the goings-on of nature, instead concentrating on the interaction between the people in the park. The fifth person, being a pickpocket, quickly takes advantage of the others' absorption to make some money. There are two lessons in this little story. The first, of course, is to watch your wallet carefully. The second is that our occupational roles govern our perceptions.

Even within the same occupational setting, the different roles that participants have can affect their experience. Consider a typical college classroom, for example: the experiences of the instructor and students often are quite dissimilar. Having dedicated a large part of their lives to their work, most professors see their subject matter—whether French literature, physics, or speech communication—as vitally important. Students who are taking the course to satisfy a general education requirement may view the subject quite differently; maybe as one of many obstacles that stand between them and a degree, maybe as a chance to meet new people. Another difference centers on the amount of knowledge possessed by the parties. To an instructor who has taught the course many times, the material probably seems extremely simple; but to students encountering it for the first time, it may seem strange and confusing. Toward the end of a semester or quarter the instructor might be pressing onward hurriedly to cover all the material in the course, while the students are fatigued from their studies and ready to move more slowly. We don't need to spell out the interpersonal strains and stresses that come from such differing perceptions.

Perhaps the most dramatic illustration of how occupational roles shape perception occurred in 1971. Stanford psychologist Philip Zimbardo recruited a group of middle-class, well-educated young men, all white except for one Oriental. He randomly chose eleven to serve as "guards" in a mock prison set up in the basement of Stanford's psychology building. He issued the guards uniforms, handcuffs, whistles, and billy clubs. The remaining ten subjects became "prisoners" and were placed in rooms with metal bars, bucket toilets, and cots.

Zimbardo let the guards establish their own rules for the experiment. The rules were tough: no talking during meals, rest periods, and after lights out. Head counts at 2:30 A.M. Troublemakers received short rations.

Faced with these conditions, the prisoners began to resist. Some barricaded their doors with beds. Others went on hunger strikes. Several ripped off their identifying number tags. The guards reacted to the rebellion by clamping down hard on protesters. Some turned sadistic, physically and verbally abusing the prisoners. They threw prisoners into solitary confinement. Others forced prisoners to call each other names and clean out toilets with their bare hands.

Within a short time the experiment had become reality for both prisoners and guards. Several inmates experienced stomach cramps and lapsed into uncontrollable weeping. Others suffered from headaches, and one broke out in a head-to-toe rash after his request for early "parole" was denied by the guards.

The experiment was scheduled to go on for two weeks, but after six days Zimbardo realized that what had started as a simulation had become too intense. "I knew by then that they were thinking like prisoners and not like people," he said. "If we were able to demonstrate that pathological behavior could be produced in so short a time, think of what damage is being done in 'real' prisons . . ."

This dramatic exercise in which twenty-one well-educated, middle-class citizens turned almost overnight into sadistic bullies and demoralized victims tells us that *how* we think is a function of our roles in society. It seems that *what* we are is determined largely by society's designation of *who* we are. Fortunately, many officials in the field of law enforcement are aware of the perceptual blindness that can come with one's job. These professionals have developed programs that help to overcome the problem, as the following reading illustrates.

Field Experiments: Preparation for the Changing Police Role

We are all aware that it is extremely difficult to immerse the average policeman into situations that will reveal the feelings of the down-and-outer, the social outcast, the have-nots, and show us their perspective of normal law-enforcement procedures. Obviously the officer, in his police role, would not fit into a ghetto of any kind. But suppose he were a man with a great deal of courage, willing for the sake of experimentation to become a bum, a skid row habitant.

Our Covina officers who were willing to become skid row habitants were carefully selected and conditioned for the role they were about to play. Each man was given three dollars with which to purchase a complete outfit of pawn shop clothing. The only new article of attire he was allowed was footwear—reject tennis shoes purchased for a few small coins. Among his other props were such items as a shopping bag filled with collected junk, and a wine bottle camouflaged with a brown paper sack.

Conditioned and ready, our men, assigned in pairs, moved into the Los Angeles skid row district. They soon discovered that when they tried to leave the area, walking a few blocks into the legitimate retail sections, they were told, "Go back where you belong!" Our men knew in reality they were not "bums," but they found that other citizens quickly categorized them and treated them accordingly. Some women, when approached on the sidewalk and asked for a match, stepped out into the street rather than offer a reply, much less a light for a smoke.

During the skid row experiment, our men ate in the rescue missions, and sat through the prayer services with other outcasts and derelicts. They roamed the streets and the alleys, and discovered many leveling experiences. Some were anticipated, others were not. Perhaps the most meaningful experience of the skid row exercise occurred to Tom Courtney, a young juvenile officer with five years' police service.

It was dusk, and Tom and his partner were sauntering back to a prearranged gathering place. Feeling a little sporty, the pair decided to "polish off" the bottle of wine. They paused in a convenient parking lot and Tom tipped the bottle up. As if from nowhere, two uniformed policemen materialized before the surprised pair. Tom and his partner were spread-eagled against a building and searched. Forgetting the admonishment not to reveal identities and purpose unless absolutely necessary, Tom panicked and identified himself.

Later, Tom found it difficult to explain why he was so quick in his revelation. "You wouldn't understand," he told me; then blurted out that he "thought he might get shot."

I found it difficult to receive this as a rational explanation, especially since Tom stated that the officers, while firm, were courteous at all times. With some additional prodding, Tom admitted that as he was being searched, he suddenly thought of every negative thing he had ever heard about a policeman. He even perceived a mental flash of a newspaper headline: "Police Officer Erroneously Shot While on Field Experiment."

"I know better now," Tom continued, "but when you feel that way about yourself, you believe—you believe."

I attempted to rationalize with Tom his reason for fear. I asked if he was certain that the officers were courteous. He replied in the affirmative, but added, "They didn't smile, or tell me what they were going to do next." Tom had discovered a new emotional reaction within his own personal make-up, and it left a telling impression.

Today, Tom Courtney is still telling our department personnel, "For God's sake, smile when you can. And above all, tell the man you're shaking down what you are going to do. Take the personal threat out of the encounter, if you can."

Equally important as Tom's experience, I believe, is the lesson we learned about personal judgments. Our men in the "Operation Empathy" experiment found they were adjudged by the so-called normal population as "being like" all the other inmates of skid row, simply because their appearance was representative.

Perhaps we would all do well to heed the lesson, for now, more than at any other time in our history, policemen must guard against the natural tendency to lump people into categories simply because they look alike.

The invisible barrier that stands between the law enforcer and the law breaker is being bridged through experimentation. Human beings are dealing with human beings, and successful field experiments, conducted by law enforcement, have shown that empathy, understanding another's emotions and feelings, can, in some potentially volatile situations, play an important role towards nonviolence in police-involved situations.

R. Fred Ferguson, *Chief of Police, Riverside Police Department, Riverside, California. Formerly Chief, Covina Police Department, Covina, California.*

23 Judges Shaken by Night in Nevada Prison

RENO (UPI)—More than one of the 23 shaken judges from across the country who spent the night at the Nevada State Prison said Thursday it should be torn down along with others in the country.

"Appalling."

"My conscience is scarred."

"Am I glad to get out of there. I didn't get five minutes sleep."

These were typical comments from the judges as they climbed off the bus in the morning after returning to Reno from the state prison in Carson City.

The judges, all attending a graduate seminar at the University of Nevada in Reno, volunteered to spend the night in prison to learn more about the prisoners' point of view.

"After that experience I'm going to work for total reform of our prisons," vowed Tom Lee of Miami.

"I was in a cage like an animal," said Newton Vickers of Topeka, who complained the prisoners "screamed and rattled cans against the wall all night and I couldn't sleep."

"Ten years in there is like 100 or maybe 200," he said. "They should take two bull-dozers out there and tear it down."

Cultural Differences

So far you've seen how both physiological factors and social roles can make the world a different place for each of us. But there's another kind of perceptual gap that often blocks communication—the gap between people from different backgrounds. Every culture has its own view, its own way of looking at the world, which is unique. When we remember these differing cultural perspectives, they can be a great way of learning more about both ourselves and others. But at times it's easy to forget that people everywhere don't see things the way we do; as the following story shows, at such times this cultural barrier can lead to trouble.

''I don't understand it. Why didn't he marry both of them?''

Beware of a Crocodile Bag

There was a girl they all said later was American. She went stepping down the street ahead of me, young, with a good figure, well covered. She was well dressed too, and she had a way of working her haunches as she walked that rather singled her out. I had been specially conscious of her for the past hundred yards or so because there was a man following along close behind her who found her irresistible—it was clear to see in the way he was jockeying for position, sidling up on her right, whipping over to the left again, only to be foiled each time by some clumsy interfering pedestrian or a lamp-standard or whatever it might be. I knew what he planned to do, too.

This was in Athens and the three of us—first the girl, next the man I speak of, and then myself bring up the rear—were walking across the top of Constitution Square along with a whole crowd of others. On we went, the girl wiggling, the man set on his little plan, head held rigid and a bit to one side, one arm behind his back—she must surely have been aware of him as over the road she wobbled and on to the further pavement, down the side of the Hotel Grande Bretagne. The man

was most certainly Greek and I guessed that the girl could not be. He was coming right up alongside her now, very close . . . and then suddenly, without warning, the girl spun on her heel in a ninety-degree turn and the next moment she would be in at the Grande Bretagne side-entrance, safe in one of the little segments of those revolving doors. It all but caught the man off-balance: but the Greek mind is very quick and he reacted instantly. He had to move before she could slip away for ever. So his arm shot out and he pinched her smartly on the behind.

What should a girl do when this happens in the public street? In Athens it is an occupational risk all girls run and I have had talks with several of them about it. They mostly give the same answer. Nothing. They are very sensible about it: they realize that if they dress provocatively and walk provocatively, someone is likely to be provoked into pinching them. An Athenian girl can recognize a pincher a block distant. He is quite easy to identify, it seems—the slightly furtive sideways advance, the hand behind the back symbolically out of sight, as it were, the manoeuvring—girls quickly learn to take evasive action, such as keeping away from shop-windows or points where they could get cornered, and the nervous ones certainly welcomed the full flaring skirts

with the layers of stiff frilly petticoat underneath when that fashion came in. But those narrow, hobbling skirts. . . . I have questioned several Athenians. They say it is better to come up from behind if you can. I can see the sense in that. *"A mezedaki,"* they are apt to call it: a little *hors d'oeuvre*. It is a game, really: a game for two persons, whether the second person wishes to play or not. And once the pincher has got his pinch in, or else the girl has outwitted him and escaped, he does not follow her up. He is content with his pinch, just as a picador is content with his pic, or the banderillero with banderillas. Most girls say there is only one rule—if she loses she must do so with grace. No shrieks, no angry cries. She must just walk on as if nothing whatever had happened. The game is over. She has lost.

The game is not always very well understood by foreign ladies visiting Athens. The case of the American girl who had fled to the safety of the Grande Bretagne underlines my point. Her thinking was confused. She was not in the wrong, maybe, but she reacted wrongly. When the man landed his pinch and won, she lost her head as well as the game. She went black in the face and did something very shocking. Everyone present gasped. She was carrying a big crocodile travel-bag—a splendid thing with metal clasps and buckles, and so on. She swung this bag of hers in a great arc and caught the man over the head with it. He went to the ground instantly. She tossed her head furiously and as she turned to wobble through the revolving doors to refuge, the man was rising to his feet again and wagging his head in his bewilderment.

"I only pinched her. . . ." he said plaintively, looking round at us.

We were quite a little crowd by now—the hotel doorman, taxi-drivers, other passersby, a policeman.

"Tch-tch! . . ." the people went, wagging their heads too and staring through the big plate-glass windows at the girl's retreating back. What sort of girl could she be? A taxi-driver helped the poor man up, brushing him down.

"Did she hurt you, then?" he asked with great solicitude.

Peter Mayne

A pinch on the behind led to one cultural misunderstanding. A student described another one, which he swears is true.

He was visiting Lagos, Nigeria, and while walking down the street one afternoon he came upon two men, one a Nigerian and the other an American. The men were fighting wildly and cursing at each other, each in his own language. The police had come and seemed to be ready to take both fighters away when an English-speaking taxi driver saved the day.

After talking to both men, he explained the story: It seems that the American was hitchhiking through town, signaling for a ride the only way he knew—standing at the roadside with his thumb sticking out where the drivers could easily see it. Unfortunately for him, in Nigeria this gesture doesn't mean the same thing as in the United States. In fact, its closest equivalent in our terms is what we call "the finger." So, although the American meant to politely ask for a ride, instead he had insulted the Nigerian's honor.

Thanks to the taxi driver, who ought to be working for the U.N., the last time our student saw the two former enemies they were heading arm in arm into a bar. They'd learned by experience that to members of different cultures even little differences can have big consequences when you're not aware of them.

After looking at these examples, you can see that different cultures have customs that can cause trouble for the unaware foreigner. But you don't have to go this far from home to come across people with differing cultural perspectives. Within this country there are many subcultures, and the members of each one have backgrounds that cause them to see things in unique ways.

Probably the clearest example of these differing perceptions is the gap between Americans of different ethnic backgrounds. Even to people of goodwill it seems that there's a barrier which makes understanding difficult; there just seem to be too many different experiences that separate us. If this is true, how can we possibly understand each other?

"Relativity." Here we have three forces of gravity working perpendicularly to one another. Three earth-planes cut across each other at right-angles, and human beings are living on each of them. It is impossible for the inhabitants of different worlds to walk or sit or stand on the same floor, because they have differing conceptions of what is horizontal and what is vertical. Yet they may well share the use of the same staircase. On the top staircase illustrated here, two people are moving side by side and in the same direction, and yet one of them is going downstairs and the other upstairs. Contact between them is out of the question, because they live in different worlds and therefore can have no knowledge of each other's existence.

M. C. Escher

Black Like Me

Writer John Howard Griffin found one way to bridge the gulf that separates whites and blacks. Realizing the impossibility of truly understanding the black experience by simply reading or talking about it, he decided to go one big step further. "How else except by becoming a Negro could a white man hope to learn the truth?" he wrote. "The only way I could see to bridge the gap was to become a Negro."

And this he did. Through a series of treatments that included doses of skin-darkening drugs, applications of stain, and shaving off the hair on his head, Griffin transformed himself into a black man—or at least a man with black skin.

In the following selections from his book you'll read some of Griffin's experiences as a black man in the southern United States in 1959. The narrative begins as he takes the first steps into a new world.

November 8 . . . I caught the bus into town, choosing a seat halfway to the rear. As we neared Canal, the car began to fill with whites. Unless they could find a place to themselves or beside another white, they stood in the aisle.

A middle-aged woman with stringy gray hair stood near my seat. She wore a clean but faded print house dress that was hoisted to one side as she clung to an overhead pendant support. Her face looked tired and I felt uncomfortable. As she staggered with the bus's movement my lack of gallantry tormented me. I half rose from my seat to give it to her, but Negroes behind me frowned disapproval. I realized I was "going against the race" and the subtle tug-of-war became instantly clear. If the whites would not sit with us, let them stand. When they became tired enough or uncomfortable enough, they would eventually take seats beside us and soon see that it was not so poisonous after all. But to give them your seat was to let them win. I slumped back under the intensity of their stares.

But my movement had attracted the white woman's attention. For an instant our eyes met. I felt sympathy for her, and thought I detected sympathy in her glance. The exchange blurred the barriers of race (so new to me) long enough for me to smile and vaguely indicate the empty seat beside me, letting her know she was welcome to accept it.

Her blue eyes, so pale before, sharpened and she spat out, "What're you looking at me like *that* for?"

I felt myself flush. Other white passengers craned to look at me. The silent onrush of hostility frightened me.

"I'm sorry," I said, staring at my knees. "I'm not from here." The pattern of her skirt turned abruptly as she faced the front.

"They're getting sassier every day," she said loudly. Another woman agreed and the two fell into conversation. . . .

I learned a strange thing—that in a jumble of unintelligible talk, the word "nigger" leaps out with electric clarity. You always hear it and always it stings. And always it casts the person using it into a category of brute ignorance. I thought with some amusement that if these two women only knew what they were revealing about themselves to every Negro on that bus, they would have been outraged.

November 10–12 Two days of incessant walking, mostly looking for jobs. I wanted to discover what sort of work an educated Negro, nicely dressed, could find. I met no rebuffs, only gentleness when they informed me they could not use my services as typist, bookkeeper, etc.

November 14 My money was running low so I decided to cash some travelers checks before leaving for Mississippi. The banks were closed, since it was past noon on Saturday, but I felt I would have no difficulty with travelers checks in any of the larger stores, especially those on Dryades where I had traded and was known as a customer.

I took the bus to Dryades and walked down it, stopping at the dime store where I'd made most of my purchases. The young white girl came forward to wait on me.

"I need to cash a travelers check," I said, smiling.

"We don't cash any checks of any kind," she said firmly.

"But a travelers check is perfectly safe," I said.

"We just don't cash checks," she said and turned away.

"Look, you know me. You've waited on me. I need some money."

"You should have gone to the bank."

"I didn't know I needed the money until after the banks closed," I said.

I knew I was making a pest of myself, but I could scarcely believe this nice young lady could be so unsympathetic, so insolent when she discovered I did not come in to buy something.

"I'll be glad to buy a few things," I said.

She called up to the bookkeeping department on an open mezzanine. "Hey! Do we cash travelers ch_____"

"No!" the white woman shouted back.

"Thank you for your kindness," I said and walked out.

I went into one store after the other along Dryades and Rampart Streets. In every store their smiles turned to grimaces when they saw I meant not to buy but to cash a check. It was not their refusal—I could understand that. It was the bad manners they displayed. I began to feel desperate and resentful. They would have

cashed a travelers check without hesitation for a white man. Each time they refused me, they implied clearly that I had probably come by these checks dishonestly and they wanted nothing to do with them or me. . . .

[Later that day Griffin takes a bus to Hattiesburg, Mississippi, which he has been told is the most oppressive part of the South for the black man.]

My room was upstairs in a wooden shanty structure that had never known paint. From the tavern below a man improvised a ballad about "poor Mack Parker . . . overcome with passion . . . his body in the creek."

"Oh Lord," a woman said in the quiet that followed, her voice full of sadness and awe.

"Lordy . . . Lordy . . ." a man said in a hushed voice, as though there were nothing more he could say.

Canned jazz blared through the street with a monstrous high-strutting rhythm that pulled at the viscera. The board floor squeaked under my footsteps. I switched on the light and looked into a cracked piece of mirror bradded with bent nails to the wall. The bald Negro stared back at me from its mottled sheen. I knew I was in hell. Hell could be no more lonely or hopeless, no more agonizingly estranged from the world of order and harmony.

The music consumed in its blatant rhythm all other rhythms, even that of the heartbeat. I wondered how all of this would look to the casual observer, or to the whites in their homes. "The niggers are whooping it up over on Mobile Street tonight," they

might say. "They're happy." Or, as one scholar put it, "Despite their lowly status, they are capable of living jubilantly." Would they see the immense melancholy that hung over the quarter, so oppressive that men had to dull their sensibilities in noise or wine or sex or gluttony in order to escape it? The laughter had to be gross or it would turn to sobs, and to sob would be to realize, and to realize would be to despair. So the noise poured forth like a jazzed-up fugue, louder and louder to cover the whisper in every man's soul, "You are black. You are condemned." This is what the white man mistook for "jubilant living" and called "whooping it up."

Words of the state song hummed through my memory:

"Way down South in Mississippi,
    Cotton blossoms white in the sun,
We all love our Mississippi,
    Here we'll stay where livin' is fun.
The evening stars shine brighter,
    And glad is every dewy morn,
For way down South in Mississippi,
    Folks are happy they have been born."

December 1 I developed the technique of zigzaggin back and forth. In my bag I kept a damp sponge, dyes, cleansing cream and Kleenex. It was hazardous, but it was the only way to traverse an area both as Negro and white. As I traveled, I would find an isolated spot, perhaps an alley at night or the brush beside a highway, and quickly apply the dye to face, hands and legs, then rub off and reapply until it was firmly anchored in my pores. I would go through the area as a Negro and then, usually at night, remove the dyes with cleansing cream and tissues and pass through the same area as a white man.

I was the same man, whether white or black. Yet when I was white, I received the brotherly-love smiles and the privileges from whites and the hate stares or obsequiousness from the Negroes. And when I was a Negro, the whites judged me fit for the junk heap, while the Negroes treated me with great warmth.

As the Negro Griffin, I walked up the steep hill to the bus station in Montgomery to get the schedule for buses to Tuskegee. I received the information from a polite clerk and turned away from the counter.

"Boy!" I heard a woman's voice, harsh and loud.

I glanced toward the door to see a large, matriarchal woman, elderly and impatient. Her pinched face grimaced and she waved me to her.

"Boy, come here. Hurry!"
Astonished, I obeyed.

"Get those bags out of the cab," she ordered testily, seeming outraged with my lack of speed.

Without thinking, I allowed my face to spread to a grin as though overjoyed to serve her. I carried her bags to the bus and received three haughty dimes. I thanked her profusely. Her eyebrows knitted with irritation and she finally waved me away. . . .

Suddenly I had had enough. Suddenly I could stomach no more of this degradation—not of myself but of all men who were black like me. Abruptly I turned and walked away. The large bus station was crowded with humanity. In the men's room, I entered one of the cubicles and locked the door. For a time I was

safe, isolated; for a time I owned the space around me, though it was scarcely more than that of a coffin. In medieval times, men sought sanctuary in churches. Nowadays, for a nickel, I could find sanctuary in a colored restroom. Then, sanctuary had the smell of incense-permeated walls. Now it had the odor of disinfectant.

The irony of it hit me. I was back in the land of my forefathers, Georgia. The town of Griffin was named for one of them. Too, I a Negro, carried the name hated by all Negroes, for former Governor Griffin (no kin that I would care to discover) devoted himself heroically to the task of keeping Negroes "in their place." Thanks in part to his efforts, this John Griffin celebrated a triumphant return to the land from which his people had sprung by seeking sanctuary in a toilet cubicle at the bus station.

John Howard Griffin

How valid do you think Griffin's experiences are in terms of your own life? His experiment took place in the Deep South of 1959, and times have certainly changed since then. But to what extent is the world still a different place to whites and blacks today? How about other groups—Mexican-Americans, Orientals, Native Americans, old people, military men and women. Do you ever find yourself prejudging or being prejudged before getting acquainted with someone from a different sector of society?

Perhaps by sharing the personal experiences of others in your group you can gain a more personal insight into how people from different subcultures view life in your community, not only in terms of discrimination, but also in terms of values, behavioral norms, and political and economic issues. How would life be different if you were of a different race or religion, social or economic class? See if you can imagine.

But talking can enable us to understand another person's viewpoint only to a certain degree. To comprehend what it's truly like to be someone else you have to almost become that person the way Griffin did. Have you ever read Mark Twain's famous story of *The Prince and the Pauper*? If you have, you'll remember what an education the young prince had when he was mistaken for a young peasant and treated accordingly. In the same way, think of the huge growth in tolerance that would result if the rich could become poor for a bit, if teachers could recall their student days, if whites could become black.

Total role reversals aren't likely to happen, but it's possible to create experiences that give a good picture of another's perspective. The story of one Iowa schoolteacher and her class illustrates the point. Shortly after Martin Luther King's assassination in 1968, Jane Elliott wanted to make sure her third graders never became prone to the sickness that caused such events. But how could she do this? Everyone in the small town of Riceville was white, and most of her eight-year-olds had never really known blacks. How could she bring home to them the nature of prejudice?

Her solution was to divide the class into two groups: one containing all the children with blue eyes, and the other made up of the brown-eyed students. Then for the next few days she treated the brown-eyes as better people. They all sat in the front of the room, had second helpings at lunch, got five extra minutes of recess, and received extra praise for their work from Mrs. Elliott. At the same time the blue-eyes were the butt of both subtle and obvious discrimination. Besides the back-row seats, skimpy meals, and other such practices, the blue-eyes never received praise for their schoolwork from Mrs. Elliott, who seemed to find something wrong with everything they did. "What can you expect from a blue-eyed person?" was her attitude. The level of the blue-eyed children's schoolwork dropped almost immediately.

At first the children treated the experiment as a game. But shortly they changed from cooperative, thoughtful people into small but very prejudiced bigots. Classmates who had always been best friends stopped playing with each other and even quit walking to school together.

After the level of intolerance had grown painfully high, Mrs. Elliott changed the rules. Now the blue-eyed people were on top and the brown-eyes were inferior. And soon the tables were turned, with children who had only days before been the object of discrimination now being bigots themselves.

Finally Mrs. Elliott ended the experiment. When she asked the children if they wanted to go back to the old days, where everyone was the same, the class answered with a resounding ''Yes!'' Now they really knew what discrimination was, and they didn't like it.

Role Reversal

Walk a mile in another person's moccasins. Find a group that is foreign to you, and try to become a member of it for a while.

If you're down on the police, see if your local department has a ride-along program where you can spend several hours on patrol with one or two officers.

If you think the present state of education is a mess, become a teacher yourself. Maybe an instructor will give you the chance to plan one or more classes.

If you're adventuresome, follow the example of the men in the preceding article and become a bum for a day. See how you're treated.

If you're a political conservative, try getting involved in a radical organization; if you're a radical, check out the conservatives.

Whatever group you join, try to become part of it as best you can. Don't just observe. Get *into* the philosophy of your new role and see how it feels. You may find that all those weird people aren't so strange after all.

Two Views

1. Choose a disagreement you presently have with another person or group. The disagreement might be a personal one—such as an argument about how to settle a financial problem or who is to blame for a present state of affairs—or it might be a dispute over a contemporary public issue, such as the right of women to obtain abortions on demand or the value of capital punishment.

2. In 300 words or so describe your side of the issue. State why you believe as you do, just as if you were presenting your position to an impartial jury.

3. Now take 300 words or so to describe in the first-person singular how the *other* person sees the same issue. For instance, if you are a religious person, write this section as if you were an atheist: For a short while get in touch with how the other person feels and thinks.

4. Now show the description you wrote in step 3 to your "opponent," the person whose beliefs are different from yours. Have that person read your account and correct any statements that don't reflect his position accurately. Remember, you're doing this so that you can more clearly understand how the issue looks to the other person.

5. Make any necessary corrections in the account you wrote in step 3, and again show it to your partner. When he agrees that you understand his position, have him sign your paper to indicate this.

6. Now record your conclusions to this experiment. Has this perceptual shift made any difference in how you view the issue or how you feel about your partner?

So far we've talked about the many ways that differing perceptions can block communication. We've tried to show you that even though we all inhabit separate worlds, understanding each other isn't a hopeless task. You've seen how many people have learned to experience perspectives different from their own and in doing so have grown closer to others.

But empathy isn't easy, especially when it's most needed. Your own experience almost certainly shows you that the times when you disagree most strongly with someone are the times when it's hardest to see the other side. The tendency is to dig in and defend your side, to show that you're right and your opponent is wrong.

We want to close this chapter on perception with a selection that shows one way to go beyond this either-or, two-valued orientation. The method that Paul Reps describes is a paradoxical tool because on the one hand it seems too simple really to work, and on the other, making the effort to try it can be difficult. As you read about these simple Japanese children, think about how you can apply their method to your life.

"You're wrong" means "I don't understand you"—I'm not seeing what you're seeing. But there is nothing wrong with you, you are simply not me and that's not wrong.

Hugh Prather

Pillow Education in Rural Japan

How do you solve your problems?

In growing up, as much as we do grow up mentally, each of us has personal difficulties and social problems in relation with those about us.

In rural Japan a group of children are meeting their difficulties in a splendid way and even teaching their parents how to do so.

They are using a method of thinking for themselves that works. If someone has done a child an injustice, if his feelings have been hurt, if he is in pain, if his or her father is quarreling—anything becomes the subject of the study. They have no name for it, but since it is done with a pillow it might be called pillow education.

A pillow has four sides and a middle. A problem has four approaches and a middle.

For example: A child is slow in his school work. It is his turn to show the group how he is thinking through this situation. He sits before the pillow, placing his hand at 1.

"Suppose I can't think quickly," he says. "If I place here at 1, "I can't think quickly,' then this may change at some time."

"Here at 2," he continues, placing his hand in the 2 position, "is the place where I can think quickly and easily."

In doing this, the child has objectified a handicap. He takes a look at it instead of letting it corrode inside. He also has imagined the possibility of his difficulty resolving.

He continues: "If 1 is where I can't think quickly and 2 is the place where I can, then I will say that here, 3, is a situation where I can think both slowly and quickly, where 1 and 2 are together."

This third step (the 3 place on the pillow) merges the opposites 1 and 2, just as 2 reverses the problem originally placed at 1. This is education in action done by the individual for himself or herself. There are as many girls as boys in the group.

It is a fact that most adults can only think to 2: white 1, black 2; right 1, wrong 2. "If I am right as I am, 1, you are wrong, 2." Entire lives are lived with this kind of thinking. Such dichotomy, either-or, right-wrong, often results in private and public unresolved differences.

When we consider the millions of dead in recent wars from a few leaders not being able to think beyond 2, we see how urgently such education is needed.

"You say you are right, father, and our neighbor is wrong," the child tells his father who is in a property dispute. "But may there not also be a place where you are wrong and he is right. And both of you may be wrong and both right. And at still another place, 4, all this may be forgotten."

"What are you talking about?" asks the father.

The child gets out a pillow. In a few weeks the father, considerably interested, has visited the school.

Such sharp thinking came from a very young child. He had a method of thinking. If he finds no difficulty to solve for himself during the week, he begins looking for one. When called on in class, he doesn't like to be without a subject he has worked on.

The child reasons not in numbers but in a relational sequence of four steps: wrong, 1; right, 2; both wrong and right, 3; and neither wrong nor right, 4. He does this as if walking a 4-step figure with his hand and with his mind.

In conclusion each child summarizes his presentation by cupping his hands in the middle of the pillow ( ), affirming an unnamed center from which 1, 2, 3, 4 emerge. It is as if he holds the complete problem in his own hands at the center of the pillow.

He then places the hand at 4, 3, 2, 1 and concludes by saying, "All these are gloriously affirmed," or "Each of these steps is good."

It is a tremendous relief to the child to be able to reverse his thinking and not be continually held in one viewpoint. In such kind of problem-solving, "nothing is the matter," their mentor says. A rebellious child joining the others invariably becomes gentle in a few weeks.

The number of students has grown from 3 to more than 30. The meetings are a happy time. Students are entirely unhesitant about making personal problems public.

All kinds of subjects come before the pillow: Hunger and not hungry, beauty and ugliness, environment and mood, a bucket of water and a sea of water, blood of Orientals and blood of Occidentals, after my death the world will be and will not be—anything that troubles or concerns the child.

Even the pillow itself is treated as a subject: "When 1, I first heard of this study, I grasped it easily. But 2, since I understand it, it never finishes in me."

Another child offers: "Here 1, I will say that American culture surpasses Japanese culture. But here 2, I will say Japanese culture surpasses American culture. And here 3, I will say that both American culture surpassing Japanese and Japanese culture surpassing American are correct. And here 4, actually neither does any such surpassing.

Moreover since all these spring from center ( ), in such a view 4, 3, 2, 1, each is fully affirmed by me."

The students' building is inadequate. They are poor. They share clothes and food with those still poorer. But they have declined publicity for the group, thinking it might only bring more problems.

"Someone else must tell others about our method, we don't know how," they say. They are too busy using it in their own lives.

Have you something troubling you? Have you a pillow? If so, you may join these children in their wide way of thinking. It is not easy to translate the feeling of one person into the language of another and to convey in words the sensible delight of gentle hands on a pillow showing parents how to think.

Paul Reps, *Square Sun, Square Moon*

Pillow Talk

Try using the pillow method in your life. It isn't easy, but once you begin to understand it, the payoff in increased understanding is great.

1. Pick a person or viewpoint with which you strongly disagree. If you've chosen a person, it's best to have him there with you; but if that's not possible, you can do it alone.

2. What disagreement should you choose? No doubt there are many in your life:

   parent-child
   teacher-student
   employer-employee
   brother-sister
   friend-friend
   nation-nation
   Republican-Democrat

3. For each problem you choose, really place yourself in each position on the pillow as you encounter it:

    a. Your position is correct and your opponent's is wrong.
    b. Your opponent's position is correct and yours is wrong.
    c. Both your positions are correct and both are wrong.
    d. It isn't important which side is right or wrong. Finally, affirm the fact that all four positions are true.

4. The more important the problem is to you, the harder you'll find it to accept positions 2, 3, and 4 as having any validity. But the exercise will work only if you can suspend your present position and imagine how it would feel to hold the other ones.

5. How can you tell if you've been successful with the pillow method? The answer is simple: If after going over the four steps you can understand—not necessarily *accept* but just *understand*—the other person's position, you've done it. After you've reached this understanding, do you notice any change in how you feel about the other person?

Pillow Education in Action

Introduction   *The problem I decided to work on involves me and my boyfriend. We have trouble deciding how serious our relationship is. I want things more casual to give both of us some freedom. Bill wants things on a one-to-one basis, not allowing either of us to go out with anyone else.*

Position 1: I'm right and Bill is wrong   *I am right in wanting the relationship more casual. Because of some bad past experiences I like my relationships to grow gradually, so that I don't get hurt as easily. Also, I like to be genuine when expressing feelings or commitments, and I don't want to say things to Bill before I really feel them. Bill should realize this and not push me.*

Position 2: Bill is right and I'm wrong   *He's right for wanting the relationship his way because this is the only way he has ever had a relationship. He likes the security of having a steady girlfriend. Since it's hard to change old habits and Bill's reasons for wanting a steady relationship make sense for him, I'm wrong for not being more sympathetic.*

Position 3: Both of us are right and both are wrong   *I'm right to want a more casual relationship because of my past experiences and present needs, but I'm wrong to ignore Bill's needs. He's right to want the security of a one-to-one relationship because he feels best with this type of arrangement, but he's wrong to push me before I'm ready.*

Position 4: It doesn't matter   *When both of us are together and enjoying each other, no thought is given to future commitments or the type of relationship we are involved in. At that moment no thought of this problem enters our minds, and for the moment it does not exist.*

Conclusion: All positions are true together   *I can see now that Bill and I are limiting ourselves by not going beyond steps 1 and 2. If we can see the rights and wrongs in each other's position, then maybe we can find an answer that both of us will feel good about.*

Introduction   *Last week I came into work expecting to work in my regular unit, but I was "floated" to another floor. When I reported there, I had a disagreement with the charge nurse over my assignment. I tried to explain to her that I felt she was giving me too heavy a workload, but she didn't seem to understand what I was trying to tell her. I was angry and upset, so I decided to give the pillow method a try to see if I could clarify the problem before I talked to her again.*

Position 1: I am right, she is wrong   *The assignment she gave me was too heavy. Patient assignments should not be made by room numbers without regard to the type of patient and the amount of care needed. She was wrong to give me the patients needing the most care in order to give her staff a break. I am justified to feel used when treated in this manner.*

Position 2: She is right and I am wrong   *I shouldn't expect any special treatment just because I'm from another floor. It is easier to assign patients by room number. It keeps the nurses in one area and saves working steps.*

Position 3: We are both right and both wrong   *I am right in saying that she did give me the hardest assignment, but I can see now that she didn't do this with the intention of being unfair: somebody had to do the work. She was right (or at least reasonable) in being cool to my complaints: they probably made me look as if I wanted special consideration. I am right in saying that assigning patients by room number is not an effective way to manage the workload.*

Position 4: It really isn't important who was right or wrong   *I was only working on that floor one night and probably won't work there for another year. The whole incident is over, and not worth worrying about. There are always going to be times when things won't work out the way I'd like them. I must admit that the majority of my assignments are fair.*

Conclusion   *I found this assignment very interesting. When I started, I was still so angry that I felt totally dumped on! By the time I had gone through the four steps I could understand why the charge nurse behaved as she did. I didn't feel so angry at her and decided to talk to her again to see if we could clear the air. We did get a chance to do this, and I was able to explain clearly how I felt in a way that didn't threaten her. What's more important, I was able to truly listen to her without becoming defensive. The outcome of our conversation was that we parted feeling good about each other. I know I couldn't have done this before looking at the issue from all sides, using the pillow method.*

Introduction   *My husband, Rick, is a dreamer of dreams. His most recent idea was to give up our house and possessions and move onto a boat in the harbor. Since I am a fairly conventional person, the idea seemed crazy to me at first. But we talked about it many times, and eventually the idea became an adventure to me, and I was comfortable considering the real possibility of making the move. I shared our idea with my mother, expecting to get a favorable reaction. Instead, I got a very negative, emotional one. She saw the idea as being just one more crazy dream that Rick was forcing upon me. I, naturally, claimed she was wrong and defended Rick.*

Position 1: I'm right and she's wrong   *After many years of close companionship I'm certain that I know Rick much better than my mother does. I have accepted the dreamer in him and realize that most of his ideas will never come to pass. When he arrives at the conclusion that one of his dreams is important enough to pursue, we discuss it. He doesn't shove the plan down my throat. We have a great deal of respect for each other, and our decision-making is always a joint effort. Therefore, I think my mother is wrong to say that any initiation of change in our marriage is always one-sided, in favor of Rick.*

Position 2: She's right and I'm wrong

My mother looks at our relationship, first, from the standpoint of how it affects me, her daughter. She loves me and is genuinely concerned about how equal my part is in our relationship. She has known me all my life and sees me as lacking assertiveness in making my ideas known. Many times in the past she has seen me sacrifice my principles to keep in good standing with a person I cared for. For this reason, she also sees me as being very fragile and easily hurt. No mother can stand by and watch her daughter walk into a possibly painful situation without trying, in some way, to shelter her from the blow. This is her way of reaching out to save me from what she thinks could be a big mistake and the hurt that would go with it.

She also admits that the idea of giving up our house and all our possessions to live on a boat rocks the very foundation upon which she has built her life. Coming from a background where security is a marriage, a house, comfortable furnishings, and kids in the future, she sees no sense in what we plan to do with our lives. She sees us throwing away a lot of positive, concrete things that we have worked hard to get, just to chase a rainbow. Therefore, she thinks that I am wrong for wanting to live out a fantasy that has potential for disappointment when I have all these comfortable, real things surrounding me and providing me with security.

Position 3: We're both right, but both wrong

I am right in defending Rick's position, as well as my own, in our relationship because I know that we share equally in ideas and decision-making. I am wrong in thinking that just because she is my mother, and she tends always to take what she sees to be my side in issues, she lacks any real sound basis for her side of the argument in this case.

She is right in being concerned about my feelings in this situation. She is wrong in overlooking the fact that I have changed through the years. My attitudes have become more open and receptive to change, and I have the courage now to challenge many aspects of life that I would never even have approached when I was younger.

Position 4: It doesn't matter

I know that my mother loves Rick and cares about his welfare, just as she cares about mine. If we pursue this dream, she won't love us any less. Even though she may disagree with us, her love is not based on whether or not we always see things her way. In the same way, I love her regardless of whether she accepts everything that I think or do. Looking at the overall picture, I can see that how we both feel about this issue really doesn't matter, because it doesn't affect our love for each other, now or in the future.

Conclusion

Now that I can see the truth in all four positions, the issue takes on a new kind of importance. It has been the tool to help me overcome my own selective perception of the boat situation, as well as others. I have also attained a greater insight into the way my mother feels about things, but more importantly, why she feels as she does. In light of this discovery, the issue does matter a great deal to me and is important.

Now we've reached the end of our look at the role perception plays in communication. Before we move to the subject of listening, we want to say one final thing about the chapter.

Lest you misunderstand, in all our talk about empathy we've never suggested that it means giving up your opinion in favor of someone else's. There's a big difference between understanding someone's position and agreeing with it; we've been advocating the first approach, not the latter.

The world would be a very dull place if everybody agreed on everything. The attitude we've suggested here is quite different from this tame, falsely accommodating one. We're convinced that the ability to empathize, to understand another's viewpoint without necessarily accepting it for your own, is a big key to effective interpersonal communication. The German poet and dramatist Goethe expressed this point most clearly when he said, ''All sects seem to me to be right in what they assert and wrong in what they deny.'' If each of us could develop this attitude, the world (to borrow an old phrase) would be a better place to live.

Roads Not Taken

1. Find someone who is color-blind and interview him. Try to find out how you and he differ in the way you see the world.

2. Interview someone who has grown up in a culture unlike yours. Before your talk select several different topics to ask about that might bring out differences in the way you each view your environments. For example, you might discuss food, women's place in society, education, religion, dating habits, and so on.

3. Check with your local police department to see if they have a program of public education whereby citizens may ride with an officer while he is on duty. If you are fortunate enough to have this experience, share with your class any changes the experience made in your views of police work and law enforcement.

4. Try to locate some establishment that deals with the public. If possible, make arrangements to observe what a person who meets and works with the public or customer goes through. Try to physically position yourself on the worker's side of the desk or counter. Places that might serve well for this experience would be Department of Motor Vehicles, License Bureau at City Hall, the post office, the returns desk of a local store, or the registrar's office of your college. If you can arrange this, share with your group any changes the experience makes in the way you view the activity you monitored.

5. Attempt to create an experiment that will point up how susceptible we are to selective perception. Can you devise an experience that individuals with different occupations, religions, philosophical beliefs, levels of knowledge, or nationalities would view differently?

6. Select a current topic of controversy. Create several questions pertinent to this topic and interview a number of people who you suspect would see the topic from different viewpoints. How do their answers agree and disagree with each other? What factors caused these variations?

7. For a one-week period apply the pillow method to issues in your life.

8. Write an account of a single event that is perceived differently by two or more people. Whether your account is fictional or based on events that actually occurred, be sure to write it in the first-person singular for each person.

More Readings in Perception

Argyle, Michael. *Social Interaction.* Chicago: Aldine-Atherton, 1969.
Argyle offers a more complete treatment of the perceptual influences that shape our perceptions of others.

Bohannon, Laura. "Shakespeare in the Bush." *Natural History* 75 (August–September 1966): 28–33
A woman who believes that Shakespeare's Hamlet has a universal theme gets a shock when she tries to describe it to a remote African tribe. A great example of culturally influenced perception.

Burke, Kenneth. *Permanence and Change.* Indianapolis: Bobbs-Merrill, 1965.
Probably the best description we've read of the process of selective perception.

Hammer, Richard. "Role Playing: A Judge Is a Con, A Con Is a Judge." *New York Times Magazine,* September 14, 1969.
The account of a role-reversal workshop that gave some judges and police a new perspective on what it means to be a prisoner.

Hastrof, Albert, David Schneider, and Judith Polefka. *Person Perception.* Reading, MA: Addison-Wesley, 1970.
A survey of research in the field.

Hastrof, Albert H., and Hadley Cantril. "They Saw a Game: A Case Study." *Journal of Abnormal and Social Psychology* 49 (January 1954).
This study clearly illustrates Goethe's remark that we quoted in our conclusion to this chapter: Shows how football fans view their home team as saints and the opposition as monsters.

Ramey, Estelle. "Mens Cycles." *Ms.,* Spring 1972.
A description of men's emotional, physical, and sexual cycles as well as the daily rhythms that both men and women undergo.

Tyler, Leona. *The Psychology of Human Differences.* New York: Appleton-Century-Crofts, 1965.
A survey of the psychological differences between people. Covers intelligence, personality, sex, age, race, class.

Wilentz, Joan S. *The Senses of Man*. New York: Thomas Y. Crowell, 1968.
This book provides a good bridge between overly simple and technical work in perception.

Loftus, Elizabeth. *Eyewitness Testimony*. Cambridge, MA: Harvard University Press, 1979.
Loftus describes the way in which events are retained in the memory and how factors can influence the way they are recalled.

Chapter Six

Listening vs. Hearing

i have just
wandered back
into our conversation
and find
that you
are still
rattling on
about something
or other
i think i must
have been gone
at least
twenty minutes
and you
never missed me

now this might say
something
about my
acting ability
or it might say
something about
your sensitivity

one thing
troubles me tho
when it
is my turn
to rattle on
for twenty minutes
which i
have been known to do
have you
been missing too

Ric Masten

There's more to listening than gazing politely at a speaker and nodding your head every so often. All of us know the frustration of not being heard, and unfortunately all of us are guilty of not listening to others at times. In fact, as you'll find out for yourself shortly, it's likely that more than half the things you say every day might as well have never been spoken because they're not understood clearly.

Maybe the reason most people listen so poorly is that they were never taught this skill. Is this true for you? Think back on your own education. You spent twelve years in classes learning how to read and write, yet you probably never had any instruction in how to listen.

In this chapter we'll introduce you to some skills that can make you a better listener. First we'll talk about poor listening. You'll see just how often you truly listen to others and how often you simply pretend—the results may surprise you. You'll learn why we don't listen much of the time and you'll see some of the bad habits we've developed in this area. After looking at this rather gloomy picture, you'll learn some ways of improving your listening skills, making sure that you understand others and that they understand you. And finally we'll show you the technique of active listening, which not only lets you understand others better but can actually show you how to help them solve their own problems.

Before we start talking about better ways of listening, here's an exercise that may remind you of some bad habits in this area.

Everybody's talkin' at me
I don't hear a word they're sayin'
Only the echoes of my mind.

from *Everybody's Talkin'*, Fred Neil

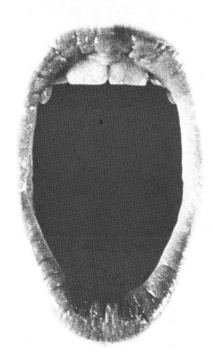

Not Listening

1. Divide the class into groups of four or five people.

2. Each person in turn should take two minutes to discuss with the group his ideas about a current issue (abortion, capital punishment, or some other idea that is personally important.) *But,* as the talker shares his ideas, the other group members should think about the unfinished business in their lives—incomplete assignments, on-the-job work, things to discuss with the family. They should try to decide what they're going to do about these situations. The group members shouldn't be rude; they should respond politely every so often to the speaker, putting on a good appearance of paying close attention to him. But they should keep their mind on their personal concerns, not the speaker's remarks.

3. After everyone in your group completes step 2, spend some time sharing the feelings you experienced when you were talking and being listened to by the others. Also discuss how you felt as you thought about your problems instead of listening to the speaker.

4. For five minutes try to have a discussion in which each member of your group shares one personal communication problem she hopes to solve. Try to be as sincere and open with your feelings as you can. But as you all talk, try to keep the discussion focused on *your* problem. Every time someone shares an idea or experience, try to turn it around to relate to your situation. Don't get sidetracked by her comments. Your task is to tell the others about *your* communication problem.

5. After your discussion, take a few minutes to talk about how you felt during the conversation—when others ignored your message and when you ignored theirs.

Types of Nonlistening

The preceding exercise demonstrated some of the most common types of poor listening. As you read on, you'll begin to recognize them as behaviors that you and those around you probably use quite often. While you'll soon learn that a certain amount of inaccurate listening is understandable, and sometimes even desirable, it's important to be aware of these styles so that you can avoid them when understanding others is important to you.

Pseudolistening   Pseudolistening is an imitation of the real thing. Good pseudolisteners give the appearance of being attentive: They look you in the eye, nod and smile at the right times, and even may answer you occasionally. Behind that appearance of interest, however, something entirely different is going on, for pseudolisteners use a polite facade to mask thoughts that have nothing to do with what the speaker is saying. Often pseudolisteners ignore you because of something on their mind that's more important to them than your remarks. Other times they may simply be bored, or think that they've heard what you have to say before, and so tune out your remarks. Whatever the reasons, the significant fact is that pseudolistening is really counterfeit communication.

Stage-hogging   The stage-hogs are only interested in expressing their ideas and don't care about what anyone else has to say. These people will allow you to speak from time to time, but only so that they can catch their breath, use your remarks as a basis for their own babbling, or to keep you from running away. Stage-hogs really aren't having a conversation when they dominate others with their talk; they're making a speech and at the same time probably making an enemy.

Selective Listening   Selective listeners respond only to the parts of our remarks that interest them, rejecting everything else. All of us are selective listeners from time to time, as for instance when we screen out radio commercials and music as we keep an ear cocked for a weather report or an announcement of the time. In other cases selective listening occurs in conversations with people who expect a thorough hearing, but only get their partner's attention when the subject turns to their favorite topic—perhaps money, sex, a hobby, or some particular person. Unless and until you bring up one of these pet subjects, you might as well talk to a tree.

Insulated Listening   Insulated listeners are almost the opposite of their selective cousins just mentioned. Instead of looking for something, these people avoid it. Whenever a topic arises which they'd rather not deal with, insulated listeners simply fail to hear, or rather acknowledge it. You remind them about a problem, perhaps—an unfinished job, poor grades, or the like— and they'll nod or answer you and then promptly forget what you've just said.

Defensive Listening   Defensive listeners take things you intended as innocent comments as personal attacks. The teenager who perceives her parents' questions about her friends and activities as distrustful snooping is a defensive listener, as is the insecure breadwinner who explodes any time his mate mentions money or the touchy parent who views any questioning by her children as a threat to her authority and parental wisdom. As your reading in Chapter 4 suggests, it's fair to assume that many defensive listeners are suffering from shaky public images, and avoid admitting this by projecting their own insecurities onto others.

Ambushing   Ambushers listen carefully to you, but only because they're collecting information that they'll use to attack what you have to say. The cross-examining prosecution attorney is a good example of an ambusher. Needless to say, using this kind of strategy will justifiably initiate defensiveness on the other's behalf.

Insensitive Listening   Insensitive listeners offer the final example of people who don't receive another person's messages clearly. As we've said before, people often don't express their thoughts or feelings open but instead communicate them through subtle and unconscious choice of words and/or nonverbal clues. Insensitive listeners aren't able to look beyond the words and behavior to understand their hidden meanings. Instead, they take a speaker's remarks at face value. The kind of companions Ralph Schoenstein described on page 000 were insensitive listeners.

*We have been given
two ears
and but a single mouth
in order that
we may hear more
and talk less*

Zeno of Citium

America has better means of communication than any nation on earth. We are constantly developing splendid new techniques for the dissemination of sound, pictures, and print. The only problem is that on the most basic level of communication—person-to-person, live, mouth-to-ear, low-frequency conversation—we're still in the dark ages; for everyone sends well enough, but very few of us are receiving.

Last week in the elevator of my mother's apartment house, a man asked her, "How are you?"

Since Mother had just spent three hours with a tax collector,

she smiled graciously and said, "Lousy, thank you."

The man returned the smile and said, "That's nice."

Mother suspected that he either had misunderstood her or was simply a sadist. However, later the same day, she passed a woman who said, "How are you?"

"Suicidally distraught," said Mother.

"Fine," said the woman. "Hope the family's well, too."

This second exchange gave Mother the kind of revelation that only scientists have known when discovering great truths. Because that man and woman weren't

people who would have wanted to see Mother out of the way (neither is in her will), she reached a profound conclusion: if you are well enough to be talking, people consider your condition superb, even if you colorfully describe an internal hemorrhage.

Mother's pioneering experimentation in the amenities has so inspired me that I have dedicated myself to continuing her work. Yesterday, I made real progress.

"How are you? asked a man in front of my house.

"I'll be dead in a week," I said.

"Glad to hear it. Take care now."

There is no known way to shake the composure of the man who makes a perfunctory inquiry about your health; he loves his lines so well that the grimmest truth can't make him revise them. Never is human communication so defeated as when someone asks casually about your condition.

Some day, perhaps when I'm under a bus getting the last rites, I expect such a man to throw me a breezy, "How are you?"

"As well as can be expected," I'll say.

"Good. And the kids?"

"The older one goes to the chair tomorrow. The little one was lost on a Scout hike."

"Swell. The wife okay?"

"She just ran off with the milkman."

"Glad to hear it. You'll have to bring the whole family over one night soon."

Ralph Schoenstein, *Time Lurches On*

Why We Don't Listen

After thinking about the styles of nonlistening described in the previous pages, most people begin to see that they listen carefully only a small percentage of the time they're with others. It's pretty discouraging to realize that much of the time you aren't hearing others and they aren't getting your messages, but this is a fact of life. Sad as it may be, it's impossible to listen *all* the time, for several reasons.

1. Message Overload   The amount of speech most of us encounter everyday makes careful listening to everything we hear impossible. According to one study, many of us spend as much as one-third of the time we're awake listening to verbal messages—from teachers, coworkers, friends, family, salesmen, and total strangers. This means we often spend five hours or more a day listening to people talk. If you add this to the amount of time we tune in radio and television, you can see that it's impossible for us to keep our attention totally focused for this amount of time. Therefore we have to let our attention wander at times.

2. Preoccupation   Another reason we don't always listen carefully is that we're often wrapped up in personal concerns that are of more immediate importance to us than the messages others are sending. It's hard to pay attention to someone else when you're anticipating an upcoming test or thinking about the wonderful time you had last night with good friends. Yet we still feel we have to "listen" politely to others, and so we continue with our charade.

3. Rapid Thought   Listening carefully is also difficult for a physiological reason. Although we're capable of understanding speech at rates up to 600 words per minute, the average person speaks between 100 and 140 words per minute. Thus we have a lot of "spare time" to spend with our minds while someone is talking. And the temptation is to use this time in ways that don't relate to the speaker's ideas, such as thinking about personal interests, daydreaming, planning a rebuttal, and so on. The trick is to use this spare time to understand the speaker's ideas better, rather than letting your attention wander.

4. Physical Noise   The physical world in which we live often presents distractions that make it hard to pay attention to others. The sound of traffic, music, others' speech, and the like interfere with our ability to hear well. Also, fatigue or other forms of discomfort can distract us from paying attention to a speaker's remarks. Consider, for example, how the efficiency of your listening decreases when you are seated in a crowded, hot, stuffy room that is surrounded by traffic and other noises. In such circumstances even the best intentions aren't enough to ensure clear understanding.

5. Hearing Problems   Sometimes a person's listening ability suffers from a physiological hearing problem. Once a hearing problem has been diagnosed it's often possible to treat it. The real tragedy occurs when a hearing loss goes undetected. In such cases both the person with the defect and others can become frustrated and annoyed at the ineffective communication which results. If you suspect that you or someone you know suffers from a hearing loss, it's wise to have a physician or audiologist perform an examination.

6. Faulty Assumptions We often make incorrect assumptions which lead us to believe that we're listening attentively when quite the opposite is true. When the subject is a familiar one, it's easy to think that you've "heard it all before," when in fact the speaker is offering new information. A related problem arises when you assume that a speaker's thoughts are too simple or obvious to deserve careful attention, when the truth is that you ought to be listening carefully. At other times just the opposite occurs: you think that another's comments are too complex to possibly understand (as in some lectures), and so give up trying to make sense of them. A final mistake people often make is to assume that a subject is unimportant and to stop paying attention when they ought to be listening carefully.

7. Talking Has More Apparent Advantages It often appears that we have more to gain by speaking than by listening. One big advantage of speaking is that it gives you a chance to control others' thoughts and actions. Whatever your goal—to have a prospective boss hire you, to convince others to vote for the candidate of your choice, or to describe the way you want your hair cut—the key to success seems to be the ability to speak well.

Another apparent advantage of speaking is the chance it provides to gain the admiration, respect, or liking of others. Tell jokes, and everyone will think you're a real wit. Offer advice, and they'll be grateful for your help. Tell them all you know, and they'll be impressed by your wisdom. But keep quiet . . . and it seems as if you'll look like a worthless nobody.

So the first simple feeling I want to share with you is my enjoyment when I can really hear someone. I think perhaps this has been a long-standing characteristic of mine. I can remember this in my early grammar school days. A child would ask the teacher a question and the teacher would give a perfectly good answer to a completely different question. A feeling of pain and distress would always strike me. My reaction was, "But you didn't hear him!" I felt a sort of childish despair at the lack of communication which was (and is) so common.

Carl R. Rogers

B.C. by Johnny Hart

© Field Enterprises, Inc., 1972

By permission of John Hart and Field Enterprises, Inc.

AT THE PARTY

Unrhymed, unrhythmical, the chatter goes:
Yet no one hears his own remarks as prose.

Beneath each topic tunelessly discussed
The ground-bass is reciprocal mistrust.

The names in fashion shuttling to and fro
Yield, when deciphered, messages of woe.

You cannot read me like an open book.

I'm more myself than you will ever look.

Will no one listen to my little song?

Perhaps I shan't be with you very long.

A howl for recognition, shrill with fear,
Shakes the jam-packed apartment, but each ear
Is listening to its hearing, so none hear.

W. H. Auden

Finally, talking gives you the chance to release energy in a way that listening can't. When you're frustrated, the chance to talk about your problems can often help you feel better. In the same way, you can often lessen your anger by letting it out verbally. It is also helpful to share your excitement with others by talking about it, for keeping it inside often leaves you feeling as if you might burst.

While it's true that talking does have many advantages, it's important to realize that listening can pay dividends, too. As you'll soon read, being a good listener is one good way to help others with their problems; and what better way is there to have others appreciate you? As for controlling others, it may be true that it's hard to be persuasive while you're listening, but your willingness to hear others out will often leave them open to thinking about your ideas in return. Like defensiveness, listening is often reciprocal: you get what you give.

8. We're Not Trained to Listen Well Even if we want to listen well, we're often hampered by a lack of skill. A common but mistaken belief is that listening is like breathing—an activity that people do well naturally. "After all," the common belief goes, "I've been listening since I was a child. I don't need to study the subject in school."

The truth is that listening is a skill much like speaking: virtually everybody does it, though few people do it well. As you read through this chapter, you'll see that one reason so much poor listening exists is because most people fail to follow the important steps that lead to real understanding.

Duet

When we speak we do not listen, my son and I.
I complain of slights, hurts inflicted on me.
He sings a counterpoint, but not in harmony.
Asking a question, he doesn't wait to hear.
Trying to answer, I interrupt his refrain.
This comic opera excels in disharmony only.

Lenni Shender Goldstein

Styles of Listening

Before going any further, we want to make it clear that it isn't always desirable to listen intently, even when the circumstances permit. Given the number of messages to which we're exposed, it's impractical to expect yourself to listen well 100 percent of the time. This fact becomes even more true when you consider how many of the messages sent at us aren't especially worthwhile: boring stories, deceitful commercials, remarks we've heard many times before, and so on. Given this deluge of relatively worthless information, it's important for you to realize that behaviors such as insulated listening, pseudolistening, and selective listening are often reasonable. But there are times when you do want very much to understand others. At times like these you may try hard to get the other person's meaning and yet *still* seem to wind up with misunderstandings.

What can you do in such cases? It takes more than good intentions to listen well—there are skills that you can learn to use. To begin understanding these skills we need to look at two styles of listening.

One-way Listening   One-way communication occurs when a listener tries to make sense out of a speaker's remarks without actively taking part in the exchange of a message. Another term that describes this style of communication is *passive listening.* Probably the most familiar examples of passive listening occur when students hear a professor lecture or when viewers watch television. One-way communication also takes place in interpersonal settings, as when one person dominates a conversation while the others fall into the role of audience members, or when some parents lecture their children without allowing them to respond.

The most important feature of one-way communication is that it contains little or no feedback. The receiver may deliberately or unintentionally send nonverbal messages that show how the speaker's ideas are being received—nods and smiles, stifled yawns, more or less eye contact—but there's no verbal response to indicate how—or even whether—the message has been received.

Since the speaker isn't interrupted in this type of lecture-conversation, one-way communication has the advantage of being relatively quick. We've all felt like telling someone, "I'm in a hurry. Just listen carefully and don't interrupt." What we're asking for here is one-way communication.

Sometimes one-way communication is an appropriate way of listening. As you'll soon read, sometimes the best way to help people with problems is to hear them out. In many cases they're not looking for, nor do they need, a verbal response. At times like these, when there's no input by the receiver, *anybody* who will serve as a sounding board will do as a "listener." This explains why some people find relief talking to a pet or a photograph.

One-way communication also works well when the listener wants to ease back mentally and be entertained. It would be a mistake to interrupt a good joke or story or to stand up in the middle of a play and shout out a question to the performers.

But outside of these cases one-way listening isn't very effective for the simple reason that it almost guarantees that the listener will misunderstand at least some of the speaker's ideas. There are at least three types of misunderstandings. As you read about each of them, think about how often they occur for you.

The first kind of misunderstanding happens when a speaker sends a clear, accurate message that the receiver simply gets wrong. Somehow a quarter-cup of sugar is transformed into four cups, or "I'll see you at twelve" is translated into "I'll see you at two."

In other cases the receiver is listening carefully enough, but the speaker sends an incorrect message. These instances are the reverse of the ones just mentioned, and their results can be just as disastrous.

The third mixup that comes from one-way communication is probably the most common: The speaker sends a message that may not be incorrect but is overly vague, and the receiver interprets the words in a manner that doesn't match the speaker's ideas. In Chapter 1 we talked about the problems that come from failing to check out interpretations. In this statement, "I'm a little confused," does "little" mean "slightly" or is it an understatement that could be translated into "very"? When a lover says, "You're my best friend," is this synonymous with the message, "Besides being such a romantic devil, I also feel comfortable with you," or does it mean, "I want to become less of a lover and more of a pal"? You could make your own personal list of confusing messages and in doing so prove the point: assuming you understand another's words isn't always a sure thing. Fortunately, there's another, usually better way of listening.

Two-way listening   The element that distinguishes two-way from one-way communication is verbal feedback. You'll recall from our communication model in Chapter 1 that feedback occurs whenever a listener sends some sort of message to the sender indicating how the original idea was received.

There are at least two types of verbal feedback you can use as a listener.

Questioning   This type of response involves asking for additional information to clarify your idea of the sender's message. In asking directions to a friend's house, typical questions might be "Is your place an apartment?" or "How long does it take to get there from here?" In more serious situations questions could include "What's bothering you?" or "Why are you so angry" or "Why is that so important?" Notice that one key element of these questions is that they request the speaker to elaborate on information already given.

Questioning is often a valuable tool for increasing understanding. Sometimes, however, it won't help you receive a speaker's ideas any more clearly, and it can even lead to further communication breakdown. To see how this can be so, consider again our example of asking directions to a friend's home. Suppose the instructions you've received are to "Drive about a mile and then turn left at the traffic signal." Now imagine that a few common problems exist in this simple message. First, suppose that your friend's idea of a mile is different from yours: Your mental picture of the distance is actually closer to two miles, while hers is closer to 300 yards. Next, consider the very likely occurrence that while your friend said "traffic signal" she meant "stop sign"; after all, it's common for us to think one thing and say another. Keeping these problems in mind, suppose you tried to verify your understanding of the directions by asking, "After I turn at the light, how far should I go?" to which your friend replied that her house is the third from the corner. Clearly, if you parted after this exchange, you would encounter a lot of frustration before finding the elusive residence.

What was the problem here? It's easy to see that questioning didn't help, for your original idea of how far to drive and where to turn were mistaken. And contained in such mistakes is the biggest problem with questioning, for such inquiries don't tell you whether you have accurately received the information that has *already* been sent.

Active listening   Now consider another kind of feedback—one that would tell you whether you understand what had already been said before you asked additional questions. This sort of feedback involves restating in your own words the message you thought the speaker has just sent, without adding anything new. In the example of seeking directions we've been using, such rephrasing might sound like this: "So you're telling me to drive down to the traffic light by the high school and turn toward the mountains, is that it?" Immediately sensing the problem, your friend could then reply, "Oh no, that's way too far. I meant that you should drive to the four-way stop by the park and turn there. Did I say stop light? I always do that when I mean stop sign!"

This simple step of restating what you thought the speaker has said before going on is commonly termed *active listening,* and it is a very important tool for effective listening. The thing to remember in active listening is to *paraphrase* the sender's words, not to parrot them. In other words, restate what you think the speaker has said in your own terms as a way of cross-checking the information. If you simply repeat the speaker's comments *verbatim,* you'll sound like you're foolish or hard of hearing, and just as importantly, you still might be misunderstanding what's been said.

The Chinese characters which make up the verb "to listen" tell us something significant about this skill.

YOU

EAR

EYES

UNDIVIDED
ATTENTION

HEART

"I have a pet at home"

"Oh, what kind of a pet?"

"It is a dog."

"What kind of a dog?"

"It is a St. Bernard."

"Grown up or a puppy?"

"It is full grown."

"What color is it?"

"It is brown and white."

"Why didn't you say you had a full-grown, brown and white St. Bernard as a pet in the first place?"

At first active listening might seem to have little to recommend it. After all, it's an unfamiliar tool, which means that you'll have to go through a stage of awkwardness while learning it. And until you become skillful at responding in this new way, you run the risk of getting odd reactions from the people to whom you're responding. In spite of these very real problems, learning to listen actively is worth the effort, for it offers some very real advantages.

First, it boosts the odds that you'll accurately and fully understand what others are saying. We've already seen that one-way listening or even asking questions may lead you to think that you've understood a speaker when in fact you haven't. Active listening, on the other hand, serves as a way of double-checking your interpretation for accuracy. A second advantage of active listening is that it guides you toward sincerely trying to understand another person instead of using nonlistening styles such as stage-hogging, selective listening, and so on. If you force yourself to reflect the other person's ideas in your own words, you'll have to spend your energy trying to understand that speaker instead of using your mental energy elsewhere: planning retorts, daydreaming, or defending yourself.

You can see for yourself what a difference active listening can make by trying the following exercise. You can do this either in class or with a companion on your own.

Active Listening

1. Find a partner, then move to a place where you can talk comfortably. Designate one person as *A* and the other *B*.

2. Find a subject on which you and your partner apparently disagree—a current events topic, a philosophical or moral issue, or perhaps simply a matter of personal taste.

3. *A* begins by making a statement on the subject. *B*'s job is then to paraphrase the idea back, beginning by saying something like "What I hear you saying is . . ." It is very important that in this step *B* feeds back only what she heard *A* say without adding any judgment or interpretation. *B*'s job is simply to *understand* here, and doing so in no way should signify agreement or disagreement with *A*'s remarks.

4. *A* then responds by telling *B* whether or not her response was accurate. If there was some misunderstanding, *A* should make the correction and *B* should feed back her new understanding of the statement. Continue this process until you're both sure that *B* understands *A*'s statement.

5. Now it's *B*'s turn to respond to *A*'s statement, and for *A* to help the process of understanding by correcting *B*.

6. Continue this process until each partner is satisfied that she has explained herself fully and has been understood by the other person.

7. Now discuss the following questions:
   a. As a listener, how accurate was your first understanding of the speaker's statements?

b. How did your understanding of the speaker's position change after you used active listening?

c. Did you find that the gap between your position and that of your partner narrowed as a result of your both using active listening?

d. How did you feel at the end of your conversation? How does this feeling compare to your usual emotional state after discussing controversial issues with others?

e. How might your life change if you used active listening at home? at work? with friends?

Listening to Help

So far we've talked about how becoming a better listener can help you to understand other people more often and more clearly. If you use the skills presented so far, you should be rewarded by communicating far more accurately with others every day. But there's another way in which listening can improve your relationships. Strange as it may sound, often you can help other people solve their own problems simply by learning to listen—actively and with concern.

To understand how listening to others can be so helpful, you need to realize that there are many times when you can't solve people's problems for them. You can, however, help them work things out for themselves. This is a difficult lesson to learn. When someone you care for is in trouble and feeling bad, your first tendency is to try and make things better—to answer questions, soothe hurts, fix whatever seems to be the problem. But even in cases when you're sure you know what's right for a person, it's often necessary to let that person discover the solution independently.

This need to let people find their own answers doesn't mean that you have to stand by and do nothing when a friend is in trouble. Fortunately there's a way of responding that you can use to help others find solutions to their problems—even when you don't know these solutions yourself. But before we introduce this technique, take a few moments to explore your present style of responding to others' problems and see how well they work. You should complete this exercise right now, before reading on.

What Would You Say?

1. In a moment you'll read a list of situations in which someone shares a problem with you. In each case write out the words you'd use in responding to this person.

2. Here are the statements:

   a. I don't know what to do about my parents. It seems like they just don't understand me. Everything I like seems to go against their values, and they just won't accept my feelings as being right for me. It's not that they don't love me—they do. But they don't accept me.

b. I've been pretty discouraged lately. I just can't get a good relationship going with any guys. . . . I mean a romantic relationship . . . you know. I have plenty of men whom I'm good friends with, but that's always as far as it goes. I'm tired of being just a pal. . . . I want to be more than that.

c. (child to parents) I hate you guys? You always go out and leave me with some stupid sitter. Why don't you like me?

d. I'm really bummed out. I don't know what I want to do with my life. I'm pretty tired of school, but there aren't any good jobs around, and I sure don't want to join the service. I could just drop out for a while, but that doesn't really sound very good either.

e. Things really seem to be kind of lousy in my marriage lately. It's not that we fight too much or anything, but all the excitement seems to be gone. It's like we're in a rut, and it keeps getting worse. . . .

f. I keep getting the feeling that my boss is angry at me. It seems like lately he hasn't been joking around very much, and he hasn't said anything at all about my work for about three weeks now. I wonder what I should do?

3. Once you've written your response to each of these messages, imagine the probable outcome of the conversation that would have followed. If you've tried this exercise in class you might have two group members role-play each statement. Based on your idea of how the conversation might have gone, decide which responses were helpful and which were unproductive.

Some Typical Ways of Responding to Problems

Most of the responses you made probably fell into one of several categories. None of these ways of responding is good or bad in itself, but it often happens that we use these ways in situations when they aren't best suited to helping someone we care about solve a problem. There's a proper time and place for each kind of response. The problem, however, usually occurs when we use them in the wrong situations or depend upon one of two styles of responses for all situations.

As you read the following description of these ways of responding, see which ones you most frequently used in the previous exercise and think about results that probably would have occurred from your response.

Advising   When approached with another's problem, the most common tendency is to try to help by offering a solution. While such a response is sometimes valuable, often it isn't as helpful as you might think.

Often your suggestion may not offer the best course to follow, in which case it can even be harmful. There's often a temptation to tell others how *we* would behave in their place, but it's important to realize that what's right for one person may not be right for another. A related consequence of advising is that it often allows others to avoid responsibility for their decisions. A

partner who follows a suggestion of yours that doesn't work out can always pin the blame on you. Finally, often people simply don't want advice: They may not be ready to accept it, instead needing simply to talk out their thoughts and feelings.

Before offering advice, then, you need to be sure that three conditions are present. First, you should be confident that your advice is correct. It's essential to resist the temptation to act like an authority on matters about which you know little. It's equally important to remember that just because a course of action worked for you doesn't guarantee that it will be correct for everybody. Second, you need to be sure that the person seeking your advice is truly ready to accept it. In this way you can avoid the frustration of making good suggestions, only to find that the person with the problem had another solution in mind all the time. Finally, when offering advice, you should be certain that the receiver won't blame you if the advice doesn't work out. You may be offering the suggestions, but the choice and responsibility of following them is up to the other person.

Judging   A judging response evaluates the sender's thoughts or behaviors in some way. The judgment may be favorable—"That's a good idea" or "You're on the right track now"—or unfavorable—"An attitude like that won't get you anywhere." But in either case it implies that the person doing the judging is in some way qualified to pass judgment on the speaker's thoughts or actions.

Sometimes negative judgments are purely critical. How many times have you heard such responses as "Well, you asked for it!" or "I *told* you so!" or "You're just feeling sorry for yourself"? While comments like these can sometimes serve as a verbal slap that brings problem-holders to their senses, they usually make matters worse. To see why, recall our discussion in Chapter 4, where we stated that judging or evaluative language is very likely to make others defensive. After all, suggesting that someone is foolish or mistaken is an attack on their public image that most people would have a hard time ignoring or accepting.

There are other cases where negative judgments are less critical. These involve what we usually call constructive criticism, which is intended to help the problem-holder improve in the future. This is the sort of response given by friends about everything from the choice of clothing to jobs to friends. Another common setting for constructive criticism occurs in school, where instructors evaluate students' work in order to help them master concepts and skills. But whether it's justified or not, even constructive criticism runs the risk of arousing defensiveness, since it may threaten the self-concept of the person at whom it is directed.

Judgments have the best chance of being received when two conditions exist. First, the person with the problem should have requested an evaluation from you. In addition, your judgments should be genuinely constructive and not designed to be "put-downs." If you can remember to follow these two guidelines, your judgments will probably be less frequent and better received.

Analyzing   In analyzing a situation the listener offers an alternative interpretation to a speaker's message. Analyses like these are probably familiar to you:

"I think what's really bothering you is . . . "

"It sounds to me like she's doing it because . . . "

"I don't think you really meant that."

"Maybe the problem started when she . . . "

Interpretations are often effective ways to help people with problems to consider alternative meanings to a situation—ways they would have never thought of without your help. Sometimes a clear analysis will make a confusing problem suddenly clear, either suggesting a solution or at least providing an understanding of what is going on.

In other cases an analysis can create more problems than it solves. There are two problems with analyzing. First, your interpretation may not be correct, in which case the sender may become even more confused by accepting it. Second, even if your analysis is accurate, sharing it with the sender might not be useful. There's a chance that it'll arouse defensiveness (since analysis implies superiority and evaluativeness), and even if this doesn't occur, the receiver may not be able to understand your view of the problem without working it out personally.

How can you know when it's helpful to offer an analysis? There are several guidelines to follow. First, it's important to offer your interpretation in a tentative way, rather than as absolute fact. There's a big difference between saying "Maybe the reason is . . . " and insisting "This is the truth." Second, your analysis ought to have a reasonable chance of being correct. We've already said that a wild, unlikely interpretation can leave a person more confused than before. Third, you ought to be sure that the other person will be receptive to your analysis. Even if you're completely accurate, your thoughts won't help if the problem-holder isn't ready to consider what you say. Finally, you should be sure that your motives for offering an analysis are truly involved with helping the other person. It's sometimes tempting to offer

an analysis to show how brilliant you are, or even to make the other person feel bad for not having thought of the right answer in the first place. Needless to say, an analysis offered under these conditions isn't very helpful.

Questioning   A few pages ago we talked about questioning as one way for you to understand others better. This type of response can also be a way of helping others think about their problem and understand it more clearly. For example, questioning can help a problem-holder define vague ideas more precisely. You might respond to a friend with a line of questioning: "You said Greg has been acting 'differently' toward you lately. What has he been doing?" Another example of a question that helps clarify is as follows: "You told your roommates that you wanted them to be more helpful in keeping the place clean. What would you like them to do?"

Questions can also encourage a problem-holder to examine a situation in more detail, either by talking about what happened or about personal feelings. For example: "How did you feel when they turned you down? What did you do then?" This type of questioning is particularly helpful when you are dealing with someone who is quiet or is unwilling under the circumstances to talk about the problem very much.

While asking questions can definitely be helpful, there are two dangers that can come from using this style too much or at the wrong times. The first is that your questions may lead the help-seeker on a wild goose chase away from a solution to the problem. For instance, asking someone "When did the problem begin?" might provide some clue about how to solve it—but it could also lead to a long digression that would only confuse matters. As with advice, it's important to be sure you're on the right track before asking questions.

A second danger is that questioning can also be a way of disguising advice or criticism. We've all been questioned by parents, teachers or other figures who seemed to be trying to trap or indirectly to guide us. In this way questioning becomes a strategy and often implies that the person doing the asking already has some idea of what direction the discussion should take.

Supporting   Support can take several forms. Sometimes it involves reassuring: "You've got nothing to worry about—I know you'll do a good job." In other cases support comes through comforting: "Don't worry, we all love you." We can also support people in need by distracting them with humor, kidding and joking.

Sometimes a person needs encouragement, and in these cases a supporting response can be the best thing. But in many instances this kind of comment isn't helpful at all: in fact, it can even make things worse. Telling a person who is obviously upset that everything is all right or joking about what seems like a serious problem can communicate the idea that you don't think the problem is really worth all the fuss. This might lead people to see your comments as a put-down, leaving them feeling worse than before. As with the other styles we've discussed, supporting *can* be helpful . . . but only in certain circumstances.

SO PENSEROSO

Come, megrims, mollygrubs and collywobbles!
Come, gloom that limps, and misery that hobbles!
Come also, most exquisite melancholiage,
As dank and decadent as November foliage!
I crave to shudder in your moist embrace,
To feel your oystery fingers on my face.
This is my hour of sadness and of soulfulness,
And cursed be he who dissipates my dolefulness.
I do not desire to be cheered,
I desire to retire, I am thinking of growing a beard,
A sorrowful beard, with a mournful, a dolorous hue in it,
With ashes and glue in it.
I want to be drunk with despair,
I want to caress my care,
I do not wish to be blithe,
I wish to recoil and writhe,
I will revel in cosmic woe,
And I want my woe to show.
This is the morbid moment,
This is the ebony hour.
Aroint thee, sweetness and light!
I want to be dark and sour!
Away with the bird that twitters!
All that glitters is jitters!
Roses, roses are gray,
Violets cry Boo! and frighten me.
Sugar is stimulating,
And people conspire to brighten me.
Go hence, people, go hence!
Go sit on a picket fence!
Go gargle with mineral oil,
Go out and develop a boil!
Melancholy is what I brag and boast of,
Melancholy I mean to make the most of,
You beaming optimists shall not destroy it.
But while I am it, I intend to enjoy it.
Go, people, stuff your mouths with soap,
And remember, please, that when I mope, I mope!

OGDEN NASH

You can get an idea of some problems that come from using the above helping styles by reading this dialog:

Tom   Boy, there must be something wrong with me. Last night I blew it on my first date with Linda. That's the way it always goes—I never seem to do anything right. I'm really a clod.

Bill   Oh, well, cheer up; you'll probably forget about it in a few days. (Supporting)

Tom   No I won't. This dating thing really has me depressed. I feel like a social outcast or something.

Bill   Well, I think you're worrying about it too much. Just forget about it. It's probably your worrying that messes things up in the first place. (Judging, advising, analyzing)

Tom   But I can't help worrying about it. How would you feel if you hadn't had a woman really like you in about three years?

Bill   Well, what do you think the problem is? Have you been polite to them? Do you get drunk or something? There must be some reason why you blow it. (Questioning)

Tom   I don't know. I've tried all kinds of approaches and none of them works.

Bill   Well, there's your problem. You're just not being yourself. You have to be natural, and then women will like you for what you are. There's really nothing to it—just be yourself and everything will be cool. (Judging, analyzing, supporting)

We've used this example to illustrate how good intentions aren't always helpful. Bill may have been right about what caused Tom's dating problem and how he could solve it, but because Tom didn't discover the answer himself, it most likely wasn't useful to him. As you know, people can often ignore the truth, even when it's so obvious that you'd think they would trip over it.

Active Listening: Another Way of Responding

What *can* you say at the times when none of the styles we've discussed so far seem to be right? Fortunately, there's another way of responding that can often be a helpful way of letting others solve their own problems. This style of responding is to *listen actively,* building upon the techniques of giving feedback we introduced earlier in this chapter. Actively listening tells the speaker that you're interested in understanding what he has to say, that you care about him. And amazingly enough, simply feeding back a person's ideas often helps him sort out and solve the problems for himself. If you're lucky, you probably know people who can help you understand things better simply by sitting and listening. These people are probably active listeners, even though they don't know it.

You can begin to see how active listening works by imagining how the previous conversation might have gone if Bill had used this method.

Tom   Boy, there must be something wrong with me. Last night I blew it on my first date with Linda. That's the way it always goes—I never seem to do anything right. I'm really a clod.

Bill   You're pretty upset because things never seem to work out on your dates, huh?

Tom   Yeah. And I don't know what my problem is. I'm not stupid or anything. I always take them to nice places, and I dont get loaded and act like a fool or anything. But I always blow it.

Bill   So you always try to do everything just right—be a gentleman and all that, but it never works out.

Tom   Yeah. I really want to make it work, and so I wind up maybe being too much of a gentleman. I don't act natural. And then when that doesn't work I get even more nervous the next time, which makes the woman uptight, and on it goes. It's a vicious circle.

Bill   So it's your nervousness that you think hangs you up? You're afraid of not being a good date, and so you try too hard, which the women don't like.

Tom   Yeah. I guess what I have to do is just be myself—not try to force things or act like I'm right out of some suave movie or something. Maybe I'll try that. . . .

While active listening won't always be this successful, it's easy to see how this style of reflecting could often work. Active listening is a useful way of responding; combined with your other ways of reacting, it can turn you into a better helper.

Active Listening Defined   When you use active listening as a helping tool, your reflection should contain two elements. The first is a restatement of the speaker's *thoughts*. While it might seem unnecessary to restate something the other person just uttered, your playing it back can often help the speaker to take a more objective look at what's been said, possibly to clarify the idea. Look at a simple example:

Other   "I can't believe my boss! She keeps piling the work on, and I'll never get caught up. What does she think I am?"

You   "It doesn't seem fair, is that it?"

Other   "Well, she isn't exactly picking on me; everybody is loaded with work, including her. It's just that I didn't expect the job would be such a hassle when I took it, and I'm wondering if it's worth the money."

You   "So you're thinking about quitting."

Other   "Well, not right now. But maybe after the school year is over and I have more time I'll look around. I can handle it for a few more months, but not another year!"

In many cases you need to go beyond reflecting thoughts and also rephrase the often unspoken *emotions* that accompany the verbal message. You read in Chapters 1 and 3 about the importance of emotions in personal relationships. This is especially true when someone has a problem. Since many people aren't aware of how they do feel, your statement can help bring the troublesome emotion to the surface and clarify it. Look at this example:

Other   "I can't believe what a thoughtless jerk my brother is. Whenever I call him to talk, he always tells me that I'm his 'special little sister,' but he hasn't called me or written in over a year. I'm always the one who's reaching out. He's such a phony!"

You   "It sounds like you're really mad at him for not making any effort to keep in touch.

Other   "Oh, I suppose it isn't the letters themselves that matter. It just makes me think he doesn't care about me."

You   "So you're not mad so much as hurt, huh?"

Other   "That's the truth. I'm not mad at all. I just wish I knew how much I really do matter to him."

Types of Active Listening   Counseling psychologist Gerard Egan describes several types of active listening (which he calls accurate empathetic understanding). For the sake of simplicity we can divide them into two categories.

Simple reflection   In this type of listening you rephrase what the speaker has *explicitly* stated. There is no digging at hidden meanings or implied messages; rather, you simply put into your own words what you've heard. You may have to verbalize a feeling that the speaker only suggests, but beyond this your goal is to serve as a verbal sounding board.

Other "My friend keeps inviting me to go to church with her, even though I've told her politely that it's not for me. I wish she'd lay off."
You "You're getting irritated at her for not respecting your decision."

Other "I can't decide whether to stay in school or skip a year to travel. The trip sounds great, but I know that if I quit I might not go back."
You "So you're afraid that this wouldn't be just a vacation."

While this type of simple reflecting might seem to be of little help, we'll soon explain several of its advantages.

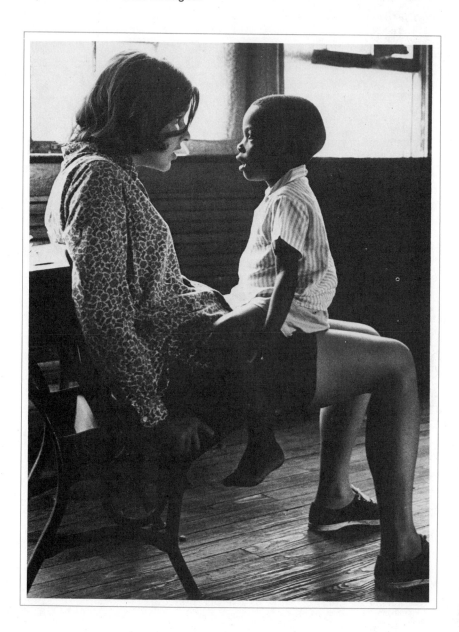

Interpretative reflection　In this second type of active listening you go beyond simply restating what the speaker has said, by instead reflecting what appears to you to be an underlying message. There are two types of interpretative reflections. The first calls for you to *summarize what the other person has been saying* and to *identify themes* in these messages. Here are some sample interpretative reflections:

"You've been talking for almost a half hour now about whether or not to move out of the apartment, and during that time the only reason you gave for staying was that moving would be a hassle. From what you've said, I get the idea that you'd really like to move. Does that make sense?"

"I've been trying to boil down what you've been saying—tell me if this is it. You're sorry that you said those things last night, but you do think you had a reason for getting angry."

In a second variety of interpretative reflection you try to paraphrase thoughts or feelings the speaker hasn't stated, but which you suspect are the real message.

"You keep telling me that everything is fine, but every time the subject of school comes up, all the enthusiasm goes out of your voice. I get the idea that something there is bothering you. Does that seem right?"

"When you talk about all the petty tasks your boss gives you and the questions he asks, I hear you saying that you're hurt and disappointed that he hasn't given you more responsibility."

You can see that responses like these contain an element of analysis. The feature that transforms them into active listening is their *tentative* quality. Notice that all the examples you just read are phrased tentatively rather than being dogmatic, mind-reading pronouncements. This conditional approach is more than a matter of choosing words carefully, for it indicates that you're simply sharing an interpretation and allowing the speaker to decide whether or not it is accurate. This approach is very different from the analyzer who states with great certainty "I know what you're *really* thinking . . . "

As with analyzing, there's a danger in doing too much interpretative reflecting. Most often your simple paraphrasing of thoughts and emotions will be sufficient to let the speaker sort out the problem. Going overboard with your helpful perceptions might add to rather than decrease the speaker's confusion. Most importantly, before you share your interpretations, you should feel confident that there is a good chance that they are accurate. This style of listening should not turn into a guessing game in which you try out every interpretation that occurs to you.

Advantages of Active Listening　When we talked about active listening as a way of understanding others, we discussed two of its advantages. We saw then that it increases the chances that you're receiving a message accurately, and it also keeps you truly paying attention instead of carrying on an act. In addition to these benefits, listening reflectively also has advantages as a tool for helping others.

The reality of the other person is not in what he reveals to you, but in what he cannot reveal to you.

Therefore, if you would understand him, listen not to what he says but rather to what he does not say.

Kahlil Gibran

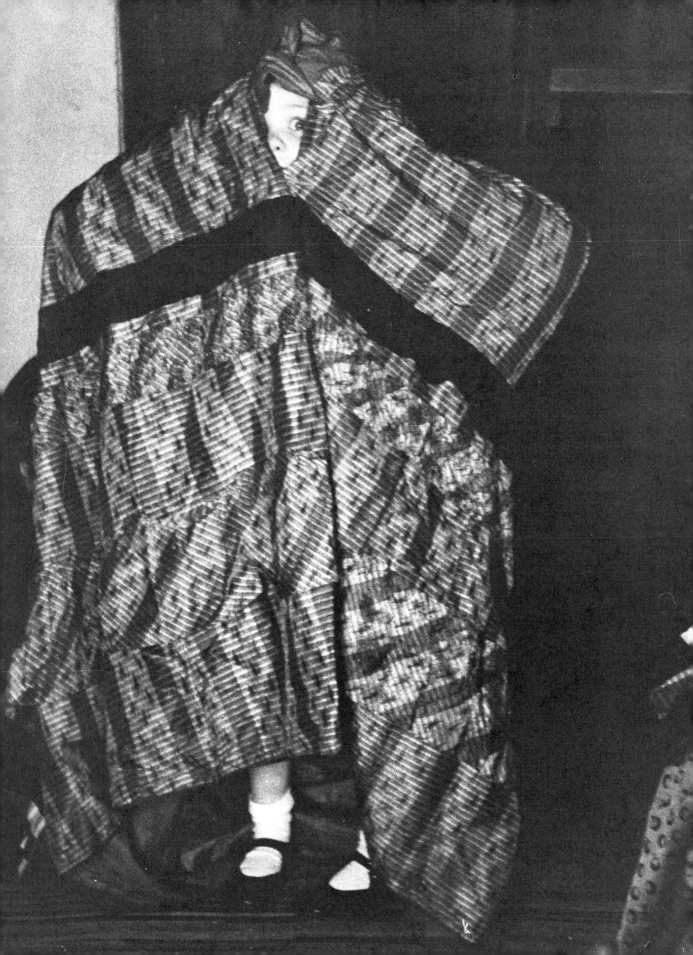

DANNY

Mother It's late. Turn out the light and go to sleep.

Danny I'm not going to sleep.

Mother You have to, it's late. You'll be tired tomorrow.

Danny I'm not going to sleep.

Mother (harshly) Turn that light off immediately!

Danny (flatly) I'm *never* goin to sleep.

Mother (I feel like strangling him. I'm so tired, I can't stand this tonight . . . I go into the kitchen, smoke a cigarette, decide that I'm going in there and try active listening even if it kills me! Entering Danny's room) C'mon, it's late but I'll sit on your bed for a while and rest my feet before I do the dishes. [She takes the book from him, turns off the light, closes the door, and sits on the bed beside him, leaning back against the wall.]

Danny Gimme that book! Don't turn off the light. Get out of here. I don't want you in here. I'm not going to sleep. I hate you!

Mother You're feeling angry.

Danny Yeah, I hate school, and I'll never go back, never!

Mother (He loves school.) You're fed up with school.

Danny It's horrible. I'm not good in school. Don't know anything. I ought to be in second grade. [He's in third.] Math, I don't know it. [He is very good at it.] The teacher must think we're in a high school or something.

Mother Math's pretty hard for you.

Danny No! It's easy. Just don't feel like doing it.

Mother Oh.

Danny (sudden shift) I sure like baseball. Much rather play baseball than go to school.

Mother You really like baseball.

Danny Do you *have* to go to college? [Oldest brother will soon enter college and there is much family talk about it.]

Mother No.

Danny How long do you have to go to school?

Mother You have to finish high school.

Danny Well, I'm not going to college. Don't have to, right?

Mother Right.

Danny Good, I'll play baseball.

Mother Baseball's really fun.

Danny Sure is. [Completely calmed down, talking comfortably, no anger.] Well, good night.

Mother Good night.

Danny Will you sit up with me some more?

Mother Uh huh.

Danny (pulls up covers which had been kicked off, carefully covers up Mother's knees and pats them) Comfortable?

Mother Yes, thank you.

Danny You're welcome. [Period of quiet, then Danny starts snorting and sniffing with much exaggerated clearing of throat and nose.] Snort, snort, snort. [Danny does have slight allergy with stuffy nose, but the symptoms are never acute. Mother has never heard Danny snort like this before.]

Mother Nose bugging you?

Danny Yeah, sure is. Think I need the stuffy nose medicine?

Mother Do you think it would help?

Danny No. (Snort, snort.)

Mother Nose really bugs you.

Danny Yeah [snort]. [Sigh of anguish.] Oh, I wish you didn't have to breathe through your nose when you sleep.

Mother (very surprised at this, tempted to ask where that idea came from): You think you have to breathe through your nose when you sleep?

Danny I *know* I have to.

Mother You feel sure about it.

Danny I know it. Tommy told me, a long time ago. [Much admired friend, two years older.] He said you have to. You can't breathe through your mouth when you sleep.

Mother You mean you aren't supposed to?

Danny You just *can't* [snort]. Mommy, that's so, isn't it? I mean, you *gotta* breathe through your nose when you sleep, don't you? [Long explanation—many questions from Danny about admired friend. "He wouldn't lie to me."]

Mother (explains that friend is probably trying to help but kids get false information sometimes. Much emphasis from Mother that everyone breathes through the mouth when sleeping.)

Danny (very relieved)   Well, good night.

Mother   Good night. [Danny breathing easily through mouth.]

Danny (suddenly)   Snort.

Mother   Still scary.

Danny   Uh huh. Mommy, what if I go to sleep breathing through my mouth—and my nose is stuffy—and what if in the middle of the night when I'm sound asleep—what if I closed my mouth?

Mother (realizes that he has been afraid to go to sleep for years because he is afraid he would choke to death; thinks, "Oh, my poor baby")   You're afraid you might choke maybe?

Danny   Uh huh. You *gotta* breathe. [He couldn't say, "I might die."]

Mother (more explaining)   It simply couldn't happen. Your mouth would open—just like your heart pumps blood or your eyes blink.

Danny   Are you *sure?*

Mother   Yes, I'm sure.

Danny   Well, good night.

Mother   Good night, dear. [Kiss. Danny is asleep in minutes.]

Thomas Gordon, *Parent Effectiveness Training*

First, it takes the burden off you as a friend. Simply being there to understand what's on other peoples' minds often makes it possible for them to clarify their own problems. This means you don't have to know all the answers to help. Also, helping by active listening means you don't need to guess at reasons or solutions that might not be correct. Thus, both you and your friend are saved from going on a wild goose chase after incorrect solutions.

A second advantage of active listening is that it's a great way to get through layers of hidden meanings. Often people express their ideas, problems, or feelings in strangely coded ways. Active listening can sometimes help cut through to the real message.

The third advantage of active listening is that it's usually the best way to encourage others to share more of themselves with you. Knowing that you're interested will encourage less feeling of threat, and leave them willing to let down some defenses. In this sense active listening is simply a good way to learn more about others and a good foundation on which to build a relationship.

Another benefit of active listening is the catharsis it provides for the person with a problem. Even when there's no apparent solution, simply having the chance to talk about what's wrong can be a tremendous relief. This sort of release often makes it easier to accept unchangeable situations rather than complaining about or resisting them.

Finally, at the very least active listening lets the other person know that you understand the problem. While this might seem true of other helping styles, understanding isn't always present. For instance, you've probably had well-intentioned helpers reassure you or offer advice in a way that left you sure they really didn't know what was upsetting you. Because it requires paraphrasing, active listening is the surest way to help you understand others' problems.

They Learn to Aid Customers by Becoming Good Listeners

Do you need someone to listen to your troubles?

Have your hair done.

Beauty salon chairs may be to today's women what conversation-centered backyard fences were to their grandmothers and psychiatrists' couches are to their wealthier contemporaries.

"We are not as family-oriented as our ancestors were," says counsellor-trainer Andy Thompson. "They listened to and helped each other. Now that we have become a society of individuals isolated from one another by cars, telephones, jobs and the like, we have had to find other listeners."

Community training program director for Crisis House, Thompson has designed and is conducting human relations training sessions for workers to whom customers tend to unburden their woes most frequently—cosmetologists, bartenders and cab-drivers.

"People can definitely help others just by letting them talk," he said. "Relatives, friends or spouses who listen do a lot to keep the mental health of this country at a reasonable rate. Workers in situations that encourage communications can make the same meaningful contribution."

Thompson explained that his training is not meant to replace, or be confused with, professional treatment or counseling. His students fill a gap between family and professionals.

"There are not enough psychiatrists or psychologists to go around," he said. "And some

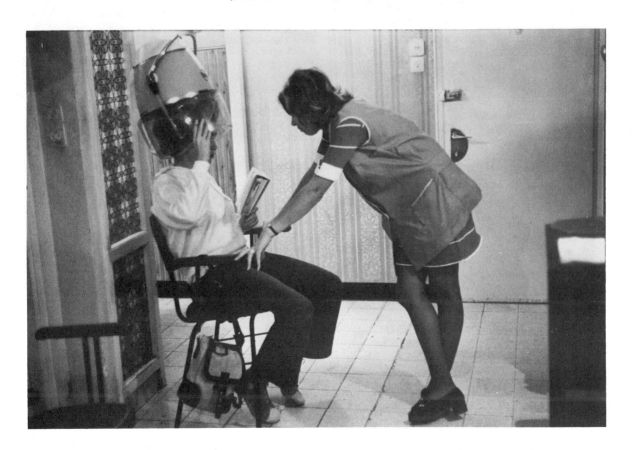

professionals become so technical that their help doesn't mean much to persons who just need a someone who will let them get problems and questions out in the open where they can look at them."

Thompson's first course of training, completed recently, was for cosmetologists.

The human relations training program attempts to make the most of these built-in assets by using a method Thompson calls "reflective listening."

"The purpose is to let the customer talk enough to clarify her own thinking," he said. "We are not interested in having cosmetologists tell women what to do, but to give them a chance to choose their own course of action.

"There is a tendency among listeners to try to rescue a person with problems and pull them out of negative situations. People don't really want that. They just want to discuss what is on their minds and reach their own conclusions."

Cosmetologists are taught to use phrases that aid customers in analyzing their thoughts. Some of the phrases are, "You seem to think . . ." "You sound like . . ." "You appear to be . . ." "As I get it, you . . ." and "It must seem to you that . . ."

There also are barriers to conversation that the cosmetologists are taught to avoid.

"A constant bombardment of questions can disrupt communications," Thompson said. "Commands will have the same effect. Many of them are impossible to follow anyway.

"How many can respond to orders to 'Stop feeling depressed,' 'Don't be so upset, or 'Don't think about it.' "

"The same applies to negative criticism, 'That's dumb,' for instance; and evaluations, such as 'Oh, you're just confused.'

"Comments that seem threatening—'You had better stop feeling sad,' as an example—will end a conversation as quickly as changing the subject or not paying attention."

San Diego Union

When to Use Active Listening

Active listening isn't appropriate in all situations when someone wants help. There are several factors to consider before you choose to use this style.

1. Is the Problem Complex Enough?   Sometimes people are simply looking for information and not trying to work out their feelings. At times like this active listening would be out of place. If someone asks you for the time of day, you'd do better to simply give her the information than to respond by saying "You want to know what time it is." If you're fixing dinner and someone wants to know when it will be ready, it would be exasperating to reply, "You're interested in knowing when we'll be eating."

2. Do You Have the Necessary Time and Concern?   The kind of paraphrasing we've been discussing here takes a good deal of time. Therefore, if you're in a hurry to do something besides listen, it's wise to avoid starting a conversation you won't be able to finish. Even more important than time is concern. It's not necessarily wrong to be too preoccupied to help, or even to be unwilling to exert the considerable effort that active listening requires: After all, you can't help everyone with every problem. It's far better

to honestly state that you're unable or unwilling to help than to pretend to care when you really don't.

3. Can You Withhold Judgment? You've already seen that an active listener allows other people to find their own answers. You should only use this style if you can comfortably paraphrase without injecting your own judgments. It's sometimes tempting to rephrase others' comments in a way that leads them toward the solution that you think is best without ever clearly stating your intentions. As you read in Chapter 4, this kind of strategy is likely to backfire by causing defensiveness if it's discovered. If you think that the situation meets the criteria for advice described earlier in this chapter, then you should offer your suggestions openly.

4. Is Your Active Listening in Proportion to Other Responses? While active listening can be a very helpful way of responding to others' problems, it can become artificial and annoying when it's overused. This is especially true if you suddenly begin to use it as a major response. Even if they're potentially helpful, this sudden switch in your behavior will be so out of character that others might find it distracting. A far better way to use active listening is gradually to introduce it into your repertoire of helpfulness, so that you can become comfortable with it without appearing too awkward. Another way to become more comfortable with this style is to start using it on real but relatively minor problems at first, so that you'll be more adept at knowing how and when to use it when a big crisis does occur.

The Superactive Listener

Just as there are those who seek cheap psychotherapy, there are others who are bent on dispensing it. Having a conversation with such an individual is like trying to punch a hole in a pond—you can try as hard as you like, but when you're done, there's just an unruffled surface reflecting your own face. "You're feeling under some pressure" is just not an appropriate response to a request for directions to the bathroom. These people are often immune to feedback. Tell them "I thought the point you made in the meeting was off-target," and they'll reply, "You thought my point was not quite on target." Get mad at them and they reflect your feelings: "You're saying you're angry because I didn't get the report I promised you in on time." You don't have to worry about excessive self-disclosure from such a person, but after dealing with him or her for a time, you may find yourself beating your head rhythmically against a wall.

Kristin Sheridan Libbee and Michael Libbee

Roads Not Taken

1. Observe the listening behavior of those around you—at home, on the job, at school, in social situations. Do the styles of listening various people use differ from one situation to another? What are the consequences of each style?

2. Work on improving your listening behavior. Begin by defining which styles you would like to use with various people in different situations. Next, keep a journal in which you record the kind of listening you actually do use. See if you can move closer to your goal over the time you keep your journal.

3. Investigate some of the studies that have been conducted on human listening. What does the information contained in these studies have to do with your listening behavior?

4. Our educational system provides many opportunities for learning how to speak, write and read, but the skill of listening is relatively neglected. Try to find information about courses on listening that exist in various educational settings. Where do such courses exist? What is taught in them?

More Readings on Listening

Axline, Virginia M. *Dibs: In Search of Self.* New York: Ballantine Books, 1967. *This is a fascinating account of a child's transition from isolation to happy normality. Beautifully illustrates how active listening can be a therapeutic tool.*

Axline, Virginia M. *Play Therapy.* New York: Ballantine Books, 1969. *A description of the author's technique for working with troubled children. An important part of her work involves the skillful use of active listening.*

Barker, Larry L. *Listening Behavior.* Englewood Cliffs, NJ: Prentice-Hall, 1971. *This book is helpful because it's concerned with just listening: the variables, identifying problems, listening to biased communication, and feedback. A good collection of recent thinking on the subject.*

Beier, Ernst G., and Evans G. Valens. *People-Reading: How We Control Others, How They Control Us.* New York: Stein and Day, 1975. *Chapter 2, How to Listen, Chapter 3, How Not to Listen, and Chapter 4, Listening to Feelings, expand on the information that we have been able to include in our one chapter. The many examples are extremely helpful in adding to your understanding of the art of listening.*

Egan, Gerard. *Interpersonal Living.* Monterey, CA: Brooks/Cole, 1976. *Egan gives a detailed description of the various types of active listening as a helping tool. Especially useful are Chapters 6, 7, and 9.*

Gordon, Thomas. *Parent Effectiveness Training.* New York: Wyden, 1970. *While Gordon's method is aimed at parents, the principles of communication he discusses are equally appropriate for other types of relationships. His treatment of active listening is clear and detailed.*

Gordon, Thomas. *P.E.T. in Action.* New York: Wyden, 1976.
   In a question-and-answer format, Gordon covers most of the problems and misunderstandings that occur when people first try active listening.

Nichols, R., and L. A. Stevens. *Are You Listening?* New York: McGraw-Hill, 1957.
   This is the pioneer book about the subject. It deals mostly with listening accurately for information.

Rogers, Carl R. *On Becoming a Person.* Boston: Houghton Mifflin, 1961.
   Rogers' technique of helping others centers around actively listening. This is a readable, helpful book.

Chapter Seven

Nonverbal Communication: Messages Without Words

Noverbal Communication Means:

smiling, frowning
laughing, crying, sighing
standing close to others
being stand-offish

the way you look:
your hair, your clothing
your face, your body

your handshake (sweaty palms?)
your postures
your gestures
your mannerisms

your voice:
soft-loud
fast-slow
smooth-jerky

the environment you create:
your home, your room
your office, your desk
your kitchen
your car

The Adventures of Sherlock Holmes

One night—it was on the twentieth of March, 1888—I was returning from a journey to a patient (for I had now returned to civil practice), when my way led me through Baker Street. As I passed the well-remembered door, which must always be associated in my mind with my wooing, and with the dark incidents of the *Study in Scarlet,* I was seized with a keen desire to see Holmes again, and to know how he was employing his extraordinary powers. His rooms were brilliantly lit, and, even as I looked up, I saw his tall, spare figure pass twice in a dark silhouette against the blind. He was pacing the room swiftly, eagerly, with his head sunk upon his chest and his hands clasped behind him. To me, who knew his every mood and habit, his attitude and manner told their own story. He was at work again. He had risen out of his drug-created dreams and was hot upon the scent of some new problem. I rang the bell and was shown up to the chamber which had formerly been in part my own.

His manner was not effusive. It seldom was; but he was glad, I think, to see me. With hardly a word spoken, but with kindly eye, he waved me to an armchair, threw across his case of cigars, and indicated a spirit case and a gasogene in the corner. Then he stood before the fire and looked me over in his singular introspective fashion.

"Wedlock suits you," he remarked. "I think, Watson, that you have put on seven and a half pounds since I saw you."

"Seven!" I answered.

"Indeed, I should have thought a little more. Just a trifle more, I fancy, Watson. And in practice again, I observe. You did not tell me that you intended to go into harness."

"Then, how do you know?"

"I see it, I deduce it. How do I know that you have been getting yourself very wet lately, and that you have a most clumsy and careless servant girl?"

"My dear Holmes," said I, "this is too much. You would certainly have been burned, had you lived a few centuries ago. It is true that I had a country walk on Thursday and came home in a dreadful mess, but as I have changed my clothes I can't imagine how you deduce it. As to Mary Jane, she is incorrigible, and my wife has given her notice; but there, again, I fail to see how you work it out."

He chuckled to himself and rubbed his long, nervous hands together.

"It is simplicity itself," said he; "my eyes tell me that on the inside of your left shoe, just where the firelight strikes it, the leather is scored by six almost parallel cuts. Obviously they have been caused by someone who has very carelessly scraped round the edges of the sole in order to remove crusted mud from it. Hence, you see, my double deduction that you had been out in vile weather, and that you had a particularly malignant boot-slitting specimen of the London slavey. As to your practice, if a gentleman walks into my rooms smelling of iodoform, with a black mark of nitrate of silver upon his right forefinger, and a bulge on the right side of his tophat to show where he has secreted his stethoscope, I must be dull, indeed, if I do not pronounce him to be an active member of the medical profession."

I could not help laughing at the ease with which he explained his process of deduction. "When I hear you give your reasons," I remarked, "the thing always appears to me to be so ridiculously simple that I could easily do it myself, though at each successive instance of your reasoning I am baffled until you explain your process. And yet I believe that my eyes are as good as yours."

"Quite so," he answered, lighting a cigarette, and throwing himself down into an armchair. "You see, but you do not observe."

Sir Arthur Conan Doyle,
A Scandal in Bohemia

S ometimes it's difficult to know how other people really feel. Often they don't know for sure themselves, and other times they have some reason for not wanting to tell us, but in either case there are times when we can't find out what is going on inside another's mind simply by asking.

What should we do in these cases? They happen every day, and often in the most important situations. Sherlock Holmes said the way to understand people was to watch them—not only to see, but to observe.

Observing yourself and others is what this chapter is about. In the following pages you'll become acquainted with the field of nonverbal communication—the way we express ourselves, not by what we say, but by what we *do*. Psychologist Albert Mehrabian claims that 93 percent of the emotional impact of a message comes from nonverbal sources, while only 7 percent is verbal. Anthropologist Ray Birdwhistell describes a 65–35 percent split between words and actions, again in favor of nonverbal messages. Whether or not we choose to argue with these precise figures, the point still remains: nonverbal communication contributes a great deal to sharing meanings. It stands to reason, then, that one skill we need to develop is the ability to understand and respond to nonverbal messages.

So let's begin.

Verbal and Nonverbal Communication

Here's an experiment you can try either at home or in class. It will help you begin learning how nonverbal communication works.

1. Pick a partner, and find a place where you have some space to yourselves.

2. Now sit back-to-back with your partner, making sure that no parts of your bodies are touching. You should be seated so that you can talk easily without seeing each other.

3. Once you're seated, take two minutes to carry on a conversation about whatever subject you like. The only requirement is that you not look at or touch each other. Communicate using words only.

4. Next, turn around so that you're facing your partner, seated at a comfortable distance. Now that you can both see and hear each other, carry on your conversation for another two minutes.

5. Continue to face each other, but for the next two minutes don't speak. Instead, join hands with your partner and communicate whatever messages you want to through sight and touch. Try to keep aware of how you feel as you go through this step. There isn't any right or wrong way to behave here—there's nothing wrong with feeling embarrassed, silly, or any other way. The only requirement is to *remain silent*.

After you've finished the experiment, take some time to talk it over with your partner. Start by sharing how you felt in each part of the experience. Were you comfortable, nervous, playful, affectionate? Did your feelings change from one step to another? Could your partner tell these feelings without our expressing them? If so, how? Did he communicate his feelings too?

Characteristics of Nonverbal Communication

If this experiment seemed strange to you, we hope you still went through with it, because it points out several things about nonverbal communication.

Nonverbal Communication Exists   Even when you were in the nontalking stage, you probably could pick up some of your partner's feelings by the touch of her hands, her posture, and expressions—maybe more than you could during your conversation. We hope that this exercise showed you that there are other languages besides words that carry messages about your relationships.

The point isn't so much *how* you or your partner behaved during the exercises—whether you were tense or relaxed, friendly or distant. We wanted to show you that even without any formal experience you can recognize and to some degree interpret messages that other people send nonverbally. In this chapter we want to sharpen the skills you already have, to give you a better grasp of the vocabulary of nonverbal language, and to show you how this understanding can help you understand yourself and others better.

You Can't Not Communicate   The fact that communication without words took place between you and your partner brings us to this second important feature of nonverbal communication. To understand what we mean here, think back to the experience you just finished. Suppose we'd asked you not to communicate any messages at all while with your partner. What would you have done? Closed your eyes? Withdrawn into a ball? Left the room? You can probably see that even these behaviors communicate messages that mean you're avoiding contact.

Take a minute now to try *not* communicating. Join with a partner and spend some time trying not to reveal any messages to one another. What happens?

This impossibility of not communicating is extremely important to understand because it means that each of us is a kind of transmitter that

> HE THAT HAS EYES TO SEE AND
> EARS TO HEAR MAY CONVINCE
> HIMSELF THAT NO MORTAL CAN
> KEEP A SECRET. IF HIS LIPS ARE
> SILENT, HE CHATTERS WITH HIS
> FINGER TIPS; BETRAYAL OOZES
> OUT OF HIM AT EVERY PORE.
>
> SIGMUND FREUD

cannot be shut off. No matter what we do, we give off information about ourselves.

Stop for a moment and examine yourself as you read this. If someone were observing you now, what nonverbal clues would they get about how you're feeling? Are you sitting forward or reclining back? Is your posture tense or relaxed? Are your eyes wide open, or do they keep closing? What does your facial expression communicate? Can you make your face expressionless? Don't people with expressionless faces communicate something to you?

Of course, we don't always intend to send nonverbal messages. Consider, for instance, behaviors like blushing, frowning, sweating, or stammering. We rarely try to act in these ways, and often we're not aware when we're doing so. Nonetheless, others recognize signs like these and make interpretations about us based on their observations.

The fact that you and everyone around you is constantly sending off nonverbal clues is important because it means that you have a constant source of information available about yourself and others. If you can tune into these signals, you'll be more aware of how those around you are feeling and thinking, and you'll be better able to respond to their behavior.

Nonverbal Communication Transmits Feelings   As you study this subject, you'll find that even though feelings are communicated quite well nonverbally, thoughts don't lend themselves to nonverbal channels.

Think back to the exercise at the beginning of the chapter. Do you recall the different kinds of messages that you sent and received in the talking and nontalking parts of it? Most people find that in the first parts (where they communicate verbally) they talk about what they *think:* ''Does the exercise seem like a good or bad one?''; ''What have you been doing lately?''; ''Did you do your reading?''; and so on. Quite different kinds of messages usually come across in the last step, however. Without being able to use words, peoples' bodies generally express how they *feel*—nervous, embarrassed, playful, friendly, etc.

You can test this another way. Here's a list that contains both thoughts and feelings. Try to express each item nonverbally, and see which ones come most easily:

You're tired.

You're in favor of capital punishment.

You're attracted to another person in the group.

You think marijuana should be legalized.

You're angry at someone in the group.

Nonverbal Communication Serves Many Functions   Just because this chapter deals with nonverbal communication, don't get the idea that our words and our actions are unrelated. Quite the opposite is true: Verbal and nonverbal communication are interconnected elements in every act of communication. Nonverbal behaviors can operate in several relationships to verbal messages.

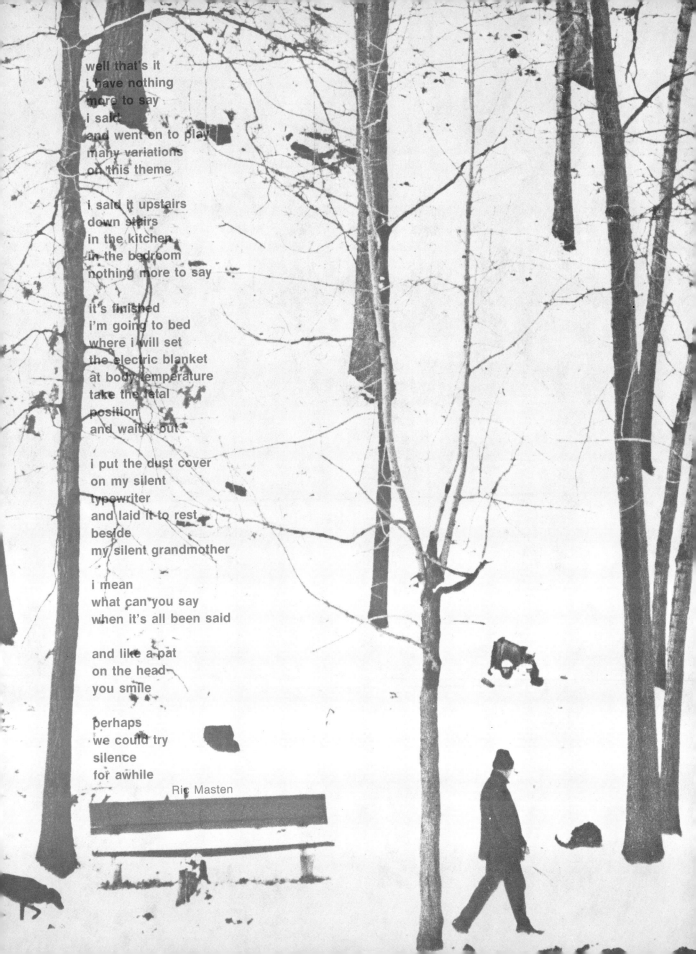

well that's it
i have nothing
more to say
i said
and went on to play
many variations
on this theme

i said it upstairs
down stairs
in the kitchen
in the bedroom
nothing more to say

it's finished
i'm going to bed
where i will set
the electric blanket
at body temperature
take the fetal
position
and wait it out

i put the dust cover
on my silent
typewriter
and laid it to rest
beside
my silent grandmother

i mean
what can you say
when it's all been said

and like a pat
on the head
you smile

perhaps
we could try
silence
for awhile

Ric Masten

she dresses in flags
comes on
like a mack truck
she paints
her eyelids green
and her mouth
is a loud speaker
rasping out
profanity

at cocktail parties
she is everywhere
like a sheep dog
working a flock
nipping at your sleeve
spilling your drink
bestowing
wet sloppy kisses

but i
have received
secret messages
carefully written
from the shy
quiet woman
who hides
in this
bizarre
gaudy castle

Ric Masten

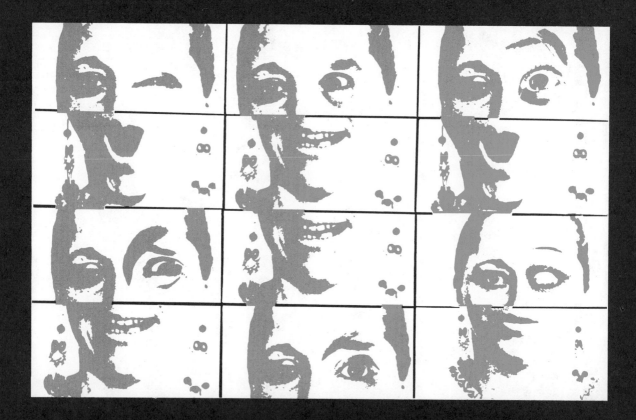

First, nonverbal behaviors can *repeat* what is said verbally. If someone asked you for directions to the nearest drugstore, you could say, ''North of here about two blocks,'' and then repeat your instructions nonverbally by pointing north.

Nonverbal messages may also *substitute* for verbal ones. When you see a familiar friend wearing a certain facial expression, you don't need to ask, ''How's it going?'' In the same way, experience has probably shown you that other kinds of looks, gestures, and other clues say, ''I'm angry at you'' or ''I feel great'' far better than words.

A third way in which verbal and nonverbal messages can relate is called *complementing.* If you saw a student talking to a teacher, and his head was bowed slightly, his voice was low and hesitating, and he shuffled slowly from foot to foot, you might conclude that he felt inferior to the teacher, possibly embarrassed about something he did. The nonverbal behaviors you observed provided the context for the verbal behaviors—they conveyed the relationship between the teacher and student. Complementing nonverbal behaviors signal the attitudes the interactants have for one another.

Nonverbal behaviors can also *accent* verbal messages. Just as we can use *italics* in print to underline an idea, we can emphasize some part of a face-to-face message in various ways. Pointing an accusing finger adds emphasis to criticism (as well as probably creating defensiveness in the receiver). Shrugging shoulders accent confusion, and hugs can highlight excitement or affection. As you'll see later in this chapter, the voice plays a big role in accenting verbal messages.

Nonverbal behavior also serves to *regulate* verbal behavior. By lowering your voice at the end of a sentence, ''trailing off,'' you indicate that the other person may speak. You can also convey this information through the use of eye contact and by the way you position your body.

Finally—and often most significantly—nonverbal behavior can often *contradict* the spoken word. People often simultaneously express different and even contradictory messages in their verbal and nonverbal behaviors. A common example of this sort of ''double message'' is the experience we've all had of hearing someone with a red face and bulging veins yelling, ''Angry? No, *I'm not angry!''*

Usually, however, the contradiction between words and nonverbal clues isn't this obvious. At times we all try to seem different than we are. There are many reasons for this contradictory behavior: to cover nervousness when giving a speech or in a job interview, to keep someone from worrying about us, or to appear more attractive than we believe we really are.

Even though some of the ways in which people contradict themselves are subtle, double messages have a strong impact. Research suggests that when a receiver perceives an inconsistency between verbal and nonverbal messages, the unspoken one carries more weight.

As we discuss the different kinds of nonverbal communication throughout this chapter, we'll point out a number of ways in which people contradict themselves by either conscious or unconscious behaviors. Thus, by the end of this chapter you should have a better idea of how others feel, even when they can't or won't tell you with their words.

Pleads he in earnest?—Look upon his
  face,
His eyes do drop no tears; his prayers are
  jest;
His words come from his mouth; ours,
  from our breast;
He prays but faintly, and would be
  denied;
We pray with heart and soul.

Shakespeare, Richard II

Nonverbal Communication Is Ambiguous   Before you get the idea that merely reading this chapter will turn you into some sort of mind reader, we want to caution you and in so doing introduce a fifth feature of nonverbal communication: A great deal of ambiguity surrounds nonverbal behavior. To understand what we mean, how would you interpret silence from your spouse, date, or companion after an evening in which you both laughed and joked a lot? Can you think of at least two possible meanings for this nonverbal behavior? Or suppose that a much admired person with whom you've worked suddenly begins paying more attention to you than ever before. What could the possible meanings of this be?

The point is that although nonverbal behavior can be very revealing, it can have so many possible meanings that it's foolish to think that your interpretations will always be correct.

When you do try to make sense out of ambiguous nonverbal behavior, you need to consider several factors: The *context* in which they occur (e.g., smiling at a joke suggests a different feeling than smiling at another's misfortune); the *history of your relationship* with the sender (friendly, hostile, etc.); *the other's mood* at the time; and *your feelings* (when you're feeling insecure, almost anything can seem like a threat).

The important idea here is that when you become aware of nonverbal messages, you should think of them not as facts, but as *clues* that need to be checked out using the sense-interpret-consequence-feel-intend format from Chapter 1.

Reading "Body Language"

In your journey through the supermarket checkout stand or while waiting for a plane you've probably noticed books that promise to teach you how to read "body language." These books claim that you can become a kind of mind reader, learning the deepest secrets of everyone around you. But, it's not quite as simple as it sounds. Here's an exercise that will both increase your skill in observing nonverbal behavior and show you the dangers of being too sure that you're a perfect reader of body language. You can try the exercise either in or out of class, and the period of time over which you do it is flexible, from a single class period to several days. In any case begin by choosing a partner, and then follow these directions:

1. For the first period of time (however long you decide to make it), observe the way your partner behaves. Notice how she moves, her mannerisms, postures, the way she speaks, how she dresses, etc. To remember your observations, jot them down. If you're doing this exercise out of class over an extended period of time, there's no need to let your observations interfere with whatever you'd normally be doing: Your only job here is to compile a list of your partner's behaviors. In this step you should be careful *not* to *interpret* your partner's actions; just record what you *see*.

2. At the end of the time period share what you've seen with your partner. She'll do the same with you.

3. For the next period of time your job is to not only observe your partner's behavior but also to *interpret* it. This time in your conference you should tell your partner what you thought her actions said about her. For example, if she dressed carelessly, did you think this meant she overslept, that she's losing interest in her appearance, or that she was trying to be more comfortable? If you noticed her yawning frequently, did you think this meant she was bored, tired from a late night, or sleepy after a big meal? Don't feel bad if your guesses weren't all correct. Remember, nonverbal clues tend to be ambiguous. You may be surprised how checking out the nonverbal clues you observe can help build a relationship with another person.

This exercise should have showed you the difference between merely observing somebody's behavior and actually interpreting it. Noticing someone's shaky hands or smile is one thing, but deciding what such behaviors mean is quite another. If you're like most people, you probably found that a lot of your guesses were incorrect. Now, if that was true here, it may also be true in your daily life. Being a sharp nonverbal observer can give you some good hunches about how people are feeling, but the only way you can find out if these hunches are correct is to *check them out* verbally.

You may also have found that sharing your feelings with your partner expanded your relationship with that person. As we said in the defensiveness chapter, simply describing your feelings using "I" language is a good way of gaining understanding.

Keeping the five characteristics of nonverbal communication in mind, let's take a look at some of the ways we communicate in addition to words.

The first area of nonverbal communication we want to talk about is the broad field of *kinesics,* or body motion. In this section we'll explore the role that posture, gestures, body orientation, facial expressions, and eye behaviors play in our relationships with each other.

I suppose it was something you said
That caused me to tighten
And pull away.
And when you asked,
"What is it?"
I, of course, said,
"Nothing."

Whenever I say, "Nothing,"
You may be very certain there is something.
The something is a cold, hard lump of
Nothing.

Lois Wyse

Body Orientation

We'll start with body orientation—the degree to which we face toward or away from someone with our body, feet, and head. To understand how this kind of physical positioning communicates nonverbal messages you might try an experiment.

You'll need two friends to help you. Imagine that two of you are in the middle of a personal conversation when a third person approaches and wants to join you. You're not especially glad to see this person, but you don't want to sound rude by asking her to leave. Your task is to signal to the intruder that you'd rather be alone, using only the position of your bodies. You can talk to the third person if you wish, but you can't verbally tell her that you want privacy.

When you've tried this experiment, or if you've ever been in a real-life situation similar to it, you know that by turning your body slightly away from an intruder you can make your feelings very clear. An intruder finds herself in the difficult position of trying to talk over your shoulder, and it isn't long before she gets the message and goes her way. The nonverbal message here is "Look, we're interested in each other right now and don't want to include you in our conversation." The general rule this situation describes is that facing someone directly signals your interest, and facing away signals a desire to avoid involvement. This explains how we can pack ourselves into intimate distance with total strangers in places like a crowded elevator without offending others. Because there's a very indirect orientation here (everyone is usually standing shoulder to shoulder, facing in the same direction), we understand that despite the close quarters everyone wants to avoid personal contact.

By observing the way people position themselves you can learn a good deal about how they feel. Next time you're in a crowded place where people can choose whom to face directly, try observing who seems to be included in the action and who is being subtly shut out. And in the same way, pay attention to your own body orientation. You may be surprised to discover that you're avoiding a certain person without being conscious of it or that at times you're "turning your back" on people altogether. If this is the case, it may be helpful to figure out why. Are you avoiding an unpleasant situation that needs clearing up, communicating your annoyance or dislike for the other, or sending some other message?

Nonverbal Feedback

1. Choose a partner, and form a group of about five pairs.
2. Sit in two concentric circles, with one partner in each circle. People on the outside should sit so they can easily see their partner.

3. Now, for fifteen minutes or so the inside group should carry on a discussion about some subject that will generate lots of personal feelings. (Some possible topics are: would you want your teenage child to smoke marijuana, and should capital punishment be abolished?)

4. During this time people in the outside circle should observe their partner, noticing as many characteristic gestures, postures, facial expressions, and other nonverbal clues as possible.

5. After fifteen minutes the partners should meet. The observer can now feed back his partner's nonverbal behavior, being careful only to describe and not to interpret it. After this description the partner who was observed may want to discuss what nonverbal messages she might have been sending.

6. Now switch places and repeat steps 2 to 5, discussing a new topic.

Posture

Another way we communicate nonverbally is through our posture.

To see if this is true, stop reading for a moment and notice how you're sitting. What does your position say nonverbally about how you feel? Are there any other people near you now? What messages do you get from their present posture? By paying attention to the postures of those around you, as well as your own, you'll find another channel of nonverbal communication that can furnish information about how people feel about themselves and each other.

An indication of how much posture communicates is shown by our language. It's full of expressions that link emotional states with body postures:

I won't take this lying down!

He can stand on his own two feet.

She has to carry a heavy burden.

Take a load off your back.

He's all wrapped up in himself.

Don't be so uptight!

Such phrases show that an awareness of posture exists for us, even if it's often unconscious. The main reason we miss most posture messages is that they aren't very obvious. It's seldom that a person who feels weighted down by a problem hunches over so much that he stands out in a crowd, and when we're bored we usually don't lean back and slump enough to embarrass the other person. In reading posture, then, the key is to look for small changes that might be shadows of the way people feel inside.

I don't want to disgrace you —

I've shined up my bones and
smoothed my skin in quiet
folds around me, arranged
my limbs tastefully
in elegant lines that none may see
elbow or knee, i've instructed
my jaw not to grin nor jape,
my lips to stay firmly in place:

I shall not blink nor stare
nor will a hair upon my head
move, and I can hold my feet
still, that not a toe will tumble:

I don't want to disgrace you —

but my hands have their own
history and instinctively
at your entrance

rise to your face

Gerald Huckaby

For example, a teacher who has a reputation for interesting classes told us how he uses his understanding of micropostures to do a better job. "Because of my large classes I have to lecture a lot," he said, "And that's an easy way to turn students off. I work hard to make my talks entertaining, but you know that nobody's perfect, and I do have my off days. I can tell when I'm not doing a good job of communicating by picking out three or four students before I start my talk and watching how they sit throughout the class period. As long as they're leaning forward in their seats, I know I'm doing okay, but if I look up and see them starting to slump back, I know I'd better change my approach."

Psychologist Albert Mehrabian has found that other postural keys to feelings are tension and relaxation. He says that we take relaxed postures in nonthreatening situations and tighten up when threatened. Based on this observation he says we can tell a good deal about how others feel simply by watching how tense or loose they seem to be. For example, he suggests that watching tenseness is a way of detecting status differences: The lower-status person is generally the more rigid, tense-appearing one, whereas the one with higher status is more relaxed. This is the kind of situation that often happens when we picture a "chat" with the boss (or professor, judge, et cetera) where we sit ramrod straight while she leans back in her chair. The same principle applies to social situations, where it's often possible to tell who's uncomfortable by looking at pictures. Often you'll see someone laughing and talking as if he were perfectly at home, but his posture almost shouts nervousness. Some people never relax, and their posture shows it.

Try spending an hour or so observing the posture of those around you. See if you can get some idea of how they're feeling by the way they carry themselves. Also, pay attention to your own posture. In what situations do you tense up? Is this a sign of anger, aggressiveness, excitement, fear? Do you ever find yourself signaling boredom, interest, attraction, or other emotions by your posture? Do the feelings you find yourself expressing posturally ever surprise you?

Gestures

Gestures are another good source of nonverbal communication. In an article titled "Nonverbal Leakage and Clues to Deception" Paul Ekman and Wallace Friesen observed how gestures transmit emotions. They explained that because most of us, at least unconsciously, know that the face is the most obvious channel of expressing emotions, we're especially careful to control our facial expressions when trying to hide our feelings. But most of us are less aware of the ways we move our hands, legs, and feet, and because of this these movements are better indicators of how we truly feel.

Probably the clearest example of someone whose feelings show through gestures is the fidgeter. They're the kind of people who assure us that "everything is fine" while almost ceaselessly biting their fingernails, flicking their cigarette, bending paperclips, and so on. Even when fidgeters are aware of these gestures and try to control them, their nervousness usually finds another way of leaking out, such as toe tapping, leg crossing and uncrossing, or other restless movements.

Besides nervousness, you can often detect other emotions from a person's gestures. It's possible to observe anger by looking beyond a smile and noticing the whitened knuckles and clenched fists. When people would like to express their friendship or attraction toward us, but for some reason feel they can't, we can sometimes notice them slightly reaching out or maybe even opening their hands. In one article, Albert Scheflen, a psychiatrist, tells how a person's sexual feelings can be signaled through gestures. He describes "preening behaviors" that draw attention to the sender's body and advertise a "come-on" message. Movements such as stroking or combing the hair, glancing in a mirror, and rearranging the clothing are sometimes signals of sexual interest in another person. (It's important not to overemphasize the sexual angle: such gestures also are more general signals of interest in the topic of conversation or one's partner.)

Ekman and Friesen describe another kind of double message—the "lie of omission." These deceivers nonverbally show their true feelings by failing to accompany their words with the appropriate gestures. This is the kind of behavior we see from a person who talks about being excited or happy while sitting almost motionless with hands, arms, legs, and posture signaling boredom, discomfort, or fatigue. In addition to sending double messages, gestures play other roles—repeating, substituting, complementing, accenting, and regulating in conversations.

Fie, fie upon her!
There's language in her eyes,
    her cheek, her lip.
Nay, her foot speaks; her wanton
    spirits look out at every
joint and motive in her body.

William Shakespeare
Troilus and Cressida

. . . the expert [poker player] is a psychologist.

He is continually studying the other players to see, first, if they have any telltale habits, and second, if there are any situations in which they act automatically.

In connection with general habits, I divide poker players into three classes

(a) the ingenuous player,

(b) the tricky, or coffee-housing player,

(c) the unreadable player.

The ingenuous player   When the ingenuous player looks worried, he probably is worried.

When he takes a long time to bet, he probably doesn't think much of his hand.

When he bets quickly, he fancies his hand.

When he bluffs, he looks a little guilty, and when he really has a good hand, you can see him mentally wishing to be called.

This ingenuousness, incidently, is seldom found in veteran players. A player of this type usually quits poker at an early stage on account of his "bad luck."

The tricky or coffee-housing player   At least ninety percent of all poker players fall into this category.

The tricky player has a great tendency to act just opposite of the way he really feels. Thus with a very good hand, he trembles a little as he bets, while with a poor hand, he fairly exudes confidence. Of course, he may be triple-crossing, but year-in and year-out I have played in a great many games, and have found that at least two times out of three when another player makes a special effort to look confident, he has nothing, while when he tries to look nervous, he is loaded.

There is one mild little coffee-housing habit that practically never fails to act as a giveaway.

That is showing too much nonchalance. For instance, it is my turn to bet, and as I am about to put my chips in the pot, one of the other players casually lights a cigarette. Experience tells me that this casual player is at least going to call me, and is very likely to raise me if I bet.

Accordingly, if I do see that sign, unless my hand is really very good, I refuse to bet for him and simply check.

The unreadable player   This particular individual is, of course, the hardest opponent of all.

Invariably, he knows all the rules of correct play, but departs from all of them on occasion. Unlike the ingenuous player, who acts the way he feels, or the coffee-house, who acts the way he doesn't feel, this player has no consistency.

Accordingly, the fact that he exudes confidence or looks nervous gives no clue to the nature of his hand.

The preceding discussion has been of a very general nature. Here are a few specific giveaway habits I have noticed.

(It should be borne in mind that poker has no ethics, except in a few obvious and specific instances and that short of actually cheating, which, by the way, includes attempting to peek at another player's hand, you have the right to any advantage you can gain.)

Glancing to the left   In the early stages of betting, a player with a normal calling hand usually comes into the pot with no fuss whatsoever. However, a player with a good hand is going to consider raising and before betting, is likely to cast a covert glance toward the players in back of him (on his left) to see if he can get any idea of what they are going to do.

If it looks to him as if two or three of them are going to call, he sandbags. If it looks as if they are all going to drop, he raises.

Accordingly, when I see this glance, even though the player merely calls, I am fairly sure that his hand is fully strong enough for a raise.

Looking at the hole card the second time   The very best stud players, of course, look at their hole card once, and then know it for the rest of the hand, but the average player, particularly with a low card in the hole, is likely to be careless and not remember it.

Accordingly, there are many instances where a second glance at the hole card gives a lot of information.

For instance:

The first bettor shows an ace. On the next card, he receives a six, and promptly looks at his hole card. At this point, there is a very strong presumption that his hole card is a six or very close to it.

Piling chips on your hole card   This is probably the most telltale giveaway habit of all.

Before the second card is dealt, a player looks at his hole card. If it is a low card, he pays no attention to it, but if it is a high card he is quite likely to put it down and pile some chips on top of it immediately, to prevent any possibility of it blowing over.

I know I must have seen chips piled on top of the hole card in that situation hundreds of times, and I do not recall more than two or three instances where the card was lower than a jack, and very few when it was not an ace or a king.

Looking at your draw   In Draw Poker, it is the exceptional player who will simply pick up the cards and look at them. The average player has various methods of mixing his draw with his hand, squeezing the cards, looking at them one at a time, etc.

While little can be learned about the nature of a player's hand from the manner in which he looks at his draw, there is one pretty general giveaway in connection with a one-card draw.

A player drawing to a flush or two pair is likely to put the card he draws in the middle of his hand A player drawing to an open straight invariably puts the card either on top or bottom.

Oswald Jacoby, *Oswald Jacoby on Poker*

The Face and Eyes

The face and eyes are probably the most noticed parts of the body, but this doesn't mean that their nonverbal messages are the easiest to read. The face is a tremendously complicated channel of expression for several reasons.

First, it's hard even to describe the number and kind of expressions we commonly produce with our face and eyes. For example, researchers have found that there are at least eight distinguishable positions of the eyebrows and forehead, eight more of the eyes and lids, and ten for the lower face. When you multiply this complexity by the number of emotions we experience, you can see why it would be almost impossible to compile a dictionary of facial expressions and their corresponding emotions.

Another reason for the difficulty in understanding facial expressions is the speed with which they can change. For example, slow-motion films have been taken that show expressions fleeting across a subject's face in as short a time as a fifth of a second. Also, it seems that different emotions show most clearly in different parts of the face: happiness and surprise in the eyes and lower face, anger in the lower face and brows and forehead, fear and sadness in the eyes, and disgust in the lower face.

Ekman and Friesen have identified six basic emotions that facial expressions reflect—surprise, fear, anger, disgust, happiness, and sadness. Expressions reflecting these feelings seem to be recognizable in and between members of all cultures. Of course, affect blends—the combination of two or more expressions in different parts of the face—are possible. For instance, it's easy to imagine how someone would look who is fearful and surprised or disgusted and angry.

Research also indicates that people are quite accurate at judging facial expressions of these emotions. Accuracy increases when judges know the target or have knowledge of the context in which the expression occurs, or when they have seen several samples of the target's expressions.

In spite of the complex way in which the face shows emotions, you can still pick up messages by watching it. One of the easiest ways is to look for expressions that seem to be overdone. Often when someone is trying to fool himself or another he'll emphasize his mask to a point where it seems too exaggerated to be true. Another way to detect a person's feelings is by watching his expression at moments when he isn't likely to be thinking about his appearance. We've all had the experience of glancing into another car while stopped in a traffic jam or looking around at a sporting event and seeing expressions that the wearer would probably never show in more guarded moments. At other times it's possible to watch a microexpression as it flashes

© 1979 United Feature Syndicate, Inc.

across a person's face. For just a moment we see a flash of emotion quite different from the one a speaker is trying to convey. Finally, you may be able to spot contradictory expressions on different parts of someone's face: His eyes say one thing, but the expression of his mouth or eyebrows might be sending quite a different message.

The eyes themselves can send several kinds of messages. Meeting someone's glance with your eyes is usually a sign of involvement, while looking away signals a desire to avoid contact. As we mentioned earlier, this is why solicitors on the street—panhandlers, salesmen, petitioners—try to catch our eye. Once they've managed to establish contact with a glance, it becomes harder for the approached person to draw away. A friend explained how to apply this principle to hitchhiking. "When I'm hitching a ride, I'm always careful to look each driver in the eye as he comes toward me. Most of them will try to look somewhere else as they pass, but if I can catch somebody's eye, he'll almost always stop." Most of us remember trying to avoid a question we didn't understand by glancing away from the teacher. At times like these we usually became very interested in our textbooks, fingernails, the clock—anything but the teacher's stare. Of course, the teacher always seemed to know the meaning of this nonverbal behavior and ended up picking on those of us who signaled our uncertainty.

Another kind of message the eyes communicate is a positive or negative attitude. When someone glances toward us with the proper facial expression, we get a clear message that the looker is interested in us, thus the expression "making eyes." At the same time, when our long glances toward someone else are avoided by him, we can be pretty sure that the other person isn't as interested in us as we are in him. (Of course, there are all sorts of courtship games in which the receiver of a glance pretends not to notice any message by glancing away, yet signals his interest with some other part of the body.)

The eyes communicate both dominance and submission. We've all played the game of trying to stare down somebody, and in real life there are also times when downcast eyes are a sign of giving in. In some religious orders, for example, subordinate members are expected to keep their eyes downcast when addressing a superior.

Even the pupils of our eyes communicate. E. H. Hess and J. M. Polt of the University of Chicago measured the amount of pupil dilation while showing men and women various types of pictures. The results of the experiment were very interesting: A person's eyes grow larger in proportion to the degree of interest they have in an object. For example, men's pupils grew about eighteen percent larger when looking at pictures of a naked woman, and the degree of dilation for women looking at a naked man's picture was twenty percent. Interestingly enough, the greatest increase in pupil size occurred when women looked at a picture of a mother and infant. A good salesman can increase his profits by being aware of pupil dilation, as Edward Hall describes. He was once in a Middle East bazaar, where an Arab merchant insisted that a customer looking at his jewelry buy a certain piece that the shopper hadn't been paying much attention to. But the vendor had been watching the pupils of the buyer's eyes and had known what the buyer really wanted.

PEOPLE ARE REALLY TWO-FACED

Normal face

Composite of right halves

Composite of left halves

Portrait painters and photographers know only too well that the human face is asymmetrical; wrinkles and eyebrow movements vary, and the smile usually breaks from one side to the other. What is more, each side seems to express a different feeling. This phenomenon can best be shown by first covering one half of the face in a portrait, then the other. In most cases, the right side of the subject's face (on the viewer's left) appears pleasant or blank; the left side looks worried, fearful or even a bit sinister. The difference is even more pronounced when a composite face made of two left sides is compared with one composed of two right sides.

Taking note of this right-left difference, Psychologist Werner Wolff of Columbia University

suggested in the 1940s that the right side is the "public" face, and the left the "private," registering emotions that are not intended to be conveyed. Yet this strategy of "hiding" unacceptable emotions on the left side of the face could be effective only if the public side had far more impact on the viewer. Wolff found this to be so; after studying the faces of others, subjects in his experiments noted that the right side of the face looked more like the whole face than the left side did. But Wolff could not explain why.

Now a team of psychologists thinks it has the answer. Writing in the journal *Science,* Harold Sackeim of Columbia and Ruben Gur and Marcel Saucy of the University of Pennsylvania report that the left side of the face is not perceived well by a viewer. The team bases its conclusion on split-brain research, which shows that the right hemisphere of the brain has predominant control over the

left side of the face and that the left hemisphere governs the right side. Other studies indicate that the right hemisphere of the brain is better than the left in recognizing faces and processing emotional information.

As the researchers explain, when two people stand face to face, the right of one studies the left side of the face of the other. The right eye, in turn, is controlled by the left hemisphere of the brain the half that is less deft at reading images. Thus people may unconsciously mislead one another by presenting a confident or blank public expression on the right side of the face, where it has a strong effect, and by "hiding" strong emotions on the poorly perceived left side.

In the course of the studies, Sackeim's team found that

negative emotions registered heavily on the left side, but positive emotions spread more evenly across the entire face. Says Sackeim: "We believe the two sides of the face are differently involved in experiencing happy and unhappy states." Other researchers have reported "small correlations" between emotional illness and a high degrees of facial asymmetry. Sackeim is currently studying these results. "Why should people with greater facial asymmetry report more neurotic symptoms?" he asks. "We don't understand the connection."

Sackeim's interpretation of the evidence is that the emotional left side of the face may have evolved to convey a clear message about feelings—the facial expression is more strongly drawn to compensate to the poor ability of the left brain to read faces. Sackeim's research has also convinced him that the brain's right hemisphere is more heavily involved in expressing emotions than the left. What does it all boil down to, in practical terms? When in doubt about anyone's feelings, just study the left side of the person's face with your left eye.

Time Magazine

Voice

The voice itself is another channel of nonverbal communication. We don't mean the words we say, which after all make up verbal communication, but rather *how* we say them. If you think about it for a moment, you'll realize that a certain way of speaking can give the same word or words many meanings. For example, look at the possible meanings from a single sentence just by changing the word emphasis:

This is a fantastic communication book.
  (Not just any book, but *this* one in particular.)

This is a *fantastic* communication book.
  (This book is superior, exciting.)

This is a fantastic *communication* book.
  (The book is good as far as communication goes; it may not be so great as literature drama, et cetera.)

This is a fantastic communication *book*.
  (It's not a play or record, it's a book.)

It's possible to get an idea across without ever expressing it outright by emphasizing a certain word in a sentence. For example, a State Department official in the Nixon administration, was able to express the government's position in an off-the-record way when answering questions. He had three different ways of saying "I would not speculate." When he added no accent, he meant the department didn't really know; when he emphasized the "I," he meant "I wouldn't, but you may—and with some assurance"; when he emphasized "speculate," he meant that the questioner's premise was probably wrong.

There are many other ways our voice communicates—through its tone, speed, pitch, and number and length of pauses, volume, find disfluencies (such as stammering, use of "uh," "um," "er," and so on). All these factors together can be called "paralanguage," and they can do a great deal to reinforce or contradict the message our words convey.

Sarcasm is one instance in which we use both emphasis and tone of voice to change a statement's meaning to the opposite of its verbal message. Experience this yourself with the following three statements. First time through mean them literally, and then say them sarcastically.

Darling, what a beautiful little gown!

I really had a wonderful time on my blind date.

There's nothing I like better than calves' brains on toast.

Albert Mehrabian and others have conducted experiments which indicate that when the vocal factors (tone of voice, disfluences, emphasis, etc.) contradict the verbal message (words), the vocal factors carry more meaning. They had subjects evaluate the degree of liking communicated by a message in which vocal clues conflicted with the words and found that the words had very little effect on the interpretation of the message.

Communication through paralanguage isn't always intentional. Often our voices give us away when we're trying to create an impression different from our actual feelings. For example, you've probably had experiences of trying to sound calm and serene when you were really exploding with inner nervousness. Maybe your deception went along perfectly for a while—just the right smile, no telltale fidgeting of the hands, posture appearing relaxed—and then, without being able to do a thing about it, right in the middle of your relaxed comments your voice squeaked! The charade was over.

The derivation of the word "personality" proves that there was originally a profound understanding of the close connection between voice and personality. The word comes from the Latin persona, which originally meant the mouthpiece of a mask used by actors (persona: the sound of the voice passes through). From the mask the term shifted to the actor; the "person" in drama. The word eventually came to mean any person and finally "personality," but over the centuries it lost its symbolic connection with the voice.

Paul Moses, M.D.
The Voice of Neurosis

Big Brother Is Listening

It could change forever the relationships between husbands and wives, witnesses and juries, political leaders and voters, businessmen and customers. It could sharply reduce the output of talk all over by making everyone think twice before speaking. It could also bring closer the Orwellian society of *1984*. The remarkable but ominous device that might cause these changes is the P.S.E. (for Psychological Stress Evaluator) which, its inventors believe, can use voice recordings to detect lies without the cooperation or even the presence of the speaker.

The new lie detector is a creation of Dektor Counterintelligence and Security, Inc. of Springfield, Va. It uses an ordinary tape recording of a voice on radio or TV or in any of the numerous settings where lies may be told: in a police station, perhaps, at a press conference, on the speaker's platform at a political meeting, or in the bedroom of a married—or unmarried—couple. The tape is fed into a machine that measures muscular microtremors in the voice, faint quivers that come from the muscles in the voice box and cause slight changes in pitch. Changes are not detectable by ear, but they can be traced on a chart by a pen linked to the machine. It is the capacity to detect and reproduce these tremors—apparently produced by the freely undulating throat muscles of a relaxed speaker—that gives the P.S.E. its awesome powers. For the throat muscles of a person under stress are so tense that they produce practically no microtremors.

Government intelligence agencies have already bought four of the machines (at $3,200 each), allegedly for testing purposes only. Also, by agreement of prosecution and defense, the P.S.E. has been used in four Maryland court cases. In three, negative findings by the device led to dropping one murder and two bad-check charges; in the fourth case, a positive report ensured conviction in a shoplifting incident. In addition, Dektor reports that it has monitored the TV program *To Tell the Truth* and been 94.7% successful in finding out who the truth tellers really were.

P.S.E.'s reliability still has not been proved. No independent agency has double checked the company's TV experiment. Moreover, some lie detector experts caution that the weakness of the stress evaluator may lie in its dependence on a single measure of bodily function (the polygraph, or conventional lie detector, records several: pulse rate, blood pressure, respiration and sweat-gland activity). Besides, experts agree that although both the old and new devices can spot stress neither can prove absolutely that the stress results from lying. The most serious objection to the P.S.E. is ethical. As the company itself suggests, the machine can be used covertly, thus invading the privacy to which, presumably, even liars are entitled.

Time Magazine

Voice Messages

Here's an experiment that can give you an idea of some messages your voice communicates.

1. Choose a partner, and find a space for yourselves.

2. Now close your eyes. You'll be focusing on the voice as a means of communication; this will help screen out other kinds of nonverbal messages.

3. For five minutes carry on a conversation about whatever you want. As you talk, listen to your partner's voice. Try not to concentrate as much on the *words* as the way your partner *sounds*. Imagine what messages you'd receive if you were listening to a foreign language.

4. Now with your eyes still shut tell your partner what messages you received from the sound of her voice. Did it sound tired, relaxed, happy, tense? Share your perceptions.

5. Still keeping your eyes closed, take turns performing the following step. The first person begins a sentence with the words "I am my voice . . . ,"

completing the statement by describing whatever he hears his voice communicating. For example: "I am my voice and I'm very excited. I'm high-pitched and fast, and I can go on and on without stopping"; or "I am my voice, and I'm tired. I hardly ever say anything, and when I do, it's very quietly. It hardly takes anything to make me stop."

6. After both partners have completed the previous step, take turns sharing your perceptions of your partner's description of her voice. Do you agree with the interpretation, or did you pick up different messages?

7. As you talk with others both in and outside of class, try to listen to the messages your voice sends. Can you tell when you're sincere and when you're being untruthful? Do you have a different voice for certain occasions with: parents, employers, teachers, certain friends? Do you have a happy, bored, angry voice? What do these different voices say about the relationships in which you use them?

An interesting variation of this exercise is to spend five minutes or so holding a conversation with your partner in gibberish. Say whatever nonsense syllables come to your mind, and see what happens. If you can get over the fear of sounding foolish for a few minutes (is this so horrible?), you'll probably find that you can communicate a great deal with your voice, even without words.

Touching

Besides being the earliest means we have of making contact with others, touching is essential to our healthy development. During the nineteenth and early twentieth centuries a large percentage of children born every year died from a disease then called *marasmus,* which translated from Greek means "wasting away." In some orphanages the mortality rate was nearly 100 percent, but even children in the most "progressive" homes, hospitals, and other institutions died regularly from the ailment. When researchers finally tracked down the causes of this disease, they found that the infants suffered from lack of physical contact with parents or nurses, rather than nutrition, medical care, or other factors. They hadn't been touched enough, and as a result they died. From this knowledge came the practice of "mothering" children in institutions—picking the baby up, carrying it around, and handling it several times each day. At one hospital that began this practice, the death rate for infants fell from between 30 and 35 percent to below 10 percent.

As a child develops, the need for being touched continues. In his excellent book *Touching: The Human Significance of the Skin,* Ashley Montagu describes research which suggests that allergies, eczema, and other health problems are in part caused by a person's lack of contact as an infant with his mother. Although Montagu says that these problems develop early in life, he also cites cases where adults suffering from conditions as diverse as asthma and schizophrenia have been successfully treated by psychiatric therapy that uses extensive physical contact.

Touch seems to increase a child's mental functioning as well as physical

> *The unconscious parental feelings communicated through touch or lack of touch can lead to feelings of confusion and conflict in a child. Sometimes a "modern" parent will say all the right things but not want to touch his child very much. The child's confusion comes from the inconsistency of levels: if they really approve of me so much like they say they do, why won't they touch me?*
>
> William Schutz, *Here Comes Everybody*

health. L. J. Yarrow has conducted surveys which show that babies who have been given plenty of physical stimulation by their mothers have significantly higher IQs than those receiving less contact.

The society we live in places less importance on touch than on other, less immediate senses such as sight or hearing. Our language is full of visual and aural figures of speech such as "Seeing is believing," "I'll be hearing from you," "Here's looking at you," and "Sounding something out." As Bernard Gunther points out, when leaving someone we say, "See you later," never "touch," "smell," or "taste" you later.

Touch can communicate many messages. Besides the nurturing/caring function we just discussed, it can convey friendship, sexual interest, and aggressiveness. In addition, Mark Knapp points out that touch can serve as a means of managing transactions, such as when we tug at another's sleeve. Context also influences the way we ascribe meaning to touch. For example, we allow physicians and haircutters to touch us in ways we usually reserve for more intimate relationships. In the same way, a hug or kiss that says "goodbye" or "thanks" in one setting might have sexual connotations at other times and places. Desmond Morris comments on the importance of context in his book *Intimate Behavior.*

> We can turn now to the safer and more tender intimacies of the dance-floor. At parties, discotheques, dance-halls and ballrooms, adults who are strangers to one another can come together and move around the room in an intimate frontal embrace. Individuals who are already friendly can also use the situation to escalate a non-touching relationship into a touching one. The special role that social dancing plays in our society is that it permits, in its special context, a sudden and dramatic increase in body intimacy in a way that would be impossible elsewhere. If the same full frontal embrace were performed between strangers, or partial strangers, outside the context of the dance-floor, the impact would be entirely different. Dancing, so to speak, devalues the significance of the embrace, lowering its threshold to a point where it can lightly be indulged in without fear of rebuff. Having permitted it to occur, it then gives a chance for it to work its powerful magic. If the magic fails to work, the formalities of the situation also permit retreat without ignominy.*

*Desmond Morris, *Intimate Behavior.* New York: Random House, 1972 (pp. 176–177 of Bantam Books edition).

"Come on, Zorba," I cried, "teach me to dance!"

Zorba leaped to his feet, his face sparkling. . .

"Watch my feet, boss," he enjoined me. "Watch!"

He put out his foot, touched the ground lightly with his toes, then pointed the other foot; the steps were mingled violently, joyously, the ground reverberated like a drum.

He shook me by the shoulder.

"Now then, my boy," he said. "Both together!"

We threw ourselves into the dance. Zorba instructed me, corrected me gravely, patiently, and with great gentleness. I grew bold and felt my heart on the wing like a bird.

"Bravo! You're a wonder!" cried Zorba, clapping his hands to mark the beat. "Bravo, youngster! To hell with paper and ink! To hell with goods and profits! To hell with mines and workmen and monasteries! And now that you, my boy, can dance as well and have learnt my language, what shan't we be able to tell each other!"

He pounded on the pebbles with his bare feet and clapped his hands.

"Boss," he said, "I've dozens of things to say to you. I've never loved anyone as much before. I've hundreds of things to say, but my tongue just can't manage them. So I'll dance them for you!

Nikos Kazantzakis, *Zorba the Greek*

Touch Sparks Love

Our little girl was retreating into a walled-off world until we found the key to unlock her love.

"Debbie, please brush that hair out of your face. It's even getting into the food on your fork!"

It was suppertime; I had been late getting home from work, and I was edgy. My irritation was apparent in my voice. Slowly, mechanically, Debbie reached up and pushed her hair back. Then The Look began to come over her face.

I had seen it before. She had been perhaps four years old when it began. Her eyes became flat and expressionless, her face lost all animation. Even her coloring seemed to fade, and with her pale lashes and brows, she looked like an unpainted wooden doll. I knew that I could pass my hand in front of her face and she wouldn't even see it. Nor would she respond to anything that was said to her.

"There she goes again, feeling sorry for herself," commented Don, her big brother.

And so it appeared. The middle child in a family of seven children, it was understandable that she might feel sorry for herself. The older children bossed her around, nagged her, and seemed to pick on everything she said. The younger children demanded their own way, and often got it through the privilege of their ages. Pushed from above, threatened from below, Debbie didn't feel that she mattered to anyone.

The rest of the family continued with supper, ignoring Debbie. From past experience, we knew that it was useless to try to bring her back into the group. As the others were excused I led Debbie away from her half-eaten dinner to the living room, where I saw her down in front of the television set. Here she would gradually forget her grievances and join in again.

I couldn't help but have mixed feelings, though. Poor little thing! Six years old, and so unhappy! I wished desperately that I had more time to spend with her as an individual. I knew I had nagged her again. But why must she resort to that "Sorrowful Sal" act at every offense, either real or imagined? It was positively exasperating for her to tune us all out when it was quite clear that she could see and hear everything around her.

When Debbie had first begun to get The Look, we thought she was funny. "Isn't she cute when she's angry? See how she refuses to pay any attention to you! She's got a mind of her own!" But as time passed, it was no longer funny. It was angering to be intentionally ignored. We coaxed. We reasoned. We scolded. We even spanked her for her stubbornness, all to no avail.

But as long as it didn't happen often, we didn't pay much attention to such behavior. In a large family, it's easy to put a problem aside when a minor crisis has passed. Our older children were starting school; we had one in the "terrible twos" and an infant, as well as a chronic invalid who required extensive home nursing care. Our hands were full. The more-urgent-appearing problems received our attention, and Debbie's increasing needs went unrecognized.

Debbie was in the first grade when one of the older children said to me one afternoon, "Mom, Debbie's teacher wants to talk to you." The normal pangs of worry hit me that night. What trouble had Debbie gotten herself into? I made an appointment for the next afternoon with her teacher.

"I'm worried about Debbie," Mrs. Voorhees told me. "She's so . . . alone. She craves attention and she desperately needs more of it from you." She was telling me as gently as she could that I was failing my daughter.

I turned the problem over and over in my mind. How could I give Debbie more attention without incurring the resentment of the other children? Knowing that siblings in a large family are intensely competitive, I decided it would be best to enlist their help. I called the older children together and repeated what Mrs. Voorhees had told me. "So I'm going to try to give Debbie what she needs. It means that she has a greater need for attention at this time, and I'm trying to help her. I'd do the same for any of you.''

For a while this seemed to help. But as weeks went by, I found that even the knowledge of reasons for my actions could not compensate for the unequal distribution of my attention. Don began to take pokes and pinches at his little sister, or to kick her as she went by, for no apparent reason.

Denise would keep track of every favor that I might give Debbie, and accused me, ''You've read to her four times in the past month, and only once to me.''

It was true. I was now working full time and trying to divide the remaining time between the children. With the small amount of time that there was to be divided, the inequality was obvious. The resentment of the other children over the extra time given to Debbie alone only made them more quarrelsome and belittling toward her. It was defeating my original purpose.

Still, I wondered, what could I do? What should I do? Debbie was getting good grades in school, so it didn't seem that she was too badly in need of attention. I began to spend more time in group activities with the family and less time with Debbie as an individual.

The Look returned more frequently, and Debbie ran away that summer—several times. ''Where will you live?'' I asked her. ''Under a bush,'' she would reply poignantly. My heart ached for her.

Her comments began to reveal her feelings. ''I wish I'd never been born.''; ''I wish I was dead.'';

Or ''Some day I'm going to kill myself.''

One afternoon she climbed up on the family car, and walked around on it in her gritty shoes, scratching the paint. Her exasperated father spanked her vigorously. Afterward I sat down beside her at the foot of the stairway, where she sat sobbing. ''Why ever did you do that, Debbie? You knew Daddy would get angry and spank you,'' I asked her.

''Because I don't like myself.''

''Why don't you like yourself?''

''Because nobody likes me.'' Because nobody likes me. Oh, Debbie!

''I like you Debbie. I love you. You're my little girl.'' Words. Just words. Again, The Look. She tuned me out. She didn't see or hear me.

What a desperate cry for help! A little girl, six years old, invoking the wrath of her parents because she didn't think she was a person worth liking!

It took me a long time to acknowledge that Debbie—that WE—needed help. ''How could a six-year-old have any serious problems?'' I would ask myself. ''How could so young a child be too much for you to manage? Don't bring outsiders into it. We can handle our own problems if we work on them.''

But we weren't handling them. By the time Debbie was seven years old, The Look became a routine part of our daily life.

After a long inner struggle I finally decided to go to the county mental-health center. ''What if someone sees me there and thinks I'm a kook?'' I wondered.

But I swallowed my pride and went. It was the turning point in Debbie's life.

After I discussed the problem with the psychiatric social worker, he set up an appointment for the entire family. ''I want to see how they interact,'' he told me. After several such appointments, he began to see Debbie alone. A few weeks later he was able to give some help.

''She's a very unhappy little girl,'' he told me. ''You must give her the love and attention she needs. If you don't, her problems will probably come to a head when she is a teenager. Then there is a strong chance that she will either commit suicide, or turn for affection to the first fellow who will give her a little attention. And you know what that means. These girls often become unwed mothers in their teens.''

''But how?'' I asked. ''I'm working full time; I must work. I've so little time to give any of the children and when I try to give Debbie a little extra attention, the other children become jealous and are cruel to her. And how do I cope with her when she tunes me out?''

''She's tuning you out to protect herself. Think about it,'' the social worker said, ''When does she do it? When you scold her or criticize her? When the other children argue with her or deride her? These things hurt her so much that she can't cope with them. But if she can't see you or hear you, then you can't hurt her like that any more. So she withdraws. It's a defense mechanism she uses to keep from being hurt by other people."

He paused, then continued gently, "But you can reach her. There is one means you haven't tried yet. And that is—touch."

Touch? A strange thought. Communication without words. She could close her eyes and her ears, but she could still feel love.

"Touch her every chance you get. Ruffle her hair when you go by her. Pat her bottom. Touch her arm when you talk to her. Caress her. Put your hand on her shoulder, your arm around her. Pat her back. Hold her. Every chance you get. Every time you talk to her."

"Even when she refuses to see or hear you, she will feel you. And, incidently, this is something you can use to communicate with all your children. But pour it on Debbie."

Pour it on I did. And in a short time the results began to show noticeably. Debbie gradually became alive again. She smiled. She laughed. She had fun. She began to talk with me again. The Look became less and less frequent. And the other children never seemed to notice a thing, nor did they show any resentment of Debbie, possibly because I was touching them too.

Debbie is nine now, and she is like a different child. In addition to her new cheerful outlook on life, she has begun to discover some self-esteem. She stood in front of the mirror recently and told me, "I like my hair. It's pretty." What she was really telling me was that she has learned to like herself again. How far she has come! How far we all have come since I finally admitted that we needed professional help for a problem we hadn't been able to solve by ourselves.

The social worker's suggestion that I begin to communicate my love to my children by touching them was not guaranteed to be a miracle cure for Debbie's problems—or anyone else's It did work for us, but not without a serious re-evaluation of ourselves as individuals and as a family unit. We have had to learn a lot about ourselves, and we had to try hard to understand one another better, to accept one another as distinctly different human beings, each with intense feelings and needs.

I know the road ahead of us will have many rough spots and that the struggle to work out family difficulties is not an easy one. Debbie's problems are not over yet by any means. Strong rivalry remains among the children and she is still right in the middle of it. She has many crucial years in front of her, and we'll have to continue to boost her ego. We'll have to pay attention to her; give her the opportunity to express her feelings and listen to her when she does.

But no matter what the future holds, I have learned at least one invaluable lesson: to let my children feel my love. Love can be shown in many ways—in facial expressions, in attitudes, in actions. Love can be heard. But— and perhaps this is most important of all—love can be felt, in one of the simplest means of communication there is: touch.

In our now more than slightly cockeyed world, there seems to be little provision for someone to get touched without having to go to bed with whoever does the touching. And that's something to think about. We have mixed up simple, healing, warm touching with sexual advances. So much so, that it often seems as if there is no middle way between "Don't you dare touch me!" and "Okay, you touched me, so now we should make love!"

A nation which is able to distinguish the fine points between offensive and defensive pass interference, bogies, birdies, and par, a schuss and a slalom, a technical, a personal, and a player-control foul should certainly be able to make some far more obvious distinctions between various sorts of body contact.

Sidney Simon
Caring, Feeling, Touching

Hospital Prescribes The Touch of Love

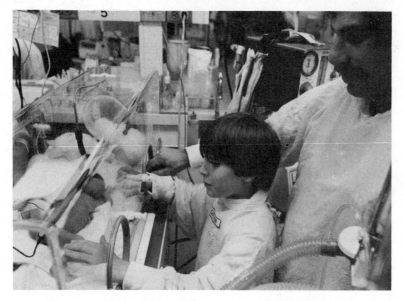

A touch, from one who loves, can do more than the most sophisticated machine or medical technique.

At least, that is the assumption Children's Hospital and Health Center is putting to the test. It is using the power of love as part of the prescription for premature babies in the 32-bed neonatal intensive-care unit.

Families are welcome at any time to touch, cuddle, and love the new baby.

Month-old Jasmine Rubin is such a tot. Confined to an incubator, she is visited often by her brother, Joe Rubin, 8, and father, Stephen, above.

The women of the family, left, grandmother Dolores Duncan and mother, Stephanie, express with happy smiles what the hospital is hoping for—the joy of loving as an avenue to health.

The San Diego Union

Clothing

Besides protecting us from catching colds, clothes can be decorative, a means of identification with groups, devices for sexual attraction, indicators of status, markers of certain roles and even means of concealment. Clothes communicate some of these functions far more clearly than others. For instance, there's little doubt that someone dressed in a uniform, wearing a badge, and carrying handcuffs and a gun is a police officer. On the other hand, while wrinkled, ill-fitting, dirty old clothes might be a sign that the wearer is a destitute drifter, they might also be the outfit of a worker on vacation, a normally stylish person who is on the way to clean a fireplace, or of an emotionally upset person, or even of an eccentric millionaire.

In spite of the ambiguity of clothing as a means of communication, people do intentionally send messages about themselves by what they wear, and we make interpretations about others on this basis. Think about the people you know. See if you can tell anything about their personal attitudes or social philosophies by the way they dress. A good place to begin your survey is with the faculty at your school. Is there any relationship between an instructor's mode of dress and teaching style? Take a look at your friends. Do you find that the people who spend time together share the same ideas about clothing? Is there a "uniform" for political radicals and one for conservatives? Is there a high fashion "uniform" that tells the public who's in style and who's out of it?

A student proved to himself how clothing labels a person's social position by trying an experiment. He spent a week hitchhiking back and forth from Santa Barbara to Los Angeles, a distance of about 100 miles. Every other day he would alternate his clothing style. On Monday, Wednesday and Friday he wore old Levi's, sandals, and a tie-dyed sweatshirt; and on Tuesday, Thursday, and Saturday he put on stay-pressed bell-bottomed pants, well-shined leather shoes, and a freshly ironed shirt. Other than his clothing, he kept all factors constant: He began at the same time each day, stood in the same spot, and signaled with his thumb in exactly the same way. The results seemed to prove how much clothes can say to others. As he described the results:

> It was incredible! On my three grubby days I got rides from people who looked just like I did. Two of them drove old V.W. buses, and the third had a '55 Ford pickup truck. They all wore Levi's, boots, et cetera, and all had pretty much the same life style. On the days when I dressed up, I got rides in shiny new Oldsmobiles and Cadillacs from people who were completely opposite from the ones I'd driven with the day before. The very first thing one guy said after picking me up was how nice it was to see a young person who wasn't one of those "hippie types"!

As well as illustrating the influence clothing has in our culture, this story points out a real danger inherent in reading many nonverbal messages. That danger is that we find ourselves stereotyping others on skimpy evidence, and often our interpretations are mistaken. By jumping to conclusions about another human from these surface appearances, we may very well be stereotyping ourselves out of some important relationships. There's an old generalization that you can't judge a book by its cover. In light of what we know about nonverbal communication we could change it to "You can tell only a little about a book from its cover; you need to have more information before you'll be able to speak with any authority about it."

The King   Louis   King Louis

AN HISTORICAL STUDY

Decoding the Runner's Wardrobe

Early in the morning a solitary figure runs down the middle of the street in a residential section of a large midwestern city. He passes another man running in the opposite direction. Each individual keeps his eyes straight ahead or on the path in front of him; although they see each other, neither acknowledges the presence of the other. A few miles farther, near the park, the runner spots another figure just over the top of the next hill. Their routes appear to cross but soon the other will be out of sight. The runner speeds up, moving to within hearing range. The other figure turns, raises a hand in a waving gesture. The runner returns the gesture calling out, "Looks good." The other person replies, "Yeah, great day." Each continues running; within a few seconds they are out of each other's sight.

A casual observer might infer that the first encounter was between strangers, the second between friends. But such is not the case. Both were strangers; our runner has never seen either person before. In the first case, communication occurred, but it was by means of a silent language alone. Our runner quickly decoded the message in the other's clothes, which said, "I'm not a runner but only someone who jogs before breakfast, probably for my health." In the

second encounter, the silent message was, "I'm a runner," and led quickly to the verbal exchange. But how did this communication occur? What silent grammar did the runner employ to interpret the clothing and the posture of these strangers? To answer these questions we must look at runners' cultural attitudes toward shoes, shirts, shorts, other paraphenalia, and posture. We need to understand also how these adornments are influenced by the weather. The answers to these questions will provide a guide to the cultural rules by which a runner's wardrobe can be decoded.

The primacy of shoes   Without doubt, it is shoes that make the runner. Their primacy derives in part from the physical punishment that the feet must endure in long runs over hard city pavement. The "good shoe" protects the foot; it is also light and well suited for the purposes of the run.

But runners do not simply go out and purchase a shoe. Function, durability, price, and weight are all important; however, overriding those considerations is the meaning of each style of shoe. Shoes communicate a message; runners select the pair that communicates the right message.

The characteristics of each shoe type are numerous and the typical runner will not be able to articulate all details of shank, heel, toe, support, durability, etc.

However, a runner will have a minimal level of knowledge that includes ability to recognize the manufacturer's logo. Manufacturers emboss this symbol on all the different kinds of shoes they make—from ultra-light spikes to heavy training flats. When our runner spots the figure at the top of the hill and suspects a runner, he moves close enough to see the Nike logo, the bold white stripe in the shape of a check mark with a rounded point; then he knows that a greeting is appropriate. This is not to say that only runners wear Nike shoes. Rather, the Nike logo is consistent with the total configuration that the runner presents. It completes the picture and may well be the definitive mark of a runner.

The same process applies for the three-striped logo of the Adidas, the distinctive double-crossed lines of the Tiger, or the muted belt with two oblong holes of the New Balance. A person running down the street wearing blue jeans and a pair of four-striped Kinney sneakers is simply not a runner, though the sneakers look much like the three-striped Adidas. A runner knows that although the cost of the Adidas, Nike, Puma, or Tiger shoes may be three times that of a discount store's "running shoe," a person who is serious about running would never use "discounted" shoes.

Although any running shoe suffices to communicate "I am a runner," the kind of shoe worn does articulate the message further. For example, a person sporting a pair of Eugen Brutting Marathons, a shoe with a distinctive diamond embossed with the letters EB, communicates that his or her commitment to running is serious. These shoes cost approximately $12 more than other popular running shoes. They are known for their ultralight yet substantive construction. A person wearing them communicates that he or she knows a great deal about shoes, that he or she trains long and hard and for fast times.

The exotic shoe may indicate that the wearer has some special need in footwear. The serious runner runs long and hard. With increased distance comes worry about the possibility of injury. The nagging knee pain or the strained tendon in the foot can interfere with preparation for racing. Runners believe that improper footwear can contribute to knee and leg problems by placing stress on these parts of the anatomy with repeated and peculiar foot-pavement contact. Thus, a runner wearing Karhu 2323s may have a knee problem that is alleviated by the high heel design of the shoe. These orange and black shoes communicate that the wearer has a special need and that this shoe fits the need. This runner knows shoes. It is not that the runner wants to acquire high status by displaying the special shoe; instead, the special shoe means that despite pain or discomfort the runner continues to run. Special shoes, then, indicate dedication toward running, and mark their wearers as the most conscientious members of the runner's culture.

Shirts as billboards Shoes may make runners, but shirts advertise their messages. The shirt is the second most important article of clothing for communicating a runner's identity. The message shirt may be displayed even in cold weather by wearing it over warm sweats or warmups. This is by no means a widespread practice, but when it is done, it is regarded as meaningful by other runners.

There are two types of shirt: the T-shirt and the tank top. T-shirts have a special significance since they are often used as prizes in races. Such shirts are embossed in letters proclaiming the name of the event—for example, Bay City 25k, AAU State Championship 10k, or the Berry City 5-Mile Open. Runners know these races. Some are very popular and attract many runners, while others are highly competitive and attract only the most committed.

Runners generally rank all races; hence, those who wear shirts proclaiming their participation in them are likewise rated. The marathons, of course, have the highest prestige. A Lake City Marathon shirt on a person running in the park is a definite sign that the person is a runner. A Berry City 5-Mile Open shirt, however, may or may not signify a runner. The Berry City race is popular and is short enough to attract the casual jogger and many part-time runners. Thus, wearers of the shirt may race only once a year; they may simply have walked across the finish line to get the shirt. Even a nonparticipant could pick up such a shirt as a discarded item from some runner's collection. Thus, decoding the runner's wardrobe requires not only an awareness of the custom of awarding shirts at races but also familiarity with the ranking of races within the runner's world.

Serious runners know that many prestigious marathons, like the Boston Marathon, do not award shirts. Those competing in such big-time races are often affiliated with a local track club. Even if the runner has never run in the Boston, wearing a shirt that bears the name of the club that sponsors a few serious runners will give him high status among fellow runners. A tank top with the words "Tri-Cities Track" says of the wearer, "I am a runner." It is more convincing than a T-shirt from a local marathon, but this is something that only experienced runners would know.

Our runner's journey through the park could bring him in contact with a serious runner adorned in Interval 3:05 shoes and a Tri-Cities Track shirt, or he could encounter a more casual but nevertheless committed runner sporting Brooks 270s and wearing a Berry City 5-Mile Open shirt. Both encounters would signal the presence of a runner and both could appropriately trigger greetings. Perhaps a hand wave would be in order to the 3:05 wearer out of deference to high accomplishment, while a conversation would be appropriate with the wearer of Brooks 270s.

Of course, the type of exchange will depend upon the relative status of the two runners. In the example above, we are assuming that our runner does not regard himself in a class with the Tri-Cities Track shirt wearer, but instead feels more comfortable around the Berry City man. Equals in the runners' world exchange greetings, whereas unequals merely acknowledge each other's identity. The higher status runner's acknowledgement demonstrates that the lower status runner is "within" the dress code of the runner, and the lower status runner's acknowledgement of the higher confirms standards for dress and appearance of the serious runner.

Jeffrey E. Nash
In *Conformity and Conflict: Readings in Cultural Anthropology*, 3rd ed. Spradley & Boston: Little, Brown, 1977 (this is an excerpt)

Proxemics—Distance as Nonverbal Communication

Proxemics is the study of the way people and animals use space. As you'll see by the end of this chapter, you can sometimes tell how people are feeling toward each other simply by noting the distance between them. To begin to understand how this is so, try this exercise:

Distance Makes a Difference

1. Choose a partner, and go to opposite sides of the room and face each other.

2. Very slowly begin walking toward each other while carrying on a conversation. You might simply talk about how you feel as you experience the activity. As you move closer, try to be aware of any change in your feelings. Continue moving slowly toward each other until you are only an inch or so apart. Remember how you feel at this point.

3. Now, while still facing each other, back up until you're at a comfortable distance for carrying on your conversation.

4. Share your feelings with each other and/or the whole group.

During this experiment your feelings most likely changed at least three times. During the first phase, when you were across the room from your partner, you probably felt unnaturally far away. Then, as you neared a point about three feet from him, you probably felt like stopping; this is the distance at which two people in our culture normally stand while conversing socially. If your partner wasn't someone you're emotionally close to, you probably began to feel quite uncomfortable as you moved through this normal range and came closer; it's possible that you had to force yourself not to move back. Some people find this phase so uncomfortable that they can't get closer than twenty inches or so to their partner.

What was happening here? Each of us carries around a sort of invisible bubble of personal space wherever we go. We think of the area inside this

Once I heard a hospital nurse describing doctors. She said there were beside-the-bed doctors, who were interested in the patient, and foot-of-the-bed doctors, who were interested in the patient's condition. They unconsciously expressed their emotional involvement — or lack of it — by where they stood.

Edward T. Hall

bubble as our private territory—almost as much a part of us as our own bodies. As you moved closer to your partner, the distance between your bubbles narrowed and at a certain point diappeared altogether: Your space had been invaded, and this is the point at which you probably felt uncomfortable. As you moved away again, your partner retreated out of your bubble, and you felt more relaxed.

Of course, if you were to try this experiment with someone very close to you—your mate, for example—you might not have felt any discomfort at all, even while touching. The reason for this is that our willingness to get close to others—physically as well as emotionally—varies according to the person we're with and the situation we're in. And it's precisely the distance that we voluntarily put between ourselves and others that gives a nonverbal clue about our feelings and the nature of the relationship.

Anthropologist Edward T. Hall has defined four distances that we use in our everyday lives. He says that we choose a particular one depending upon how we feel toward the other person at a given time, the context of the conversation, and what our interpersonal goals are.

Intimate Distance   The first of Hall's zones begins with skin contact and ranges out to about eighteen inches. We usually use intimate distance with people who are emotionally very close to us, and then mostly in private situations—making love, caressing, comforting, protecting. By allowing someone to move into our intimate distance we're letting them enter our territory. When we do this voluntarily, it's usually a sign of trust: We've willingly lowered our defenses. On the other hand, when someone invades this most personal area without our consent, we usually feel threatened. This explains the feeling you may have had during the last exercise when your partner intruded into your space without any real invitation from you. It also explains the discomfort we sometimes feel when forced into crowded places like buses or elevators with strangers. At times like these the standard behavior in our society is to draw away or tense our muscles and avoid eye contact. This is a nonverbal way of signaling, ''I'm sorry for invading your territory, but the situation forced it.''

In courtship situations a critical moment usually occurs when one member of a couple first moves into the other's intimate zone. If the partner being approached does not retreat, this usually signals that the relationship is moving into a new stage. On the other hand, if the reaction to the advance is withdrawal to a greater distance, the initiator should get the message that it isn't yet time to get more intimate. We remember from our dating experiences the significance of where on the car seat our companions chose to sit. If they moved close to us, it meant one thing; if they stayed jammed against the passenger's door, we got quite a different message.

Personal Distance   This second spatial zone ranges from eighteen inches at its closest point to four feet at its farthest. Its closer phase is the distance at which most couples stand in public. But if someone of the opposite sex stands this near one partner at a party, the other partner is likely to feel uncomfortable. This ''moving in'' often is taken to mean that something more

Some thirty inches from my nose
The frontier of my Person goes,
And all the untilled air between
Is private *pagus* or demense.
Stranger, unless with bedroom eyes
I beckon you to fraternize,
Beware of rudely crossing it:
I have no gun, but I can spit.

W. H. Auden

287

than casual conversation is taking place. The far range of personal distance runs from about two and a half to four feet. It's the zone just beyond the other person's reach. As Hall puts it, at this distance we can keep someone "at arm's length." This choice of words suggests the type of communication that goes on at this range: The contacts are still reasonably close, but they're much less personal than the ones that occur a foot or so closer.

Test this for yourself. Start a conversation with someone at a distance of about three feet, and slowly move a foot or so closer. Do you notice a difference? Does the distance affect your conversation?

Social Distance   This third zone ranges from four to about twelve feet out. Within it are the kinds of communication that usually occur in business situations. Its closer phase, from four to seven feet, is the distance at which conversations usually occur between salespeople and customers and between people who work together. Most people feel uncomfortable when a salesclerk comes as close as three feet, whereas four or five feet nonverbally signals "I'm here to help you, but I dont mean to be too personal or pushy."

Take a minute now to role play a customer-salesperson scene. Try it first at five feet and then at three. Which one seems most natural?

We use the far range of social distance—seven to twelve feet—for more formal and impersonal situations. This is the range at which we sit from our boss (or other authority figure) as he stares across his desk at us. Sitting at this distance signals a far different and less relaxed type of conversation than if we were to pull a chair around to the boss's side of the desk and sit only three or so feet away.

Public Distance   This is Hall's term for the farthest zone, running outward from twelve feet. The closer range of public distance is the one that most teachers use in the classroom. In the farther reaches of public space—twenty-five feet and beyond—two-way communication is almost impossible. In some

The interrogator should sit fairly close to the subject, and between the two there should be no table, desk, or other piece of furniture. Distance or the presence of an obstruction of any sort constitutes a serious psychological barrier and also affords the subject a certain degree of relief and confidence not otherwise attainable. . . .

As to the psychological validity of the above suggested seating arrangement, reference may be made to the commonplace but yet meaningful expressions such as "getting next" to a person, or the "buttonholing" of a customer by a salesman. These expressions signify that when a person is close to another one physically, he is closer to him psychologically. Anything such as a desk or a table between the interrogator and the subject defeats the purpose and should be avoided.

INBAU AND REID, *Criminal Interrogation and Confessions*

cases it's necessary for speakers to use public distance due to the size of their audience, but we can assume that anyone who voluntarily chooses to use it when he could be closer is not interested in having a dialog.

Physical invasion isn't the only way people penetrate our spatial bubble; we're just as uncomfortable when someone intrudes on your visual territory. If you've had the unpleasant experience of being stared at, you know this can be just as threatening as having someone get too close. In most situations, however, people respect each others' visual privacy. You can test this the next time you're walking in public. As you approach another person notice how he'll shift his glance away from you at a distance of a few paces, almost like a visual dimming of headlights. Generally, strangers maintain eye contact at a close distance only when they want something—information, assistance, signatures on a petition, recognition, a handout, etc.

Territoriality

Whereas personal space is the invisible bubble we carry around as an extension of our physical being, territory remains stationary. Any geographical area such as a room, house, neighborhood, or country to which we assume some kind of "rights" is our territory. What's interesting about territoriality is that there is no real basis for the assumption of proprietary rights of "owning" some area, but the feeling of "owning" exists nonetheless. Your room in the house is *your room* whether you're there or not (unlike personal space, which is carried around with you), and it's your room because you say it is. Although you could probably make a case for your room *really being* your room (and not the family's, or the mortgage holder on the house), what about the desk you sit at in each class? You feel the same way about the desk, that it's yours, even though it's certain that the desk is owned by the school and is in no way really yours.

The way people use space can communicate a good deal about power and status relationships. Generally we grant people with higher status more personal territory and greater privacy. We knock before entering our boss's office, whereas she can usually walk into our work area without hesitating. In traditional schools professors have offices, dining rooms, and even toilets that are private, while the students, who are presumably less important, have no such sanctuaries. In the military greater space and privacy usually come with rank: Privates sleep forty to a barracks, sergeants have their own private rooms, and generals have government-provided houses.

Environment and Nonverbal Communication

To conclude our look at nonverbal communication we want to emphasize the ways in which physical settings, architecture, and interior design affect our communication. Begin your thinking by recalling for a moment the different homes you've visited lately. Were some of these homes more comfortable to be in than others? Certainly a lot of these kinds of feelings are shaped by the people you were with, but there are some houses where it seems impossible to relax, no matter how friendly the hosts are. We've spent what seemed like endless evenings in what Mark Knapp calls "unliving rooms," where the spotless ashtrays, furniture coverings, and plastic lamp covers seem to send nonverbal messages telling us not to touch anything, not to put our feet up, and not to be comfortable. People who live in houses like this probably wonder why nobody ever seems to relax and enjoy themselves at their parties. One thing is quite certain: They don't understand that this environment they have created can communicate discomfort to their guests.

There's a large amount of research that shows how the design of an environment can shape the kind of communication that takes place in it. In one experiment at Brandeis University Maslow and Mintz found that the attractiveness of a room influenced the happiness and energy of people working in it. The experimenters set up three rooms: an "ugly" one, which resembled a janitor's closet in the basement of a campus building; an "average" room, which was a professor's office; and a "beautiful" room, which was furnished with carpeting, drapes, and comfortable furniture. The subjects in the experiment were asked to rate a series of pictures as a way of measuring their energy and feelings of well-being while at work. Results of the experiment showed that while in the ugly room, the subjects became tired and bored more quickly and took longer to complete their task. When they moved to the beautiful room, however, they rated the faces they were judging higher, showed a greater desire to work, and expressed feelings of importance, comfort, and enjoyment. The results teach a lesson that isn't surprising: Workers generally feel better and do a better job when they're in an attractive environment.

Many business people show an understanding of how environment can influence communication. Robert Sommer, a leading environmental psychologist, described several such cases. In his book *Personal Space: the Behavioral basis for Design,* he points out that dim lighting, subdued noise levels, and comfortable seats encourage people to spend more time in a restaurant or bar. Knowing this, the management can control the amount of customer turnover. If the goal is to run a high-volume business that tries to move people in and out quickly, it's necessary to keep the lights shining brightly and not worry too much about soundproofing. On the other hand, if the goal is to keep customers in the bar or restaurant for a long time, the proper technique is to lower the lighting and use absorbent building materials that will keep down the noise level.

Furniture design can control the amount of time a person spends in an environment too. From this knowledge came the Larsen chair, which was designed for Copenhagen restaurant owners who felt their customers were occupying their seats too long without spending enough money. The chair is constructed to put an uncomfortable pressure on the sitter's back if occupied for more than a few minutes. (We suspect that many people who are careless in buying furniture for their homes get much the same result without trying. One environmental psychologist we know refuses to buy a chair or couch without sitting in it for a least half an hour to test its comfort.)

Sommer also describes how airports are designed to discourage people from spending too much time in waiting areas. The uncomfortable chairs, bolted shoulder to shoulder in rows facing outward, make conversation and relaxation next to impossible. Faced with this situation, travelers are forced to move to restaurants and bars in the terminal, where they're not only more comfortable but where they're also likely to spend money.

Casino owners in places such as Las Vegas also know how to use the environment to control behavior. To keep gamblers from noticing how long they've been shooting craps, playing roulette and blackjack, and feeding slot machines, they build their casinos without windows or clocks. Unless he has his own watch, the customer has no way of knowing how long he has been gambling, or, for that matter, whether it's day or night.

In a more therapeutic and less commercial way physicians have also shaped environments to improve communications. One study showed that simply removing a doctor's desk made patients feel almost five times more at ease during office visits. Sommer found that redesigning a convalescent ward of a hospital greatly increased the interaction between patients. In the old design seats were placed shoulder to shoulder around the edges of the ward. By grouping the chairs around small tables so that patients faced each other at a comfortable distance, the amount of conversations doubled.

The exterior design of a building often communicates a message about its occupants. Banks, for example, have traditionally used imposing elements such as large marble columns and open spaces to convey an image of strength and security to their customers. As tastes and attitudes change, however, architecture follows. (Some architects would argue that it also leads at times.) Banks built within the last ten or fifteen years reflect a newer approach, which stresses the institution's friendliness and openness, as conveyed by greater use of glass, landscaping, and lower barriers between customers and bank personnel.

A good house is planned from the inside out. First, you decide what it has to do for its occupants. Then, you let the functions determine the form. The more numerous and various those functions, the more responsive and interesting the house should be. And it may not look at all like you expect.

Dan MacMasters, *Los Angeles Times*

The hospital building disregards physical factors that might promote recovery. Colors are bland, but instead of being restful, are more often depressing; space is badly distributed, so that a patient may be stranded in a large room, or crowded in a small one; private and semi-private patients often feel isolated in their rooms. . . . Windows are badly placed, and the view most often shows an adjacent large hospital building or a parking lot. . . .

One may immediately object that despite all this, the majority of patients adjust well to the hospital, recover, and go home. That is true, but as an argument it is a little like saying that the world got on perfectly well without electricity, which is also true.

Michael Crichton, M.D., *Five Patients*

The design of an entire building can shape communication among its users. Architects have learned that the way housing projects are designed will control to a great extent the contact neighbors will have with each other. People who live in apartments near stairways and mailboxes have many more neighbor contacts than do those living in less heavily traveled parts of the building, and tenants generally have more contacts with immediate neighbors than with people even a few doors away. Architects now use this information to design buildings that either encourage communication or increase privacy, and house hunters can use the same knowledge to choose a home that gives them the neighborhood relationships they want.

Sometimes the matter of designing an environment can become absurd. During 1968 the United States, South Vietnam, and North Vietnam spent eight months arguing over the shape of the table at which they would hold their peace talks. The argument centered on the nonverbal statement that the design of the conference room would make. The North Vietnamese wanted a square table, which would have given the National Liberation Front (NLF) guerillas a separate side all to themselves. As the Communists saw it, this arrangement would have given the guerillas equal status as an independent government. The United States and South Vietnam were not about to give in to the demand. They wanted two rectangular tables, one seating themselves and the other for the North Vietnamese and NLF. This design would have kept the guerillas from having a whole table side to themselves, and symbolically denied them clear-cut status as an equal power. Several thousand lives later both sides finally compromised on a round table, which, having no sides at all, allowed each side to claim victory.

So far we've talked about how designing an environment can shape communication, but there's another side to consider. Watching how people use an already existing environment can be a way of telling what kind of relationships they want. For example, Sommer watched students in a college library and found that there's a definite pattern for people who want to study alone. While the library was uncrowded, students almost always chose corner seats at one of the empty rectangular tables. Finally each table was occupied by one reader. New readers would then choose a seat on the opposite side and far end of an occupied table, thus keeping the maximum distance between themselves and the other readers. One of Sommer's associates tried violating these "rules" by sitting next to and across from other female readers when more distant seats were available. She found that the approached women reacted defensively, either by signalling their discomfort through shifts in posture, gesturing, or by eventually moving away.

A person's position in a room can also communicate his status. Research shows that during conferences people who take leadership roles usually seat themselves at the ends of a meeting table. This pattern carries over to many households, where the father as head of the family sits at the end of the dinner table.

As we draw this discussion of nonverbal communication to a close, there are some points we'd like to reemphasize. First, in a normal two-person conversation the words or verbal components of the message carry far less of the social meaning of the situation than do the nonverbal components. This statistic may have been difficult for you to believe when we cited it at the beginning of the chapter, but by this time you know how many channels nonverbal communication includes: spatial distance, touch, body posture and tension, facial expression, hand and body movement, dress, physique, tone of voice, speed of speech, as well as disfluencies of speech and even the environment we create. Our hope is that the information and experiences of the chapter have placed some importance on nonverbal communication in your life.

We also want to reemphasize that when we compare nonverbal behavior with verbal language it's very limited. Our nonverbal communication is concerned mostly with the expression of feelings, likings, or preferences, and these usually *reinforce* or *contradict* the message we're expressing verbally.

Third, we need to realize that although nonverbal behaviors are more powerful in expressing feelings than are words, they're ambiguous and difficult to "read" accurately. They'll always stand checking out.

Our fourth point is to remind you that many of the gestures, glances, postures, and other behavior we've discussed here are culturally learned and don't necessarily apply to other cultures or even to subcultures within our society. At this point most nonverbal research has been done on middle- and upper-middle-class college students and shouldn't be automatically generalized to other groups.

Finally, we hope you now understand the importance of *congruency*—the matching of your verbal and nonverbal expressions. Contradicting messages from two channels are a pretty good indication of deliberate or unconscious deception, and matching signals reinforce your messages.

We haven't tried to teach you *how* to communicate nonverbally in this chapter—you've always known this. What we do hope you've gained here is a greater *awareness* of the messages you and others send, and we further hope that you can use this new awareness to understand and improve your relationships.

Roads Not Taken

1. Research such as that cited in the readings section of this chapter shows that the design of an environment can have a great effect on what takes place within it. Investigate some of the studies that have been done in this area and report your findings.

2. Touching plays a necessary role in human relationships and adjustment. Familiarize yourself with some research in this area and report your findings.

3. Apply the statement, "It's easier to lie verbally than nonverbally," to various communication settings—business, school, social, family, and romantic relationships, and the legal system.

4. Gestures are a large part of nonverbal language. Make an investigation into the universality of the meaning of gestures. Do the same movements have the same meanings around the world?

5. Report on the different nonverbal customs and rules in various cultures and subcultures that interest you. What is the importance of knowing these rules for travelers from one culture to another?

More Readings on Nonverbal Communication

Burgoon, Judee, and Thomas Saine. *The Unspoken Dialogue: An Introduction to Nonverbal Communication.* Boston: Houghton Mifflin, 1978. *A comprehensive, well-organized introduction.*

Deasy, C. M. "When Architects Consult People." *Psychology Today,* 3:10 (March, 1970).
A readable article that discusses how architects can design buildings to encourage certain types of relationships. It shows how social science applies to the "real world."

Ekman, Paul, and Wallace V. Friesen, "Nonverbal Leakage and Clues to Deception." *Psychiatry,* 32 (1969):88–106.
The title of this article is self-explanatory. Ekman and Friesen discuss the various types of nonverbal emotional clues that people unintentionally send as well as indicators of deliberate deception.

——. *Unmasking the Face.* Englewood Cliffs, NJ: Prentice-Hall, 1975.
Two leading researchers in nonverbal communication discuss the research and speculation surrounding this highly visible means of expression.

Hall, Edward T. *The Hidden Dimension.* Garden City, NY: Anchor Books, Doubleday, 1969.

Hall has probably done more work on proxemics than anyone else, and this book gives you a good survey of the field, including the research with animals that led to our knowledge about how humans use space. It also contains chapters on how different cultures handle space.

———. *The Silent Language.* New York: Fawcett Books, 1959.
A good blend of theory and anecdotes, this book introduces several kinds of nonverbal communication and their cultural implications. As a quote on the cover says, "Diplomats could study this book with profit."

Knapp, Mark L. *Nonverbal Communication in Human Interaction.* New York: Holt, Rinehart and Winston, 1972.
If you're interested in finding out how much and what kinds of work have been done in nonverbal communication, this is the book to read. As we go to press this is the most complete survey of the field and a book you should have if you're seriously interested in the subject.

Mehrabian, Albert. *Nonverbal Communication.* Chicago: Aldine-Atherton, 1972.
This book falls into the same category as Knapp's, although it's organized differently. Mehrabian has probably written more articles and books about nonverbal communication than anyone else, and this work reviews his and most everyone else's work in this area.

Montagu, Ashley, *Touching: The Human Significance of the Skin.* New York: Harper & Row, 1971.
Montagu has written 335 mostly fascinating pages about our skins and the importance they have in our development. It's a book you'll probably want to read before you plan to have children.

Rosenfeld, Lawrence B., and Jean M. Civikly. *With Words Unspoken: The Nonverbal Experience.* New York: Holt, Rinehart and Winston, 1976.
This is a new text for a study of the importance of the nonverbal in our lives. The treatment of the material is contemporary and inviting to the college student. Materials are drawn from all parts of our society. Subjects covered range from biorhythm cycles to weight. The book is hard to put down once you pick it up.

Scheflen, Albert E. *How Behavior Means.* Garden City, NY: Anchor Books, 1974.
This book explores kinesics, posture, interaction, setting, and culture as to their importance in human communication.

Sommer, Robert. *Personal Space: The Behavioral Basis of Design.* Englewood Cliffs, NJ: Prentice-Hall, 1969.
Sommer is a leading authority on environmental psychology, and this book is a good introduction to the field. It shows how manipulating space controls communication.

Thompson, James J. *Beyond Words: Nonverbal Communication in the Classroom.* New York: Citation Press, 1973.
This is a highly readable, nontechnical explanation of the many ways nonverbal communication affects the performances of both students and teachers.

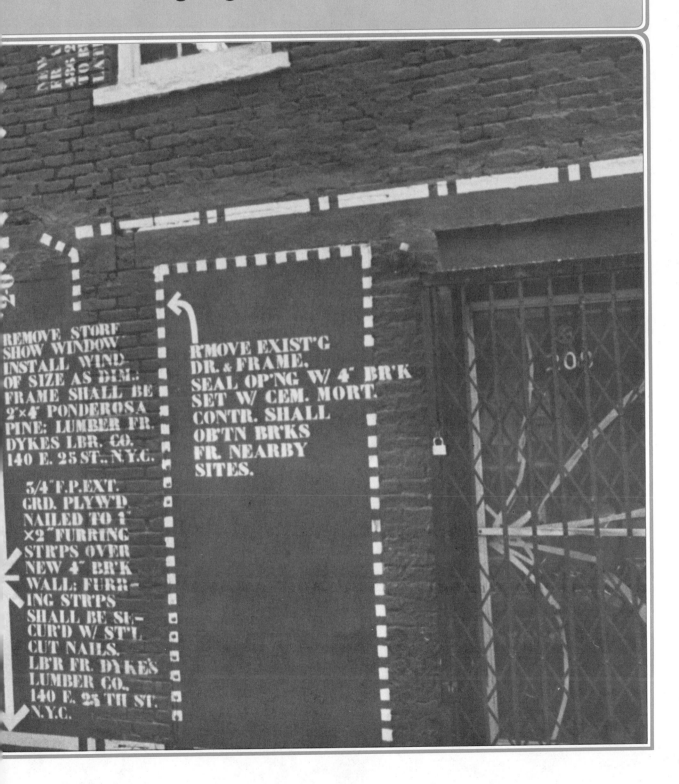

Chapter Eight

*A*ND THE WHOLE EARTH WAS OF ONE LANGUAGE AND ONE SPEECH. AND IT CAME TO PASS, AS THEY JOURNEYED FROM THE EAST, THAT THEY FOUND A PLAIN IN THE LAND OF SHINAR; AND THEY DWELT THERE.

2 AND THEY SAID TO ONE ANOTHER, GO TO, LET US MAKE BRICK, AND BURN THEM THOROUGHLY. AND THEY HAD BRICK FOR STONE, AND SLIME HAD THEY FOR MORTAR.

3 AND THEY SAID, GO TO, LET US BUILD US A CITY AND A TOWER, WHOSE TOP MAY REACH UNTO HEAVEN; AND LET US MAKE US A NAME, LEST WE BE SCATTERED ABROAD UPON THE FACE OF THE WHOLE EARTH.

4 AND THE LORD CAME DOWN TO SEE THE CITY AND THE TOWER, WHICH THE CHILDREN OF MEN BUILDED.

5 AND THE LORD SAID, BEHOLD, THE PEOPLE IS ONE, AND THEY HAVE ALL ONE LANGUAGE; AND THIS THEY BEGIN TO DO: AND NOW NOTHING WILL BE RESTRAINED FROM THEM, WHICH THEY HAVE IMAGINED TO DO.

6 GO TO, LET US GO DOWN, AND THERE CONFOUND THEIR LANGUAGE, THAT THEY MAY NOT UNDERSTAND ONE ANOTHER'S SPEECH.

7 SO THE LORD SCATTERED THEM ABROAD FROM THENCE UPON THE FACE OF ALL THE EARTH; AND THEY LEFT OFF TO BUILD THE CITY.

8 THEREFORE IS THE NAME OF IT CALLED BABEL; BECAUSE THE LORD DID THERE CONFOUND THE LANGUAGE OF ALL THE EARTH; AND FROM THENCE DID THE LORD SCATTER THEM ABROAD UPON THE FACE OF ALL THE EARTH.

Genesis 11:1–9

S ometimes it seems as if *none* of us speak the same language. How often have you felt that nobody understood what you were saying? *You* knew what you meant, but people just didn't seem to understand you. How often have the tables been turned—you couldn't understand somebody else's ideas? And how many times have you had the feeling that others were deliberately playing tricks with words—using language to fool you or hide what was on their minds?

In this chapter we'll examine these problems by taking a quick look at the subject of semantics—the relationship between words and things. We'll try to show you some of the ways language can trip us up and some of the things you can do to make it work better. We'll also talk about how language not only describes how we see the world but shapes our view of it.

Words and Meanings

Let's begin our study of semantics by looking at some characteristics of language. Because we use words almost constantly, we tend to assume that they are ideally suited to convey meaning. Actually, there are several points to keep in mind if your verbal messages are going to be accurate and successful.

Language Is Symbolic   The first thing to realize is that meanings rest more in people than in words themselves. Words are *symbols* that represent ideas; they aren't the ideas themselves. For instance, it's obvious that the word *coat* is not the same as the piece of clothing it describes. You'd be a fool to expect the letters c–o–a–t to keep you warm in a snowstorm. Yet people often forget the symbolic nature of language and confuse words with their referents. For example, some students will cram facts into their heads just long enough to regurgitate them into a blue book in order to receive a high grade. They forget that the letters like *A* or *B* are only symbols, that a few lines of ink on paper doesn't necessarily represent true learning. In the same way, simply saying the words "I care about you" isn't necessarily a reflection of the truth, although for many dissappointed lovers this lesson is a painful one.

Meanings Are In People, Not Words   Show a dozen people the same symbol and ask them what it means, and you're likely to get twelve different answers. Does an American flag bring up associations of soldiers giving their lives for their country? Fourth of July parades? Institutionalized bigotry? Mom's apple pie? How about a cross: what does it represent? The gentleness and wisdom of Jesus Christ? Fire-lit rallies of Ku Klux Klansmen? Your childhood Sunday school? The necklace your sister always wears?

Like these symbols, words can be interpreted in many different ways. And of course this is the basis for many misunderstandings. It's possible to have an argument about feminism without ever realizing that you and the other person are using the word to represent entirely different things. The same goes for *communism, Republicans, health food,* and thousands upon thousands of other symbols. Words don't mean, people do—and often in widely different ways.

COON!!   **HONKIE!!**

Words don't mean—people mean!

Just Look It Up . . .   It might seem as if one remedy to misunderstandings like these would be to have more respect for the dictionary meanings of words. After all, you might think, if people would just consult a dictionary whenever they send or receive a potentially confusing message, there would be little problem.

This approach has two shortcomings. First, dictionaries show that many words have multiple definitions, and it isn't always clear which one applies in a given situation. The 500 words most commonly used in everyday communication have over 14,000 dictionary definitions which should give you an idea of the limitations of this approach.

A second problem is that people often use words in ways you'd never be able to look up. Sometimes the misuse of words is due to a lack of knowledge, as when you might ask your auto parts dealer for a new generator when you really need an alternator. As you'll read later in this chapter, there are other cases in which people deliberately use words in unconventional ways in order to mislead or to confuse.

The third shortcoming of dictionaries is that they define most words in terms of *other* words, and this process often won't tell you any more about a term than you already know. In fact, it's possible to talk endlessly about a subject and sound very knowledgeable without ever having the slightest idea of what your words refer to. Jessica Davidson's quiz is an example of this. Read the paragraph and see if you can answer the questons:*

Because public opinion is sometimes marsiflate, empetricious insoculences are frequently zophilimized. Nevertheless, it cannot be overemphasized that carpoflansibles are highly traculate.

*Jessica Davidson, "How to Translate English," in Joseph Fletcher Littell, ed., *The Language of Man,* vol. 4 (Evanston, IL: McDougal Littell, 1971).

1. In the authors' opinion, carpoflansibles are
   a. Empetricious
   b. Traculate
   c. Zophilimized
2. Public opinion is sometimes
   a. Insoculent
   b. Variable
   c. Marsiflate
3. According to the text insoculences are zophilimized
   a. Often
   b. Never
   c. Sometimes

You can see that the correct answers are 1(b), 2(c), and 3(a). But even if you scored perfectly on the quiz, do you know the meaning of the paragraph? Of course not, for the words are gibberish. But if you look closely, you'll find that many people use their own language in the same way, talking in terms which they can define only by other terms.

After reading this far, you should be aware that language isn't the simple thing it at first seems to be. You've already seen that a failure to use language with the care and caution it deserves can lead to problems. Sometimes these problems are relatively minor, but in other cases they can be disastrous, as the following account shows.

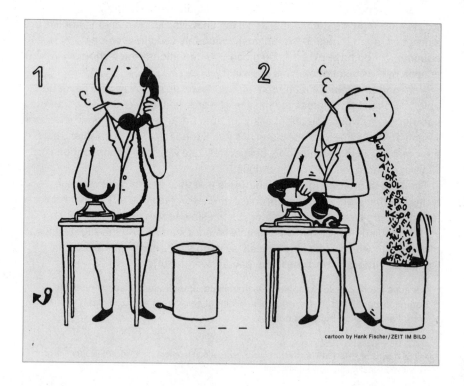

cartoon by Hank Fischer/ZEIT IM BILD

The Great Mokusatsu Mistake
Was This the Deadliest Error of Our Time?

For many months after the Japanese collapse in 1945, people wondered whether it was the atomic bomb or Russia's entry into the war that had brought to an end the fighting in the Pacific. But it gradually became clear that the importance of these two events in persuading Japan to surrender had been overrated; that Japan had been a defeated nation long before August 1945.

"The Japanese had, in fact, already sued for peace before the Atomic Age was announced to the world with the destruction of Hiroshima, and before the Russian entry into the war," Fleet Admiral Chester W. Nimitz told Congress; and other American military leaders confirmed this report.

Why, then, did not Japan accept the Potsdam Declaration, which called upon Japan to surrender, when it was issued in late July of 1945, instead of waiting until the second week in August, after Hiroshima and Nagasaki had been blasted into radioactive rubble and the Russians had begun their drive into Manchuria? That question has never been satisfactorily answered.

The true story of Japan's rejection of the Potsdam Declaration *may* be the story of an incredible mistake—a mistake which so altered the course of history in the Far East that we shall never be able to estimate its full effect on our nation—a mistake which, ironically, was made by a Japanese and involved just one Japanese word.

I say that it "may be" because part of the actual truth lies buried in human motivations which will probably always puzzle historians. But another part of it is clearly demonstrable. Let me tell the story; then you can judge for yourself what really happened.

By the spring of 1945 there was no question in the minds of Japan's leaders that their nation had been badly beaten.

The plight of the nation was so desperate that the actual figures were kept secret even from some of the cabinet ministers. Japan's industrial complex had crumbled under the aerial assault. Steel production was down 79 percent, aircraft production down 64 percent. By September a lack of aluminum would halt the building of planes entirely.

Allied air attacks were destroying railroads, highways, and bridges faster than they could be replaced. Hundreds of thousands of bodies were buried in the smoking ruins of cities and towns. Millions were homeless. In Tokyo alone, almost half of the homes had been leveled. People were fleeing the cities. A combination of American surface, air, and undersea attack had cut off shipments from the occupied regions on which Japan depended for her life. Food was running out.

American planes destroyed the last of Japan's fleet in a battle off Kyushu on the very day in April when Suzuki took office. The aged Premier was an admiral without a navy.

"We must stop the war at the earliest opportunity," he said when he learned the true condition of his nation's war potential. The *jushin,* the senior statesmen, had advised the Emperor in February of 1945 that surrender was necessary *no matter what the cost.*

The Potsdam Declaration was issued on July 26, 1945. It was signed by the United States, Great Britain, and (to the surprise of the Japanese) China. The reaction among Japanese leaders was one of exultation. The terms were far more lenient than had been expected. The Japanese were quick to note that instead of demanding unconditional surrender from the *government,* the last item of the proclamation called upon the government to proclaim the unconditional surrender of the *armed forces.*

The document also promised that Japan would not be destroyed as a nation, that the Japanese would be free to choose their own form of government, that sovereignty over the home islands would be returned to them after occupation, that they would be allowed access to raw materials for industry, and that Japanese forces would be allowed to return home.

Most important of all, the phrasing of the proclamation hinted strongly that the Emperor would be left on the throne, the one point which had been of most concern to the cabinet in all its discussions of surrender. The Japanese were expected to read between the lines, which they very quickly did.

Upon receiving the text of the proclamation, the Emperor told Foreign Minister Togo without hesitation that he deemed it acceptable. The full cabinet then met to discuss the Allied ultimatum.

Despite the fact that the cabinet members were considering acceptance of the Potsdam terms, they could not at first decide whether the news of the Allied proclamation should be released to the Japanese public. Foreign Minister Togo, anxious to prepare the people for the surrender, argued for four hours for its prompt release to the press. At six in the evening he won his point over strong army objections and late that night the declaration was released to the newspapers.

But there was another factor which the cabinet also was forced to consider. As yet the Japanese had received news of the statement of Allied policy at Potsdam only through their radio listening posts. It was not addressed to their government and the ultimatum had not yet reached them through official channels. Could the cabinet act on the basis of such unofficial information?

"After mature deliberation the hastily convened cabinet decided to keep silence for a while about the Potsdam proclamation pending further developments," says Kase.

The delay in announcing acceptance of the Allied terms was not expected to be long, but Prime Minister Suzuki was to meet the very next day with the press. The Japanese newsmen undoubtedly would question him about the proclamation. What should he say?

Hiroshi Shimomura, president of the powerful Board of Information—counterpart of Germany's propaganda ministry—and a member of the cabinet, recalls in his account of this fateful session that it was decided that the prime minister, if asked, should treat the subject lightly.

"This was to be done in order not to upset the surrender negotiations then under way through Russia," says Shimomura.

Premier Suzuki was to say merely that the cabinet had reached no decision on the Allied demands and that the discussion was continuing. Although the policy was to be one of silence, the very fact that the cabinet did not reject the ultimatum at once would make it clear to the Japanese people what was in the wind.

When Premier Suzuki confronted the press on July 28, he said that the cabinet was holding to a policy of *mokusatsu.* The word *mokusatsu* not only has no exact counterpart in English but it is ambiguous even in Japanese. Suzuki, as we know, meant that the cabinet had decided to make no comment on the Potsdam proclamation, with the implication that something significant was impending. But the Japanese were tricked by their own language. For in addition to meaning "to withhold comment," *mokusatsu* may also be translated as "to ignore."

The word has two characters in Japanese. *Moku* means "silence" and *satsu* means "kill," thus implying in an absolutely literal sense "to kill with silence." This can mean—to a Japanese—either to ignore or to refrain from comment.

Unfortunately the translators at the Domei News Agency could not know what Suzuki had in mind. As they hastily translated the prime minister's statement into English, they chose the wrong meaning. From the towers of Radio Tokyo

the news crackled to the Allied world that the Suzuki cabinet had decided to "ignore" the Potsdam ultimatum.

The cabinet was furious at Suzuki's choice of words and the subsequent error by Domei. The reaction of Kase, who had fought long and hard for peace, was one of dismay.

"This was a piece of foolhardiness," he says. "When I heard of this I strongly remonstrated with the cabinet chief secretary, but it was too late. . . . Tokyo radio flashed it—to America! The punishment came swiftly. An atomic bomb was dropped on Hiroshima on August 6 by the Allies, who were led by Suzuki's outrageous statement into the belief that our government had refused to accept the Potsdam proclamation."

But for this tragic mistake, Kase laments, Japan might have been spared the atomic attack and the Russian declaration of war.

William J. Coughlin

Where Words Go Astray

One word, one mistaken interpretation by a news reporter, and the cost may have been tens of thousands of lives. Add to this the literally hundreds of small misunderstandings that almost certainly come between you and other people every week and you can probably begin to see the need for taking a close look at how our language works.

What are some of the most common problems we have in understanding each other? We'll start our survey of semantics by listing the most important ones and after doing so try to show you how you can keep them from occurring in your life.

Attitude Survey

Begin by filling out the following questionnaire. It's a series of statements someone might make while discussing politics; you've probably heard comments like these many times. Signify your response by putting a number next to each statement according to the following scale:

5 strongly agree
4 agree
3 undecided
2 disagree
1 strongly disagree

1. _____ In many cases revolutions are justifiable ways of getting rid of repressive governments.

2. _____ All groups can live in harmony in this country without changing the system very much.

3. _____ It's not really undemocratic to recognize that the world is divided into superior and inferior people.

4. _____ If you start trying to change things very much, you usually make them worse.

5. _____ You can usually depend more on a person who owns property than one who doesn't.

6. _____ Freedom is worth fighting for—sometimes even to death.

7. _____ I prefer the practical person anytime to the intellectual.

8. _____ Private ownership of property is necessary if we're to have a strong nation.

9. _____ No matter what ordinary people may think, political power doesn't come from them but from some higher source.

10. _____ It's better to stick with what you have than to be trying new things you don't really know.

11. _____ Increasing government control in our lives is taking away our freedom.

12. _____ A person has the right to protect himself from physical threats, no matter what the law says.

13. _____ It's never wise to introduce changes rapidly, in government or in the economic system.

14. _____ Our society is so complicated that if you try to reform parts of it, you're likely to upset the whole system.

15. _____ A person doesn't really get much wisdom until he's well along in years.

16. _____ If something grows up over a long time, there's bound to be much wisdom in it.

17. _____ I'd want to be sure that something would really work before I'd be willing to take chances on it.

18. _____ You can't change human nature.

19. _____ The heart is as good a guide as the head.

After writing down your response to the questions, compare them with the answers of other people who have taken the survey. Where do you agree? disagree? Talk over your responses and see if anyone's mind is changed. Do you ever get the feeling in such conversations that all you're doing is talking in circles? Why do you think this is so?

What happened when you discussed the survey? It's likely that you found yourself in one of those unsatisfying arguments where you not only disagreed with other respondants about the answers you gave, but you couldn't even be sure you were talking about the same questions.

If this did happen, you can probably see why. The statements you responded to were so vague that they meant different things to every person who read them. Take question 1, for example. What kind of revolution were you thinking about—violent or nonviolent? Are all revolutions alike? If so, to defend one means you have to defend them all. If you don't believe all revolutions are justified, did you explain in your discussion which ones you do support? And what about "repressive governments"? Do you think everybody you argued with shared the same idea of what constitutes one? Probably not, but did you take much time trying to find a common definition for this term? In discussions like the ones you probably had here it almost seems sometimes that the people involved are speaking different languages which only look alike.

Now you might say that this vague kind of language in the survey was obvious, that in your everyday communications you'd never be this careless in your use of language. But would this really be true? How often do you recall arguing with someone about one or more of these topics, and how many times have such discussions turned into frustrating arguments?

In the next pages we'll take a look at some common semantic problems. As you read about them, think about how they influenced your response to the preceding survey and how they occur in your everyday encounters.

Equivocal Words   One kind of semantic misunderstanding is caused by equivocal words, that is, words that can be interpreted in more than one way. Equivocal misunderstandings happen almost every day, usually when we least expect them. Not long ago we were ordering dinner in a Mexican restaurant and noticed that the menu described each item as coming with rice or beans. We asked the waitress for "a tostada with beans," but when the order came we were surprised to find that instead of a beef tostada with beans on the side as we expected, the waitress had brought a tostada _filled_ with beans. At first we were angry at her for botching a simple order, but then we realized that it was as much our fault for not making the order clear as it was hers for not checking.

"I know you believe you understand what you think I said, but I'm not sure you realize that what you heard is not what I meant."

. . . Considerably more serious is the frequent mistake committed by translators with the number word billion, which in the United States and France means a thousand millions (10^9) but in England and most continental European countries means a million millions (10^{12}). There the U.S. billion is called miliardo, Milliarde, etc. The reader will appreciate that . . . the difference between 10^9 and 10^{12} can mean disaster if hidden in, say, a textbook on nuclear physics.

Paul Watzlawick
How Real Is Real?

The Semantics of
"I Love You"

. . . "I love you" [is] a statement that can be expressed in so many varied ways. It may be a stage song, repeated daily without any meaning, or a barely audible murmur, full of surrender. Sometimes it means: I desire you or I want you sexually. It may mean: I hope you love me or I hope that I will be able to love you. Often it means: It may be that a love relationship can develop between us or even I hate you. Often it is a wish for emotional exchange: I want your admiration in exchange for mine or I give my love in exchange for some passion or I want to feel cozy and at home with you or I admire some of your qualities: A declaration of love is mostly a request: I desire you or I want you to gratify me, or I want your protection or I want to be intimate with you or I want to exploit your loveliness.

Sometimes it is the need for security and tenderness, for parental treatment. It may mean: My self-love goes out to you. But it may also express submissiveness: Please take me as I am, or I feel guilty about you, I want, through you, to correct the mistakes I have made in human relations. It may be self-sacrifice and a masochistic wish for dependency. However, it may also be a full affirmation of the other, taking the responsibility for mutual exchange of feelings. It may be a weak feeling of friendliness, it may be the scarcely even whispered expression of ecstasy. "I love you,"—wish, desire, submission, conquest; it is never the word itself that tells the real meaning here.

J. A. M. Meerloo, *Conversation and Communication*

Often equivocal misunderstandings are more serious. A nurse gave one of her patients a real scare when she told him that he "wouldn't be needing" his robe, books, and shaving materials any more. After that statement the patient became quiet and moody for no apparent reason. When the nurse finally asked why, she found out that her statement had led the poor man to think he was going to die immediately; she really meant that he'd be going home soon.

As we mentioned earlier, most of the words we use can be interpreted in a number of ways. A good rule to remember if you want to keep misunderstandings to a minimum is "If a word can be interpreted in more than one way, it probably will be."

Relative Words   Relative words are ones that gain their meaning by comparison. For example, is the school you attend a large or small one? This depends on what you compare it to: Alongside a campus like UCLA, with its almost 28,000 students, it probably looks pretty small; but compared with a smaller institution it might seem quite large. In the same way relative words like fast and slow, smart and stupid, short and long depend for their meaning upon what they're compared to. (The "large" size can of olives is the smallest you can buy; the larger ones are "giant," "colossal," and "supercolossal.")

Using relative terms without explaining them can lead to communication problems. Have you ever responded to someone's question about the weather by telling her it was warm, only to find out that she thought it was cold? Or have you followed a friend's advice and gone to a "cheap" restaurant only to find that it was twice as expensive as you expected? Have you been disappointed to learn that classes you've heard were "easy" turned out to be hard, that journeys you were told would be "short" were long, that "unusual" ideas were really quite ordinary? The problem in each case came from failing to anchor the relative term used to a more precisely measurable one.

Last night while Roy and I were preparing dinner, four-year-old Michael yelled from the family room, "Hey mom, how do you make love, again?" The expression on Roy's face clearly said, "What have you been teaching this kid?" I calmly answered Michael's question with "L–O–V–E." He had been drawing a picture for a friend and wanted to sign it "Love, Michael," but had forgotten how to "make" love. I wonder how Roy would have answered Michael's question if I hadn't been around!

Liddy Error Alleged: Thought He Must Kill

NEW YORK (UPI)—Convicted Watergate conspirator G. Gordan Liddy thought he had been ordered to assassinate columnist Jack Anderson during the 1972 campaign, Parade magazine reported Saturday.

The magazine said that during the course of a meeting with Jeb Stuart Magruder, deputy director of the Committee for the Reelection of the President, Magruder mentioned Anderson and told Liddy: "We've got to get rid of this guy."

Liddy, according to Parade, left the meeting and ran into Robert Reisner, Magruder's assistant.

"I've just been ordered to kill Jack Anderson," the magazine quoted Liddy as telling him.

Alarmed, Reisner ran back into Magruder's office and confronted Magruder.

"Magruder and Reisner immediately got hold of Liddy," the magazine said. "Magruder explained that he had just been talking figuratively.

He didn't want Anderson assassinated . . . all he meant was that Anderson's incisive reporting constituted a problem that he would prefer to be rid of."

According to Parade, Liddy answered: "Where I come from that means a rubout."

Emotive Language To understand how emotive language works we need to distinguish between *denotative* and *connotative* meanings. A denotative definition describes an event in purely objective terms, while connotative interpretations contain an emotional element. Consider, for example, the term *pregnant*. The denotative meaning of this word involves a condition in which a female is carrying her offspring during a gestation period. When used in this purely biological sense, most people could hear the term without a strong emotional reaction. But imagine the additional turmoil this word would create when an unmarried teenage couple find it stamped on the young woman's lab report. Certainly the meaning to these people would go far beyond the dictionary definition.

Some words have little or no connotative meaning: *the, it, as,* and so on. Others are likely to evoke both denotative and connotative reactions: *cancer, income tax,* and *final examination,* for example. There are also terms that are almost exclusively connotative, such as the *damn!* (or other oath) you would probably utter if you hammered your thumb instead of a nail.

Connotative meanings are a necessary and important part of human communication. Being creatures with emotions, it's a fact of life that people will use some words that will evoke strong reactions. Without connotative meanings we'd be unable to describe ourselves fully or have others understand us.

Problems occur, however, when people claim to use words in a purely denotative way when they are really expressing their attitudes. *Emotive language,* then, contains words that sound as if they're describing something when they are really announcing the speaker's attitude toward something. Do you like that old picture frame? If so, you'd probably call it "an antique," but if you think it's ugly you'd likely describe it as "a piece of junk." Now whether the picture frame belongs on the mantle or in the garbage can is a matter of opinion, not fact, but it's easy to forget this when you use emotive words. Emotive words may sound like statements of fact, but they're always opinions.

Here's a list of other emotive words:

If you approve, say	If you disapprove, say
Thrifty	Cheap
Traditional	Old-fashioned
Extrovert	Loudmouth
Cautious	Coward
Progressive	Radical
Information	Propaganda
Determined	Stubborn
Slender	Skinny

Problems occur when people use emotive terms without labeling them as such. You might have a long and bitter argument with a friend about whether a third person was "assertive" or "obnoxious," when a more accurate and peaceable way to handle the issue would be to acknowledge that one of you approves of the behavior while the other doesn't.

A businessman	A businesswoman
He is aggressive	She is pushy
He is careful about details	She's picky
He loses his temper because he's so involved in his job	She's bitchy
He's depressed (or hung over), so everyone tiptoes past his office	She's moody, so it must be her time of the month
He follows through	She doesn't know when to quit
He's firm	She's stubborn
He makes wise judgments	She reveals her prejudices
He is a man of the world	She's been around
He isn't afraid to say what he thinks	She's opinionated
He exercises authority	She's tyrannical
He's discrete	She's secretive
He's a stern taskmaster	She's difficult to work for

Overly Broad Terms Sometimes we use a word that says more to others than we intend it to. In such cases we've unintentionally chosen a word that covers a whole class of objects, but we only meant to describe some members of that class. For example, how many times has an instructor told you to study "everything we've covered so far" for an exam (causing you to lose sleep, neglect your other work, and generally ruin part of your life)? Then, when the day of the test came, you found he really meant you should study everything since the last midterm. In this case the words "everything we've covered so far" were too broad.

Fiction Words Semanticists use the label "fiction word" to describe terms such as freedom, truth, communism, democracy, justice, and so on. Fiction words make communication difficult because they have so many meanings that no two people use them the same way. The danger in using such words comes from assuming that their meaning is clear. For example, many voters will hear a candidate for office declare that he's in favor of "peace" and automatically vote for him, assuming his election will bring on a new era of international friendship. Later they may be disappointed to learn that their candidates' idea of peace involves bombing into submission any country whose governmental policies differ from his.

We'll have more to say about fiction words later in this chapter.

Abstraction in Language

Toward the beginning of this chapter we said that words represent things, rather than being things themselves. This fact leads to the critically important idea that language can describe events on many levels, some of which are more abstract than others.

To understand the concept of abstraction, consider the object you're reading now. What would you call it? Probably a book. But you could narrow your description by calling it a "communication book," or even more specifically, *Looking Out/Looking In*. You could be even more precise than this if you wanted: You could say that you're reading Chapter 8 of *Looking Out/Looking In,* or even page 312 of Chapter 8 of *Looking Out/Looking In.* In each case your description would be more precise, focusing more specifically on the object we asked you about while excluding other things that were members of the same categories but didn't apply in this case.

Instead of going down the abstraction ladder to more basic terms, you could go the other way. Rather than talking about this thing you're reading as a book, you could describe it as educational literature, nonfiction writing, or printed material, each description being less and less specific.

Semanticist (and later U.S. Senator) S. I. Hayakawa created an "abstraction ladder" to describe this process. This ladder consists of a number of descriptions of the same person, object, or event. The lowest description on the ladder describes the phenomenon at its most basic level: atoms and molecules interacting, nerve synapses operating, magnetic waves moving through space, and so on.

Further up the ladder come visually observable aspects of the event: specifically what words are said, what movements made, what colors or sizes are present, and so on. Moving still higher up the ladder, we come to increasingly general descriptions. The sample abstraction ladder illustrated here is an example of the many levels on which a phenomenon can be described.

Another way of thinking about abstractions is to realize that they're generalizations. Hayakawa gives an example to illustrate this principle:

> . . . suppose that we live in an isolated village of four families, each owning a house. A's house is referred to as *maga;* B's house is *biyo*; C's is *kata,* D's is *pelel.* This is quite satisfactory for ordinary purposes of communication in the village, unless a

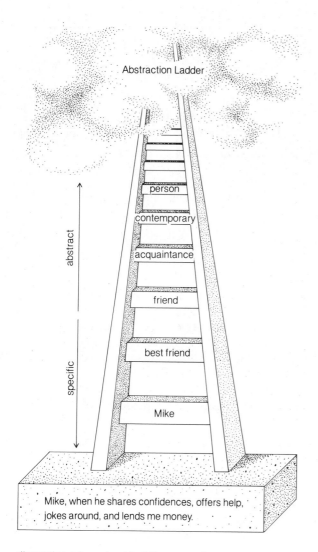

Abstraction Ladder

person

contemporary

acquaintance

friend

best friend

Mike

abstract

specific

Mike, when he shares confidences, offers help, jokes around, and lends me money.

discussion arises about building a new house—a spare one, let us say. We cannot refer to the projected house by any one of the four words we have for the existing houses, since each of these has too specific a meaning. We must find a *general* term, at a higher level of abstraction, that means "something that has certain characteristics in common with maga, biyo, kata, and pelel, and yet is not A's, B's, C's, or D's." Since this is much too complicated to say each time, an *abbreviation* must be invented. So we choose the noise, *house.* Out of such needs do our words come—they are a form of shorthand.*

Thus, abstractions are generalizations that let us talk about the similarities between several objects or events. But at the same time these abstractions allow us to focus on similarities, they also cause us to ignore differences between the objects being described in a category. This can lead to communication problems, as we'll now see.

*S. I. Hayakawa, *Language in Thought and Action* (New York: Harcourt Brace Jovanovich, 1964).

© 1972 United Feature Syndicate, Inc.

Problems With Abstractions Most problems in this area come from using terms that are too high on the abstraction ladder. This lack of specificity causes trouble in four ways.

Stereotyping Imagine someone who has had a bad experience while traveling abroad and as a result blames an entire country. "Yeah, those damn Hottentots are a bunch of thieves. If you're not careful they'll steal you blind. I know, because one of 'em stole my camera last year." You can see here how lumping people into highly abstract categories ignores the fact that for every thieving Hottentot there are probably 100 honest ones. It's this kind of thinking that leads to mistaken assumptions that keep people apart: "None of those kids are any damn good!"; "You can't trust anybody in business."; "Those cops are all a bunch of goons." Each of these statements ignores the very important fact that sometimes our descriptions are too general, that they say more than we really mean.

Kleindienst, Favoring Gray, Says FBI Chief Should Be a "Patriot"

BY RONALD J. OSTROW

WASHINGTON—Saying the FBI directorship calls for "a patriot of America . . . with a religious sense," Atty. Gen. Richard G. Kleindienst disclosed Thursday he had recommended acting FBI director L. Patrick Gray III for the job.

Kleindienst told newsmen that the FBI post, which will be subject to Senate confirmation for the first time, calls for "a broad reference person," not one with "a limited or myopic background."

In saying the director should be a patriot, Kleindienst said he did not mean "a silly flag-waver," but a man who believed the nation's institutions were "worth preserving and defending."

On the religious qualification, Kleindienst said he meant a man who was "capable of compassion and understanding." Asked if he would rule out an agnostic, Kleindienst said he would not "if he had love of his fellow man, "but added

with a laugh: "I don't believe an agnostic can."

"You have to have a basic love for your fellow human being if you are going to be entrusted with the tremendous power" of the FBI, Kleindienst said.

He said the FBI chief should be a lawyer and a disciplinarian.

Los Angeles Times

On the basis of this article, explain in low-level terms Kleindienst's definition of the words *patriot, religious sense, broad reference person, compassion,* and *understanding.*

When you think about examples like these, you begin to see how thinking in abstract terms can lead to ignoring individual differences, which can be as important as similarities. In this sense semantics isn't "just" a matter of words. People in the habit of using highly abstract language begin to *think* in generalities, ignoring uniqueness. And as we discussed in Chapters 2 and 4, expecting people to be a certain way can become a self-fulfilling prophecy. If I think all policemen are brutal, I'm more likely to react in a defensive, hostile way toward them, which in turn increases the chance that they'll react to me as a threat. If I think that no teachers care about their classes, then my defensive indifference is likely to make a potentially helpful instructor into someone who truly doesn't care.

Failing to recognize abstractions for what they are can lead to a great deal of unnecessary grief. We know a couple who were convinced that their child was abnormal because she hadn't learned to talk by the age of two. When we tried to tell them that some kids begin talking later than others and that there was nothing to worry about, the parents wouldn't accept our help. "But something must be wrong with Sally," they said, pointing to a book on child development. "It says right here that children should be talking by one year, and Sally only makes funny noises." What the parent had failed to do was read the first chapters of the book, in which the authors stressed that the term "child" is an abstraction—that there's no such thing as the "typical" child because each one is an individual.

In many situations it's important to be specific, but I can't think of any examples offhand.

Ashleigh Brilliant

Confusing others   Have you ever been disappointed with the way a haircut turned out? In spite of your instructions—"not too short," for example—you got up from the chair with a style unlike anything you wanted. Although the problem might have come from choosing a stylist who should have become a butcher, it's more likely that your instructions weren't clear enough. Terms like "not too short" or "more casual" are just too abstract to paint a clear picture of what you had in mind.

Of course, overly abstract explanations can cause problems of a more serious nature. Imagine the lack of understanding that could come from vague complaints such as:

A   We never do anything that's fun anymore.

B   What do you mean?

A   We used to do lots of unusual things, but now it's the same old stuff, over and over.

B   But last week we went on that camping trip, and tomorrow we're going to that party where we'll meet all sorts of new people. Those are new things.

A   That's not what I mean. I'm talking about *really* unusual stuff.

B   (becoming confused and a little impatient)   Like what? Taking hard drugs or going over Niagara Falls in a barrel?

A   Don't be stupid. All I'm saying is that we're in a rut. We should be living more exciting lives.

B   Well, I don't know what you want.

. . . it is doubtful if a people learned in semantics would tolerate any sort of supreme political dictator. . . . A typical speech by an aspiring Hitler would be translated into its intrinsic meaning, if any. Abstract words and phrases without discoverable referents would register a semantic blank, noises without meaning. For instance:

> The Aryan Fatherland, which has nursed the souls of heroes, calls upon you for the supreme sacrifice which you, in whom flows heroic blood, will not fail, and which will echo forever down the corridors of history.

This would be translated:

> The blab, blab, which has nursed the blabs of blabs, calls upon you for the blab blab which you, in whom flows blab blood, will not fail, and which will echo down the blabs of blab.

The "blab" is not an attempt to be funny; it is a semantic blank. Nothing comes through. The hearer, versed in reducing high-order abstractions to either nil or a series of roughly similar events in the real world of experience, and protected from emotive associations with such words, simply hears nothing comprehensible. The demagogue might as well have used Sanskrit.

Stuart Chase, The Tyranny of Words

Overly abstract language also leads to confusing directions:

Teacher   I hope you'll do a thorough job on this paper.

Student   When you say thorough, how long should it be?

T   Long enough to cover the topic thoroughly.

S   How many sources should I look at when I'm researching it?

T   You should use several—enough to show me that you've really explored the subject.

S   And what style should I use to write it?

T   One that's scholarly but not too formal.

S   Arrgh!!!

Along with unclear complaints and vague instructions, even appreciations can suffer from being expressed in overly abstract terms. Psychologists have established that behaviors that are reinforced will recur with increased frequency. This means that your statements of appreciation will encourage others to keep acting in ways you like. But if they don't know just what it is that you appreciate, the chances of that behavior being repeated are lessened. There's a big difference between "I appreciate your being so nice" and "I appreciate the way you spent that time talking to me when I was upset."

Bypassing   Bypassing occurs when people unintentionally use the same word to mean different things or use different words to represent the same thing. Have you ever gotten angry at a friend who calls to say, "I'll be a little late for our date," and then keeps you waiting an hour? This mix-up about the relative term *little* typifies bypassing. So does the argument we once heard between two students, one black and one white, who were talking about a particular model of car. The black student insisted the car was "bad," while the white claimed it was "great." After a few minutes they finally realized that they both liked the auto, but that the terms they chose to express themselves suggested a disagreement. Problems of bypassing such as these are much more likely to occur when we use abstract language, since there's less possibility of checking terms against observable events.

Confusing yourself   Overly abstract language can even leave you unclear about your own thoughts. At one time or another we've all felt dissatisfied with ourselves and others. Often these dissatisfaction show up as thoughts such as "I've got to get better organized" or "She's been acting strangely lately." Sometimes abstract statements such as these are shorthand for specific behaviors that we can easily identify; but in other cases we'd have a hard time clearly explaining what you'd have to do to get organized or what the strange behavior is. And without clear ideas of these concepts it's hard to begin changing matters. Instead, the tendency is to go around in mental circles, feeling vaguely dissatisfied without knowing exactly what is wrong or how to improve matters.

> *A group of synonyms does not define an object. A careful description may help bring it into focus for the listener, but is not conclusive. Final identification is achieved only by pointing to the apple, touching it with the hand, seeing it with the eyes, tasting it with the mouth, and so recognizing it as noverbal. Here is the base from which all our proud words rise — every last one of them — and to it they must constantly return and be refreshed. Failing this, they wander into regions where there are no apples, no objects, no acts, and so they become symbols for airy chunks of nothing at all. . . .*
>
> Stuart Chase, *The Tyranny of Words*

Down to Specifics: Avoiding Abstract Thinking and Language   If abstract language is often a problem, what can you do to reduce its inappropriate use in your life? Probably the best answer is to pay attention to your everyday conversations and thoughts. Every so often—especially when your emotions are strong—ask yourself whether you can translate your language down the abstraction ladder to less vague terms.

You can do this by learning to make *behavioral descriptions* of your problems, goals, appreciations, complaints, and requests. We use the word *behavioral* because descriptions of this sort move down the abstraction ladder to describe the specific, observable objects and actions about which we're thinking.

It's hard to overestimate the value of specific, behavioral language, for speaking in this way vastly increases the chance not only of you thinking clearly about what's on your mind, but also of others understanding you. A behavioral description should include three elements.

Who is involved?   At first the answer to this question might seem simple. If you're thinking about a personal problem or goal, you might reply "I am"; if you're expressing appreciation, complaining, or making a request of another person, then he or she would be the one who is involved. Although the question of involvement may be easy, it often calls for more detail. Ask yourself whether the problem or goal you're thinking about involves an entire category of people (women, salespeople, strangers), a subclass of the group (attractive women, rude salespeople, strangers you'd like to meet), or a specific person (Jane Doe, the salesclerk at a particular store, a new person in your neighborhood). If you're talking to another person, consider whether your appreciation, complaint, or request is directed solely at him or her or whether it also involves others.

In what circumstances does the behavior occur?   You can identify the circumstances by answering several questions. In what places does the behavior occur? Does it occur at any particular times? When you are discussing particular subjects? Is there anything special about you when it occurs: are you tired, embarrassed, busy? Is there any common trait shared by the other person or people involved? Are they friendly or hostile, straightforward or manipulative, nervous or confident? In other words, if the behavior you're describing doesn't occur all the time (and few do), you need to pin down what circumstances set this situation apart from other ones.

What behaviors are involved?　While terms such as "more cooperative" and "helpful" might sound like they're concrete descriptions of behavior, they are usually too vague to do a clear job of explaining what's on your mind. Behaviors must be *observable,* ideally both to you and to others. For instance, moving down the abstraction ladder from the relatively vague term "helpful," you might come to behaviors such as "does the dishes every other day," "volunteers to help me with my studies," or "fixes dinner once or twice a week without being asked." It's easy to see that terms like these are easier for both you and others to understand than are more vague abstractions.

There is one exception to the rule that behaviors should be observable, and that involves the internal processes of thoughts and emotions. For instance, in describing what happens to you when a friend has kept you waiting for a long time, you might say "My stomach felt like it was in knots—I was really worried. I kept thinking that you had forgotten and that I wasn't important enough to you for you to remember our date." What you're doing when offering such a description is to make unobservable events clear.

You can get a clearer idea of the value of behavioral descriptions by looking at the examples we've provided on page 320. Notice how much more clearly they explain the speaker's thought than do the more vague terms. Clear behavioral descriptions form the basis for accurate "sensing statements" such as we described in Chapter 1.

One valuable type of behavioral description is the *operational definition.* Instead of defining a word with more words, an operational definition points, as it were, to the behaviors, actions, or properties that a word signifies.

We use operational definitions all the time: "The student union is that building with all the bikes in front"; "What I'd like more than anything is 30 acres of land on the Columbia River"; "My idea of a good time is eating a triple-decker, three-flavor, chocolate-dipped ice cream cone." Each of these statements is relatively clear; rather than using vague, more abstract language they tell in observable terms just what the speaker is talking about. Hayakawa points out that the best examples of operational definitions in our everyday lives are found in cookbooks. They describe a dish by telling you what ingredients are combined in what amounts by what operations. ("To make a pizza, begin with the crust. Mix ¼ cup water with 2 cups flour. . . .")

But as we've already seen, some definitions aren't operational. They never point down the ladder of abstraction to more clearly understandable operations; instead, they only explain words with more words. A nonoperational, highly abstract cookbook might define a pizza as "a delectable, flavorful treat that is both hearty and subtle."

"In that case," said the Dodo solemnly, rising to its feet, "I move that the meeting adjourn, for the immediate adoption of more energetic remedies—"

"Speak English!" said the Eaglet. "I don't know the meaning of half those long words, and, what's more, I don't believe you do either!" And the Eaglet bent down its head to hide a smile: some of the other birds tittered audibly.

"What I was going to say," said the Dodo in an offended tone, "was that the best thing to get us dry would be a Caucus-race."

"What is a Caucus-race?" said Alice.

"Why," said the Dodo, "the best way to explain it is to do it."

Lewis Carroll, *Alice's Adventures in Wonderland*

Abstract Description	Behavioral Description			Remarks
	Who Is Involved	**In What Circumstances**	**Specific Behaviors**	
Problem I'm no good at meeting strangers.	People I'd like to date	When I meet them at parties or at school	Think to myself, "They'd never want to date me." Also, I don't originate conversations.	Behavioral description more clearly identifies thoughts and behaviors to change.
Goal I'd like to be more assertive.	Telephone and door-to-door solicitors	When I don't want the product or can't afford it	Instead of apologizing or explaining, say "I'm not interested" and keep repeating this until they go away.	Behavioral description clearly outlines how to act; abstract description doesn't.
Appreciation "You've been a great boss."	(no clarification necessary)	When I've needed to change my schedule because of school exams or assignments	"You've rearranged my hours cheerfully."	Give both abstract and behavioral descriptions for best results.
Complaint "I don't like some of the instructors around here."	Professors A and B	In class when students ask questions the professors think are stupid	Either answer in a sarcastic voice (you might demonstrate), or accuse us of not studying hard enough	If talking to A or B, use only behavioral description. With others, use both abstract and behavioral descriptions.
Request "Quit bothering me!"	You and your friends, X and Y	When I'm studying for exams	Instead of asking me over and over to party with you, I wish you'd accept my comment that I need to study and leave me to do it.	Behavioral description will reduce defensiveness and make it clear that you don't *always* want to be left alone.

This example illustrates both the advantages and limitations of operational definitions. On one hand, they paint a very clear picture of what you're talking about, leaving very little to the listener's imagination. This is important when you remember our discussion in Chapter 6 of how easy it is for others to misinterpret our words. On the other hand, operational definitions leave out some qualities that lend an emotional element to communication. While the recipe for pizza might tell you *how* to make one, it's not likely to make you *want* to eat it. Figurative language is appropriate at times. You're much more likely to win your true love's affection by reciting poetry than by talking about how your blood pressure changes whenever you're together. The trick, then, isn't to use just abstract or only specific language, but rather to use each when it will best suit your needs.

The Language of Deception

So far we've been talking about cases where people use unclear language unintentionally. But there are other instances when vague or misleading terms can be used deliberately to obscure someone's intentions.

Probably the most widespread instance of this deliberate muddying of the waters is in the field of politics. People running for elective offices often use what we earlier termed fiction words to start the voters' glands working. Take Candidate *X;* he needs the support both of people who favor capital punishment and those who oppose it. How can he make a statement on the subject that won't cost him any votes? He can't say we should string up every felon in the state, yet he doesn't want to look "soft on crime" either. So after much deliberation, his office issues the following news release: "Candidate *X* declared today that under our great system of laws each man and woman must be guaranteed due process, with those found guilty receiving treatment which is both swift and fair. To do any less would be contrary to the principles of this nation."

Now what do statements like this say? It's no accident that we don't know. In this age of widespread telecommunications every word a candidate speaks can be heard by anyone who cares to listen. In a statement like this candidates often are tempted to water down their words so that they sound good but say nothing . . . or everything.

Although more and more people are developing a healthy skepticism toward such statements, there's still a danger of a few high-level abstractions slipping through. Because of this it's necessary to keep on guard—to ask what those fine-sounding words refer to, what they mean in specific, operational terms to the person who spoke them.

Many times we use high-level abstractions to fool ourselves as well as others. When faced with a truth we'd rather ignore, often the easiest thing to do is rename it and in so doing remove some of its distastefulness. One way is through the use of euphemisms, words that soften the bluntness of unpleasant ideas. Often euphemisms are merely ways of avoiding shocking friends, as, for example, asking where the "rest rooms" are instead of asking "Where's the toilet?" In such cases there's nothing especially dangerous about using euphemisms instead of more straightforward language.

But there are many instances in which using vague, inoffensive terms instead of "telling it like it is" can block our thinking in important ways. Speaking of poor people as being "disadvantaged" somehow makes their plight less disturbing. Referring to "senior citizens' retirement communities" presents a happier picture than "old peoples' homes." And talking about someone's "passing on" instead of dying allows us to avoid facing and preparing for the eventual deaths of ourselves and our friends.

But it's in the field of international politics and war that euphemisms are probably most dangerous. As Aldous Huxley shows in the following reading, high-sounding phrases and noble generalities can lead to disastrous consequences.

Political language—and with variations this is true of all political parties, from Conservatives to Anarchists—is designed to make lies sound truthful and murder respectable, and to give an appearance of solidarity to pure wind.

George Orwell, *Politics and the English Language*

THE LANGUAGE OF WAR

Words form the thread on which we string our experiences. Without them we should live spasmodically and intermittently. If, as so often happens, we choose to give continuity to our experience by means of words which falsify the facts, this is because the falsification is somehow to our advantage as egotists.

Consider, for example, the case of war. War is enormously discreditable to those who order it to be waged and even to those who merely tolerate its existence. Furthermore, to developed sensibilities the facts of war are revolting and horrifying. To falsify these facts, and by so doing to make war seem less evil than it really is, and our own responsibility in tolerating war less heavy, is doubly to our advantage. By suppressing and distorting the truth, we protect our sensibilities and preserve our self-esteem. Now, language is, among other things, a device which men use for suppressing and distorting the truth. Finding the reality of war too unpleasant to contemplate, we create a verbal alternative to that reality, parallel with it, but in quality quite different from it. That which we contemplate thenceforward is not that to which we react emotionally and upon which we pass our moral judgments, is not war as it is in fact, but the fiction of war as it exists in our pleasantly falsifying verbiage. Our stupidity in using inappropriate language turns out, on analysis, to be the most refined cunning.

The most shocking fact about war is that its victims and its instruments are individual human beings, and that these individual human beings are condemned by the monstrous conventions of politics to murder or be murdered in quarrels not their own, to inflict upon the innocent and, innocent themselves of any crime against their enemies, to suffer cruelties of every kind.

The language of strategy and politics is designed, so far as it is possible, to conceal this fact, to make it appear as though wars were not fought by individuals drilled to murder one another in cold blood and without provocation, but either by impersonal and therefore wholly non-moral and impassible forces, or else by personified abstractions.

Ignoring the facts, so far as we possibly can, we imply that battles are not fought by soldiers, but by things, principles, allegories, personified collectivities, or (at the most human) by opposing commanders, pitched against one another in single combat. For the same reason, when we have to describe the processes and the results of war, we employ a rich variety of euphemisms. Even the most violently patriotic and militaristic are reluctant to call a spade by its own name. To conceal their intentions even from themselves, they make use of picturesque metaphors. We find them, for example, clamouring for war planes numerous and powerful enough to go and "destroy the hornets in their nests"—in other words, to go and throw thermite, high explosives and vesicants upon the inhabitants of neighbouring countries before they have time to come and do the same to us. And how reassuring is the language of historians and strategists! They write admiringly of those military geniuses who know "when to strike at the enemy's line" (a single combatant deranges the geometrical constructions of a personification); when to "turn his flank"; when to "execute an enveloping movement." As though they were engineers discussing the strength of materials and the distribution of stresses, they talk of abstract entities called "man power" and "fire power." They sum up the long-drawn sufferings and atrocities of trench warfare in the phrase, "a war of attrition"; the massacre and mangling of human beings is assimilated to the grinding of a lens.

A dangerously abstract word, which figures in all discussions about war, is "force." Those who believe in organizing collective security by means of military pacts against a possible aggressor are particularly fond of this word. "You cannot," they say, "have international justice unless you are prepared to impose it by force." "Peace-loving countries must unite to use force against aggressive dictatorships." "Democratic institutions must be protected, if need be, by force." And so on.

Let us take the sentences quoted above and translate the abstract word "force" into language that will render (however inadequately) the concrete and particular realities of contemporary warfare.

"You cannot have international justice, unless you are prepared to impose it by force." Translated, this becomes: "You cannot have international justice unless you are prepared, with a view to imposing a just settlement, to drop thermite, high explosives and vesicants upon the inhabitants of foreign cities and to have thermite, high explosives and vesicants dropped in return upon the inhabitants of your cities." At the end of this proceeding, justice is to be imposed by the victorious party—that is, if there is a victorious party.

The next two sentences may be taken together. "Peace-loving countries must unite to use force against aggressive dictatorships. Democratic institutions must be protected, if need be, by force." Let us translate. "Peace-loving countries must unite to throw thermite, high explosives and vesicants on the inhabitants of countries ruled by aggressive dictators. They must do this, and of course abide the consequences, in order to preserve peace and democratic institutions."

The alternatives confronting us seem to be plain enough. Either we invent and conscientiously employ a new technique for making revolutions and settling international disputes; or else we cling to the old technique and, using "force" (that is to say, thermite, high explosives and vesicants), destroy ourselves. Those who, for whatever motive, disguise the nature of the second alternative under inappropriate language, render the world a grave disservice. They lead us into one of the temptations we find it hardest to resist—the temptation to run away from reality, to pretend that facts are not what they are. Like Shelley (but without Shelley's acute awareness of what he was doing) we are perpetually weaving

A shroud of talk to hide us from the sun
Of this familiar life.

We protect our minds by an elaborate system of abstractions, ambiguities, metaphors and similes from the reality we do not wish to know too clearly; we lie to ourselves, in order that we may still have the excuse of ignorance, the alibi of stupidity and incomprehension, possessing which we can continue with a good conscience to commit and tolerate the most monstrous crimes.

Aldous Huxley, *Words and Behaviour*

Language Shapes Our World

At the beginning of this chapter we said that meanings rest more in people than words. Although this statement is true, it shouldn't lead you to think that labels are unimportant; just the opposite is true. In many cases the name we give something determines the way we'll look at it—whether we'll regard it as attractive or unpleasant, respectable or contemptible, desirable or repellent. For the next few pages we'll explore the way in which language shapes ideas.

We already hinted at how this process works when we talked about euphemisms and how they can make an unattractive idea or thing more pleasant. By changing the labels we use, the euphemism changes our perception of the world and thus our behavior. But language shapes our attitudes in other ways too.

Advertisements are probably the best example of how attitudes can be created through the use of words. Semanticists like to tell a story that illustrates this point: In a department store experimenters set up two stacks of handkerchiefs side by side on a table. The merchandise in each was identical, the only difference being the signs above each pile. One read "Fine Linen Handkerchiefs—$1.50 each," while the other said "Nose Rags—35¢." As you might expect, the "handkerchiefs" sold out quickly, and the "nose rags" were hardly touched. In this case names didn't reflect reality so much as create it.

Another example of labels reshaping perceptions occurred at a Virginia high school, where a course called "home economics for boys" drew very few students. Instead of dropping the course, someone with at least an intuitive knowledge of semantics retitled it. The new name was the more glamorous "bachelor living." With nothing more than this verbal facelift the class drew 120 students.

We don't give names only to things. The words we use to describe the functions people fill in society can shape the way they feel about themselves and others. We call reading a letter to the editor in the journal *ETC: A Review of General Semantics* which illustrated this point. The author described how her formerly friendly and comfortable relationship with her daughter's fiance had changed soon after the wedding. The new husband began to act ill at ease when around his wife's mother and avoided her whenever possible. Recalling the principle of names influencing behavior, she suspected what the problem was. The next time the husband visited her house, the woman reported saying, "I'm so glad I'm not really your mother-in-law so that we can be friends." Incredibly enough, this simple statement worked like magic; he began to relax and behave as he did before the wedding. The woman certainly had not changed, but once rid of the unpleasant connotations of "mother-in-law," the man's perception of her shifted radically.

The same principle applies in the working world. Much of our self-esteem comes from the importance we feel our work has, and this perception of importance often comes from the title our role has. For example, we've heard of a theater owner who had trouble keeping ushers working for him for more than a week or two. They seemed to tire quickly of their work, which consisted mostly of taking tickets, selling popcorn, and showing people to their seats. Then, with only one change, the manager ended his personnel problems: He simply "promoted" all his ushers to the "new" position of "assistant manager." And believe it or not, the new title was sufficient to make the employees happy. It seemed that the new name made them think more highly of themselves and take new pride in their work.

This power of labeling extends even to our personal names. Research shows that these names are more than just simple means of identification: that in fact they shape the way others think of us, the way we view ourselves, and our behavior.

Different names have different connotations. Psychologists Barbara Buchanan and James Bruning asked college students to rate over a thousand

Alice: *"Must a name mean something?"*
Humpty-Dumpty: *"Of course it must . . .*

My name means the shape I am . . . With a name like yours, you might be any shape, almost."

Lewis Carroll,
Through The Looking Glass

Franchising: What's in a Name?

There are Halston suitcases, his-and-hers Halston towels, Halston Ultrasuede quilts, Halston wigs and Halston gloves. The Bill Blass name and his back-to-back initials appear on fur coats, after-shave cologne and Lincoln Continentals. Anne Klein's "Mark of the Lion" decorates umbrellas, belts, espadrille shoes and clutch purses. And John Weitz's imprint graces bathing suits, ties, shirts and even cigars. American designers seem to be slapping their signatures on high-ticket products of virtually every description in hopes that the name of the game is a famous name.

European designers learned long ago that selling their names to an independent soap or perfume manufacturer was much easier—and almost as lucrative—as coming up with new clothing styles each season. But most American designers are just beginning to catch on to the license ploy.

There are many different licensing contracts but the format is basically the same. As a binder when the contract is signed, the designer is either paid "front money" from the distributor, ranging from $5,000 to $50,000 depending on the status of his name, or a percentage of the projected first-year royalties. From then on, royalty contracts pay the designer from 5 to 10 percent of net wholesale sales, and there is usually a guaranteed annual minimum. "Royalties are all gravy," says Jack Maurer, business manager of Bill Blass, whose twelve licenses brought in nearly $2 million last year. "No costs are taken out."

John Weitz, one of the founding fathers of American franchising, has grown less particular and more practical over the years. "I'll put my name on a product if the company convinces me it will make money even if I don't find it particularly palatable—as long as it's not vulgar," says the 54-year-old Weitz, whose 48 accounts, including cigars, generate $100 million in worldwide retail sales a year. "I mean how much design goes into a navy-blue tie?" Sometimes nothing extra goes into a franchise product except the signature. "Most customers who buy designer names are being ripped off," says Vince Thurston, manager of T. Anthony, a top New York luggage shop. "I've got an all-leather knapsack for $65, and the same one is selling with Cassini's name on it for $95." What's in a name? Says Thurston: "A 35 percent markup."

Newsweek

"It's called bananas flambeau, not a bunch of
burned bananas."

names according to their likability, how active or passive they seemed, and
their masculinity or femininity. In spite of the large number of subjects, the
responses were quite similar. Michael, John, and Wendy were likable and
active and were rated as possessing the masculine or feminine traits of their
sex. Percival, Isadore, and Alfreda were less likable, and their sexuality was
more suspect. Other research also suggests that names have strong
connotative meanings. More common names are generally viewed as being
more active, stronger, and better than unusual ones.

The preconceptions we hold about people due to their names influence our
behavior toward them. In a well-known study Herbert Harari and John
McDavid asked a number of teachers to read several essays supposedly
written by fifth-grade students. The researchers found that certain names—
generally the most popular ones such as Lisa, Michael, and Karen—received
higher grades, regardless of which essay they were attached to, while other
less popular names—Elmer, Bertha, Hubert—were consistently graded as
inferior. There was one exception to the link between popular names and
high grades: unpopular Adelle received the highest evaluation of all. Harari
and McDavid speculated that the teachers saw her as more ''scholarly.''

It's not surprising to find that the attitudes others hold toward a person due
to his or her name have an effect on that person's self-concept. Forty years
ago B. M. Savage and F. L. Wells found that students at Harvard who had
unusual names were more likely to be neurotic and to flunk out of school. The
negative effect of unusual names seems to be more damaging to men than
women, perhaps due to our social convention that makes such labels
acceptable for females. At any rate, research such as this makes it clear that
the question ''What shall we name the baby?'' is an important one for more
than aesthetic reasons.

Along with personal names, the labels we choose to describe certain
groups also affects our perceptions, as the following article shows.

IDENTITY CRISIS

Black? Afro-American? Negro? Or colored?

The *Newsweek* Poll shows that name calling is a matter of considerable concern to the sampling of 22 million U.S. citizens. And news media mirror this concern, shifting from black to Negro and back frequently in the same story (colored seems passé).

This identity crisis seems superficial, but beneath the surface are far more complex questions of how white men view non-white men—and how non-whites view themselves. Involved too is a largely unconscious set of perceptions sometimes used by white newsmen to describe what they think they see.

Throughout American history words of racial identification have gone through cycles of popularity and disrepute. The first freed slaves preferred to be called "Africans" and periodically there have been attempts to establish the term "Afro-American." But even though Afro-American parallels such expressions as Irish-American and Italian-American, such attempts have never been very successful. *The Amsterdam News* in Harlem momentarily tried Afro-American, but dropped it in favor of black.

"Colored" was a respectable word in the last century but is now avoided almost everywhere. (An exception: The National Association for the Advancement of Colored People, founded in 1909.)

Until the twentieth century, the lower-case "negro" was considered derogatory. But in the early 1900s civil-rights activists campaigned for and successfully popularized "Negro." And the word achieved a certain legitimacy in the white community when in a March 7, 1930, editorial *The New York Times* noted: "In our stylebook 'Negro' is now added to the list of words to be capitalized . . . it is an act of recognition of racial self-respect for those who have been for generations in "the lower case'."

More and more these days newsmen and broadcasters are using "black," a word that only a few years ago was considered contemptuous. Beginning with Stokely Carmichael's speeches in Mississippi in 1966, "black" has become increasingly acceptable and now many newsmen (*Newsweek's* among them) use Negro and black interchangeably. The momentum has been shifting to black and, significantly, it is black newsmen who are leading the way. "Black is more prominent, it's easier to say and the young people prefer it," observes Tom Picour, editor of *The Chicago Defender,* a black daily.

Pride "Black" is now associated with youth, with unity, with militancy (black power), and with pride ("Black is beautiful"). At the same time, "Negro" has come more and more to connote middle age, the status quo, complacency. "At one time it didn't matter to me whether I was called Negro or black," says Hans Massaquoi, managing editor of *Ebony.* "But now it does matter and I prefer to be called black. As I read copy, I am aware that when certain writers say Negro they are describing someone they *see* as a Negro—an Uncle Tom."

" 'Black' is a much more honest word for us," says Henry Hampton, 28, a political commentator for WGBH in Boston. "It conjures a state of mind to cope with the long tradition of what the word used to mean. When I was 12 my mother used to play 'Old Black Joe' on the piano. Black used to be a word that was used against us. Now we've turned it around and made it into a positive weapon."

On most "white" publications, editors are taking their cue from black reporters. "One of our black reporters turned in a story and in the rewrite where he had used black it was changed to Negro," recalls Ed Cony, managing editor of *The Wall Street Journal.* "When he saw the rewrite he said he'd like all those 'Negroes' changed back to 'blacks' and we did it."

William Raspberry, a black columnist for *The Washington Post,* believes that in general people who are over 30 prefer "Negro," while most who are under 30 would rather be called "black." "Only the older generation would accept the term 'colored'," says Raspberry, "and Afro-American is just too unwieldy." Leo Addie, director of WTOP-TV News in Washington, says that the station generally uses the word "Negro," but adds, "We leave it up to the reporter's judgment in cases where the subject insists on being called 'black'."

Heritage Chris Borgen, a 38-year-old CBS-TV newsman, says that his rule-of-thumb is that no militant will be offended by the word "black" and that anyone displaying signs of African heritage, such as wearing a Dashiki, can properly be called an Afro-American. "To the militant," he explains, "any person of color in the U.S. who is, by his own choice a member of the Establishment and does not agree with the militant, is a Negro." Borgen adds that he considers himself a Negro. "Black and Afro-American imply to me that I need an identity which transcends the one that I already have."

Often the galling thing to blacks—and Negroes—is the over-all context and tone of a story or broadcast.

White writers and editors, it seems, tend to put out papers that have a distinctly "white" viewpoint. The current issue of the *Columbia Journalism Review* cites several not so subtle examples. An editorial in *The New Haven Register* stated that the community had tried to give "its Negro citizens the things they have asked." The implication, the *Review* points out, is that "those" people are not really part of "our" community. Well-intentioned white reporters take great pains to point out that a certain Negro is "well-dressed" or "articulate" but in so doing they imply that most other Negroes are not. A *New York Times* article wrote of the white female lead in *The Great White Hope:* "Playing a part in which she has to kiss a Negro doesn't faze her." The *Journalism Review* advised that "white readers should substitute 'white' for 'Negro' to understand the insult." Fortunately, there are indications that whites are beginning to understand. The man who culled the samples of "white thinking" is Robert E. Smith. He is an editor for the *Newsday* feature syndicate, 28 years old—and white.

Newsweek

KELLY   by Jack Moore

♪IN TH' EV'NIN♪ MMM♪ BY TH' MOONLIGHT♪ MMM♪

QUIET NOW BLACK MOVIE NOW SHOOTING

♪YOU CAN♪ ♪HEAR♪

♪THOSE BLACKS, NEGROES, OR♪ AFRO-AMERICANS WHICHEVER ♪YOU PREFER♪

♪SINGIN'♪ ♪MMMM♪

Different Language, Different World

Anthropologists know that the culture in which we live influences our perception of reality. Some social scientists believe that this cultural perspective is at least partially shaped by the very language the members of that culture speak. This idea has been most widely circulated in the writings of Benjamin Lee Whorf and Edward Sapir.

After spending several years studying various North American Indian cultures, Whorf found that their entire way of thinking was shaped by the language they spoke. For example, Nootka, a language spoken on Vancouver Island, contains no distinction between nouns and verbs. Because of this the Indians who speak it view the entire world as being constantly in process. Where we see a thing as fixed or constant (noun), they view it as constantly changing. Thus, instead of calling something a "fire," the Nootka speaker might call it a "burning"; where we see a house, he would see a "house-ing." In this sense our language operates much like a snapshot camera, while Nootka works more like a moving-picture camera.

What does this have to do with communication? How does our language influence the way we relate with each other? Because of the static, unchanging nature of English grammar, we often regard people and things as never-changing. Someone who spoke a more process-oriented language would view people quite differently, better recognizing their changeable nature.

The Sapir-Whorf hypothesis has never been conclusively proved or disproved. In spite of its intellectual appeal, some critics point out that it is possible to conceive of flux even in static languages like English. They suggest that Sapir and Whorf overstated the importance of their idea. Supporters of the hypothesis respond that while it is *possible* to conceptualize an idea in different languages, some make it much easier to recognize a term than do others.

For example, suppose that you, an English speaker, have just returned from a visit to New York and someone asks you what kind of place it is. "Oh, it's a terrible place," you say. Now look at this response. By saying that New York *is* terrible (or great, or any other adjective), your language implies two things: First, that your judgment is a total one—that it covers everything about the city—and second, that New York is an unchanging place. The word *is* implies eternal sameness, when in fact the "things" we give names to are really changing, dynamic processes. New York today isn't the same place it was last year or will be tomorrow, and your experiences there aren't the same ones that other people might have had. You'd have been more correct if you'd answered by saying, "My experiences while visiting New York in January 1981 were that the streets were crowded, the people I encountered behaved rudely, and that the prices for food, lodging, and entertainment were too high." Now of course this way of talking isn't always practical, but it's certainly more accurate than judging New York in absolute terms.

The real culprit we're talking about is the word *is*. It leads us to think of people or things as if they were absolute and unchanging. Saying that "John

> *The labels we attach to people, the names and all the other things that identify the individual by distinguishing him from the masses, are just what prevent genuine knowing. For labels and classifications make it appear that we know the other, when actually we have caught the outline and not the substance. Since we are convinced we know ourselves and others, since we take this knowledge for granted, we fail to recognize that our perceptions are often only habits growing out of routines and familiar forms of expression. We no longer actually see what is happening before us and in us, and, not knowing that we do not know, we make no effort to be in contact with the real. We continue to use labels to stereotype ourselves and others, and these labels have replaced human meanings, unique feelings, and growing life within and between persons.*
>
> Clark Moustakas

is handsome, boring, or immature isn't as correct as saying "The John I encountered yesterday seemed to be . . ." There's a big difference between saying "Beth is a phony" and "Beth seemed phony the other night." The second statement describes the way someone behaved at one point in time, and the first categorizes her as if she had always been a phony. It's this kind of verbal generalizing that causes teachers to think of students as "slow learners" or "troublemakers" because of past test scores or reports.

Alfred Korzybski, who originated the discipline of General Semantics, suggested a linguistic device to remind us of the way all things change. He proposed that we qualify important words by attaching subscripts to them. For example, instead of saying "I didn't like Joe," you might say "I didn't like Joe $_{last\ Tuesday}$." This would make it harder to think in abstract, overly general terms.

The following article is one example of how subscripting helps avoid the idea that people act or should be expected to act consistently. As you read it, imagine how you could apply this way of thinking to one or two people you know. How would doing this affect your relationships with them?

The Husbands in My Life

A Greek named Heraclitus claimed that you never see the same river twice because the water that was there one minute is not there the next. In this respect, it seems to me, husbands are like rivers. For example, my husband Tom.

Tom$_1$ is of course the lover; Tom$_2$, the man of business. Both these Toms are substantially the same today as when we were married in 1948.

Tom$_3$, the father, is different. He wasn't born until 1950. I watched his birth with some pity, a little resentment, and a strong upsurge of motherly feeling toward him. He was almost as bewildered as was Tom, Jr. But, whereas the baby took strong hold in his new world, Tom$_3$ stood at the edge of fatherhood for a while, until I felt like taking him by the ear with an old-fashioned motherly grip and leading him to his son. Today, though, Tom$_3$ bears little resemblance to Tom$_{3\ (1950)}$. Actually, I feel a little shut out now when Tom$_3$ and Tom, Jr. are especially close, as when they're planning a fishing trip.

Tom$_4$, the fisherman, is a loathsome person—an adolescent, self-centered, unpredictable, thoughtless, utterly selfish braggart. Yesterday, he bought Junior a fishing rod.

"Pampering him," I said. "He needs other things so much more—his teeth straightened, summer camp."

"He needs a fishing rod." Tom$_4$ said.

"You're teaching him to become a thoughtless husband," I charged.

"Oh, I don't know," Tom$_4$ said. "Maybe he'll marry a girl who likes to fish."

That stopped me for a minute. I'd never thought of there being such girls. Perhaps Tom$_4$ was disappointed in me. I was just wondering what I could wear on a fishing trip when Tom$_4$ shattered my good intentions by saying, "A fishing trip for Junior is a good deal more important than a permanent for Nancy."

This came as a surprise. Tom$_{3b}$ as father of Nancy was not the Tom$_{3a}$ father of Junior. Usually Nancy could get away with anything. At five, she had known better than to cut up the evening paper before her father had seen it, but Tom$_{3b}$ had just laughed. He was certainly no relation to the husband-at-breakfast Tom who would scream if his wife got the pages of the morning paper out of place. He'd always been a little too indulgent with Nancy and too severe with Junior, but now he was begrudging Nancy a permanent.

"Do you want to have an unattractive daughter?" I asked, but Tom$_{3b}$ wasn't there. Tom$_5$, the amateur plumber and ardent do-it-yourselfer, had taken over. He was at the sink fussing with the garbage disposer, promising to fix it Saturday.

"Why don't you buy Nancy a fishing rod?" I suggested.

And who looked back at me? Tom$_6$ the bewildered husband. "Are you joking?" he asked.

"Certainty not," I said indignantly. "You should train her to make a good wife."

Tom$_6$ laughed. Then Tom$_7$ took over. Tom$_7$ is the appreciative husband. He's a very determined fellow. He laughs loud and long.

"Very funny," he said. "I always appreciate your sense of humor. I always tell my—"

"Don't overdo it," I snarled. "I'm not being funny. Maybe she should have a fishing rod."

"She has her permanent," Tom$_8$ said with a laugh. "When she gets a little older she can fish with that." Tom$_6$ is a clown, the life of the party. Some day I may murder him.

I poured the coffee and resisted the temptation to drip a little on Tom$_8$'s balding head. "Polygamy's wonderful," I murmured with a sigh, as I set the coffee pot down.

Tom$_7$ looked at me with concern. "Have you seen your doctor lately?" he asked.

"No, there are enough men in my life," I answered. But Tom$_2$ was looking at his watch. I realized that my remark had been wasted. Not one of my husbands was listening.

Mary Graham Lund

The Un-Isness of Is

For several years now, D. David Bourland Jr. has conscientiously scrubbed from his discourse and his writing all forms of the verb "to be." The first time he tried to do this, it gave him a headache. Now the practice comes so naturally that Bourland's listeners and readers are not likely to notice the omission. On the contrary, they are likely to be struck by the lucidity of his expression, which is commendably unambiguous if not always very lyrical. Where most people might render harsh judgment on themselves with "I'm no good at math," Bourland would express the thought with far less immutability: "I did not receive good grades in math," or "I did less well at math than at other subjects."

Unlike the California musician who once wrote a novel without the letter "e" just to see if it could be done, Bourland, 40, is not an eccentric visionary. He is the highly skilled president of Information Research Associates, a McLean, Va., think tank that does classified systems development for the U.S. Navy. Bourland, who has a master's degree in business administration from Harvard, was also a student at the Institute of General Semantics in Lakeville, Conn., where be became an ardent disciple of the linguistic theories of the leading prophet of general semantics, Alfred Korzybski. In Korzybski's view, the verb "to be" was a dangerous and frequently misused word that was responsible for much of mankind's semantic difficulties. Going the master one better, Bourland has led a one-man crusade for the adoption of "E-prime"—which is his name for the English language minus "to be."

All Is Change The semanticist's objection to the verb "to be" is based on certain philosophical convictions. One is a stern rejection of an axiom of classical logic, the principle of identity— that A is A, or a rose is a rose. In fact, argued Korzybski, the basic principle of life is not identity but, as the elliptical pre-socratic philosopher Heraclitus put it, that all is change. Time and movement are inexorable, and in the fraction of a second that a rose is described it has already begun to alter.

The second philosophical conviction is that language influences behavior. Mankind is much less aware of the implacable reality of change simply because his language is dominated by the verb "to be," which implies a static quality of illusory permanence. "Our language," says Bourland, "remains the language of absolutes. The chief offender remains the verb 'to be.' The spurious identity it so readily connotes perverts our perception of reality."

One semantic harm done by "to be" is that it tempts man into erroneous value judgments. Korzybski noted dryly that a rose is not at all "red" to those afflicted by color blindness, and that redness itself is not a reality but a quality of reflected light to which the description "red" is arbitrarily assigned. Better to say, Korzybski suggested, "I classify the rose as red," or "I see the rose as red."

Undemonstrated Conclusions E-prime, Bourland firmly insists, has certain advantages over conventional English. Certain questions that semanticists as well as many analytical philosophers regard as poorly structured— "What is man?", "What is art?", or Hamlet's famous "To be or not to be"—simply disappear as unaskable. Another is the elimination of essentially empty phrases—"Boys will be boys," for example, or "We know this is the right thing to do." A third advantage is that the E-prime user cannot blandly take refuge in waffling statements based on factually undemonstrated conclusions—sentences that begin with, say, "It is known that," or "It is certain."

Despite the stirring rhetorical flair of the Declaration of Independence, Bourland is even willing to rewrite it, in the interest of semantic clarity. In the standard text, the first sentence reads: "We hold these truths to be self-evident, that all men are created equal, that they are endowed by their creator with certain inalienable rights, that among these are Life, Liberty and the pursuit of Happiness." A somewhat more prosaic E-Prime version: "We make the following assumptions: All citizens have equal political rights. All citizens simply by virtue of their existence have certain inalienable rights, including life, liberty and the pursuit of happiness."

Bourland notes with some satisfaction that a number of scientific papers, not all done by Korzybski disciples, are now being written in E-prime; he is currently writing a book on how to speak and write without recourse to Isness. From personal experience, he claims that the use of E-prime can force a self-conscious but salutary revision in the speaker's oulook on life. "Once you realize that every time you say 'is' you tell a lie," he says, "you begin to think less of a thing's identity and more of its function. I find it much harder to be dishonest now."

Time Magazine

We live in a time of increasing sensitivity to various types of discrimination. Some of the most strenuous battles have been fought in order to give women rights and opportunities equal to those of men. Observers of language—not all of them female—have noted that the very nature of English as it is usually written and spoken discriminates against women. One subtle but pervasive habit has been to use the personal pronoun "he" when talking about people in general. As you have probably noticed, we have tried to avoid this misleading style in *Looking Out/Looking In* by using several approaches: using the sexually neutral "they" whenever it was grammatically correct, switching between "he" and "she," or writing "he or she" when the singular form was necessary, using the passive voice when this didn't make the text too dry and boring, and even rewriting many passages to eliminate any specific sexual reference. We've tried to make these changes unobtrusive, for we believe that the style of a textbook shouldn't call attention to itself. But many people believe that a more radical solution is appropriate. They suggest that since language shapes perceptions, we need to change our grammar in order to change our thinking. Read the following article and see whether you agree.

Is Is What Was Was?

An is is just a was that was
and that is very small. . .
And is is was so soon it almost
wasn't is at all.
For is is only is until
it is a was—you see. . .
And as an is advances—to
remain an is can't be. . .
'cause if is is to stay an is
it isn't is because
another is is where it was
and is is then a was.

Tom Hicks, *Etc.*

DE~SEXING THE ENGLISH LANGUAGE

On the television screen, a teacher of first-graders who has just won a national award is describing her way of teaching. "You take each child where you find him," she says. "You watch to see what he's interested in, and then you build on his interests."

A five-year-old looking at the program asks her mother, "Do only boys go to that school?"

"No," her mother begins, "she's talking about girls too, but—"

But what? The teacher being interviewed on television is speaking correct English. What can the mother tell her daughter about why a child, in any generalization, is always *he* rather than *she?* How does a five-year-old comprehend the generic personal pronoun?

The effect on personality development of this one part of speech was recognized by thoughtful people long before the present assault on the English language by the forces of Women's Liberation. Fifteen years ago, Lynn T. White, then president of Mills College, wrote:

The grammar of English dictates that when a referent is either of indeterminate sex or both sexes, it shall be considered masculine. The penetration of this habit of language into the minds of little girls as they grow up to be women is more

profound than most people, including most women, have recognized: for it implies that personality is really a male attribute, and that women are a human subspecies. . . . It would be a miracle if a girl-baby, learning to use the symbols of our tongue, could escape some wound to her self-respect: whereas a boy-baby's ego is bolstered by the pattern of our language.

Now that our language has begun to respond to the justice of Women's Liberation, a lot of people apparently are trying to kick the habit of using *he* when they mean anyone, male or female. In fact, there is mounting evidence that a major renovation of the language is in progress with respect to this pronoun. It is especially noticeable in the speeches of politicians up for election: "And as for every citizen who pays taxes, I say that he or she deserves an accounting!" A variation of the tandem form is also cropping up in print, like the copy on a coupon that offers the bearer a 20 percent saving on "the cost of his/her meal." A writer in the New York newspaper *The Village Voice* adopts the same form to comment "that every artist of major stature is actually a school in him/herself."

Adding the feminine pronoun to the masculine whenever the generic form is called for may be politically smart and morally right, but the result is often awkward.

Some of the devices used to get around the problem are even less acceptable, at least to grammarians. It is one thing for a student to announce in assembly that "Anybody can join the Glee Club as long as they can carry a tune," but when this patchwork solution begins to appear in print, the language is in trouble. In blatant defiance of every teacher of freshman English, a full-page advertisement in *The New York Times* for its college and school subscription service begins with this headline: "If someone you know is attending one of these colleges, here's something they should know that can save them money." Although the grammatical inconsistency of the *Times's* claim offends the ear—especially since "they" in the headline can refer only to "colleges"—the alternatives would present insurmountable problems for the writer. For example, the sentence might read, "If someone you know . . . etc., here's something he or she should know that can save him/her money." Or, in order to keep the plural subject in the second clause, the writer might have begun, "If several people you know are attending one or more of these colleges. . . ." But by that time will the reader still care?

In the long run, the problem of the generic personal pronoun is a problem of the status of women. But it is more immediately a matter of common sense and clear communication. Absurd examples of the burdens now placed upon masculine pronouns pop up everywhere. "The next time you meet a handicapped person, don't make up your mind about him in advance," admonishes a radio public service announcement. A medical school bulletin, apparently caught by surprise, reports that a certain scholarship given annually "to a student of unquestioned ability and character who has completed his first year" was awarded to one Barbara Kinder.

Since there is no way in English to solve problems like these with felicity and grace, it is becoming obvious that what we need is a new singular personal pronoun that is truly generic: a common-gender pronoun. Several have been proposed, but so far none appears to have the transparently

SINGULAR			PLURAL
	Distinct Gender	Common Gender	Common Gender
Nominative	*he* and *she*	*tey*	*they*
Possessive	*his* and *her* (or *hers*)	*ter* (or *ters*)	*their* (or *theirs*)
Objective	*him* and *her*	*tem*	*them*

logical relationship to existing pronouns that is necessary if a new word is to gain wide acceptance. Perhaps a clue to the solution is to be found in people's persistent use of *they* as a singular pronoun.

In the plural forms, both genders are included in one word: *they* can refer to males or females or a mixed group. So why not derive the needed singular common-gender pronouns from the plural? *They, their,* and *them* suggest *tey, ter,* and *tem.* With its inflected forms pronounced to rhyme with the existing plural forms, the new word would join the family of third person pronouns as shown in the box below.

Someone will probably object to the idea of a common-gender pronoun in the mistaken belief that it is a neuter form and therefore underrates sexual differences. The opposite is true.

Once *tey* or a similar word is adopted, *he* can become exclusively masculine, just as *she* is now exclusively feminine. The new pronoun will thus accentuate the significant and valuable differences between females and males—those of reproductive function and form—while affirming the essential unity and equality of the two sexes within the species.

Language constantly evolves in response to need. It is groping today for ways to accommodate the new recognition of women as full-fledged members of the human race. If the new pronoun helps anyone toward that end, tey should be free to adopt it.

If anyone objects, it is certainly ter right—but in that case let tem come up with a better solution.

Casey Miller and Kate Swift

In Conclusion

Now we've come to the end of our short look at the subject of language. We hope that after reading this chapter you aren't as inclined as before to take words for granted.

We've pointed out the simple but tremendously important fact that meanings rest more in people than in words themselves. Because of this fact it's especially important to find out whether someone is using a word the same way we are before we jump to conclusions.

We've listed a few of the most common ways that language can trip us up if we're unaware—equivocation, overly broad terms, relative words, fiction words, and emotive terms.

We've shown how using overly abstract terms can lead you to think of people as being similar when they're really quite unique.

You've seen how we can go around in verbal circles by looking for meanings in a dictionary, and how much more precise communication can be when we use operational definitions.

You've learned how euphemisms are devices that can serve as defense mechanisms, helping us avoid facing facts we'd rather ignore.

And finally, you should see now that although words don't mean anything in themselves, the labels we attach to our experiences can shape the attitudes we hold.

Trying to cover so much ground in so short a space is a very frustrating thing. You probably still have many unanswered questions about semantics, and there may be things we've covered that you simply don't understand or see as important. If you're willing to dig deeper and learn more, both your instructor and the following list of readings are good places to go from here.

Roads Not Taken

1. Develop case studies to show that communication can break down due to one or more of the following problems:
   a. equivocation
   b. use of relative words
   c. use of emotive words
   d. use of fiction words

2. Observe the use of euphemisms in your everyday life. Describe the impact such language has on your thoughts and those of others.

3. Research the charge that some school textbooks use sexist language. What evidence exists to demonstrate that such language exists and that it affects the perceptions of the people reading it?

4. Investigate other languages to see how they deal with the issue of pronouns for nonsexual objects. Based on your study, what do you think is the best method for dealing with this problem?

5. Explore research in anthropology and linguistics that describes ways in which various languages shape the world view of their users.

6. Write a story or essay in E prime language, and comment on how its use changes the narration.

More Readings on Semantics

Bois, J. Samuel. *The Art of Awareness.* Dubuque, IA: Wm. C. Brown Company, 1973.
General semantics (as opposed to just plain semantics) is a discipline that goes beyond studying language. It attempts to explore the ways in which we look at the world and to suggest some better alternatives. This college-level text about the subject provides a thorough introduction.

Carroll, John B., ed. *Language, Thought, and Reality: Selected Writings of Benjamin Lee Whorf.* Cambridge, MA: M.I.T., 1966.
Writings of the most widely recognized authority about how language shapes our world view.

Chase, Stuart. *The Tyranny of Words.* New York: Harvest Books, 1938.
A very readable account of the many ways in which semantic problems cause fuzzy thinking and get us into trouble.

Condon, John C. *Semantics and Communication,* 2nd ed. New York: Macmillan, 1975.
The clearest introduction to the field of semantics we've found. It's neither too long nor too short and gives good overview.

Fabun, Don. *Communications: The Transfer of Meaning.* Beverly Hills, CA: Glencoe Press, 1968.
This pamphlet is an attractive, very short introduction to the study of language. If you're trying to explain some of the things in this chapter to a friend who doesn't have time to read it, this booklet might be just the thing.

Hayakawa, S. I. *Language in Thought and Action.* New York: Harcourt Brace Jovanovich, 1964.
A clear, detailed treatment of many topics introduced in this chapter.

————. *The Use and Misuse of Language.* New York: Fawcett Books, 1962.
A collection of essays from ETC.: A Review of General Semantics, which illustrate how topics introduced in this chapter apply to everyday situations.

Lakoff, Robin. *Language and Woman's Place.* New York: Harper Colophon Books, 1975.
Lakoff investigates those roots of our language that give us parallel words for male and the female. The structure may be parallel, but she argues that the range of use and connotation are not.

Mager, Robert. *Goal Analysis.* Belmont, CA: Fearon, 1972.
An entertaining, valuable guide for defining vague, abstract aims (called "Fuzzies") into specific behavioral targets. The book was written primarily for teachers to use in improving their instruction, but you should have no problem applying the ideas here to your own communication goals.

Marcus, Mary G. "The Power of a Name." *Psychology Today* (October, 1976), pp. 75–77, 108.
This interesting article illustrates how the principle of language-shaping perception applies to the names parents give their children. Do you want your son or daughter to be regarded as intelligent, clumsy, well adjusted, or neurotic? The name you choose may make a difference.

Miller, Casey, and Kate Swift. *Words and Women.* Garden City, NY: Anchor Press, 1976.
Miller and Swift provide the evidence that point out how our everyday language communicates much about male and female role biases.

Newman, Edwin. *A Civil Tongue.* Indianapolis: Bobbs-Merrill, 1976.
Newman cites hundreds of examples of the semantic atrocities listed in this chapter. His stories come from politics, academia, business, and many other settings. After reading them, one doesn't know whether to laugh or cry.

Sagarian, Edward. "The High Cost of Wearing a Label." *Psychology Today* (March, 1976), pp. 25–27.
This article shows some of the dangers of the word is, as described in Chapter 8. As Sagarian suggests, believing one's self *to be* a deviant can lend to an unnecessary self-fulfilling prophecy.

Chapter Nine

Not everything that is faced can be changed,
But nothing can be changed until it is faced.

James Baldwin

You've almost finished this first look at interpersonal communication. You've seen the major barriers that keep us from understanding each other, and you've practiced some ways to overcome them. If you've learned to use the skills presented in this book, you should now find that your relationships with others are everything you've ever wanted, free from any problems, right?

Wrong!

We'd only be kidding you if we pretended that it's possible to live a life without any conflicts, because just the opposite is true. Problems are bound to come up any time two people get together for more than a short while, and sooner or later some will arise that are serious enough to wreck the relationship unless you know how to handle them.

Unfortunately, we can't offer you any magic tricks to resolve all the conflicts in your life; at this stage, the social sciences just aren't advanced enough. On the other hand, we can show you some ways that constructively expressed conflict can strengthen your relationships much of the time.

Conflict is Natural

We'll start by saying that without exception *every* relationship of any depth at all has conflict. No matter how close, how understanding, how compatible you are, there will be times when your ideas or actions or needs or goals won't match those of others around you. You like rock music, but your companions prefer Beethoven; you want to date other people, but your partner wants to keep the relationship exclusive; you think a paper you've done is fine, but your instructor wants it changed; you like to sleep in on Sunday mornings, but your roommate likes to play the stereo—loudly! There's no end to the number or kinds of disagreements that are possible.

And just as conflict is a fact of life, so are the feelings that go along with it—hurt, anger, frustration, resentment, disappointment. Because these feelings are usually unpleasant, there is a temptation to avoid them or pretend they don't exist. But as sure as conflicts are bound to come up, so are the emotions that go along with them.

At first this might seem pretty depressing. If problems are inevitable in even the best relationships, does this mean that you're doomed to relive the same arguments, the same hurt feelings over and over? Fortunately, the answer to this question is a definite No. Even though conflict is part of a meaningful relationship, you can change the way you deal with it.

The reason most of us fear conflict is that we've been conditioned to believe that it's bad to disagree, argue, or fight. We've seen conflict force people apart and damage their relationships. It's our belief that this happens most of the time because conflict is not handled constructively.

How can facing up to problems and disagreements bring people together? How can feelings like anger and hurt make a relationship stronger? Answering these questions will take some time, so let's get started. The first step is to take a look at some of the present ways you handle conflict.

Styles of Conflict

There are four ways in which people can act when their needs aren't met. Each one has very different characteristics, as we can show by describing a common problem. At one time or another almost everyone has been bothered by a neighbor's barking dog. You know the story: every passing car, distant siren, pedestrian, and falling leaf seems to set off a fit of barking that leaves you unable to sleep, socialize, or study. By describing the possible ways of handling this kind of situation, the differences between nonassertive, directly aggressive, indirectly aggressive, and assertive behavior should become clear.

Nonassertive Behavior   There are two ways in which nonasserters manage a conflict. Sometimes they ignore their needs. Faced with the dog, for instance, a nonassertive person would try to forget the barking by closing the windows and trying to concentrate even harder. Another form of denial would be to claim that no problem exists—that a little barking never bothered anyone. To the degree that it's possible to make problems disappear by ignoring them, such an approach is probably advisable. In many cases, however, it simply isn't realistic to claim that nothing is wrong. For instance, if your health is being jeopardized by the cigarette smoke from someone nearby, you are clearly punishing yourself by remaining silent. If you need to learn more information from a supervisor before undertaking a project, you reduce the

© 1963 United Feature Syndicate, Inc.

quality of your work by pretending that you understand it at all. If you claim that an unsatisfactory repair job is acceptable, you are paying good money for nothing. In all these and many more cases simply pretending that nothing is the matter when your needs continue to go unmet is clearly not the answer.

A second nonassertive course of action is to acknowledge your needs are not being met but simply to accept the situation, hoping that it might clear up without any action on your part. You could, for instance, wait for the neighbor who owns the barking dog to move. You could wait for the dog to be run over by a passing car or to die of old age. You could hope that your neighbor will realize how noisy the dog is and do something to keep it quiet. Each of these occurrences is a possibility, of course, but it would be unrealistic to count on one of them to solve your problem. And even if by chance you were lucky enough for the dog problem to be solved without taking action, you couldn't expect to be so fortunate in other parts of your life.

In addition, while waiting for one of these eventualities, you would undoubtedly grow more and more angry at your neighbor, making a friendly relationship between the two of you impossible. You would also lose a degree of self-respect, since you would see yourself as the kind of person who can't cope with even a common everyday irritation. Clearly, nonassertion is not a very satisfying course of action—either in this case or in other instances.

Direct Aggression   Where the nonasserter underreacts, a directly aggressive person overreacts. The usual consequences of aggressive behaviors are anger and defensiveness or hurt and humiliation. In either case aggressive communicators build themselves up at the expense of others.

You could handle the dog problem with direct aggression by abusively confronting your neighbors, calling them names and threatening to call the dogcatcher the next time you see their hound running loose. If the town in which you live has a leash law, you would be within your legal rights to do so, and thus you would gain your goal of bringing peace and quiet to the neighborhood. Unfortunately, your direct aggression would have other, less productive consequences. Your neighbors and you would probably cease to be on speaking terms, and you could expect a complaint from them the first time you violated even the most inconsequential of city ordinances. If you live in the neighborhood for any time at all, this state of hostilities isn't very appealing.

Indirect Aggression   In several of his works psychologist George Bach describes behavior that he terms "crazymaking." Crazymaking occurs when people have feelings of resentment, anger, or rage that they are unable or unwilling to express directly. Instead of keeping these feelings to themselves, the crazymakers send these aggressive messages in subtle, indirect ways, thus maintaining the front of kindness. This amiable façade eventually crumbles, however, leaving the crazymaker's victim confused and angry at having been fooled. The targets of the crazymaker can either react with aggressive behavior of their own or retreat to nurse their hurt feelings. In either case indirect aggression seldom has anything but harmful effects on a relationship.

What's your conflict style? To give you a better idea of some unproductive ways you may be handling your conflicts, we'll describe some typical conflict behaviors that can weaken relationships. In our survey we'll follow the fascinating work of George Bach, a leading authority on conflict and communication.

Bach explains that there are two types of aggression—clean fighting and dirty fighting. Either because they can't or won't express their feelings openly and constructively, dirty fighters sometimes resort to ''crazymaking'' techniques to vent their resentments. Instead of openly and caringly expressing their emotions, crazymakers (often unconsciously) use a variety of indirect tricks to get at their opponent. Because these ''sneak attacks'' don't usually get to the root of the problem, and because of their power to create a great deal of hurt, crazymakers can destroy communication. Let's take a look at some of them.

The avoider   The avoider refuses to fight. When a conflict arises, he'll leave, fall asleep, pretend to be busy at work, or keep from facing the problem in some other way. This behavior makes it very difficult for the partner to express his feelings of anger, hurt, etc., because the avoider won't fight back. Arguing with an avoider is like trying to box with a person who won't even put up his gloves.

The pseudoaccommodator   The pseudoaccommodator refuses to face up to a conflict either by giving in or by pretending that there's nothing at all wrong. This really drives the partner, who definitely feels there's a problem, crazy and causes him to feel both guilt and resentment toward the accommodator.

The guiltmaker   Instead of saying straight out that she doesn't want or approve of something, the guiltmaker tries to change her partner's behavior by making him feel responsible for causing pain. The guiltmaker's favorite line is ''It's o.k., don't worry about me. . . .'' accompanied by a big sigh.

The subject changer   Really a type of avoider, the subject changer escapes facing up to aggression by shifting the conversation whenever it approaches an area of conflict. Because of his tactics, the subject changer and his partner never have the chance to explore their problem and do something about it.

The distracter   Rather than come out and express his feelings about the object of his dissatisfaction, the distracter attacks other parts of his partner's life. Thus he never has to share what's really on his mind and can avoid dealing with painful parts of his relationships.

The mind reader   Instead of allowing her partner to express her feelings honestly, the mind reader goes into character analysis, explaining what the other person really means or what's wrong with the other person. By behaving this way the mind reader refuses to handle her own feelings and leaves no room for her partner to express himself.

The trapper   The trapper plays an especially dirty trick by setting up a desired behavior for her partner, and then when it's met, attacking the very thing she requested. An example of this technique is for the trapper to say ''Let's be totally honest with each other,'' and then when the partner shares his feelings, he finds himself attacked for having feelings that the trapper doesn't want to accept.

The crisis tickler   This person almost brings what's bothering him to the surface, but he never quite comes out and expresses himself. Instead of admitting his concern about the finances he innocently asks ''Gee, how much did that cost?'', dropping a rather obvious hint but never really dealing with the crisis.

The gunnysacker   This person doesn't respond immediately when she's angry. Instead, she puts her resentment into her gunnysack, which after a while begins to bulge with large and small gripes. Then, when the sack is about to burst, the gunnysacker pours out all her pent-up aggressions on the overwhelmed and unsuspecting victim.

The trivial tyrannizer Instead of honestly sharing his resentments, the trivial tyrannizer does things he knows will get his partner's goat—leaving dirty dishes in the sink, clipping his fingernails in bed, belching out loud, turning up the television too loud, and so on.

The joker Because she's afraid to face conflicts squarely, the joker kids around when her partner wants to be serious, thus blocking the expression of important feelings.

The beltliner Everyone has a psychological "beltline," and below it are subjects too sensitive to be approached without damaging the relationship.

Beltlines may have to do with physical characteristics, intelligence, past behavior, or deeply ingrained personality traits a person is trying to overcome. In an attempt to "get even" or hurt his partner the beltliner will use his intimate knowledge to hit below the belt, where he knows it will hurt.

The blamer The blamer is more interested in finding fault than in solving a conflict. Needless to say, she usually doesn't blame herself. Blaming behavior almost never solves a conflict and is an almost surefire way to make the receiver defensive.

The contract tyrannizer This person will not allow his relationship to change from the way it once was. Whatever the agreements the partners had as to roles and responsibilities at one time, they'll remain unchanged. "It's your job to . . . feed the baby, wash the dishes, discipline the kids. . . ."

The kitchen sink fighter This person is so named because in an argument he brings up things that are totally off the subject ("everything but the kitchen sink"): the way his partner behaved last New Year's eve, the unbalanced checkbook, bad breath—anything.

The withholder Instead of expressing her anger honestly and directly, the withholder punishes her partner by keeping back something—courtesy, affection, good cooking, humor, sex. As you can imagine, this is likely to build up even greater resentments in the relationship.

The Benedict Arnold This character gets back at his partner by sabotage, by failing to defend him from attackers, and even by encouraging ridicule or disregard from outside the relationship.

Your Crazymakers

1. **Pick the three crazymakers you use most often and give three recent examples of each.**

2. **For each example, describe**
   a. the situation in which you used the crazymaker
   b. the consequences of using it, including the other person's behavior and your feelings
   c. your level of satisfaction with having used the crazymaker
   d. any alternate style of expressing your problem which might have been more satisfying

Crazymaking Diary

1. **Look over the previous pages and think about the crazymakers you use. (You may want to look back at the chart you made earlier describing your conflict styles to recall some.)**

Are there genuinely nice, sweet people in this world? Yes, absolutely yes, and they get angry as often as you and I. They must—otherwise they would be full of vindictive feelings and slush, which would prevent genuine sweetness.

Theodore Isaac Rubin

2. For a week keep a record of the way you handle conflicts, focusing especially on any crazymakers you use.

3. What are the consequences of your behaviors? That is, do your crazymaking actions do anything to strengthen your relationships? to weaken them?

4. If you can, take time to talk with the person or people most important to you about the crazymakers you both use. Can you agree to try expressing your conflicts in more honest and direct ways from now on?

You could respond to your neighbors and their dog in several crazymaking, indirectly aggressive ways. One strategy would be to complain anonymously to the city pound and then, after the dog has been hauled away, express your sympathy. Or you could complain to everyone else in the neighborhood, hoping that their hostility would force the offending neighbors to quiet the dog or face being a social outcast. A third possibility would be to strike up a friendly conversation with one of the owners and casually remark about the terrible neighborhood you had just left, in which noisy dogs roamed the streets, uncontrolled by their thoughtless owners. (Or perhaps you could be more subtle and talk about noisy children instead!)

There are a number of shortcomings to such approaches as these, each of which illustrate the risks of indirect aggression. First, there is the chance that the crazymaking won't work: the neighbors might simply miss the point of your veiled attacks and continue to ignore the barking. On the other hand, they might get your message clearly, but either because of your lack of sincerity or out of sheer stubbornness, they might simply refuse to do anything about the complaining. In either case it's likely that in this and other instances indirect aggression won't satisfy your unmet need.

Even when indirect aggression proves successful in the short run, a second shortcoming lies in its consequences over the longer range. You might manage to intimidate your neighbors into shutting up their mutt, for instance, but in winning that battle you could lose what would become a war. As a means of revenge, it's possible that they would wage their own campaign of crazymaking by such tactics as badmouthing things like your sloppy gardening to other neighbors or by phoning in false complaints about your allegedly loud parties. It's obvious that feuds such as this one are counter-productive and outweigh the apparent advantages of indirect aggression.

DEAR ABBY: I am desperate. After 15 years of a very stormy off-again, on-again marriage, my husband has asked me for a divorce. It all started a year ago when, in the middle of a heated argument, I told him that his lovemaking did nothing for me—I had only been putting on an act. It wasn't even the truth. Knowing how proud he is of his masculinity, I said it because I knew it would hurt him. I never realized it would hurt him so much that it would destroy all his feeling for me. He hasn't kissed me or touched me since that terrible argument, and now he says he wants a divorce.

Abby, I'll do anything in the world to get my husband back. I don't want a divorce. Please, please tell me what to do.

RAZOR SHARP-TONGUE

DEAR TONGUE: Unless you can convince your husband that you spoke in anger and didn't mean what you said, there may be no way you can get your husband back. This may not help much, but it may serve to let others know that one seldom regrets unspoken words.

Abigail Van Buren

Who's Afraid of Virginia Woolf?

Martha Hey, put some more ice in my drink, will you? You never put any ice in my drink. Why is that, hunh?

George (*Takes her drink*) I always put ice in your drink. You eat it, that's all. It's that habit you have . . . chewing your ice cubes . . . like a cocker spaniel. You'll crack your big teeth.

Martha THEY'RE MY BIG TEETH!

George Some of them . . . some of them.

Martha I've got more teeth than you've got.

George Two more.

Martha Well, two more's a lot more.

George I suppose it is. I suppose it's pretty remarkable . . . considering how old you are.

Martha YOU CUT THAT OUT! (*Pause*) You're not so young yourself.

George (*With boyish pleasure . . . a chant*) I'm six years younger than you are. . . . I always have been and I always will be.

Martha (*Glumly*) Well . . . you're going bald.

George So are you. (*Pause . . . they both laugh*) Hello, honey.

Martha Hello. C'mon over here and give your Mommy a big sloppy kiss.

George . . . oh, now . . .

Martha I WANT A BIG SLOPPY KISS!

George (*Preoccupied*) I don't *want* to kiss you, Martha. Where *are* these people? Where are these *people* you invited over?

Martha They stayed on to talk to Daddy. . . . They'll be here. . . . *Why* don't you want to kiss me?

George (*Too matter-of-fact*) Well, dear, if I kissed you I'd get all excited . . . I'd get beside myself, and I'd take you, by force, right here on the living room rug, and then our little guests would walk in, and . . . well, just think what your father would say about *that.*

Martha You pig!

George (*Haughtily*) Oink! Oink!

Martha Ha, ha, ha, HA! Make me another drink . . . lover.

George (*Taking her glass*) My God, you can swill it down, can't you?

Martha (*Imitating a tiny child*) I'm firsty.

George Jesus!

Martha (*Swinging around*) Look, sweetheart, I can drink you under any goddamn table you want . . . so don't worry about me!

George Martha, I gave you the prize years ago. . . . There isn't an abomination award going that you. . . .

Martha I swear . . . if you existed I'd divorce you. . . .

George Well, just stay on your feet, that's all.. . . These people are your guests, you know, and. . . .

Martha I can't even see you. . . . I haven't been able to see you for years. . . .

George . . . if you pass out, or throw up, or something. . . .

Martha . . . I mean, you're a blank, a cipher. . . .

George . . . and try to keep your clothes on, too. There aren't any more sickening sights than you with a couple of drinks in you and your skirt up over your head, you know. . . .

Martha . . . a zero. . . .

George . . . your *heads,* I should say. . . . (*The front doorbell chimes*)

Martha Party! Party!

George (*Murderously*) I'm really looking forward to this, Martha. . . .

Martha (*Same*) Go answer the door.

George (*Not moving*) You answer it.

Martha Get to that door, you. (*He does not move*) I'll fix you, you. . . .

George (*Fake-spits*) . . . to you. . . .

Edward Albee

In addition to these unpleasant possibilities, a third shortcoming of indirect aggression is that it denies the people involved a chance of building any kind of honest relationship with each other. As long as you treat your neighbors as if they were an obstacle to be removed from your path, there's little likelihood that you'll get to know them as people. While this thought may not bother you, the principle that indirect aggression prevents intimacy holds true in other important areas of life. To the degree that you try to manipulate friends, they won't know the real you. The fewer of your needs you share directly with your coworkers, the less chance you have of becoming true friends and colleagues. The same principle holds for those people you hope to meet in the future. Indirect aggression denies closeness.

Assertion   Assertive people handle conflicts skillfully by expressing their needs, thoughts, and feelings clearly and directly, but without judging others or dictating to them. They have the attitude that most of the time it is possible to resolve problems to everyone's satisfaction. Possessing this attitude and the skills to bring it about doesn't guarantee that assertive communicators will always get what they want, but it does give them the best chance of doing so. An additional benefit of such an approach is that whether or not it satisfies a particular need, it maintains the self-respect of both the asserters and those with whom they interact. As a result, people who manage their conflicts assertively may experience feelings of discomfort while they are working through the problem. They usually feel better about themselves and each

Styles of Conflict

	Nonassertive	Directly Aggressive	Indirectly Aggressive	Assertive
Approach to Others	I'm not O.K., You're O.K.	I'm O.K,. You're not O.K.	I'm O.K., You're not O.K. (But I'll let you think you are.)	I'm O.K, You're O.K,
Decision Making	Let others choose	Choose for others. They know it.	Chooses for others They don't know it.	Chooses for self
Self-Sufficiency	Low	High or low	Looks high but usually low	Usually high
Behavior in Problem Situations	Flees, gives in	Outright attack	Concealed attack	Direct confrontation
Response of Others	Disrespect, guilt, anger, frustration	Hurt, defensiveness, humiliation	Confusion, frustration, feelings of manipulation	Mutual respect
Success Pattern	Succeeds by luck or charity of others	Beats out others	Wins by manipulation	Attempts ''no lose'' solutions

Adapted with permission from S. Phelps and N. Austin, *The Assertive Woman.* San Luis Obispo, CA: Impact, 1974 p. 11, and Gerald Piaget, American Orthopsychiatric Association, 1974.

other afterward—quite a change from the outcomes of no assertiveness and aggression.

An assertive course of action in the case of the barking dog would be to wait a few days to make sure that the noise is not just a fluke. If things continue in the present way, you could introduce yourself to your neighbors and explain your problem. You could tell them that although they might not notice it, the dog often plays in the street and keeps barking at passing cars. You could tell them why this behavior bothers you. It keeps you awake at night and makes it hard for you to do your work. You could point out that you don't want to be a grouch and call the pound. Rather than behaving in these ways, you could tell them that you've come to see what kind of solution you can find that will satisfy both of you. This approach may not work, and you might then have to decide whether it is more important to avoid bad feelings or to have peace and quiet. But the chances for a happy ending are best with this assertive approach. And no matter what happens, you can keep your self-respect by behaving directly and honestly.

Your Conflict Style

1. Think back over your recent history and recall five conflicts you've had. The more current they are the better, and they should be ones that occurred with people who are important to you, people with whom your relationship matters.

2. Turn an 8½-by-11-inch sheet of paper horizontally, and copy the following chart. To give yourself plenty of room you might extend your chart onto a second page.

I The Conflict	II How I Managed It	III The Results
(Describe whom it was with; what it was about.)	(What did you say? How did you act?)	(How you felt. How the others involved felt. Are you happy with the results?)

3. For each of the conflicts, fill in the appropriate spaces on your chart.

4. Based on what you've written here, answer the following questions:
   a. Are you happy with the way you've handled your conflicts? Do you come away from them feeling better or worse than before?
   b. Have your conflicts left your relationships stronger or weaker?
   c. Do you recognize any patterns in your conflict style? For example, do you hold your angry feelings inside, are you sarcastic, do you lose your temper easily?
   d. If you could, would you like to change the way you deal with your conflicts?

Types of Conflict Resolution

So far, we've looked at individual styles of communication. While assertive problem-solving may be the most satisfying and productive of these, it's obvious that not everyone uses it. Even when one person behaves assertively, there's no guarantee that others will do so. There are three quite different outcomes of the various interactions between nonassertive, indirectly aggressive, directly aggressive, and assertive communicators. By looking at each of them, you can decide which ones you'll seek when you find yourself facing an interpersonal conflict.

Win-lose

Win-lose conflicts are ones in which one party gets what he or she wants while the other comes up short. People resort to this method of resolving disputes when they perceive a situation as being an ''either-or'' one: either I get what I want or you get your way. The most clear-cut examples of win-lose situations are certain games such as baseball or poker in which the rules require a winner and a loser. Some interpersonal issues seem to fit into this win-lose framework: two coworkers seeking a promotion to the same job or a couple who disagree on how to spend their limited money.

Power is the distinguishing characteristic in win-lose problem-solving, for it is necessary to defeat an opponent to get what you want. The most obvious kind of power is physical. Some parents threaten their children with warnings such as ''Stop misbehaving or I'll send you to your room.'' Adults who use physical power to deal with each other usually aren't so blunt, but the legal system is the implied threat: ''Follow the rules or we'll lock you up.''

Real or implied force isn't the only kind of power used in conflicts. People who rely on authority of many types engage in win-lose methods without ever threatening physical coercion. In most jobs supervisors have the potential to use authority in the assignment of working hours, job promotions, desirable or undesirable tasks, and, of course, in the power to fire an unsatisfactory employee. Teachers can use the power of grades to coerce students to act in desired ways.

Intellectual or mental power can also be a tool for conquering an opponent. Everyone is familiar with stories of how a seemingly weak hero defeats a stronger enemy through cleverness, showing that brains are more important than brawn. In a less admirable way indirectly aggressive crazymakers such as you've read about earlier in this chapter can defeat their partners by inducing guilt, avoiding issues, withholding desired behaviors, pseudoaccommodating, and so on.

Even the usually admired democratic principle of majority rule is a win-lose method of resolving conflicts. However fair it may be, this system results in one group getting its way and another being unsatisfied.

There are some circumstances when the win-lose method may be necessary, as when there are truly scarce resources and where only one party can achieve satisfaction. For instance, if two suitors want to marry the same person, only one can succeed. And to return to an earlier example, it's often true that only one applicant can be hired for a job. But don't be too

I was angry with my friend.
I told my wrath, my wrath did end.
I was angry with my foe:
I told it not, my wrath did grow.

And I watered it in fears,
Night and morning with my tears;
And I sunned it with smiles,
And with soft deceitful wiles.

And it grew both day and night,
Till it bore an apple bright;
And my foe beheld it shine,
And he knew that it was mine,

And into my garden stole
When the night had veiled the pole:
In the morning glad I see
My foe outstretched beneath the tree.

William Blake

willing to assume that your conflicts are necessarily win-lose: as you'll soon read, many situations that seem to require a loser can be resolved to everyone's satisfaction.

There is a second kind of situation when win-lose is the best method. Even when cooperation is possible, if the other person insists on trying to defeat you, then the most logical response might be to defend yourself by fighting back. "It takes two to tango," the old cliché goes, and it also often takes two to cooperate.

A final and much less frequent justification for trying to defeat another person occurs when the other party is clearly behaving in a wrong manner, and where defeating that person is the only way to stop the wrongful behavior. Few people would deny the importance of restraining a person who is deliberately harming others, even if the aggressor's freedom is sacrificed in the process. The danger of forcing wrongdoers to behave themselves is the wide difference in opinion between people about who is wrong and who is right. Given this difference, it would only seem justifiable to coerce others into behaving as we think they should in the most extreme circumstances.

Lose-lose   In lose-lose methods of problem-solving, neither side is satisfied with the outcome. While the name of this approach is so discouraging that it's hard to imagine how anyone could willingly use the method, in truth lose-lose is a fairly common approach to handling conflicts.

Compromise is the most respectable form of lose-lose conflict resolution. In it, all the parties are willing to settle for less than they want because they believe that partial satisfaction is the best result they can hope for.

In his valuable book on conflict resolution Albert Filley points out an interesting observation about our attitudes toward this method. Why is it, he asks, that if someone says, "I will compromise my values," we view the action unfavorably, yet we talk admiringly about parties in a conflict who compromise to reach a solution? While compromises may be the best obtainable result in some conflicts, it's important to realize that both people in a dispute can often work together to find much better solutions. In such cases *compromise* is a negative word.

Most of us are surrounded by the results of bad compromises. Consider a common example, the conflict between one person's desire to smoke cigarettes and another's need for clean air. The win-lose outcomes on this issue are obvious: either the smoker abstains or the nonsmoker gets polluted lungs—neither very satisfying. But a compromise in which the smoker only gets to enjoy a rare cigarette or must retreat outdoors and in which the nonsmoker still must inhale some fumes or feel like an ogre is hardly better. Both sides have lost a considerable amount of both comfort and goodwill. Of course the costs involved in other compromises are even greater. For example, if a divorced couple compromise on child care by haggling over custody and then finally grudgingly agrees to split the time with their youngsters, it's hard to say that anybody has won.

Compromises aren't the only lose-lose solutions, or even the worst ones. There are many instances in which the parties will both strive to be winners, but as a result of the struggle, both wind up losers. On the international scene many wars illustrate this sad point. A nation that gains military victory at the cost of thousands of lives, large amounts of resources, and a damaged national consciousness hasn't truly won much. On an interpersonal level the same principle holds true. Most of us have seen battles of pride in which both parties strike out and both suffer. It seems as if there should be a better alternative, and fortunately there often is.

No-lose   In this type of problem-solving the goal is to find a solution that satisfies the needs of everyone involved. Not only do the partners avoid trying to win at the other's expense, there's a belief that by working together it's possible to find a solution in which everybody reaches their goals without needing to compromise.

One way to understand how no-lose problem-solving works is to look at a few examples.

Gordon was a stamp collector; his wife Elaine loved to raise and show championship beagles. Their income didn't leave enough money for both to practice their hobbies, and splitting the cash they did have wouldn't have left enough for either. Solution: Put all the first year's money into the puppies, and then after they were grown use the income from their litters and show prizes to pay for Gordon's stamps.

Mac loved to spend his evenings talking to people all over the world on his ham radio set, but his wife Marilyn felt cheated out of the few hours of each day they could spend together. Mac didn't want to give up his hobby, and Marilyn wasn't willing to sacrifice the time she needed alone with her husband. Solution: Three or four nights each week Mac stayed up late and talked on his radio after spending the evening with Marilyn. On the following mornings she drove him to work instead of his taking the bus, which allowed him to sleep later.

Wendy and Kathy were roommates who had different studying habits. Wendy liked to do her work in the evenings, which left her days free for other things, but Kathy felt that night time was party time. Solution: Monday through Wednesday evenings Wendy studied at her boyfriend's place, while Kathy did anything she wanted. Thursday and Sunday Kathy agreed to keep things quiet around the house, and Friday and Saturday they both partied together.

The point here isn't that these solutions are the correct ones for everybody with similar problems: the no-lose approach doesn't work that way. Different people might have found other solutions that suited them better. What the no-lose method does is give you an approach—a way of creatively finding just the right answer for your unique problem. By using it you can tailor-make a way of resolving your conflicts that everyone can live with comfortably.

You should understand that the no-lose approach doesn't call for compromises in which the participants give up something they really want or need. Sometimes a compromise is the only alternative, but in the method we're talking about you find a solution that satisfies everyone—one in which nobody had to lose.

No-Lose Problem-Solving

Of these three styles the no-lose approach is clearly the most desirable one in most cases. It is also the hardest one to achieve—for two reasons. First, it requires a noncompetitive attitude and a number of skills that we'll soon discuss. Second, it requires a certain amount of cooperation from the other person, for it's difficult to arrive at a no-lose solution with somebody who insists on trying to defeat you.

In spite of these challenges it is definitely possible to become better at resolving conflicts. In the following pages we will outline a method to increase your chances of being able to handle your conflicts in a no-lose manner, so that both you and others have your needs met. As you learn to use this approach, you should find that more and more of your conflicts wind up with no-lose solutions. And even when total satisfaction isn't possible, this method can help by showing you how to solve problems in the most satisfying way possible and also by preventing individual conflict from spoiling your future interactions with the person involved.

The method is patterned after techniques developed by George Bach and Thomas Gordon, and it has proved successful with many people, both young and old, in a variety of settings.

Before we introduce you to this method, there are a few ideas you should keep in mind. This technique is a highly structured activity. While you're learning how to use it, it's important that you follow all the stages carefully. Each step is essential to the success of your encounter, and skipping one or more can lead to misunderstandings that might threaten your meeting and even cause a "dirty fight." After you've practiced the method a number of times and are familiar with it, this style of conflict will become almost second nature to you. You'll then be able to approach your conflicts without the need to follow the step-by-step approach. But for the time being try to be patient and trust the value of the following pattern.

As you read the following steps, try to imagine yourself applying them to a problem that's bothering you now.

Step 1—Identify Your Problem and Unmet Needs   Before speaking out, it's important to realize that the problem that is causing conflict is yours. Whether you want to return an unsatisfactory piece of merchandise, complain to a noisy neighbor because your sleep is being disturbed, or request a change in working conditions from your employer, the problem is yours. Why? Because in each case *you* are the person who is dissatisfied. You are the one who has paid for the defective article; the merchant who sold it to you has the use of your good money. You are the one who is losing sleep as a result of your

No Victor, So No Spoils

In these games, the idea is cooperation, not competition

"Vampire blob" is a tag game. Anyone tagged, with a mock bite on the neck, joins hands with the biter and becomes part of the monster. "The lap game" is even simpler: a crowd forms a huge ring, and everyone sits down simultaneously on the player behind. Though "blob" and "lap" may seem like innocent cavorting, they are serious business to San Francisco's New Games Foundation. An offshoot of a 1973 New Games Tournament, staged by *Whole Earth Catalog* Creator Stewart Brand, the foundation is now a growing national enterprise. Its goal is nothing less than to change the way Americans play, mainly by replacing competitive games with cooperative "no win" pastimes.

Psychologist John O'Connell, 29, codirector of the foundation, wants to see the nation playing less baseball and more blob. Says he: "In traditional team games like baseball, it usually becomes apparent halfway through the game who the winners and losers will be. Then the losers play badly and have a miserable time." But O'Connell and the foundation want to restructure these time-honored sports activities so that everyone plays and no one loses. In a version of "new volleyball," the aim is to keep the ball from hitting the ground rather than to score points by zinging it at the feet of opponents across the net. Says Jeff McKay, a San Francisco teacher and baseball coach who

subscribes to the foundation's theory of no winners or losers: "If the game doesn't fit the players, we change the game, not the players."

Assistant Intramural Director Lou Fabian and Student Kathy Evans, of the University of Pittsburgh, have found an ingenious way to curb competitiveness in basketball. Last year they introduced an intramural program in which the scores of both teams were added together. Two opposing teams win a joint victory when their total score is higher than those in other games played at the same hour. The goal of the program is to eliminate scorekeeping altogether.

The foundation's philosophy owes something to the distaste for competitiveness that rose out of the 1960s counterculture. But the "new games" are catching on in the mainstream. The foundation,

with an annual budget of about $400,000, conducts a hundred or more weekend workshops round the country for recreation specialists, educators and health care professionals; many of them are paid by their employers to learn the new nonwinning ways. Explains O'Connell: "The games are especially popular in the Midwest, where people still have lots of community picnics and family days. They're a lot more fun than spitting watermelon seeds at each other."

Another pundit of new games is Sports Psychologist Terry Orlick, 33, of the University of Ottawa. He thinks that the foundation has not gone far enough. He notes, for example, that the foundation's tug of war encourages players to switch sides to prevent a victory. Orlick, in his new *Cooperative Sports & Games Book,* promotes a "tug of peace," in which children are arrayed not in two teams

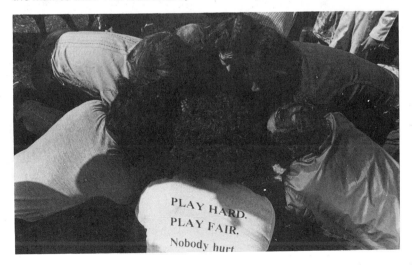

PLAY HARD.
PLAY FAIR.
Nobody hurt

pulling against each other at opposite ends of a single rope, but hauling at various ropes to form stars, triangles and other designs. Orlick has even invented a cooperative version of musical chairs and a tame version of the board game Monopoly, called Community. Says Orlick: "We've become fixated on numerical outcomes of games. Losers feel rejected, not worthy. The point is to have fun interacting, not to put someone else down."

Agreeing with the foundation, Orlick wants to adapt traditional sports so that all players are equally involved in the action. In volleyball, for instance, he suggests that all six players on a team hit the ball before it goes over the net; and in basketball he encourages more balanced scoring by subtracting the points made by the highest and lowest scorers of each team. Other popular games are manipulated so the final score is a tie.

Such ideas would make a shambles of most American sports programs, geared as they are to encouraging youngsters to test themselves and develop skills through competition. Not to worry, says Orlick: "Those kinds of games will always be around. It's just that we've gone overboard on competitiveness, aggressiveness and the 'me' ethic."

Orlick has a point. Little League fathers who abuse their kids for striking out are surely grostesque. So are football coaches who risk crippling a youngster to win a game. But some athletic supervisors see no reason to go overboard in the opposite direction. Says Roswell Merrick, executive secretary of the National Association for Sport and Physical Education in Washington, D.C.: "I can't go the Orlick route. That's extreme. You want to continue to challenge kids. Sure you want to cooperate and have fun, but you never want to not keep score." With proper supervision, he says, competitive games are not damaging to children above the age of 7 or 8. Walter Cooper, head of the health and physical education school at the University of Southern Mississippi, has attended a New Games Foundation workshop and liked its emphasis on involving people of all ages in physical activity. "But," he adds, "the new games are only a leisure pastime and have no relationship to competitive sports." Says Morgan Wootten, a successful basketball coach and athletic director at De Matha High School in Hyattsville, Md.: "We live in a competitive society. You don't have to win every time, but you have to care about winning. If we don't care, we can become a society of people who don't strive for excellence."

In fact, the "laid back" counterculture opposition to striving seems central to no-win sports. The foundation's John O'Connell insists that the aim is not to win but to catch "the flow." And what is the flow? "Being so involved you lose track of time," he says. "Feeling light, as if in love." Which, as everybody knows, is usually a no-win game.

Time Magazine

---

neighbors' activities; they are content to go on as before. You are the one who is unhappy with your working conditions, not your boss.*

Realizing that the problem is yours will make a big difference when the time comes to approach your partner. Instead of feeling and acting in an evaluative way, you'll be more likely to share your problem in a descriptive way, which will not only be more accurate, but will also reduce the chance of a defensive reaction.

*Of course, others involved in the confict may have problems of their own. For instance, the shopkeeper, noisy neighbor, and your boss may all be bothered by your requests. But the fact still remains that the reason you are speaking up about these matters is because *you* are dissatisfied. Thus, the problem is at least initially yours.

Once you realize that the problem is yours, the next step is to identify the unmet needs that leave you feeling dissatisfied. For instance, in the barking dog incident, your need may be to get some sleep or to study without interruptions. In the case of a friend who teases you in public your need would probably be to avoid embarrassment.

Sometimes the task of identifying your needs isn't as simple as it first seems. Consider these cases:

A friend hasn't returned some money you loaned long ago. Your apparent need in this situation might be to get the cash back. But a little thought will probably show that this isn't the only, or even the main, thing you want. Even if you were rolling in money, you'd probably want the loan repaid because of your most important need: *to avoid feeling victimized by your friend's taking advantage of you.*

Someone you care about who lives in a distant city has failed to respond to several letters. Your apparent need may be to get answers to the questions you've written about, but it's likely that there's another, more fundamental need: *the reassurance that you're still important enough to deserve a response.*

As you'll soon see, the ability to identify your real needs plays a key role in solving interpersonal problems. For now, the point to remember is that before you voice your problem to your partner, you ought to be clear about which of your needs aren't being met.

Step 2—Make a Date   Unconstructive fights often start because the initiator confronts a partner who isn't ready. There are many times when a person isn't in the right frame of mind to face a conflict: perhaps due to fatigue, being in too much of a hurry to take the necessary time, upset over another problem, or not feeling well. At times like these it's unfair to "jump" a person without notice and expect to get full attention for your problem. If you do persist, you'll probably have an ugly fight on your hands.

After you have a clear idea of the problem, approach your partner with a request to try and solve it. For example: "Something's been bothering me. Can we talk about it?" If the answer is Yes, then you're ready to go further. If it isn't the right time to confront your partner, find a time that's agreeable to both of you.

Step 3—Describe Your Problem and Needs   Your partner can't possibly meet your needs without knowing why you're upset and what you want. Therefore it's up to you to describe your problem as specifically as possible. The best way to deliver a complete, accurate message is to use the sense-interpret-feel-consequence-intend format described in Chapter 1. Notice how well this approach works in the following examples:

"I have a problem. It's about your leaving dirty clothes around the house after I've told you how much it bothers me *(sense)*. It's a problem because I have to run around like crazy and pick things up whenever guests come, which is no fun at all *(consequence)*. I'm starting to think that you're either not paying attention to my requests or you're trying to drive me crazy

We struggled together, knowing. We prattled, pretended, fought bitterly, laughed, wept over sad books or old movies, nagged, supported, gave, took, demanded, forgave, resented—hating the ugliness in each other, yet cherishing that which we were. . . . Will I ever find someone to battle with as we battled, love as we loved, share with as we shared, challenge as we challenged, forgive as we forgave? You used to say that I saved up all of my feelings so that I could spew forth when I got home. The anger I experienced in school I could not vent there. How many times have I heard you chuckle as you remembered the day I would come home from school and share with you all of the feelings I had kept in. "If anyone had been listening they would have thought you were punishing me, striking out at me. I always survived and you always knew that I would still be with you when you were through." There was an honesty about our relationship that may never exist again.

Vian Catrell

(thoughts), and either way I'm getting more and more resentful *(feeling).* I'd like to find some way to have a neat place without my having to be a maid or a nag.'' *(Example 1)*

''I have a problem. When you drop by without calling ahead and I'm studying *(sense),* I don't know whether to visit or ask you to leave *(thought).* Either way, I get uncomfortable *(feeling),* and it seems like whatever I do, I lose: either I have to put you off or get behind in my work *(consequences).* I'd like to find a way to get my studying done and still socialize with you *(intention).'' (Example 2)*

''Something is bothering me. When you tell me you love me and yet spend almost all your free time with your other friends *(sense),* I wonder whether you mean it *(thought).* I get insecure *(feeling),* and then I start acting moody *(consequence).* I need some way of finding out for sure how you feel about me *(intention).'' (Example 3)*

By expressing yourself in this way, you're opening up yourself to your partner, explaining just what's going on inside you and how important it is to you. It's surprising how often people argue without ever sharing with each other the extent of their feelings and thoughts.

Means and Ends   One of the most important parts of this step is to describe your needs clearly in the intention phase of your message. The biggest danger here is to confuse your true needs, which we can call ends, with one or more means that might satisfy these ends. This distinction requires some definitions.

Ends are the goals you are seeking, and not having them met is what leads you to feel that a problem exists in the first place. In the examples you just read the desired ends were as follows:

Example 1: A house free of dirty clothes. No need to nag or do more than your own share of housekeeping.
Example 2: The chance to study without sending away friends who drop by.
Example 3: A definite reassurance of love (or a definite statement of nonlove).

Means are ways of achieving ends. For instance, if your goal was to become rich, some possible means might include investing in the stock market, robbing banks, gambling for high stakes, or marrying a wealthy person with a short time to live.

We can go back to our previous examples and see that there are many possible means that could achieve the ends we identified.

Example 1

end: House free of dirty clothes. No need to nag or do more than own share of housework.

means: a. Partner agrees to clean up without being reminded.
       b. Hire a housekeeper
       c. You pick up clothes in exchange for partner's doing a share of your work.

Example 2

end: A chance to study without sending away friends who drop by.

means: a. You do all your studying at school.
       b. Study at home when friends aren't likely to drop by (e.g., late at night).
       c. Ask friends to phone before dropping by.

Example 3

end: A definite reassurance of love (or definite statement of nonlove).

means: a. Companion regularly schedules time to see you.
       b. You learn to accept loving messages, which your partner has been sending already.
       c. You ask friend for reassurance whenever feeling insecure.

You might have found some of these means personally unacceptable, and you probably could think of others to add to the list. That's fine! For now, the important point to remember is that you should approach your partner in a conflict by describing your ends rather than focusing on one or more means. When people mistakenly identify means as ends, they usually increase the level of hostility and resistance. Insisting on specific means is a perfect example of defense-arousing controlling behavior, such as you read about in Chapter 4; and concentrating on working with your partner to achieve a mutually satisfactory end constitutes the more supportive attitude of problem orientation.

Step 4—Partner Checks Back After you've shared your problem and described what you need, it's important to make sure that your partner has understood what you've said. As you can remember from our discussion of listening in Chapter 6, there's a good chance—especially in a stressful conflict situation—of your words being misinterpreted.

It's usually unrealistic to insist that your partner paraphrase your problem statement, and fortunately there are more tactful and subtle ways to make sure you've been understood. For instance, you might try saying, "I'm not sure I expressed myself very well just now—maybe you should tell me what you heard me say so I can be sure I got it right." In any case be absolutely sure that your partner understands your whole message before going any further. Legitimate agreements are tough enough, but there's no point in getting upset about a conflict that doesn't even exist.

HUG O' WAR

I will not play at tug o' war.
I'd rather play at hug o' war,
Where everyone hugs
Instead of tugs,
Where everyone giggles
And rolls on the rug,
Where everyone kisses,
And everyone grins,
And everyone cuddles,
And everyone wins.

Shel Silverstein

Training Lovers to Be Fighters

To confirm our suspicion that intimacy problems are common and not confined to "problem couples" who come to our Institute, we conducted an experiment. We asked people whom we knew through our business consulting, research, graduate teaching, and through social contacts, to help us recruit "normally happy" couples for detailed study. Our contacts were instructed: "Think of all the married couples you know. Then select the happiest of them for nomination to a 'Marriage Elite,' the imaginary Phi Beta Kappa of true intimacy."

We selected 50 "elite" couples and asked them, among other things, how they handled conflict situations. One question was: "On the few occasions when your husband is angry with you, what does he do?" Then we asked: "What do you think he would like to do?"

When such questions were put to these "happy" husbands and wives separately, the result was distressing: almost none had any notion of what was going on in the inner world of the other. Typically, the wife said: "When he does get miffed about something, he is very forgiving and thinks nothing of it"; yet the husband told us that he fought an appalling fight within himself in order to control his annoyance; and he maintained control mostly because he feared his wife might reject him for breaking their unspoken taboo against conflict.

Three groups emerged from our experiment: card-house marriages, game-playing marriages, and true intimates. The card-house partners were the largest group. They put on a fake front. They were almost totally lacking in intimacy and were held together largely by the partners' neurotic concern for appearances, social success, status, and "respectability."

The partners in the second (and smaller) group were somewhat more intimate. But essentially they had resigned themselves to game-playing and other ritualized routines. Many of these unions were held together by such outside pressures as economic advantage and fear of change. They were mutual protective associations who looked on their marriage as pretty much of a lost cause but felt that it would be disloyal and ill-mannered to complain about it, especially since the loneliness of being unmarried would probably be worse.

The third group consisted of only two couples. They checked out as natural geniuses at maintaining realistic intimacy. But when we asked them for the secret of their marital success, they said they had no idea what it was. All we discovered was that these marriage champions—unlike the other couples in our experiment but like successfully married pairs whom everybody occasionally encounters—argued constantly. They thought conflict was as natural as eating.

"Of course," they said, "we argue about practically everything!" Their special characteristic was that they had learned to live with agression comfortably.

As we continued to study our clients' fights, evidence began to accumulate that couples who can't display their hostilities are not polite but phony. Gradually we started to distinguish between constructive and destructive aggression and learned that anger is manageable—not a dark, uncontrollable "mean streak."

George R. Bach and Peter Wyden,
The Intimate Enemy

George Bach suggests a very good idea at this point. Because being really understood is so rare and gratifying, once you're sure your partner understands you, why not express your appreciation with a thank you"? Besides reinforcing the importance of good listening, such a gesture can show caring at what is probably a tense time.

Step 5—Solicit Partner's Needs   Now that you've made your position clear, it's time to find out what your partner needs in order to feel satisfied about this issue. There are two reasons why it's important to discover your partner's needs. First, it's fair. After all, the other person has just as much right as you to feel satisfied, and if you expect help in meeting your needs, then it's reasonable that you behave in the same way. But in addition to decency, there's another, practical reason for concerning yourself with what the other person wants. Just as an unhappy partner will make it hard for you to become satisfied, a happy one will be more likely to cooperate in letting you reach your goals. Thus, it's in your own self-interest to discover and meet your partner's needs.

You can learn about your partner's needs simply by asking about them: "Now I've told you what I want and why. Tell me what you need to feel o.k. about this." Once your partner begins to talk, your job is to use the listening skills discussed earlier in this book to make sure you understand.

Not having studied interpersonal communication, your partner might state intentions in terms of means rather than ends; for instance, saying things like "I want you to be around when I call' instead of "I need to know where you are when I need you." In such cases it's a good idea to rephrase the statements in terms of ends, thus making it clear to both yourself and your partner what he or she really needs to feel satisfied.

Step 6—Check Your Understanding of Partner's Needs   Reverse the procedure in Step 4 by paraphrasing your partner's needs until you're certain you understand them. The surest way to accomplish this step is to use the active listening skills you learned in Chapter 6.

Step 7—Negotiate a Solution   Now that you and your partner understand each other's needs, the goal becomes finding a way to meet them. This is done by trying to develop as many potential solutions as possible and then evaluating them to decide which one best meets everyone's needs. Perhaps you can best appreciate how the no-lose method works by looking at one example.

Not long ago Ron and his wife Sherri used the no-lose approach to solve a problem that had been causing friction between them. To understand the problem you have to know that Ron is basically a tightwad, while Sherri isn't nearly as concerned with finances and doesn't worry as much as Ron does about budgets, savings accounts, or balanced checkbooks. This difference led to their problem: Every month Sherri would come home from shopping expeditions with antiques, new clothes, and other goodies. It wasn't that these things were very expensive, but it bothered Ron that Sherri seemed to think there was something wrong with coming home empty-handed.

It got so that Ron dreaded the times Sherri would walk into the house carrying a shopping bag; and of course Ron's constant worrying about money bothered Sherri too. After what seemed like an endless number of "discussions" about the problem, they didn't seem to be getting anywhere. This was one area in which their needs came into conflict.

Let us begin anew, remembering on both sides that civility is not a sign of weakness.

John F. Kennedy

Eventually both Ron and Sherri realized that they had to find a solution that both could live with. So one evening they sat down and wrote all the alternatives they could think of:

1. Ron learns not to worry about money.
2. Sherri stops being a compulsive shopper.
3. Sherri and Ron discuss each purchase before it's made.
4. Sherri waits a day after first seeing something before buying it.

None of these ideas seemed workable. Since neither Ron nor Sherri could change their personalities overnight, solutions 1 and 2 were out. They had tried number 3 once or twice before and found it caused just as many disagreements as the original problem. The fourth alternative made sense, but it didn't sound like much fun, nor would it always be practical. Fortunately after some more brainstorming they came up with another alternative:

5. Each month they would set aside a certain amount of money for Sherri to spend any way she wanted.

This sounded good to both Ron and Sherri, and after figuring the best amount for this "discretionary fund," things worked well. Now Sherri can buy most of the things she wants, and Ron can enjoy Sherri's shopping sprees without worrying about the budget.

Probably the best description of the no-lose approach has been written by Thomas Gordon in his book *Parent Effectiveness Training.* The following steps are a modification of his approach.

A. Identify and define the conflict   We've discussed this process in the preceding pages. It consists of discovering each person's problem and needs, setting the stage for meeting all of them.

B. Generate a number of possible solutions   In this step the partners work together to think of as many means as possible to reach their stated ends. The key word here is *quantity:* it's important to generate as many ideas as you can think of without worrying about which ones are good or bad. Write down every thought that comes up, no matter how unworkable: sometimes a farfetched idea will lead to a more workable one.

C. Evaluate the alternative solutions   This is the time to talk about which solutions will work and which ones won't. It's important for everyone to be honest about their willingness to accept an idea. If a solution is going to work, everyone involved has to support it.

D. Decide on the best solution   Now that you've looked at all the alternatives, pick the one that looks best to everyone. It's important to be sure everybody understands the solution and is willing to try it out. Remember, your decision doesn't have to be final, but it should look potentially successful.

Step 8—Follow Up the Solution   You can't be sure the solution will work until you try it out. After you've tested it for a while, it's a good idea to set aside some time to talk over how things are going. You may find that you need to make some changes or even rethink the whole problem. The idea is to keep on top of the problem, to keep using creativity to solve it.

No-lose solutions aren't always possible. There will be times when even the best intentioned people simply won't be able to find a way of meeting all their needs. In cases like this the process of negotiation has to include some compromising. But even then the preceding steps haven't been wasted. The genuine desire to learn what the other person wants and to try and satisfy those desires will build a climate of goodwill that can help you find the best solution to the present problem and also improve your relationship in the future.

No-Lose Solutions and You

1. Make a list of the situations in your life where there's a conflict of needs that's creating tension between you and someone else.

2. Analyze what you're doing at present to resolve such conflicts, and describe whether your behavior is meeting with any success.

3. Pick at least one of the problems you listed above, and together with the other people involved, try to develop a no-lose solution by following the steps listed above.

4. After working through Steps 1 to 7, share the results of your conference with the class. After you've had time to test your solution, report the progress you've made and discuss the follow-up conference described in Step 8.

Letting Go

One typical comment people have after trying a few growth fights is "This is a helpful thing sometimes, but it's so rational! Sometimes I'm so uptight I don't care about defensiveness or listening or anything . . . I just want to yell and get it off my chest!"

When you feel like this it's almost impossible to be rational. At times like these probably the most therapeutic thing to do is to get your feelings off your chest in what Bach calls a "Vesuvius"—an uncontrolled, spontaneous explosion. A Vesuvius can be a terrific way of blowing off steam, and after doing so it's often much easier to figure out a rational solution to your problem.

So we encourage you to have a Vesuvius, with the following qualifications: Be sure your partner understands what you're doing and realizes that whatever you say doesn't call for a response. He should let you rant and rave for as long as you want without getting defensive or "tying in." Then, when

your eruption subsides, you can take steps to work through whatever still troubles you.

There you have it—probably some new and different ways of looking at conflict. We've tried to show you how disagreements are a natural part of life and how handling them well can turn what used to be frustrating experiences into encounters that can make your relationships stronger than they were before.

Of course the ideas we've presented here are only a beginning for you; you'll have to tailor them to suit your own personality. But we do believe that the general approach we've showed here works; it has for us and many people we know, and we hope it will for you.

Roads Not Taken

1. Keep a journal of the conflicts that arise in your life and the lives of those around you. Using the information you've learned in this book (defensive behaviors, listening styles, perceptual factors, crazymakers, growth fight, and no-lose) explore the ways in which these conflicts are handled and the results of such handling. How might the conflicts you observed be resolved more successfully?

2. Make it your goal to use no-lose problem-solving whenever possible over a two-week period. Keep a journal recording your successes, failures, and what you've learned.

3. Explore the concepts of zero-sum and nonzero-sum games as they relate to conflict resolution.

4. Research the subject of assertiveness training, focusing on the differences between assertiveness, direct aggression, indirect aggression, and unassertiveness.

5. Collect examples from films, poetry, and literature illustrating various conflict styles.

6. Agree with an important person in your life to apply the growth-fight method to your conflicts for a period of time. Report on the results.

More Readings on Conflict

Albee, Edward, *Who's Afraid of Virginia Woolf?* New York: Pocket Books, 1963.
In this famous play about George and Martha, a very unhappy couple, you can find nearly every type of "dirty fighting" we've talked about in the chapter.

Bach, George R., and Peter Wyden. *The Intimate Enemy.* New York: Avon, 1968.
In this very readable bestseller Bach and Wyden detail the destructive styles of dealing with conflict most marriage partners use. They then present the "fair fight" as an alternative. They present many examples of how couples have learned to deal constructively and successfully with conflicts they face in their lives.

Bach, George R., and Ronald M. Deutsch. *Pairing.* New York: Avon, 1970.
This book does for the singles, or nomarried persons, what The Intimate Enemy *does for the married. Bach and Deutsch apply their methods of facing conflict to the problem that a single person has in finding and building intimate relationships. They attack the problems that our marriage-prone society puts on the shoulders of the single.*

Filley, Alan C. *Interpersonal Conflict Resolution.* Glenview, IL: Scott, Foresman, 1975.
This book was written for use in the field of organizational management and is aimed at helping the reader learn to solve problems of interpersonal conflict in business. The book's strength lies in that the material presented is immediately applicable to other settings as well.

Frost, Joyce H., and Wilmot, William W. *Interpersonal Conflict* Dubuque, IA: William C. Brown, 1978.
A useful survey of the nature of interpersonal conflict and some effective (and ineffective) ways of handling it. This book is a good second step for students who want to learn more about this important topic.

Gordon, Thomas. *Parent Effectiveness Training.* New York: Wyden, 1970.
The best-written book we've seen dealing with communication between parents and kids. An excellent introduction to no-lose styles of handling conflict.

Jandt, Fred E. *Conflict Resolution Through Communication.* New York: Harper & Row, 1973.
This is a collection of readings that are more theoretical than the other titles listed here. The first article by Jandt, "Simulation and Conflict," contains a good simulation for groups.

Who am I? I am not sure.

    Once I was a rabbit's grave and a basketball hoop on the garage, a cucumber patch, lilac trees and peonies crawling with ants. I was stepping stones and a mysterious cistern, grass fires, water fights and ping pong in the basement. I was a picket fence, a bed and maple chest of drawers I shared with brothers, a dog named Sandy who danced. Friends were easy to find. We climbed trees, built grass huts, chased snakes—and we dreamed a lot.

                                        WILL YOU BE MY FRIEND? Beyond childhood.

Who am I? I am not sure.

    Once I was predictable. I was educated, trained, loved-not as I was, but as I seemed to be. My role was my safe way of hiding. There was no reason to change. I was approved. I pleased. Then, almost suddenly, I changed. Now I am less sure, more myself. My role has almost disappeared. My roots are not in my church, my job, my city; even my world. They are in me. Friends are not so easy to find—and I dream a lot.

                                        WILL YOU BE MY FRIEND? Beyond roles.

Who am I? I am not sure.

    I am more alone than before, part animal, but not protected by his instincts or restricted by his vision. I am part spirit as well, yet scarcely free, limited by taste and touch and time-yearning for all of life. There is no security. Security is sameness and fear, the postponing of life. Security is expectations and commitments and premature death. I live with uncertainty. There are mountains yet to climb, clouds to ride, stars to explore, and friends to find. I am all alone. There is only me—and I dream a lot.

                                        WILL YOU BE MY FRIEND? Beyond security.

Who am I? I am not sure.

    I do not search in emptiness and need, but in increasing fullness and desire. Emptiness seeks any voice to fill a void, and face to dispel darkness. Emptiness brings crowds and shadows easy to replace. Fullness brings a friend, unique, irreplaceable. I am not as empty as I was. There are the wind and the ocean, books and music, strength and joys within, and the night. Friendship is less a request than a celebration, less a ritual than a reality, less a need than a want. Friendship is you and me—and I dream a lot.

                                        WILL YOU BE MY FRIEND? Beyond need.

Who am I? I am not sure.

    We didn't sell Kool-aid together or hitchhike to school. We're not from the same town, the same God, hardly the same world. There is no role to play, no security to provide, no commitment to make. I expect no answer save your presence, your eyes, your self. Friendship is freedom, is flowing, is rare. It does not need stimulation, it stimulates itself. It trusts, understands, grows, explores, it smiles and weeps. It does not exhaust or cling, expect or demand. It is—and that is enough—and it dreams a lot.

                                        WILL YOU BE MY FRIEND?

James Kavanaugh

Index

Entries in bold type refer to exercises.